On Nixon's Madness

On Nixon's Madness

An Emotional History

Zachary Jonathan Jacobson

Johns Hopkins University Press
Baltimore

© 2023 Johns Hopkins University Press
All rights reserved. Published 2023
Printed in the United States of America on acid-free paper
9 8 7 6 5 4 3 2 1

Johns Hopkins University Press
2715 North Charles Street
Baltimore, Maryland 21218
www.press.jhu.edu

Library of Congress Cataloging-in-Publication Data is available.
ISBN-13: 978-1-4214-4553-3 (hardcover)
ISBN-13: 978-1-4214-4554-0 (electronic)

A catalog record for this book is available from the British Library.

Special discounts are available for bulk purchases of this book.
For more information, please contact Special Sales at specialsales@jh.edu.

I am an emotional man. I—I just believe in controlling it, and I'm pretty good at it.

Richard Nixon
1983

Contents

Acknowledgments

I WISH TO THANK Michael Sherry, John Bushnell, and Sarah Maza, my graduate school mentors at Northwestern University, for their long-time support and for their opening new vistas of thought to me in the realms of historical study and cultural imaginings, in how people and their times jointly make each other, for how they jointly raised my critical thinking. This book delves into the potency of emotion, the power of performance and the strategies to cope and wield such force. My thanks to Toni Dorfman, my undergraduate mentor at Yale University, for inspiring me with the power and empathy in the theater and in performance, and to Clark Murdock, who introduced me to the intricacies of nuclear strategy, of strategies of force and coercion, at the Center for Strategic and International Studies. I am indebted to Richard Ellis, my editor at *Presidential Studies Quarterly*, which published the article from which this book grew.

The archivists at the Richard Nixon Presidential Library and Museum, the National Security Archive at George Washington University, and Claremont College Library's Special Collections provided me invaluable assistance. My great gratitude goes to the staff at Johns Hopkins University Press for ushering forth this book, in particular my fine editor, Laura Davulis, and assistant editor Ezra Rodriguez, and to my terrific copyeditor, Robin Surratt, and the peer reviewers, who provided key, thoughtful, and detailed feedback that enriched both the scope and the intricacy of the work.

The time that William Burr and Jeffrey P. Kimball—two giants in the field of nuclear strategy and Nixonology—took with me to review the history of the madman theory helped build my core understanding of the theory and the intellectual atmosphere of the Cold War in which it developed. In addition, I wish to express my appreciation to David Brown, Mark Fenster, David Greenberg, Brian Keeley, and Deborah Knight for reading and commenting on different parts of the manuscript.

Thanks to my darlings Blix and Mattis; to my lifetime partners through this journey—Karen, Nick, Jessie, and Alex; to my dearest friends, who have kept me a practicing sentimentalist from New Haven to Brooklyn, Washington, DC, to Evanston, and on to Cambridge. Most of all, I want to thank my parents for their love and faith in me.

On Nixon's Madness

Introduction

IT WAS FOGGY as they strolled the beach. The pair had taken a break from speech writing. Little doubt, Richard Nixon was tense about the upcoming presidential election and tired from the unrelenting politicking of the campaign. He had a tendency to overwork himself, or perhaps more aptly, he had a tendency to overthink. Nixon found some relief padding along the ocean shoreline; he found the rhythm of the waves soothed him. His companion that midsummer's day, his personal chief of staff, H. R. "Bob" Haldeman, recounted that Nixon's mind strayed to a foreign policy lark, a secret plan he had been mulling over.

By 1968 the Vietnam War had reached a destructive stalemate of bombings, offensives and insurrection. The conflict had handicapped one U.S. president in John F. Kennedy, only to fell his successor, Lyndon B. Johnson. With the unpopular Johnson deciding not to run for re-election, the next commander in chief would face a nation all too done with marching, protesting, even rioting over a war halfway around the world that everyone wanted over but no one seemed to know how to end. Nixon had been campaigning on the promise of a swift peace in Vietnam, but the question weighing on the prospective front-runner was how to de-escalate the conflict once he entered the Oval Office. Ultimately, it became a matter of taking the rational route, of settling for a "peace with honor."[1]

Yet as Haldeman recalled, Nixon had a different idea as they paced the beach. What about the irrational route? Instead of halting the bombing, as Johnson had done but to no avail, what of escalating? Instead of winding down the conflict, what of ramping up. The Republican candidate spoke of upping the ante on the Indochinese Peninsula. "I want the North Vietnamese to believe I've reached the point where I might do *anything* to stop the war," Nixon explained. He would play a kind of latter-day ogre, a bully—in his words, "obsessed," "angry"—not able to be restrained. An American president acting with abandon could scare Hanoi to the peace table, Nixon told his chief aide. Just tell them "he has his hand on the nuclear button—and Ho Chi Minh himself will be in Paris in two days begging for peace." Nixon proposed he could finally extract the United States from the Vietnam quagmire with crazed strategic bluster. He called it his "madman theory."[2]

Although Haldeman did not offer an opinion on Nixon's plan in his memoir, he likely assented eagerly to the idea that day on the beach, and not merely due to his tendency toward solicitousness toward his boss, but because the idea spoke to his political instincts. To the former advertising executive with a signature brush cut, it had muscle and brawn. Haldeman preferred Nixon's swaggering moods, and beyond strong-arm tactics, the madman theory was based on pretense. The point of the scheme was not to blow up the world, the schemer would simply appear willing to do so. That was the key distinction of the strategy—acting suicidal rather than committing the act of nuclear suicide. This flair for the dramatic jibed with Haldeman's very joie de vivre. For all his apparent squareness, Nixon's chief of staff had something of the postmodern in him. During his days in advertising in Los Angeles, Haldeman had embraced the notion that image could define reality, the postmodern idea that presentation, as much as Truth and Reason, could matter as much as what was being presented, that as the veteran newsman and Nixon-watcher Marvin Kalb wrote, "The perception of reality is as acceptable as reality itself." And just so, Nixon's madman scheme was a play for the postmodern age, the idea that power is essentially a great game of feints and double-talk, of mystique both remote and overwhelming. "The whole point of it," the historian Jeffrey P. Kimball noted, was that "Nixon didn't consider himself to be crazy." He considered himself crafty.[3]

The key to the madman theory was acting mad, and even if not a first-rate actor, Nixon was perpetually performing. Haldeman called his boss the Man of a Thousand Facets. Born and raised in near poverty, Nixon fancied himself a Horatio Alger, pulling himself up by his bootstraps, his shoes never quite polished, never quite clean. Upon entering the Capitol in 1947 as a young congressional representative, he quickly gained a reputation in equal parts for blandness and for "eager beaver hustle." Nixon's critics considered him an inveterate backroom gossip, fatuous to the powerful, devoid of principle. He became known as a "sweaty striver," undeterred by ethics, all too malleable, on a permanent campaign. Kennedy had watched Nixon since they entered the House of Representatives together. "He felt sorry for Nixon," Kennedy later told his confidant, the economist John Kenneth Galbraith, "because Nixon did not know who he was, and at each stop he would have to decide which Nixon he was at that moment." It seemed, to Kennedy, "exhausting," for Nixon sold versions of himself—from communist-baiting wunderkind of the Red Scare to just your average Joe of the silent majority, from crazed carpet-bomber to elder statesman. Some thought Nixon a political genius, a "scrapper and a fighter," a "tough guy." Others thought him a little man and a great coward. Still others found him a joke. When Nixon wrote or spoke of his life, he became a great sentimentalist, peppering his speeches and memoirs with old saws, mantras and maudlin tales of impossibly good children. The madman, the part of the raging ogre, was another role to play.[4]

As for Nixon's temper, when unloosed, it was not one of mere free-radical bluster. Instead, his mind was drawn to recurrent scripts, as persistently, he perceived nefarious designs and plots against him. The conspiring cast of characters who needed unmasking shifted over time: the communists, the press, anti-war protestors, professors, Jews. Yet, consistently, he identified stories of personal dispossession and disloy-alty, if not treason. Throughout his political career, beginning with his first congressional campaign, he preached in populist fashion that the enemy, a "conspiratorial network," a cabal of conniving elites needed to be exposed to the masses and soon. The historian Richard Hofstadter described such an ethos as Nixon's a "paranoid style." It did not so much cohere to singular form as bear a rash of features: The tune was Mani-chean. The tenor resonated with a bitterness, as if something had been unfairly lost or, more precisely, stolen. A "paranoid" charismatic like Nixon rehearsed an oft-told tale to his constituents: "America has been largely taken away from them and their kind." In so identifying a con-spiracy, Nixon did not just unleash his anger, he arranged his flurry of resentment into rational and repetitive narratives, bringing structure to his disorganizing moods. In turn, as with the madman theory, Nixon found a way to make his anger useful. For rather than reaching higher, there was a stoop to his paranoid style—a desire not only to lift one's con-dition but to pull others down.[5] He transformed himself from victim to agent, from one of the woeful many to stand with the powerful and con-spiring few. From one who is enraged, he became the one who enrages.

This study intersects biography and intellectual and cultural history. It is a history of emotions in its attempt to understand Nixon through his affective life, what the French scholar Lucien Febvre described as that "darkness where psychology wrestles with history."[6] It is a psycho-history, but not in the classic sense of pursuing an analytical diagno-sis. Instead, the work examines one of Nixon's ideas—the madman theory—as an avenue to understanding his subjectivity, perspectives and motivations. The madman theory consists of two poles: perfor-mance and madness, that is, control and temper. As Nixon envisioned the strategy, his anger had to be performative so as to convince, yet his performance had to be constrained lest he risk catastrophe. In this book, I examine how Nixon saw himself as a man in such extreme tension—one of dangerous emotions, the other affective inhibition—how he constructed his life around this dialectic, struggling between hiding his hand and going all in.

In the international arena, Nixon depended on his enemies' inability to discern which of his actions were rational and which were reckless. Behind closed doors, with his clutch of confidants, he weighed the advantages of displaying control or temper, advocating the "subtle" manner of the Chinese only then to declare his admiration for what he saw as the Soviets' brute force. Nixon could be the cold realist, or he could wield his reputation for rage to strategic advantage. At times, he advanced the notion that international order was necessary for progress, but at others, he looked to conflict as the engine for change. In the name of stability, he signed strategic arms limitations agreements with the Soviets, but then in short order, unleashed a degree of excessive force against the North Vietnamese that appeared unhinged. Nixon's vision proved to be less a coherent worldview than the view through a pair of glasses with mismatched lenses, less a rational integration of ideas than a cognitive dissonance. His foreign policy depended both on his overtures as a great and reliable peacemaker and on his reputation as a bloody tyrant. He had to be "Tricky Dick" to disarm his opponents, but also honest Dick, trusted to stand by his word and stick to deals. Through the sheer unpredictability of his actions, employing strategic thrusts and nuclear bluffs, Nixon attempted to coerce his adversaries. Henry Kissinger, Nixon's national security advisor, noted that his game plan often resembled a poker match in which he "push[ed] so many chips into the pot" that the United States' foes would think the president had gone "crazy."[7] Thus, ironically, in the pursuit of stability, Nixon took great risks.

The "madman theory," Haldeman confessed in his memoirs, was a "phrase . . . which I'm sure will bring smiles of delight to Nixon-haters everywhere." Yet in 1978, when he first told the story of his stroll on the beach with Nixon, few historians took serious note. Nixon's maneuvers remained still cloaked in secrecy, filed away in archives, still largely unrelated by his contemporaries, undigested by academics. When Haldeman's account of the fog-shrouded talk appeared, there were no other sources yet declassified or otherwise available to scholars on the madman strategy. For those who did process Haldeman's account, many if not most assumed that the former chief of staff was merely taking a potshot, calling his old boss crazy. After all, Nixon had watched Haldeman go to jail for the Watergate scandal. Moreover, since the madman idea sounded like a description of just another of Nixon's well-known tantrums, few historians paid it much regard as serious, foreign policy ingenuity. Experts questioned its import. Nixon denied and denied. Measured against his triumphs of détente with the Soviets and the Chinese, the landmark successes of his nuclear limitation treaties, or the devastation wrought by his escalatory bombings in Southeast Asia, the nuclear ruse appeared an inconsequential blip of an idea, a bit of bullying bluster. The ploy remained uncorroborated, and certainly misunderstood, until three decades after its execution.[8]

Yet, Nixon did indeed test his scheme. In secretly implementing the madman theory in October 1969, Nixon, with Kissinger by his side, boldly bluffed on the international stage. After five long years of stalled warfare on the Indochinese Peninsula, the president attempted to convince Soviet and North Vietnamese leaders that he was crazy enough to unleash a nuclear holocaust. The operation remained top secret. Unbeknownst to the American people, the military went on full nuclear alert. Nixon sent formations of B-52s loaded with nuclear weapons to circle the Arctic. He deployed aircraft carriers as if the ultimate strike against the North Vietnamese were imminent. He believed he could scare Hanoi into peace, but he couldn't, and he didn't. The communists refused to flinch, as the war ground on and on. Notably, the historians William

Burr and Kimball, the most significant historians of Nixon's madman theory, made the convincing case that, if anything, Nixon's nuclear saber-rattling sufficiently scared the Soviets and Chinese into enlarging their nuclear arsenals.[9] Nonetheless, through his presidential tenure, whether elated or aggravated, Nixon returned spiritedly to this coercive scheme, which reflected not only his predilection for acting and for secrecy, but also his penchant for taking great gambles in pursuit of ever-greater gains. For the exercise in rashness tested his striving and determination. It was another version of the story he told of his own life, of the lonely, bootstrapped Dick Nixon risking everything as he lurched from crisis to crisis, struggling breakneck against a dangerous and threatening world.

Political scientists embraced the utility of madness earlier than their historian counterparts, dating back to the 1950s, to the beginning of the Cold War, and far before Nixon's scheme. They focused on the notion of the "rational" mind as able to perform cost-benefit analyses. They reasoned that if an actor's maneuvering attempted to advance his interests, weighing strategic options in a stable and consistent manner, then he was acting rationally; if the actor's costs could not logically serve the desired benefits, then the choice was irrational and deemed madness. For example, if a president threatened nuclear war to halt imminent nuclear war, his actions were rational. That is, his moves were clearly calculated and proportionate; they made sense. But if he appeared to act unreasonably, if he saber-rattled as if out of control—for example negotiating at the peace table one day only then threatening nuclear cataclysm over a conflict on the tiny Indochinese Peninsula the next—then his strategy only confused his enemy. He was acting like a madman because the potential costs of his action far mismatched its benefits and his maneuvers could not be predicted. Game theorists contemporary with Nixon were fascinated by the threatening feint able to coerce an opposing army. According to game theorists, such apparent irrationality was a matter of risk, a matter, as the Nobel Prize–winning economist Thomas Schelling wrote, that circumstances "*might* get out of control."[10]

The notion of feigning such insanity for strategic advantage steadily gained steam with time. Despite initial wariness among historians, the madman theory became a phrase that launched a thousand think pieces. During President Donald J. Trump's tenure, articles from a broad spectrum of newspapers and magazines, from *U.S. News & World Report* to the *Washington Post*, from the *Atlantic* to *Forbes*, debated whether Trump was employing the ruse against the North Koreans, Chinese and Iranians. They postured over "Trump's Madman Gambit" and "The Return of the Madman Theory."[11] Was Trump's talk of "fire and fury" mere bluster, or was he willing to let loose the United States' nuclear arsenal? Was Nixon's nuclear feint against the Vietnamese a canny strategy or did it dementedly tempt nuclear catastrophe? Trump's over-the-top rhetoric elicited trepidation among journalists and policy makers, whereas Nixon's "tricky" notion enticed. In both instances, the key and the conundrum of the nuclear gambit remained—the difficulty for onlookers to determine whether the madman persona was an act for gaining strategic advantage or if the actor was truly mad. The more difficult the distinction, the more effective the bluff. The better the actor, the crazier he seems. At a certain point, the distinction between crazed and controlled craze shrinks, collapsing on itself, as the risk of losing control becomes too great. At a certain point, the rationalized irrational simply gets out of hand.

The question for political and social scientists has been whether acting mad works. Scholarly opinion in this regard has varied. One camp contends that such seemingly out-of-control leveraging can be useful as a strategy of coercion. In short, throw a tantrum, be placated. Antithetically, other scholars insist that mad maneuvering invariably leads to bad outcomes, such as mass casualties or eventual self-destruction—see Adolf Hitler, Mao Zedong, Idi Amin, Saddam Hussein, Muammar al-Qaddafi. The political scientists Andrew Little and Thomas Zeitzoff developed an intriguing "evolutionary" model: If rewarded for risky behavior, an actor will press further. He pushes boundaries at the bargaining table to gather more and more chips, raising the stakes higher and higher. In an evolution of increasingly risky and riskier behavior, the actor ups the ante (like Hitler), and in other cases, a regime passes along such learned behavior to the next generation (like the Kim family in North Korea).[12]

In analyzing the madman theory, these contemporary political scientists have narrowly defined madness as acting irrationally tough, as an all-too-eager propensity to play Russian roulette. Nixon's thinking aligned with this framework and with foreign policy makers and intellectuals who thought of the logically oriented aspect of the mind as a cost-benefit apparatus, along the lines of the rational versus the irrational, delineating between the reasonable and the emotional. The critic Lionel Trilling, a Nixon contemporary, saw this duality as "integral to our cultural disposition." He examined how the notion of thoughtful order battling chaotic emotion in the human mind had been codified over centuries into a "doctrine that . . . there are two systems, one manifest, the other latent or covert," one logical and conscious, the other "instinctual and libidinal" and unconscious. This conceptual binary of sentiment harkens back to Victorian melodrama, to Manichean madmen like Dr. Frankenstein and Dr. Jekyll, to Freudian standoffs between the abiding superego and the unrestrained id.[13]

In the 1970s, many social scientists proposed an alternative, cognitive understanding of emotion, viewing it not as an inner force threatening to be released, but as an ongoing "process of perception and appraisal," a series of internal judgments about good and harm attuned to external stimuli and events. In the 1980s in the history of emotions, a relatively new field at the time, scholars wrote of "emotionologies" or "emotional regimes" to examine how feelings flowed not from within but were pressed upon the individual from without. According to this view, historians considered how "social communities" encouraged and policed emotions as preferable, acceptable, unwanted, or a threat. The key supposition was that like war, race, or gender, emotional experiences have changed over time. Today, scientists have linked certain regions of the neuroanatomy, for example the limbic system, to emotion. They have found a clear differentiation in brain function between primarily cognitive areas versus affectively charged brain regions. Rather than separate spheres, the pure cognitive, or non-emotional, areas of the brain often fire in concert with the limbic. Recent scholars consider how emotion acts in a loop between the cognitive, social and neurological, between external stimuli, societal conditioning and the brain's pathways.[14]

For a liberal such as Trilling, writing in Nixon's day, as he hewed to concerns between the irrational and rational, between Eros and civilization, the central modern quest appeared to be the pursuit of a "sincerity" in which the inner emotive self and external expression united. He pointed to Polonius's entreaty to his son Laertes in *Hamlet*: "To thine own self be true." Going further, Trilling traced a contemporary affective concern that seemed to dominate those on the American left in the 1960s—an ever-more penetrating pursuit of emotional "authenticity" free of social judgment, of free spirits, of the freedom to feel. By contrast, the temperamentally conservative Nixon sought to maintain control of his deepest of feelings lest he risk uncomfortable or even dangerous exposure. Easy to irritate, and at times prone to soaring sentiment, at times to tears, Nixon saw the effusion of such feelings as what the historian Barbara H. Rosenwein has described as a "hydraulic model." His thinking was akin to the medieval concept of humors, whereby emotions, like "great liquids within each person, heaving and frothing, [are] eager to be let out." Rather than digging deeper into his psyche as Trilling advocated, Nixon recoiled. He found such emotional demonstrations inappropriate and embarrassing. "I can't confide absolutely in anyone, even in [my wife] Pat," he explained. "It's something like wearing clothing. If you let your hair down, you feel too naked."[15]

Since 1946, the year of Nixon's election to the House of Representatives, journalists, scholars and the intelligentsia have searched for the "authentic" or "real Nixon" behind the shifting roles and performance, inhibitions and secrecy. In January 1969, the journalist-turned-historian Garry Wills wrote in anticipation of Nixon's first presidential term that the "secret of Nixon's durability resides largely in his willingness to sacrifice former selves to the self of the moment." Four years later, Wills found himself still trying to solve the riddle of the actorly Nixon. In anticipation of the president's second inaugural, still backfooted, Wills again wavered: "There is one Nixon only, though there seem to be new ones all the time." Frustrated for decades, scholars could not allow the indeterminacy to ride. Through waves of Nixon hunting, they sought to enlighten, digging through archives to uncover what the "real Nixon" so scrupulously (and unscrupulously) concealed. The historian Stanley I. Kutler captured the essence of this biographical project when he wrote, "Portraying Nixon demands a *Rashomon*-like approach if one is to understand those varied images he projected."[16] Just as one works to synthesize the various perspectives presented in Akira Kurosawa's film *Rashomon*, the mission for Nixon watchers was to assemble his multiple guises to find the one, true, "authentic" version.

Scholars, critics and journalists have offered four ways to understand this "real Nixon" in all his madness. One can broadly characterize these four schools of Nixonology as the temperamental, developmental, revisionist and cultural. In the 1970s, psychohistorians sought to locate the roots of Nixon's ire in his childhood. They pointed to his temperament, focusing on his stubbornness, standoffishness and anger, said to be embittered by an inadequate attachment to a brutish father and an emotionally distant and distracted mother. Nixon's hurt was compounded by the deprivations of poverty and the deaths of two brothers from tuberculosis. In the 1980s and 1990s, while long-form biographies still lingered on Nixon's childhood pain, they laid out a trail of ever-accumulating woe. According to this developmental approach, rather than Nixon's frustrations, disappointments and cynicism being set in his earliest years, they accumulated during his determined, ragged political ascent as he targeted the liberals and elite who round-by-round rejected him.[17]

In countering these temperamental and developmental accounts in the 1990s, revisionist historians focused on Nixon's broad, progressive record rather than on his anger. They reviewed his reform measures—ranging from protection of the environment to Native American rights to affirmative action—arguing that the image of a wrathful Nixon was largely a fabrication by his enemies. From this revisionist perspective, Nixon was, above all, a "dedicated, efficient public servant." More recently, beginning in the 2000s, unwilling to dismiss the force of Nixon's mad and varying identities, cultural historians focused not on the "real Nixon" but on the multiplicity of Nixon incarnations as they developed from anticommunist to everyman to crook. As the historian David Greenberg wrote, "[Nixon's] images overlapped, mingled, coexisted, . . . constantly changing, always contested." Cultural historians have taken a step back to view Nixon's ire not as exceptional to his character and circumstance, but as "something in the air." His pain resembled that of his constituents, reflecting a worry over the rising tide of global communism, the wave of discontent among conservatives against the New Deal domestic order and seeming flood of liberalizing social reforms from the 1930s through the 1960s.[18]

On Nixon's Madness is indebted to temperamental, developmental and revisionist approaches, benefitting considerably from the scores of Nixonologists and the seemingly bottomless wells of research on the former president. There are those who rooted through the record of his childhood years, interviewing his acquaintances and family, and those who parsed his professional years of letters, memos and accounts of colleagues, confidants and rivals. There is the knowledge recorded in scholarly journals, the reportage of roadie journalists and the voluminous tapes housed in the Nixon archive. Moreover, this work builds on the cultural historians' turn to the multiplicity of Nixon's image, a study on how his reputation has been fought over and wrestled with for generations. It is also an inversion of such cultural history as it rests not on how others projected meaning onto Nixon but on how Nixon projected meaning onto the world, on how he struggled. He was a product of great suffering, but he also employed his suffering to great effect. He was beaten down by the game of dirty politics, but he, too, soiled politics with his gamesmanship. He winced at the notion of his madman reputation, yet he played on that ill repute. He was turned off by the display of emotion even as he was titillated to use it.

Instead of pursuing the "real Nixon," *On Nixon's Madness* lets stand his dynamic secrecy as an elusive performer and in his whirling anger. Having interviewed Nixon for sixty hours in 1993, Jonathan Aitken, a former conservative British member of Parliament and a Nixon admirer turned biographer, conceded, "You are too complicated a character to be captured accurately by the pen of a mortal writer." Nixon chuckled, and enjoying the jousting, replied, "Now I know you are really getting somewhere." For Nixon's elusiveness was key to his character. He courted secrecy—cloakroom maneuvering, shuttle diplomacy, hush money and nuclear blustery. He touted his reserve as key to retaining a winning mystique in political campaigns. He relished the need for private negotiation and the chance to obfuscate, to create a space out of which accord with the Chinese, Soviets and Vietnamese could be reached. And further, Nixon's secretiveness, his jealously guarded scheming and his need for performance extended beyond politics, strategy and national security. His secrecy was also a tool to seek out refuge. Over and again, his close aides described him as a man of seclusion, how at every opportunity he fled to his "hideaway" office in the Executive Office Building, ever the "hunched figure trying to skulk off down the back ways." For all Nixon's grandstanding, if anything, he was awkward. Reporters and raconteurs describe a physical incongruity between his script and his movements, as if he had never quite mastered the role of Dick Nixon. He exhibited a slight delay, a stuttered effect, as if before each movement, he needed to consider each action in advance. He needed not merely to live but to perform.[19]

This book is organized in two parts, reflecting the two poles of the madman theory. Part one, "On Acting," examines Nixon's performance, his control. Part two, "On Madness," looks at his temper, his conspiracism, jealousies and deceit. In broad terms, the story begins with a focus on Nixon's youth and then moves on to his early career and the presidency. Structured like a contained essay or a short story, each chapter follows a generally chronological approach and develops a theme or a case study, an intellectual history or historiography in addressing various aspects of Nixon's acting and madness.

Chapter one looks at the roles Nixon adopted during the period prior to his presidency. In this first pole of the madman theory, in his varying performances, Nixon was quintessentially a "man of many masks"—red-baiter, master debater, diplomat. In these shifting incarnations, he saw himself ever under attack, always needing to fight back, forever needing to take great risks. Each posture, each inflection, Nixon believed, could prove pivotal to rising or being felled. In this, he has come to be portrayed popularly as peevish, as ever the striver, the hard-hearted strategist envisaging a world of balanced powers, not of human rights but of exigencies. Chapter two examines an alternative and unappreciated Nixonian guise: the sentimental. Once hailed by the likes of eighteenth-century philosophers David Hume and Adam Smith, the sentimentalist calls for a great rousing of feeling, for understanding life not through logic or divine law but through emotion. Nixon littered his speeches with appeals to sentiment, trotting out maudlin anecdotes and treacly parables. He also turned the sentimental lens on himself, as when he idealized his terribly difficult childhood. Over and again, he told the story of his life as a neat Horatio Alger epic of due reward. For Nixon, the sentimental was a space in which he could unleash great emotion, but at the same time, he could control feeling by smoothing over the turbulence of his life with ersatz sentiment.

The first of three interludes examines Nixon's wife, Pat, in her own striving and reserve. She endeavored to construct a "space of her own" for personal improvement and progressive change. Her spine stiff, smile ever present, she was popularly known as "Plastic Pat"—fake, cheap. She steeled herself, defending against devastating loss, social upheaval and stinging criticism leveled at her by feminist contemporaries appalled by her constrained demeanor. Chapter three examines how Nixon suffered through clumsiness, inhibitions and loneliness and how, like Pat, he built his own wall. His ceaseless desire for advancement, his work, his need to perform served as counterweights to his inability to relax. Particularly, in his programs for affirmative action and the Family Assistance Plan, Nixon applied his faith in hard work, in his own Horatio Alger story. He wanted not to reward the purportedly lazy and undeserving; rather he wanted "workfare," not welfare, as he advocated a life of action, of performance and hard-knuckled striving.

Part two, "On Madness," focuses on the other pole of the madman theory, on Nixon's temper, tracing the inchoate components of the strategy of feigned insanity as he played on fears of the communist menace in the early years of the Cold War, then examining his own madness, jealousies and conspiracism and, finally, how he employed and struggled over such dogged feelings. Chapter four dissects Nixon's first campaign for Congress, in 1946, in which he ran for a House of Representatives seat from Southern California, challenging the heavily favored incumbent,

Jerry Voorhis. He centered his stumping around the accusation that his Democratic opponent was a Soviet sympathizer, echoing and amplifying the Red Scare of the period. He played with the usefulness of paranoia as a political strategy in warning of Voorhis's collusion with the communists, fomenting a conspiracism that he did not even believe. The second interlude examines the history of political, cultural, artistic and mythic figures who, like Nixon or Hamlet, have been said to wield such madness to their advantage. Nixon's madman theory drew on a long tradition venerating the power of the mentally infirmed in strength, sight and creativity, from Homer to John Milton, from Machiavelli to Michel Foucault.

Chapter five explores how Nixon deployed his anger, and how, as one deputy put it, "He hated."[20] Despite Nixon's best effort to assume actorly poses, he could not quell his rage and jealousies. Casting himself in a morality play of conspiracy and class, he attributed his overwhelming moods to a range of culprits. To Nixon, there was always someone to suss out, someone who bore greater culpability—longhairs, intellectuals, Jews, homosexuals, Kennedys. The third interlude examines the proximate precursors of Nixon's madman theory, how game theorists in the 1950s and 1960s conceptualized the usefulness of risk in the nuclear age, how they played with the power of the unpredictable. Chapter six delves into Nixon's implementation of the madman theory, how he used his reputation for rage and his willingness to act unpredictably to coerce foreign adversaries. Nixon applied gaming theory to real-world standoffs from the Middle East to India to Vietnam, teetering repeatedly on the edge of nuclear war. Far from a one-off tactic, nuclear saber-rattling became a key tool in Nixon's conduct of international affairs. For him, the superpower standoff was not a steady march toward détente, but rather an ongoing test of mettle. He saw the Cold War as he saw his life—as a series of ordeals that demanded great risk, the grand gesture, the "big play."

Chapter seven examines Nixon's trip to China and how he juggled roles, trying to control the furious gamesman and channel the hallowed peacemaker. No one guise quite fit. At times he attempted to emulate the crafty Prince Klemens von Metternich, foreswearing virtue for the artful deal, yet at times he waxed on about universal ideals and self-determination in the fashion of President Woodrow Wilson. He considered his continuation of the forceful bombing of Vietnam as both a pragmatic grand strategy and as a "moral" choice for ensuring a just peace. Only then, in in his visit to Beijing, so far from relishing in his madness, Nixon was taken by the outwardly stoic Mao and Premier Zhou Enlai, their control of sentiment and also their control over their people. As a fascinated Nixon saw it, instead of unleashing their wrath, instead of saber-rattling, instead of acting mad, the great power of the Chinese came from how they manipulated their emotion artfully.

In the seminal 1941 essay "Sensibility and History: How to Reconstitute the Affective Life of the Past," Febvre described emotion as Nixon might have—as a "disturbance, as something dangerous, troublesome and ugly, at least, one might say, as something that ought not to appear naked." Nixon described his letting loose in public as a rare aberration of lost inhibition. "I am emotional," he explained, yet he preferred performative means, values of self-mastery and ascetic aloofness. He insisted, "I have always sort of prided myself on self-control . . . I am a great believer in privacy." For Nixon saw such discipline as a matter of retaining a sense of mystery, of keeping others ever at a distance, both impressed and confused. That is what his idol Charles de Gaulle had done. "You can be human and still have the mystique," Nixon calculated. "The thing is, you have to be considered an *homme sérieux*."[21] For Nixon's well-known anger was not simply due to a tainted temperament or a learned moral corruption resulting from his years in politics. Instead, his ire had an additional, instrumental component. It, too, was a tool, one more of Tricky Dick's political tricks. After all, did Nixon, like Joseph McCarthy, really think the State Department was riddled with communist traitors? Was he really as racist as the former Dixiecrats with whom he lit celebratory cigars? Did he really so revile the North Vietnamese? In his performative acts and in his swirling rage, the "authentic" and "real" Nixon eludes; the answers to such questions elude.

As Haldeman and Nixon strolled across the fog-shrouded beach during the homestretch of the 1968 presidential campaign, the soon-to-be president revealed to his square-shouldered chief aide that he was convinced he could wrap up the Vietnam War within his first year in office. The communists would "believe any threat of force that Nixon makes," Nixon insisted. And indeed, the madman seemed to resemble Haldeman's boss quite a bit or, at the least, it seemed a caricature of the famously frustrated politician: smirched by sweat, slouching under the weight of innumerable grudges, grumbling, growling, grousing, jowls aflap. It was Nixon who baited the Reds furiously. It was he who would not be contained; he who would not be kicked around anymore. Charm did not come easily to Nixon. He bore all of the stiffness of JFK with little of the ease. He exuded the gruff bearing of LBJ without the magnetic appeal. And just so, on that day kicking the sand on break from speechwriting, Nixon insisted to the former adman Haldeman that the foremost reason the madman strategy would work was the reputation he had rehearsed his whole life. The crazed bluffing, like a glove, fit the man: fury, calculation and inhibition, the propensity for the gambling play. "I'm the one man in this country who can do it," Nixon told his lead lieutenant. The crucial factor that could make the nuclear ruse work, he proposed, was "because it's Nixon."[22]

Part I: On Acting

1 | The Acting Life of Richard Nixon

> MacArthur with his riding crop and corncob pipe, Patton with his
> pearl-handled revolvers, Churchill with his strut, FDR with
> his jaunty cigarette lighter—all were acting.
> —Richard Nixon, 1990

THE TWO MET in 1947 as junior members of the House Committee
on Education and Labor. Nixon remembered one train trip in particular that he shared with John F. Kennedy. They were riding back from
McKeesport, Pennsylvania, where they had debated the Taft-Hartley
bill. "It was a night train because we had to get back for a vote the next
day," Nixon recalled. It was still years before easy air travel between
Pittsburgh and Washington. The pair drew for the upper and lower
berth, yet neither slept. Instead, the freshmen congressmen stayed up
all night talking, "particularly about the world and where we were going,"
Nixon remembered. He talked to Kennedy about his days at Vella
Lavella, in the Solomon Islands, during World War II; Kennedy relayed
the tale of his PT cruiser. They might have even met in their naval days,
they imagined. The two young men grew excited. They spoke of their
chief interests: foreign policy, Asia, Europe. Both were anti-communist,
pro–foreign aid, interventionist if necessary. Both were wary of labor
leaders, and, as one conservative scholar complained in *Commentary* of
their shared progressive shopping lists, "[Nixon] favored spending federal funds on school construction, whereas Kennedy wanted money for
teachers' salaries as well."[1]

It is easy to forget: Nixon burst onto the national political scene, just like Kennedy, as a swift up-and-comer. By accounts, before their 1960 election standoff, the two young guns had formed a genuine if mild friendship as at once colleagues, peers and competitors. They both seemed on a mission, impatient to climb to the highest of offices. Both also had overbearing fathers, hallowed but difficult mothers, and brothers who had died young—two Nixons to tuberculosis, a Kennedy in war. The two men shared an emotional reserve, a self-control. Slight of build, they were "essentially quite shy," Nixon remarked. They saw themselves as "studious, intellectual." As Nixon recalled of their connection, far different than their politician peers, "Neither of us was a back-slapper, and we both were uncomfortable with boisterous displays of superficial camaraderie."[2]

Nonetheless, the pair diverged in reputation. Kennedy needed pomp to fortify his boyish image, while Nixon needed a bit more frivolity to loosen his ever-serious mien. William Safire captured the dueling double standard of class and charisma that separated the would-be 1960 presidential nominees. "'[L]oner,' [when] applied to a picture of John Kennedy walking pensively down a beach, is a romantic word," noted the speechwriter, but when "applied to Nixon, the word seems to gain a sinister connotation." Admirers swooned at a "bookish" Jack, but stared askance at the "bookish" Dick. For Nixon, the 1960 presidential campaign would become an unwinnable bind of personality contortion and distortion. Nixon's eventual loss would be attributed to his literal performance in the first televised debate with Kennedy. To viewers at home, Kennedy came across as assured and vigorous, while Nixon was panned as sallow, sickly looking, and fumbling.[3]

The irony was that for all the talk of Kennedy's glamorous made-for-Hollywood lifestyle, it was Nixon who turned out to be the real performer. The irony was that for all of Nixon's complaints about his colleagues' "displays of superficial camaraderie," he had no equal in

Entering the House of Representatives in January 1947 as freshman up-and-comers, Nixon and John F. Kennedy developed a relationship as peers, competitors, and to a certain degree friends. *Courtesy of the National Archives.*

reinvention. Nixon was, as Safire wrote, "loser, loner, winner, leader . . . always boring in, always coming back." At times, he played the part of the philosopher-statesman, liberal and optimistic; at points, he acted the reckless warmonger, careless and nihilistic. He could climb onto the soapbox to save the forests and the seas, or he could slump around for hours on end, sulking and grumbling about the elite, the intellectual, the effete, only to turn around bedecked and bow-tied to escort his daughter Tricia to her debutante ball. One leading critic described Nixon as the heartless Tin Man of Oz, while more than a decade later, others thought him the Wizard himself, furiously coordinating world events behind thick curtain. Only then, Nixon pivoted once more. "He has been written off as finished, *kaput*, done for, washed up and all through in national politics more often by more people and more erroneously than anyone else in American life," the *Washington Post* wrote, yet back on the political stage there was that familiar face stretched from chin to brow, like Bob Hope's, like the long curve of an early moon but "carved out of a walnut." One "new Nixon" took center stage, only then another "new Nixon" appeared—new but still familiar, new yet with that same tart mien.[4]

Nixon acted for a living, for a life. He was a man of inhibition, rarely letting loose with joy or grief, with spontaneous candor. He insisted on maintaining that first pole of the "madman theory," that of performance and control of emotion, a calculated expression of affect. For Nixon did not simply project roles; he hid behind them, selling multiple versions of himself. With talking points, he could entrance a crowd of 30,000, or he could lean in to mesmerize the "smallest radio station in Rhine-lander, Wisconsin," one deputy recalled. He could charm a room from the mike. To act, however, he needed a script. Without preparation, an-other deputy added, without hours of what Nixon termed "homework," "if he's surprise[d] . . . He actually cannot utter a discernible word." A terribly shy man, Nixon was ever preparing for the performance. As one reporter remarked of his actorly chops, "I had the impression he would even practice his inflection [for] when he said 'hello.'"[5]

Nixon was not alone among presidents in possessing a penchant for acting. President Ronald Reagan once told ABC's David Brinkley that he "wondered how you could do the job if you hadn't been an actor." Gov-erning takes on a multitude of guises for a range of audiences and agen-das. Politicians need to orate, and, at times, they need to pander. In the classic study *Presidential Power and the Modern Presidents,* Richard Neu-stadt stressed "reputation" as the honed aura of the statesman imbuing him the power to govern. All modern-day presidents adopted roles to fit the situation, to build that "reputation," to wield the power of the exe-cutive or to mask weaknesses of the office and personal limitations. In the age of mass media, as the distance between ruler and the ruled seemed to shrink, aloof power no longer appeared to be sufficient. The political increasingly became personal even as the personal was countermanded for political purpose. To reach beyond Washington and at the same time to assemble a constituency to influence Washington, President Franklin D. Roosevelt saturated American culture with the power of his performance. In place of the rousing vibrato of nineteenth-century orators, FDR rallied the public with the seemingly personal aside of a fireside chat. His national radio addresses, instrumental in political persuasion, were what he deemed the "greatest force for molding public opinion."[6]

Still, what remained notable about these modern-day performances was that for all their air of familiarity, they retained a formal and aspirational tone. Roosevelt's perfectly rounded mid-Atlantic cant set him apart from the masses listening at home, while his rousing words were aptly conveyed in near-poetic verse. For all his purported candor, he dared not display actual disability, never chancing to let on that he did not have the use of his legs. Subsequently, President Dwight D. Eisenhower played the part of the "elegant amateur," wielding a casual and reassured touch even as he steered the nation with what the historian Fred Greenstein called his "hidden hand." Ike balanced an avuncular innocence in public with a toughness in private, presenting himself as ever above the fray of the political mud. In his own ersatz display, JFK affected an "elusive detachment" to burnish the myth of Camelot. The historian Steven Watts described Kennedy's duel-sided image as "inspiration and emotional sustenance on the one hand, obfuscation and self-delusion on the other." Kennedy was viewed as a man of intense vigor even though saddled with Addison's disease. He sold himself as a man of peace even as he increased U.S. military commitments during the developing Cold War. He crusaded for civil rights while slow-walking reform. He presented himself as a "family man" while being a known womanizer.[7]

By one measure, Nixon was just not as honed a performer as his predecessors, but by another, he was all too practiced. Parts of the American public caught on to the act. Nixon appeared both all too regular and all too different, too awkward, too aloof, too baldly calculating in his image making, so obviously playing a political game. In this respect, Nixon was ill-calibrated. Maddeningly, he was insufficiently remote yet too remote, unfamiliar yet somehow too candid and crass. As Safire described, "When [Nixon] was controlled, they said he was phony; when he was open, they said he was crazed."[8]

Nixon's political ascendence came at a turning point in American culture. Just as television literally became part of the furniture, a shifty but shrouded Dick Nixon came to play a central role in the American zeitgeist. By the late 1960s, the ever-reinventive Nixon had become an avatar of the new, suspect television age and the mass marketed. The burgeoning questions of the mutability of images crisscrossed with the mutability of Nixon's persona. His ever-shifting performance became a subject in and of itself. What had been the attractive, elusive power of Roosevelt, Eisenhower and Kennedy became suspect politicking by the performative and often stiff Nixon. The power of his acting was not so much a talent to respect, but a manipulation to question or even fear. The press corps nicknamed him the "cardboard man." The folk singer Country Joe McDonald crowned the president a "mechanical man . . . the genuine plastic man," the most malleable of performers for a purportedly soulless era. For years, leading columnists copped their best impressions of the Canadian philosopher of postmodernism, Marshall McLuhan, to describe his ever-distant, ever-inscrutable image. The *Wall Street Journal's* Douglas Hallett noted the "artificial spontaneity of the Nixon media," how the president's press apparatus so fastidiously staged his moments of candor. Hallett remarked on how the new medium of television both revealed the man to the masses and, at the same time, hid the candidate's true face. Even Safire's sharp pen struggled to capture how "the real Nixon, the real Nixon [wa]s not the real Nixon" for "what Nixon saw to be the real Nixon was not the real Nixon." Trying again, Safire summoned the words of Gertrude Stein, asserting that Nixon "reflected those he wanted to reflect, when he wanted to reflect them."[9]

In December 1967, Stephen Hess and David Broder wrote in the *Washington Post* that the hunt for the "real Nixon" had already been a "popular pastime" for a decade and a half, since his vice presidential days, under Eisenhower. As the historian David Greenberg charted, a cottage industry sprung up early on with the agenda of sleuthing out the true Nixon within: *The Real Nixon* (1960), *The Man Behind the Mask* (1971), *The Nixon Nobody Knows* (1972). There was a flood of think pieces with headlines like "Golf as a Clue to the Real Nixon" (1969) and "Will the Real Nixon Now Stand Up" (1972) and "There's Something about the Guy I Just Don't Like" (1971). The search for the "authentic" Nixon became a national preoccupation, Broder and Hess concluded, because the very "something [Nixon was] withholding [was] the essence of himself." Indeed, a year later, in 1968 a month before Nixon was elected president, the *Post* remained stymied, headlining a front page story "The 'Real Nixon' an Enigma."[10]

One Nixon aide floated what amounted to the "observer effect" in physics—that is, an isolated phenomenon cannot be exactly measured because the phenomenon behaves differently when under investigation. The observer, inevitably, has an effect on the observed. The aide asserted, "All those journalists looking for the 'real Nixon,' seemed not to understand." As long as reporters had Nixon under their gaze, they altered his behavior. When around the news media, the aide relayed, the boss was constantly "working." Around others, "he's not the 'real Nixon.'"[11]

With postmodern thinking at peak popularity, speculation about image and imitation, of art and artifice, circulated around Nixon's White House press office. The postmodern turn undercut singular, coherent narratives in favor of multiple, competing perspectives, digressing from the "real" and underlying truth to focus on the fabricated subjectivity of perception. In 1964 McLuhan famously posited that the key to understanding was grasping that the "medium is the message." And just so, Raymond Price Jr., one of Nixon's young speechwriters, noted in a memo that it was not reality but "the image of the candidate" that was important: "We have to be very clear on this point: that the response [of the voting public] is to the image, not to the man." Every aural aspect, every visual nuance, seemed to observers of this first television generation to influence how audiences processed the message. Rather than craning to see from the back of a rally's bleachers, suddenly with television, the viewer was thrust into front row seats, able to pick out the candidate's pores. As Neustadt wrote at the time, "Everything [a leader] personally says or does (or fails to say, omits to do) becomes significant in everyone's appraisals." For both the famed scholar as for Nixon's eager, young press team, a president's political survival became a matter of presenting an immaculate representation of himself.[12]

Yet, although a live and better image connoted an enhanced verisimilitude, the slick novel medium of television also opened opportunities for slick new tricks. Truth for the gang in the Nixon press shop would become artifice. "To put it another way," the speechwriter Price said, "it's simply not true that honesty is its own salesman . . . [I]t takes art to convey the truth from us to the viewer." For Price, the one on the team who sprinkled soaring rhetoric into Nixon's speeches, truth was a matter of performance: "It's not what's there that counts, it's what's projected . . . [I]t's not what he projects, but rather what the voter receives." Thus, Price went on, ideating of the postmodern, "It's not the man we have to change, but rather the received impression. And this impression often depends more on the medium and its use than it does on the candidate himself."[13]

Nixon's critics, rather than exhibiting enthusiasm over the possibilities of relating style through the new medium, saw Nixon in the television age as a threat. He was a carnival barker, luring the masses into a big but empty tent, an illusionist distracting the audience while selling himself as the product. To his naysayers, television allowed for sheer demagogic trickery. "If generally adopted," the liberal critic Arthur Schlesinger Jr. warned, Nixon's televised hoodwinking of the American populace would prove ultimately dangerous. Through reflections of representations and representations of reflections, through the arts of hidden persuasion, through parts switched for parts, the difference between artifice, art and the "real" would collapse, Schlesinger argued. The truth could be fabricated; the news faked. Authoritarian manipulation would overtake republican virtue. Nixon and his political trickery, Schlesinger wrote, so threatened that they stood to "destroy the whole fabric of mutual confidence on which democracy rests."[14]

Greenberg has noted that this postmodernist spin seemed to peak in the mid-1970s and 1980s with the popularity among political protestors, petty criminals, movie stars and Halloween revelers alike of the actual Nixon mask, his signature features accentuated: the deeply receded hairline, temples touched with gray, the ski-jump nose, a horse-toothed smirk, all cast in thick latex. The Nixon enigma seemed a circular maze, a mask fashioned from the face of a mask. The *Washington Post*'s Don Oberdorfer grasped to quote T.S. Eliot to describe the candidate's uncannily canned visage. Nixon's was "a face to meet the faces that you meet." Indeed, Nixon appeared to have wholly transformed into an actor. Exchanging mask for mask, as his erstwhile Democratic opponent Adlai Stevenson remarked, Nixon was the "kind of politician who would cut down a redwood tree, then mount the stump for a speech on conservation." As Stevenson swiped, "This is a man of many masks, but who can say they have seen his real face?"[15]

The ever-elusive Nixon was first drawn to acting as a senior in his high school Latin Club's celebration on the occasion of the 2000th anniversary of Virgil's birth. His class's stage adaptation of the *Aeneid* starred Nixon as Aeneas, the founder of Rome. With costume shoes two sizes too small, he found the performance "excruciating[ly] pain[ful]." The audience found themselves "bored stiff" except for the moment he had to hug the girl who played Dido. That, in the stolid atmosphere of their Quaker school, they found hilarious. Nixon would later recall the "hoots and catcalls and whistles" and how "both turned red." It was a fitting memory that Nixon liked to recount, a stage introduction of exhilaration and humiliation that would twine through his career's performances. For even as his classmates laughed, Nixon fell in love with the stage and with his scene partner. His co-star, Ola Florence, became his first girlfriend. They dated for seven years. He had little if any social life outside their courtship. Still Florence remarked, "Sometimes I think I never really knew him," speaking of the young, distant and guarded Nixon. "And I was as close to him as anyone," she added. "I still feel some of that—he was a mystery."[16]

Nixon continued to enjoy the excitement of acting in plays in college. "Dick loved the stage," his drama teacher Albert Upton remembered. "Nixon was the easiest person to direct I've ever dealt with. He'd come to class with his lines memorized [and] do what I told him to do." He was usually cast as older men—a middle-age gentlemen or an elderly British innkeeper—due to his dark features, sonorous voice and, no doubt, his seriousness of purpose. On the stage, he found the connection he lacked in the quotidian. It was "a thrill of getting to an audience," Nixon remembered. He found the theater a test of his inhibitions. "I can still remember thinking my legs would give out or I would lose my voice at some crucial moment," he remarked. Like so many trials in his life, acting was a painful but enticing feat to conquer. There is little evidence that Nixon was any good at acting in the theater, although it was said that he had an uncanny ability to cry on cue. As he so often did, he persevered, continuing to act in local theater as a young lawyer. It was while a member of the Community Players in Whittier, California, that he met

Pat Ryan, his future wife. The play was *The Dark Tower* by George S. Kaufman and Alexander Woollcott. He had the role of a playwright; she played a flirt. As Nixon remembered, he knew at once he was going to marry her. For there, again, on the stage, he had fallen in love.[17]

Nixon also found outlets for performing as an avid and successful debater in high school and college. It was when alone onstage that he excelled. He entered the Constitutional Oratorical Contest three times, and he swept, winning three times. Nixon honed "the ability to get his opponent off-balance," the manager of his university team, Kenneth Ball, recalled. "He would so fluster the other speaker with his steady attack that his opposition would become emotional and stop thinking clearly." What was more, Nixon discovered a skill: He could contort to take either side of an argument. In his first debate, in seventh grade, he argued, "Resolved: that insects are more beneficial than harmful." In college he argued that "despotic kings [are] those priceless guarantees of freedom." His flair for the dramatic continued through his days as a young lawyer. "As to his courtroom psychology," one partner in his firm said in describing Nixon's smooth, varied performances, "he could present his case so butter wouldn't melt in his mouth," or in assaultive cross examination, "he could take hold of a cantankerous witness and shake him like a dog."[18] And, indeed, Nixon made a political career of performing: the speeches, the glad-handing, the tricks and the scheming, the dance of diplomacy, more debates.

The performance that launched the young Nixon on the national stage was as a congressman on the House Un-American Activities Committee (HUAC), where he played the detective and dogged prosecutor. Selected by the Republican Party leadership in the House of Representatives, Nixon stepped in to perform the part of the young, swaggering and resolute inquisitor. Far from the cantankerous image he would later come to embody, Nixon added a sensible face to the cast. The antisubversive HUAC had become its own fief of misanthropic malcontents, neither easily dismissed nor held in much esteem. The staff of the committee consisted of a mash of penitent former communists and retired FBI agents, an underworld network of seedy witnesses disenchanted with the communist cause, self-certified experts on the "Red menace," toady patriots and low-rent lawyers pumping information on and off the congressional record. "Not all Jews are Communist, but my information is that 75 percent of the members of the Communist Party in this country are Yiddish," clucked one member, who also considered the Ku Klux Klan an "old American institution."[19]

By contrast, Nixon was the levelheaded front man. It was a plum role for the eager, new congressman. In the national spotlight during the first wave of the Red Scare, Nixon took center stage in 1948 and made his name on the Alger Hiss case. A senior editor at *Time* magazine who went by the half-concocted name Whittaker Chambers was the lead accuser against Hiss, a renowned diplomat. Journalists commonly described the hunched Chambers as "slovenly," overweight and sweating, his most distinguishing trait a garbled mash of browning teeth. A zealous former communist, he exuded the enthusiasm of the apostate, harboring what one associate judged "the conscience of Raskolnikov and the mission of Jesus Christ." Chambers had a flair for the dramatically turned phrase, the heightened pause, the elevated ring to his stories that reverberated across the hearing room and into newspapers to theatrical effect. Slouching, head ducked, his eyes pinned to the floor, he muttered his account softly to the committee. At times, over the "hum of movie cameras and the pop of flashbulbs," so apparently overwhelmed with doubt or shame or diffidence, he whispered. He was a slob "except when he spoke," Nixon noted, only then he was "a genius without question." His performance mesmerized Nixon. He could appreciate an actorly turn. Chambers outlined a communist conspiracy of one-time New Deal bureaucrats and labor leaders from the top ranks whose foremost aim was the "infiltration of the American government." He claimed to have served as a courier for the group and accused Hiss of being a "liar and a spy." In finishing, Chambers' voice croaked. The hearing's packed chamber was silent. Reporters scooted out to file under blazing headlines the machinations of an attempted Red coup.[20]

Chambers could not have targeted a man more unlike himself. Dapper and exquisitely articulate, a former mentee of Felix Frankfurter at Harvard and once a clerk for Supreme Court Justice Oliver Wendel Holmes, Hiss was the very picture of the elite Eastern bureaucrat. Nixon described the diplomat as "good-looking, suave, [an] Ivy League manner." He was far more FDR than Harry Truman. In the thick summer air of the cavernous Caucus Room, even through the faltering ventilation, Hiss rounded and clicked each syllable of his slightly high-pitched mid-Atlantic accent. "I am not and have never been a member of the Communist Party," he began. In late 1944, as executive secretary, he had helped organize the Dumbarton Oaks Conference to form the United Nations. In February 1945, Hiss served as a key aide at the tripartite Yalta Conference, where the peace terms of World War II were decided. Two months later, he acted as temporary secretary-general for the inaugural gathering of the United Nation in San Francisco. Amid rumors of communist ties, Hiss left the State Department for a still-plush seat as president of the Carnegie Endowment for International Peace in early 1946. Hiss represented a prized scalp for Chambers and the committee. If not for the communist rumors, his career had progressed such that many predicted he would have become secretary of state.[21]

Driven by sympathy for the plight of factory workers, miners and slum-dwellers, young men of Chambers and Hiss's generation had found hope and direction in the calls for justice by socialists, communist and organized labor. "Practically every young man has been through a phase when he has been interested in Communist activities of some kind," commented one prominent State Department intelligence official. The alluring propaganda of the Soviet Union offered an alternative to the suffering of America's destitute in the industrial age, a utopic vision of fairer distribution of wealth by a centrally organized state. It was a heady mix of revolution, righteousness and stern discipline. Having traveled in elite circles, Hiss knew several of the men accused of treason—one from summer camp while a boy, one on the Harvard Law Review, a couple more from legal circles—but the charges against him, he denied. The crowd met the end of his testimony with delighted laughter as he coyly concluded about the disheveled Chambers, "[He] looks like a lot of people. I might even mistake him for the chairman of this committee."[22]

In light of Hiss's impressive testimony, HUAC appeared deflated and defeated. They were tempted to drop the case. Compared to the composed Hiss, the "slovenly" Chambers seemed clearly outmatched. Truman dismissed the investigation as a "red herring." Rumor suggested that Chambers was an "incurable drunkard." There were whispers of mental illness and homosexuality. Under the glare of national coverage, HUAC needed to overcome what reporters described as its casual relationship with the truth and unhealthy attachment to con jobs and smears. "This case is going to kill the Committee unless you can prove Chambers' story," one *Washington Post* reporter muttered in an aside to Nixon, who remained dogged. He found Hiss's "show" on the stand "too sensitive," too "smooth." Something "doesn't ring true," Nixon thought. If he failed to prove Hiss a communist, he could at least undercut him as a liar—and through extension of the syllogism, if a liar, why not a communist? A determined Nixon took to the starring role of communist fighter, casting himself as the defender of truth and justice and the American way. His plan: to catch Hiss perjuring himself to Congress for denying ever setting sight on his accuser. He needed to prove that Hiss had known Chambers.[23]

To prepare for the hearing, Nixon privately grilled the accuser. "[What] did [Hiss's] wife look like, where did he live, can you describe his houses?" "What were [Hiss's] eating habits . . . What kind of clothes did he wear, did he have a car?" Chambers asserted that not only had the two been acquaintances, but that in their younger days when both traveled secretly in socialist circles, he had rented an apartment for a summer from the Hisses. Chambers further asserted that Hiss "threw in" his Model A Ford Roadster as part of the deal. When the two finally circled around to the hobbies of the accused, Nixon recalled Chambers' eyes lighting up. Well, Chambers told him, Hiss was an amateur ornithologist. They both were, he continued. "I remember how excited he was one day when he came back to the apartment in which we were both living at that time and said that he had seen a prothonotary warbler."[24]

In turn, Nixon grilled Hiss on the committee's stand. "We went over the same ground with him, and as the answers came back from him with regard to the places he lived, with regard to his car, with regard to all of these matters, we recognized . . . that Chambers had been right," that Hiss had lied to Congress, that the two had known each other well. Slipping on a familiar guise, Nixon the trial lawyer tied the two together with the leasing of the apartment and the shared broken-down Roadster. Chambers produced a letter with secret State Department codes that he claimed Hiss's wife had typed. The envelope was marked with an idiosyncratic script made by an old Woodstock typewriter that the committee traced back to the Hisses. Hiss claimed that they had sold the Woodstock years before. Had he ever seen the prothonotary warbler? Nixon poked. "I have right here on the Potomac," Hiss answered.[25]

Finally, Nixon recalled, Hiss admitted that it was "possible" that he knew "this man Chambers . . . [as] a freelance writer" for the Nye Committee on disarmament in the mid-1930s and that Chambers, then using the name George Crosley, had stayed "on occasion" in Hiss and his wife's apartment. For the last major disclosure, under Nixon's pressing, Chambers retrieved microfilm he had hidden in a carved-out pumpkin in a field on his family farm. It included classified material on trade negotiations between the United States and Nazi Germany on the precipice of World

War II, information that no doubt would have interested the Soviets. The story of the so-called Pumpkin Papers became a national sensation, the pumpkin, itself, photographed for all to behold. Playing to the rowdy press gathered at HUAC's doors, the much-ballyhooed congressman-turned-detective with a theatrical esprit touted Chambers' top-secret material as "conclusive proof of the greatest treason conspiracy in this nation's history."[26]

Hiss would spend forty-four months in prison after being convicted of perjury. He maintained his innocence and was never convicted of espionage. The Hiss case, however, made Nixon a household name as a valiant fighter of communists and prosecutor extraordinaire. It would be touted as the prime example of righteousness in the fight against the communist-infiltrated ranks of the federal government. By contrast to the overblown and outlandish accusations leveled by HUAC against targets before Hiss, Nixon had succeeded in portraying the debonair diplomat as every bit the guilty subversive. "One man. Richard Nixon argued quietly but firmly [during] . . . the Hiss case," Chambers would later assert. In continuing to fight fire, Nixon played with fire. He breathed it. After Dean Acheson refused to denounce Hiss at his own confirmation hearing for secretary of state, Nixon rolled off an alliterative barb for the ages. He declared the longtime statesman the "Red Dean of the College of Cowardly Containment." Moreover, the young congressman railed, Acheson's "clipped mustache, his British tweeds, and his haughty manner made him the perfect foil for the snobbish kind of foreign service personality and mentality that had been taken in hook, line, and sinker by the Communists."[27]

The case turned out to be a double-edged sword. As with Nixon's stage acting, some spectators admired it, while others crowed. It was then, with the Hiss case, that Nixon believed he had made enemies. Nixon had given anti-communism a respectable face, but foreign policy doves resented him deeply for it. The case that emblazoned his name in headlines also linked Nixon to the McCarthyite fringe. For years, the consensus in liberal circles was that Hiss had been wronged—smeared by anti-communist extremists—and condemned for his devotion to internationalism and an international world order. They blamed Nixon and his polished act. More than the plaudits that greeted him from conservatives, Nixon focused on the "charges," the "whispers." He obsessed over how his opponents had "hurled against me . . . bigamy, forgery, drunkenness, insanity, thievery, anti-Semitism."[28] He resented being marked as little different from the red-hunting hacks seated next to him on the committee, and it was this last strain of victimization, the sense of being attacked, of being bleeding prey that presaged if not produced Nixon's next starring role. For, in it, he would not be the smearing, but the smeared.

As a vice presidential candidate, Nixon altered his approach in 1952, transforming his role from ardent accuser to victim wronged. The one-time communist inquisitor was accused of corruption himself. Nixon was alleged to have a personal "secret fund" containing $18,000 collected from a shady group of Californian bankers, industrialists and real estate brokers. Democrats called him a crook. Prominent Republicans were split. Some wanted his name struck from Eisenhower's ticket. Nixon insisted it was a political trap.[29]

Ike had recruited Nixon as a "bridge to younger people," a "good answer to extremist[s]," the one who "got Hiss fairly." Nixon recalled the excitement even to be considered for the vice presidency at the age of thirty-nine and by General Eisenhower. It was "something you only dreamed about." But then, on his first whistle-stop tour up the coast of California, Nixon read a *New York Post* headline: "Secret Rich Men's Trust Fund Keeps Nixon in Style Far Beyond His Salary." Eisenhower was running on an Honest Deal, a challenge to Roosevelt's New Deal and Truman's Fair Deal. Eisenhower's campaign against government graft and "bossism" seemed to strike at the heart of what his proposed vice president was being accused. "[W]hat is it for us to carry on this crusade against this business . . . in Washington if we, ourselves, aren't as clean as a hound's tooth?" Ike implored his chief aides. With regard to Nixon, hedging, Eisenhower struck an ambivalent tone. "You've got a big following in this country," he told his running mate. Nixon had attracted loyal supporters among conservatives and Cold War hawks. "If the impression got around that you got off the ticket because I forced you off, it is going to be very bad," Eisenhower reasoned. "On the other hand, if I issue a statement now backing you up, in effect people will accuse me of condoning wrongdoing." Nixon pledged complete disclosure, but Eisenhower offered no assurances.[30]

The episode, what French diplomats in Washington were calling "L'affaire Neexon," took on an air of conspiracy and criminality. As the days passed, the press lathered. "'Nixon Affair' Deflates Happy Mood," the *Wall Street Journal* declared. "Nixon Should Withdraw," wrote the *Washington Post* editorial board, which had already endorsed the Eisenhower slate. One Republican operative recalled showing the headlines to Nixon. "So when I handed him that paper he almost needed intensive care," he said of the vice presidential candidate. "They almost had to take him off the train." Nixon thought about quitting. He seized up. His neck stiffened. Another smear by the Hiss crowd, he believed, State Department types, the liberal press, communist sympathizers. On a stop in Marysville, California, Nixon hit back: "The more they smear me the more I'm going to expose the Communists and the crooks and those that defend them until they throw them all out of Washington!" A matter of class also seemed in play. Nixon was the impatient up-and-comer, a partisan tosser of red meat. He had gained fame as the overeager redbaiter. In climbing so fast, Nixon screamed hunger, need, ambition. "How could Eisenhower stand this tense, insecure, self-absorbed man, always looking for marks for favor?" one wife of a senator later remarked. "Eisenhower liked rich, self-assured, relaxed people."[31]

Nixon released a list of contributions, the highest group donating in the range of $200. He drafted a typewritten itemized statement of expenses—"Stationery, printing . . . $6166.60 . . . Reports and communications . . . $2017.79 . . . Advertising . . . $764.68—but Eisenhower was more concerned about reading the country's mood. He wanted Nixon to go on nationwide television, an idea presented to his running mate as both advice and an order. To defend himself against the charge of corruption, the young politico needed not only to present his case, he also needed to transform his image from that of a tenacious prosecutor. Nixon secluded himself for twenty-seven straight hours to prepare his new guise. He wrote outline after outline on omnipresent yellow legal pads, dividing the pages, separating out pros and cons, developing his argument and then committing the words to memory. He practiced his lines: the money in the fund was to "meet my speaking and mailing schedule" and not for "personal use"; it was from "long time supporters" and a "matter of public knowledge." Nixon was said to have become "edgy and short-tempered." He ate and slept little. He timed the speech to the second.[32]

Interrupting the campaign schedule in Portland, Nixon flew to a Hollywood studio to make his case before the cameras. Thirty minutes before the speech, as Nixon continued to fiddle with the text, Republican elders backing Eisenhower's campaign, headed by New York governor Thomas Dewey, telephoned him. They insisted that he finish the address by announcing his resignation from the ticket. "Governor," Nixon responded, "I don't know what I'm going to do. Just tell your friends to listen to the broadcast." It was the end of the conversation. Once again, Nixon experienced terror mixed within the thrill of performance. He recalled the talk with Dewey as "traumatic." Sitting in the control room minutes before the fund speech, Nixon turned to his wife. He despaired. "I just don't think I can go through with this," he said. "Of course you can," Pat insisted. "If you withdraw under fire, you will carry the scar for the rest of your life."[33]

Through the still novel and somewhat enigmatic medium of television, Nixon addressed, 50,000,000 viewers, 48.9 percent of U.S. television households, at 9:00 p.m., prime time, from New York, on a Tuesday night in early September. To suggest his modest worth, the set was constructed to appear that the vice presidential candidate was opening his home, an amply curtained library, to the nation. In a twenty-six-minute speech, Nixon emphatically sought not only the audience's respect, but their pity. He was just a "poor but honest," run-of-the-mill, hard-hatted average American Joe who was nice to his secretaries. He maintained that he was, basically, an unexceptional family man with a wife who wore not mink but a "respectable Republican cloth coat."[34]

"Believe me, folks," Nixon insisted, he was a target of the communists. The whole fund affair was a vicious smear job. He simply used the money to defray the costs of being a politician. The donations covered only the price of mail, travel expenses, printing documents and clerical help. As a senator, he made only $15,000 a year in salary. He was in debt, and he refused to put his wife on the payroll, unlike some of his colleagues. Nixon had received one gift from a donor, a "little cocker spaniel dog" named Checkers, but he refused to return the puppy. That would be cruel. His two young daughters, "like all kids, loved the dog." To put a bow on this new guise, "honest Dick" added a likely apocryphal and certainly saccharine quote from Lincoln: "God must have loved the common people, he made so many of them."[35]

As Nixon finished, one confidant recalled his being in a "complete emotional daze." The weeks of upheaval and accusation, of swarming thoughts and indecision, cramped sides and stiff necks, the attention and tension had caught up with him, but his image had changed. No longer the red-baiter, the avid prosecutor, he was now the victim of unfair accusations, an everyman, a man of the television age, a true performer. The *New York Times*' David Halberstam, a leading chronicler of his day, wrote that Nixon had found a medium, a new stage: "Suddenly television was magic." Nixon, he asserted, could "go over the heads" of the press, of the political power brokers, even of the great General Eisenhower. Nixon had drawn the biggest audience to ever watch a political address. One Hollywood mogul declared the speech the "greatest production I have ever seen."[36]

While Nixon's real audience ultimately consisted of one—he only needed Eisenhower's approval to stay on the ticket—his performance met with overwhelming popular approval. In the following two days, a quarter of a million telegrams and letters, with a reported 200 to 1 in support, poured into the headquarters of the Republican National Committee. Nixon was so utterly sincere that no one could doubt his honesty, went one common refrain. I always thought such funds were evil, but now he has shown that they are a necessary evil, went another. Opinion was predictably split over the controversial young candidate. Democrats considered the whole act a "soap opera." There were catcalls of "Poor Richard." *Variety* called it "schmaltz." It was all a hoax, artifice, his naysayers complained, an illusion of the television, a sly act. It was at this time that the first reported use of the term the "new Nixon" appeared, as a pejorative jab by the *Advertiser* from Montgomery, Alabama.[37]

By Nixon's recounting, he fell asleep on the flight back to Washington. Upon landing, as he fumbled with his tie, pulled on his jacket and helped Pat with hers, his publicity man, Murray Chotiner, ran up to tell him that the general had arrived. "I was taken completely by surprise . . . when I saw him walking toward me up the aisle of the plane, smiling, with his hand out-stretched," Nixon later wrote. "General, you didn't need to come out to the airport," he mustered. "Why not?," the recently aloof Eisenhower said, smiling back. "You're my boy.'" Indeed, during the "Checkers speech," Ike had jotted down a note to himself, "I've . . . seen brave men in tough situations—None ever came through better."[38]

The following morning, newspapers across the country ran a photograph of the young candidate crying on the shoulder of a mentor, California senator William Knowland. It was, one enthusiastic commentator dubbed, a round of suffering, a "Golgotha." The fund episode, however successful in Nixon's defense, made him even more embittered following the revelation that Ike's opponent, Adlai Stevenson, had his own political fund flush with $146,000 compared to Nixon's relatively meager $18,000. The Democratic candidate claimed that his fund was necessary to supplement salaries for campaign staff, whose compensation was markedly lower than if they had remained employed in the private sector. "The press treated Stevenson with kid gloves," Nixon protested in response to the imbalance in scrutiny. The episode made Nixon all the more convinced that a liberal media had become his enemy. As had become a pattern throughout Nixon's life, even in his great success, he found himself aggrieved, somehow deprived of recognition.[39]

The aw-shucks performance of humility by "Honest Dick" did not last long. Nixon soon retired his average Joe routine and once again raised the Red flag to partisan crowds in the thousands. As the historian Irwin Gellman wrote, "Eisenhower kept himself above the fray," while Nixon turned into an attack dog. He began letting loose with seemingly offhanded but practiced barbs in an often-snide, full-throated tenor. Having stripped Hiss of his reputation, Nixon accused Stevenson of being a traitor to the country. Stevenson was nothing more than a "graduate of [Secretary of State] Dean Acheson's spineless school of diplomacy." Nixon blamed the Truman administration for "losing" half of Europe and China to the Soviets in the post–World War II scramble, the communists allegedly having outwitted the Americans at the conference tables in Yalta and Potsdam. The weak Truman, Acheson and, by extension, Stevenson had cost the free world 600 million allies. Nixon proclaimed that under a Stevenson presidency, communist cells would run rampant through the government's ranks, generating "more Alger Hisses, more atomic spies, more crises." After Stevenson rebuked Eisenhower as a "fancy khaki-colored package," the red-baiting Nixon quipped, "I'd rather have good old American khaki than State Department pink."[40]

Once a victorious Eisenhower was installed in the White House, Nixon adopted yet another new guise, taking advantage of the opportunity for international travel as vice president. It proved to be a rehearsal for his presidency. Nixon and Pat cavorted across Asia in 1953 on a 40,000-mile, country-hopping sojourn to visit dictators and potentates, sites from Angkor Wat to the Taj Mahal. At each stop, Nixon and Pat greeted crowds of commoners, shaking hands with big-bearded Muslims and turbaned Sikhs. The *New York Times* reported, "The common man of Asia liked this big, friendly, informal, democratic, serious young American." A far cry from his belligerent red-baiting and average Joe modes, early into his vice presidency, Nixon had become the heroic ambassador—spreading the word of democracy.[41]

"Revolution was sweeping over Latin America," Nixon recalled. To the right, he was a stolid Cold Warrior maintaining the bulwark of freedom. To the left, he was the very symbol of American imperialism, the leader of Yankee bandits stealing the natural wealth of the developing world. First Hiss, then Checkers and here again Nixon's triumphant performance was undercut by protest, another role he saw as marred by leftist sympathizers. On Nixon's eighteen-day goodwill tour through South America in 1958, he was met by demonstrations in Argentina, Colombia and Uruguay. Protestors tossed oranges and stones during the Lima stop. Demonstrations had been building by the day in anticipation of Nixon's arrival in Caracas. Officials cleared the Maiquetia Airport, but as Nixon and Pat stepped onto the airport's balcony, youthful crowds that had gathered hissed "Fuera Nixon—oust Nixon." He recalled them spitting tobacco juice, staining his suit and Pat's bright red dress. There had been intelligence reports the night before of an assassination plot. Two white-helmeted infantry companies on motorcycles, with fixed bayonets, escorted the Americans. Thousands lined the route of the motorcade taking Nixon to lay a ceremonial wreath at the tomb of Simón Bolívar and then to meet with Venezuela's five-man ruling junta.[42]

On the way from the airport, Nixon remembered rocks slamming into their four-and-half-ton armored limousines, shattering some of the purportedly unbreakable windows. Seemingly hundreds leapt out of buildings and storefronts in Nixon's memory. Bottles, eggs and tomatoes flew. "Here they come," Nixon recalled his secret service agent saying. Mobs besieged the motorcade. Many wore handkerchiefs on the lower half of their faces in case of tear gas. He recalled one man, a "great big guy" with a "great big steel pipe . . . bash[ing] the windows." The *New York Times* described a "lynching mood." Nixon's security detail unholstered their weapons as the crowd, throwing rocks and sticks, turned to shouting "Muerta Nixon, Muerta Nixon." Nixon recounted an agent saying, "Let's get some of these sons-of-bitches." Casting himself in a Cool Hand Luke role, Nixon recalled holding the agent back by his arm. "Don't do it," he told the antsy guard. "If you do, they'll tear us to pieces."[43]

The motorcade stalled for twelve minutes. Demonstrators ripped the American and Venezuelan flags from the limousines. The cars rocked; three windows smashed, with glass landing in Nixon's lap; then the traffic opened, and the motorcade sped off. "It certainly is not pleasant to be covered from head to foot with spit and to have a man spit directly in the face of my wife," Nixon reflected, reinventing himself once again. The harrowing images of a valiant "new Nixon," holding up the torch of democracy, splashed across the front pages of U.S. newspapers the next morning. He was now a courageous, if not swashbuckling, world traveler, a diplomatic martyr.[44]

Still, for all Nixon's performances, for all his practiced quips and grand orations, ironically, or perhaps tragically, his most remembered role arguably came not at the height of his success as a dogged prosecutor or an eloquent statesman, but ultimately when he faltered. Nixon had

Nixon's limousine after it was attacked by a mob in Caracas, Venezuela, when he traveled there as vice president, in 1958. *Courtesy of the National Archives.*

been on a steady, forceful upward trajectory since 1947, since the time he and JFK entered Congress. Yet it was in the standoff between the two hotshot up-and-comers during the 1960 presidential election campaign that Nixon's performance failed him. William Rogers, Nixon's his close friend and secretary of state, remarked of the aftermath of the Kennedy loss, "It's hard now to understand how far down he was. He was broke. He had no future in the field he knew best. He was . . . cut off." Nixon recalled feeling numb. One senator and friend remembered Pat in her hotel room "lying like a cadaver . . . with this bitter desperate face."[45]

The first presidential debate in 1960 cast an indelible image of a dashing young Kennedy and Nixon as the grump. The television viewing audience numbered 70 to 80 million out of a population of 107 million adults, or some 88 percent of households. There were no painful gaffes, no memorable blunders. "To compare them—as contemporaries did—to the Lincoln-Douglas debates of 1858 only mocks history," wrote the historian Stanley I. Kutler. Most memorable was Nixon's pallid visage—the flop sweat, a mottled upper lip, fidgety and shifty eyes, darkened cheeks that made his mother think him sickly. "My God," said a gleeful Chicago mayor and Kennedy partisan Richard Daley, "they've embalmed him before he even died." Nixon had forgone makeup, thinking the pancake powder made him look feminine. Herb Klein, his communications director, recounted that during the Democratic primary when Hubert Humphrey had debated Kennedy in Wisconsin, "Humphrey had appeared with too much make-up, and Nixon felt that made him look like a sissy." Nixon wanted his performance to appear tough, mature, what he thought of as masculine.[46]

For a man who had tried on and shed one role for another and another, the loss to Kennedy was a terribly harsh awakening to the limits of his performing abilities. The arrival of the television age had undone him. In Kennedy, Nixon had met a better actor. As he wrote two years later with a note of dripping ironic acrimony, "I believe I spent too much time in the last campaign on substance and too little time on appearance: I paid too much attention to what I was going to say and too little to how I would look." He had been beaten at his own game of transformation. For Nixon, the lesson of 1960 was that veneer had won. The elite, the vacuous, had won, and in this, Nixon could not hide his bitterness. If appearance was the trump card, Nixon would invest even more in appearance, in artifice. He determined never again to allow himself to be so vulnerable. From then on, as one top deputy noted, "[He] worked on keeping the tan alive." Self-mastery and reserve would become Nixon's campaign strategies as well as his defenses. Nixon had the vim of a convert. By the time he reached the presidency, he had digested the lesson. "Elections are not won or lost by programs," he proclaimed to H. R. Haldeman, his chief of staff. It was a matter of creating a "mystique" of "dignity and distance." Nixon dove into the postmodern talk of representation and reception, of medium over message, with which his young White House press staff was so taken. Elections, he asserted, were "won or lost on how these programs are presented to the country." The lesson from the 1960 election was well inculcated: politics was just another show, another role to play. As his younger brother Edward remembered, the loss to Kennedy "was his awakening."[47]

Nixon himself was well known for his dull, gray look—nothing fancy. He seemed not to care an ounce for fashion. Beltway reporters were flummoxed by the *homme sérieux* in his costume of grays, browns and more gray. His Washington colleagues were "respectful of Nixon the politician and puzzled about Nixon the man." A young Roger Ailes, who ran Nixon's 1968 television campaign, called Nixon "the kind of kid . . . who was 42 years old the day he was born." Ailes added, "Other kids got footballs for Christmas, Nixon got a briefcase . . . and he'd never let you copy."[48] Yet on this, too, Nixon worked. He made sure photographs were not shot from too high—a "bad angle." He most preferred a blue velvet smoking jacket, puffing a cigar. For grand occasions, he chose a white shirt with a wide tie, not his usual narrow tie with a blue shirt. Black tie for dinners, but white tie if with women, and business suits for luncheons and afternoon receptions. His assistant Alexander Butterfield remembered, "The President was concerned with whether the shades were closed or open. Social functions were always reviewed with him." In addition, Butterfield noted that with staff, Nixon "debated whether we should have a U-shaped table or a round one . . . He was very interested in meals and how they were served . . . in whether not salad should be served."[49]

Nixon "never took his coat off . . . even on the hottest Washington, D.C., night," one aide recalled, and he steadfastly changed clothes between events. Despite his reputation for having a five o'clock shadow, he shaved three times a day—an electric razor before appearances, shave stick rather than pancake makeup for the cameras. The pancake makeup, he thought, made him look clammy and overemphasized his famous jowls. Nixon was exacting in his presentation. He hated being televised from his left side. "Now when you give me the fifteen-second cue, give it to me right under the camera. So I don't shift my eyes," he directed. Even outdoors, in wind or rain, Nixon wore two coats of shave stick. To swim, he wore a bathing cap because his barber had instructed him that the chlorine would damage his hair. Nixon strictly monitored his Spartan diet, maintaining a weight of 175 pounds. As his mother once commented, "[He] has little respect for people who overeat." The journalist Hunter S. Thompson, trailing the candidate in 1972 for a profile, noted his strict meal plan. "Breakfast is juice, cereal, and milk; lunch is a sandwich [or cottage cheese with ketchup], and dinner might be roast beef or steak, which he doesn't finish." Nixon rarely drank. He passed on desserts.[50]

At the same time—ever the mutable performer, ever uncomfortable, ever ambivalent about the role he was playing—Nixon tried to counter this stolid image. He wanted to appear spontaneous while maintaining utmost control. For fundraising, for cocktail parties, for television, Nixon worked hard to counter the well-ingrained impression of the "Humorless Nixon." His run against Kennedy in 1960 was judged "just too serious." To loosen up his image, Nixon practiced. He added jokes to his new script, mining his staff for punchlines. For one, he remarked, "'A little girl came up to me in New York the other day and asked me to autograph a picture in a news magazine.' She said, 'It's an awfully good picture. It doesn't look like you at all.'" But here, too, he was strictly analytical. He had a theory for why he needed to be funnier, why he had been developing his laugh lines. "This is a generation that wants to laugh, a generation that wants to be entertained," Nixon explained. He blamed television.[51]

Nixon's penchant to perform was not limited to the public stage, not just when squaring off against the likes of a Kennedy or Soviet Premier Nikita Khrushchev. He transformed himself even in private parlays. Nixon mastered the manipulative art of misdirection, another matter of control. His conversations meandered from a morsel of gossip to a headline he had read. Nixon-speak was another trial for him and his interlocutors, both exhilarating and exhausting. He circled around issues, avoiding a direct knock, shuffling through thoughts to see how others reacted, or he took an extreme stance before retreating to play the other side. "One view in one meeting and quite a different view in the next," was how Haldeman described the pattern. That was, until "the last possible moment," Kissinger recalled, after which "he would put forward several often contradictory options."[52]

Nixon often preferred to pick one person out of the crowd to huddle with in a corner, to talk shop and then talk some more. At other times, however, savoring the "clash of ideas," he pitted one staffer against another—the fiery Pat Buchanan on the hard right against the jocular centrist Safire, the "bright and sparkly" professorial Daniel Patrick Moynihan against the stately businessman Arthur Burns. Leonard Garment, Nixon's close counsel, recalled the "interminable meetings" at the White House. The president would say, "We'll do this. No, we'll do that. No, we'll do this." Bomb Laos, no, negotiate; deploy troops to the South to enforce desegregation, no, stall for time. John Ehrlichman, Nixon's chief domestic advisor, reached for metaphor to capture his boss's conversational habits. "[He] turn[ed] the same rock over a dozen times . . . [only to] come back to it two weeks later and turn it over another dozen times." Kissinger remembered, "One almost began to hope that some catastrophe would provide a pretext for going back to one's own office to get to work."[53]

It was only after 1960, during his years in the political wilderness, when he stepped back from politics, that Nixon finally found his prime role. As a writer, he could maintain control. It was a part he could conceive himself; it was a dynamic he relished. No president has written more about himself. He composed ten books, including three stabs at autobiography. His biographer Stephen Ambrose compared Nixon to Samuel Taylor Coleridge's Ancient Mariner, "forever tugging at our sleeve, anxious to tell his story." Nixon wrote and rewrote the definitive and then, again, the more definitive account of his life's work. Nixon the writer was another "new Nixon." What the reader discovered, that is, how he chose to represent himself, was deliberately blanched of color. His prose exhibited little beauty or excitement or glee. Apart from a steady stream of gripes about the press, the memoirs were carefully devoid of anger, disappointment and guilt. Nixon was courteous, rather than generous, his words constrained by comportment.[54]

"We sense," the distinguished political scientist James MacGregor Burns observed in reviewing Nixon's writing, "the brooding presence of a man constantly standing guard over his own image." For here, Nixon adopted a temper altogether controlled. It was a bit of an irony—a buttoned-up tell-all. In Nixon's retellings, Kissinger was "fair-minded." Joseph McCarthy was just a fellow dedicated to winning the Cold War who, in the end, had a tendency toward "overstating." Nixon omitted how, in his own Senate campaign, he had smeared his opponent, Helen Douglas Gahagan, as "pink right down to her underwear."[55] Instead, he played up the part of the courteous statesman. In narrating his life in *Six Crises*, his first autobiography, Nixon portrayed himself as a performer. From role to role, he took the stage, cast in parts centered on dramatic oration—anti-communist prosecutor, world-traipsing diplomat, master debater promoting the ideals of democracy to Soviet premier Nikita Khrushchev in a mock American kitchen in the heart of Moscow. For in Nixon's telling of crisis after crisis, his was a circular feat: the performance of performance.

In mid-March 1971, Ronald Ziegler, Nixon's young press secretary, dashed off a memo to Haldeman. He wrote, "The great leaders have always stage-managed their events . . . He must know when to dissemble, when to be frank." Haldeman had poached Ziegler from his advertising agency, as he had much of his White House staff and the press office. Just as they were drawn to postmodernism's exaltation of the power of the image and representation, Nixon's young public relations stable developed a fascination with "mystique" of remote charisma. In place of the bulwarks of modernity—directness, Truth and authenticity—Haldeman acolytes, like the speechwriter Pat Buchanan, underscored the irony that "power . . . adheres in the *distance* between the Presidency and the people."[56] As in the case of Nixon's idol de Gaulle, the politics required of the president was a magnetic performance at once familiar, at once lofty and removed.

At twenty-nine years of age, a chubby-cheeked, seemingly boyish Ziegler waited, watching. He had set up an interview for Nixon with Barbara Walters in Washington. The *Today Show* had been asking for a sit-down with the president for months, and now the administration had decided to go on a public relations blitz. Recession threatened. Nixon's polls were sliding among all but loyal Republicans. As part of the communications campaign, Nixon sat for an interview with the *London Sunday Telegraph* and one with C. L. Sulzberger of the *New York Times*. The same day as the Walters interview, the president would have a live, one-hour conversation with ABC's Howard K. Smith. According to the White House public relations team, Americans needed Nixon to take on a role different from those of his vaunted predecessors, one in which he would descend from the presidential mountaintop of grand oration. They would trade in "mystique" for intimacy. They wanted him to reprise the average Joe persona of the Checkers speech, to act "more human."[57]

Herbert Klein held the new post of director of communications. While Ziegler fielded questions from the podium at press conferences, Klein's job was to spread the Nixon gospel across the country. He briefed the press on background. From time to time, he showed the administration's face, dropping in on the popular, late-night "Dick Cavett Show." Before taking the White House job, Klein had worked his way up to editor of the conservative *San Diego Union*, a decidedly less sexy outfit than

Haldeman and Ziegler's advertising firm, J. Walter Thompson. Klein had, nonetheless, been key to Nixon's climb, orchestrating the Checkers speech, the "kitchen debate" with Khrushchev, and the 1960 presidential campaign.

With a dozen staff for Klein, fourteen for Ziegler, a sixteen-person speech-writing shop plus photographers, the public relations team had ballooned to sixty. They had a "ten o'clock" and a "five o'clock" crew, each to manage the flow of information to the noon and evening news. Ziegler's press team and Klein's communications gang developed a rivalry for the king's ear. Klein, at fifty, was ever the old man in the room. He knew his access was slipping. They had begun calling him the administration's "traveling salesman," the "ambassador to the boondocks." With little "mystique," Klein stubbornly continued to push a more-modern-than-postmodern motto: "Truth will be the hallmark of the Nixon Administration."[58]

Walters, at forty years old, was not yet the "queen of interviewers," not yet the "first lady of chat." She had gotten her start in television selling dog food but went on to become the first female regular reporter on *Today*, the first not confined to reading a script. Walters had already interviewed Pat Nixon and daughter Tricia. She had also scored interviews with Israeli prime minister Golda Meir and the shah of Iran. Still, she was criticized as "mock critical," "mediocritized" with banal patter, sometimes deemed insufficiently supportive of the student rights movements, sometimes called anti-feminist. No slacks, she insisted, up before dawn, clothes laid out the night before—signature brightly colored blouses, "skirts long enough to cover her knees as she sat." Like Nixon, Walters spoke of power as "the ability to control, to direct or coerce."[59]

On a divan in the Blue Room of the White House, Walters and Nixon sat face-to-face, each with a prop of morning coffee in hand. The setup made the president appear familiar, as if the audience had caught him and the interviewer in a candid moment. The political was meant to seem personal. They spoke briefly of the war in Vietnam. They touched on the issues of drugs, American youth culture, but only tangentially, nothing too in depth. Roy Cohn, an informal advisor to the president known for his own political dirty tricks, would call Nixon and Walters "two of a kind" for their "no-glamour approach," their "cool, fast, undramatic presentation." One prominent television critic would years later dub the pair "Monsieur Nixon and Madame La Tube"—the "optimal pairing of folks one loves to hate."[60]

Walters arched her neck at an angle. "There has been a lot of talk, Mr. President, about your image," she began, with her faint lisp. Her *w*'s sometimes sounded like *s*'s, sometimes like *v*'s; her upper lip ever tense, her accent was somewhere between Boston and the Bronx. *Today*, in its twentieth season and broadcast 7:00–9:00 a.m., attracted an audience of more than 8 million each morning. "Forgive me, Mr. President," Walters pressed. "[Americans] see you as rather a stuffy man and not a human man. Are you—oh dear. Are you worried about your image, Mr. President?" The whole point of the interview with Walters was to make Nixon appear more relatable, more transparent. His strategy was to appear spontaneous, candid, to project the image of someone who cared nothing about appearance, to deny the constructed nature of his political relations game. As Ziegler looked on, as Klein and their staff in the press office hovered, the president waved Walters off. "I don't worry about images," the president remarked. "I am not going to start . . . Never have."[61]

Even as Nixon shifted roles variously, there remained an inflexibility in the themes he scripted. He was on guard, ever under strict scrutiny, ever alone on stage defending his scruples, battling on the streets of Caracas, guarding his reputation against accusations of being a grump or a crook or a sissy. His mission was to maintain a moral core against corroding forces out to get, to sabotage and to corrupt Dick Nixon. He quoted the British essayist-turned-adventurer Rudyard

Kipling: "The test of leadership is whether one has the ability . . . to keep his head while others are losing theirs." In Nixon's experience of life, each inflected expression could prove critical. As he lectured in his first memoir while still a young man, "An unconscious, unintentional upturning of the lips can appear in a picture as a smile at so grave a moment." Then again, he wrote, "Too serious an expression could create an impression of fear and concern." He had to keep control of his emotions against the likes of Hiss and Khrushchev, and even in the purportedly personal interaction with Walters, lest they thwart his better angels. Lest he get too mad.[62]

In 1982, well into retirement, Nixon returned to the same theme in the book he simply titled *Leaders*. He defied the borrowed wisdom that "the key to success in any field . . . is to 'be yourself.'" No, the former president insisted, "Most of the great leaders I have known were accomplished actors." He opined, "You can be human and still have the mystique. The thing is, you have to be considered an *homme sérieux*." Such was the experience he had as a young actor playing Achilles amid the crows and the applause. It was the lesson he learned sweating out the first debate with Kennedy. He was but one twitch away from revealing weakness on the dais, there for all to see him grandly succeed or fail miserably. Nixon turned philosophic. "Beneath that phony image of character *is* character." The act was the act; greatness perceived was greatness itself, no more, no less. Power was a matter of reputation, and for Nixon, reputation was reality itself.[63]

2 | The Sentimental Life of Richard Nixon

HIS HOSTS POINTED to various unmarked graves, mounds extending fifty feet across, as they wandered the grounds. The Piskaryovskoye Memorial Cemetery, just outside Leningrad, was filled with 470,000 dead from Germany's siege of the city during World War II. Security was tight. The Soviet crowds were held back, nearly out of view. The day before, May 26, 1972, the superpowers had signed the first strategic arms limitation treaty, SALT I. The dignitaries marched, not quite in lock step. Nixon paused. As he looked over the acres of dead, it was drizzling. He laid a wreath of roses.[1]

The Soviet hosts directed the American president to a small chapel where a few pages torn from a diary were on display. It was a slim volume by a little girl named Tanya Savicheva. Each page was alphabetized with a Cyrillic letter in the top right corner. On the page marked Ж (Zh), in pencil, she recorded that her older sister "Zhenya died on 28 December at 12 P.M." In a large looping cursive on the page labeled "д" (D, for dyadya): "Uncle Vasya died 13 April at 2:00 after midnight 1942." There was a clinical quality as Tanya ticked off the death of each Savichev family member, six in all. In later entries foreshortened, her prepositions became confused. "Mother at 13 May at 7:30 A.M. 1942." Then three quick lines from the diary were translated for Nixon: "The Savichevs died. Everyone died. Only Tanya is left." The president interjected, the girl was a "beautiful child—brown eyes, a pretty face," adding color to her black-and-white photograph where there was none.[2]

At the Marinsky Palace during a luncheon that same day in Leningrad, the president toasted, "As I think of Tanya, that twelve-year-old girl in Leningrad . . . I only hope that the visit . . . will have contributed to that kind of world in which the little Tanyas and their brothers and their sisters will be able to grow up in a world of peace." As Nixon saluted his adversaries with Tanya's tale, those in attendance communed in the wake of a past brutality, a time of their joint suffering. Around the memory of Tanya, the Soviet and American *apparatchiki* could look back at their alliance against Germany, the Allies assailed, besieged like Leningrad, by the Nazis. Soviets and Americans might hope for a renewal of their pacts of World War II, as if time had ticked back to that moment when Tanya was still "left," still a "beautiful child." Nixon's salute evoked what American revolutionaries had once celebrated as a "sentimental political union," a compact based on good feeling and companionship rather than reason or law or human right.[3]

Nixon was taken with the story of the suffering girl. He returned to it once more in the spotlight, recounting her sad lot as the capstone to his address at the Republican National Convention in Miami later that summer. That August night in 1972, Nixon once again accepted his party's nomination for the presidency. In front of a blue screen, he stood in a navy blue suit with a navy blue tie faintly spotted. He lacked the awkward giddiness of his acceptance speech four years prior. He seemed tired, managing a forced smile, his flashing half-toothed grin not as quick. Thick makeup concealed his pores and any blemishes from his long years of political battle. He spoke against the country's rebellious youth, and the cameras spotted a young woman. He spoke against quotas, and the cameras turned to a young black woman. The camera caught his advisers John Ehrlichman and Henry Kissinger anxiously leaning over a balcony. Nixon spoke of a "new American majority" gathering to restore a sense of patriotism, of pride. He lamented that taxes were too high, inflation soaring. Turning to law and order, he called for "peace officers."[4]

Tanya's story—the scraps of scrawling in her diary—was the last section of his speech. As the faithful watched on their curved and pix-

Tanya Savicheva, at six-years-old in 1936, who kept a diary documenting the loss of her family members during the Nazi siege of Leningrad, 1941–44, and whose story the sentimental Nixon invoked at the 1972 Republican National Convention, in Miami. *Courtesy of the Richard Nixon Presidential Library and Museum.*

elated television screens, he read the foreign and unfamiliar names of Tanya's dead relatives. His clipped list lilted, "Zhenya in December. Grannie in January. Then Leka. Then Uncle Vasya. Then Uncle Lyosha. Then Mama in May." The life of the dead girl from Leningrad "tells the terrible story of war," Nixon imparted, dropping to the lower edges of his baritone. Softly and haltingly, his tone turned as it did in grave moments. Tanya, he sketched her with a fierce pity. The last trailing words in her diary proclaimed, "Tanya is left." She became a symbol of war transformed into a hopeful emblem of peace, of innocence, of endurance. "Let us build a peace that our children and all the children of the world can enjoy for generations," Nixon urged. "Let us think of Tanya and of the other Tanyas and their brothers and sisters . . . everywhere in Russia, in China, in America."[5]

Nixon transformed himself, performing various parts. He was the "new Nixon" and then the new "new Nixon"—statesman, carpet bomber, progressive reformer. He was a man, he liked to say, of the "big play." At the convention, Nixon had another script with which to persuade. The sentimental was one of Nixon's favored modes. He peppered his speeches with portraits of children like Tanya to conjure the innocent and the untainted. He pressed his speechwriters to find a note of "heart, anecdotes, parables" in his scripts. He wanted "color." Far from the red-baiting Nixon, the caricature of a grumpy, middle-aged man, the remotely pragmatic practitioner of realpolitik, in Nixon's toughest hours and often during his greatest conquests, he turned to his sentimental mode, to expressions and anecdotes he believed brought forth great feeling. He tasked his staff to add "more schmaltz," more "warm instead of brittle."[6]

Derived from "sentire in mente" or "*feeling in idea*," sentimentalism had a short yet blazing heyday in the second half of the eighteenth century, during what became known as the Age of Feeling. David Hume, Adam Smith and the third Earl of Shaftesbury (the legal ward of John Locke) laid the framework for a morality of Sentiment, for the evaluation of morals not through cold calculation but through feeling. Sentimentalism challenged the primacy of dry reason, bare materialism and Thomas Hobbes's forfeit of human goodness. The Sentimentalists challenged the traditional Christian chastising of feeling as fault, the condemning of passion as sin. According to Sentimentalists like Hume and Smith, only feeling could distinguish good from evil. Theirs was a Rousseauean "je sens, donc je suis." The Sentimentalists attempted to evoke empathy from the spectator, relishing the idea that felt communion in turn generated more good feeling and more communion. A rightful indignation sprung from the fortunate for those burdened by misfortune, encouraging those fortunate to rise up to erase misfortune. As the French philosopher Denis Diderot beseeched of such work, "Move me, astonish me, break my heart."[7]

In the convention hall of Republican sympathizers in Miami, in the thick of sentimentalism, to capture Tanya's suffering in Leningrad, Nixon glossed over the grainy details of realism. A coating of filth had blanketed Tanya's frozen and encircled city for nearly 900 days. The surviving slept dressed in all their clothes to try to fend off the cold. For heat, they burned their bureaus, sofas and books. There was no water for showers or laundry. Yet from the podium in the convention center, Nixon erased the grime. He elided their starvation, how Leningraders like Tanya resorted to eating boiled leather, Vaseline, the glue that held the wallpaper to the walls. The besieged scavenged for rats and pigeons. They ate their pets. Nixon did not mention how bodies were hauled to mass graves through the icy streets on children's sleds.[8]

Nixon also omitted telling the crowd in Miami the ending to Tanya's story. After Tanya lost her mother, an aunt took her in. In January 1944, a brigade of civil defense workers, mostly young nurses, women, streamed into a liberated Leningrad after the two-and-a-half-year siege. They scoured the city, searching the "dead flats" to find surviving children. Tanya was evacuated in a train full of children ages three to thirteen, en route to one of 130 new orphanages. She ended up twelve miles away, in Children's Home 48, in the village of Shakhty, near Gorky. Having developed intestinal tuberculosis, she was soon taken to a hospital, where she began to recover, walking on crutches, bracing herself against the wall when the disease recurred. She survived but for less than six months after the freeing of Leningrad. Similar to her diary's terse reports, a short record read, "Savicheva T. N. Ponaevka. Tuberculosis of the Intestines. Died 07/07/44."[9]

Nixon's portrait of Tanya elicited a grief without qualification, empty of context or complexity, of the short ending of her story. Hers was a suffering offstage. The familial, the most cherished of sentimental bonds, was severed for Tanya, and yet she persisted. By Nixon's telling, her hurt was beatified. The words from Tanya's diary became the portrait of a pietà as she, impossibly virtuous, played both parts—as if a mother holding dearly to her suffering family and, at the same time, the child being held dear by the reader. For if the sentimental need be tragic, it is of beautiful design. If it need be painful, tears shed are salutary, as proof of conscience; they are cathartic, even enjoyable, a good cry. "Unhappiness is celebrated," the noted critic David Denby wrote. "Misfortune is seen as setting the victims apart from the rest of society and conferring upon them a superior status." A beautiful agony like Tanya's, an unjust misery, brings out exquisite emotion. Agony as much as innocence is a sign of the good. The sentimentalist's intent is not to provide greater understanding or abstract knowledge, but to elicit moral, in particular communal, action against the producers of agony, on behalf of the agonized. Indeed, it was the heyday of Sentimentalism that generated terms for the sentimental entrepreneur: *philanthropist* (1730–36), *philanthrope* (*circa* 1734), *philanthropically* (1787), and *philanthropic* (1789).[10]

In Nixon's day, critics dismissed his sentimentality as cloying flourishes from an awkward man ill-suited to write or speak of his emotional life. When he invoked Tanya's ghost or his daughters' love for their dog Checkers, they called his performance "tear-jerking soap opera." They scorned "Poor Richard's" reaching for feeling as "transparent demagog[uery] and fraud." Naysayers considered his lamentations not-very-convincing distractions from his down-and-dirty politics. He appeared, after all, so very performative as he shifted from part to part, as he stiffly invoked sentiment. One cannot discount the strategic value of Nixon's playing on his audiences' emotions. As he slipped into sentimental mode, with appeals to innocence, love and emotion, Nixon was trying to tap into what he saw as his constituents' deeply felt experience. William Gavin, the still-green, pinch-hitter on Nixon's speechwriting team, recalled, "The few times I talked with him, it seem[ed] odd that in almost every one of them he was talking about the need for 'heart.'"

Nixon wanted, as he tasked his speech writers, to sound just like the persuasive, charismatic and home-spun evangelism of his friend Rev. Billy Graham.[11]

Yet one should also not discount the instrumental value sentimentalism played for Nixon himself. Sentimentalism was more than merely a guise. His affective mode was no mere distraction, not just for public display, but a key aspect of his own affective experience. For Nixon, it was an exhibition from a man saddled by inhibition. A lonesome figure, the sentimental route was a way he tried to connect. For Nixon wrestled with an emotional force of his own. The historian Garry Wills famously dubbed him *Nixon Agonistes*. He agonized over the loss of his brothers, a lost partial scholarship to Harvard due to insufficient family funds to supplement it, the Checkers scandal, the loss to John F. Kennedy, the defeat in the California governorship race, the protracted ordeal of Watergate. After each loss, he experienced recurring bouts of depression, of melancholic sentiment, of being overwhelmed by feeling. After his youngest brother's death, his mother, Hannah, remembered Richard sinking "into a deep impenetrable silence." Nixon recounted how "for weeks after Arthur's funeral there was not a day that I did not think about [him] and cry."[12]

Nixon was no cynic, for the cynic lacks feeling. Nixon felt. He felt through music, having had an ear for classical music, favoring Chopin and Brahms. As one music teacher remarked of the young Nixon, "He is a romanticist at heart, but he doesn't like to let this show." He preferred the saccharine—Christmas carols and Broadway show tunes, from *South Pacific* and Ginger Roger belting songs from *Mame*. "You'll Never Walk Alone," from the musical *Carousel*, brought tears to Nixon's eyes. He thought the show's strapping lead, Billy Bigelow, resembled his older brother, Harold, who died of tuberculosis. He chose the tune for Pat's funeral. The song bursts with emotion: "Walk on, walk on / With hope in your heart / And you'll never walk alone," the chorus calls out. Its simple message touched a terribly troubled man. The exhortations of optimism and constant companionship made it a painfully ironic choice. For Nixon—the same man who teared up at the notion of "walking alone," who ruminated compulsively for hours into the night to confidants, who divulged thousands of pages of thoughts in ten books, three of them memoirs—insisted he had, by his own definition, no close friends. Despite constantly reaching out, he thought of himself as a loner. "I believe you should keep your troubles to yourself," he said. "I never wanted to be buddy-buddy . . . I don't believe in letting your hair down, confiding this and that and the other thing."[13]

Wills examined Nixon's fervent desire for the stoic, for "self-mastery" to muffle his pain. Nixon's approach was ever to maintain control, to tamp down his maddening moods, his bouts of rage and despair. Yet, seemingly concurrent but quite the opposite of the anesthetic of "self-mastery" that Wills describes, a deeply felt sentimentalism tantalized Nixon. Not simply a tool for persuading the masses, sentimentalism diverted Nixon from bouts he called his "fatalism." Under the guise of sentimentalism, he recast his rough childhood as a blessing. The tragic deaths of his brothers, he insisted, the suffering, had purpose. Loss could lead to still greater heights. His family could be ideal—his father a stolid yeoman, his mother a saint. Later, his marriage and his relationship with his daughters were nothing but ideal. Most intimately to Chinese prime minister Zhou Enlai, whom he had just met, Nixon admitted, "An election loss was really more painful than a physical wound in war," one not of body but of spirit. He did so a dozen years after his 1960 defeat to Kennedy. Nixon's confidants, too, remembered his loss in the 1962 California governor race as "shattering," but Nixon admitting as such was rare. In his memoirs, he asserted, "The hardest thing about losing is not how it affects you personally but to see the terrible disappointment in the eyes of those who have been at your side." Nixon spun defeat into a yarn. He clothed his own hurt in the sweetly sentimental, diverting his distress outward. It was his brother Don who took the defeat the hardest, Nixon insisted, and as for his daughters, his wife and secretaries, "Women basically find it much harder to lose than men."[14]

Sentimentalism fit with Nixon's "hydraulic model" of understanding human emotion as welling from a deep human reserve. Even as he tried to fend off strong feelings, they threatened to overwhelm. It was, as in the "madman theory," that delicate balance between control and the effusion of emotion, manipulation and release, the mastery of the self and the overwhelming of the other. Paradoxically, the sentimental rang with feeling unleashed and unfiltered, even as it provided a way to stifle feeling by glossing over the sting of turbulence and cognitive confusion. The scholar Anthony Savile described sentimentalism as bearing a "protective function," a feeling of being "cocooned" to guard against painful memory. Ira Newman has gone a step further, suggesting that the sentimental offers an avenue of recollection that makes such painful memory more bearable. There is a "psychologically practical" aspect to sentimentalism; it is not only a matter of looking away. Sentimentalizing discourages retreating and permits viewing aslant so as to rescue memories from the mud. The soft focus, the simpler view, Newman suggests, allows for leaving "oneself vulnerable to the pain of memory, rather than inuring oneself to loss by refusing to dwell on any thought."[15]

The sentimental provided a mold out of which Nixon fashioned the story of himself. "If you are reasonably intelligent and if your anger is deep enough," Nixon maintained, "you learn that you can change those attitudes by excellence, personal gut performance, while those who have everything are sitting on their fat butts." Nixon believed that he worked harder than the rich set, who simply hoarded "what they already had." The pain of derision and recriminations by his enemies, he insisted, could be turned to advantage. "Adversity breaks the weak but makes the strong," he wrote. This doctrine became the emotional narrative of Nixon's life. For he did not simply resort to neat feeling, he was tantalized by it. His hope depended on the idea of a Dickensian moral reckoning, in which light could be made from dark, sweet sentiment from rough beginnings. He traded snarling fury and ache for cloying innocence. Complex culpability dissolved into sweet, fathomless self-pity. Nixon cast his tough political climb as an adventure; crisis was adventure. His enemies were perfidious, while he was a victim of the system. He wrote and rewrote his life's story, trying to contain his "fatalism" in simple formulas while using the great effusion of emotion to propel him forward.[16]

In examining Nixon, one of his biographers quoted Winston Churchill: "Behind every extraordinary man is an unhappy childhood." Leo Tolstoy might have proposed that each extraordinary man's childhood was unhappy in its own way. But not Nixon. He depicted his family with dearness, fondness and grace. Nixon began his long second memoir, "I was born in a house my father built," bringing to mind the hallowed log cabin, connecting his sentimental yarn to another. Life was "family, church and school." It was "hard but happy." Nixon painted a portrait of full bellies and full minds. Of his first home, Nixon told one interviewer, "It didn't seem small then." To the end, he held, "It was not an easy life," adding simply, "But it was a good one, centered around a loving family and a small, tight-knit, Quaker community."[17]

Yorba Linda, thirty miles outside Los Angeles, was a fruit-picking town, mainly citrus groves. As Nixon's neighbors and cousins recalled with their own fondness, the town consisted of backroads. Indeed, Nixon hailed from a community that spoke of itself in sentimental fashion. It was a town, they recalled, where people wore hand-me-down overalls and Levi's. In school, children went barefoot. In their spare time they hiked the wild terrain speckled with orange blossom. Nixon described "idyllic" sprints through "avocado and citrus groves." The townspeople remembered Tom Sawyeresque youths, how the more adventurous boys went "frog gigging," cutting off a switch five or six inches long and tapered to a point so they could spear one and then another frog, frying them up.[18]

In Nixon's longest public palaver—a nine-day, thirty-four-hour interview with former aide Frank Gannon in 1983—he rattled off story after story, revealing a remarkable memory for places and names from his childhood. He had a kind word for each, for his great grandmother, his uncle with the marvelous butterfly collection, the concert pianist who taught him in college, his Native American football coach, the "Chief." He spoke kindly of the Korean family that took over the Nixon family store, the Paks. He recalled Christmases, believing in Santa Claus. Nixon recounted a childhood nourished, tickling piano keys, "lively discussions of politics," reading newspapers by the fireplace. In his final memoir as a seventy-seven-year-old man, he insisted "that the five Nixon boys were the luckiest boys in the world."[19]

In particular, Nixon remembered hearing the train whistles from the Santa Fe line. The sound was, to him, the "sweetest music I ever heard." It counted among one of his earliest memories. Union Station was a couple of miles from his family's store, Nixon's Market, in East Whittier. The red train cars were packed with boxes of lumber and fertilizer for the groves and, weekly, refrigerated cars also arrived with big barrels stuffed full of ice cream from Los Angeles. The train connected Nixon's small hometown to the outside world. It brought newspapers, even the *New York Times*. Nixon recalled wanting to be a railroad engineer, to leave the isolation of backward southern California, to travel the United States and the world. It was a fantasy of adventure, of upward mobility, and underneath the patina of the sentimental, a fantasy of escape. In Yorba Linda, a Quaker town, there was little drinking, little dancing. First came Prohibition and then the Great Depression. Sentiment was to be rationed. For big bands and the casino boats, for Saturday nights, you had to drive outside the city limits. There was no dating the Japanese or Mexican migrants about town, not in those days, not in those parts.[20]

The scholar I. A. Richards wrote, "If a man can only thin[k] of his childhood as a lost heaven it is probably because he is afraid to think of its other aspects." Far from Nixon being a man satisfied by outsized success, and far from experiencing a contented childhood, his speechwriter Pat Buchanan painted a portrait of the president not as a man happily reared as a child, satisfied by his outsized success, but as a "brood[ing] soldier who had been wounded badly in a war long ago." As Buchanan put it, "When the weather turned, the pain returned." Nixon's longtime advisor Bryce Harlow, a political realist who had the president's ear, came to believe that "as a young person, [Nixon] was hurt deeply by somebody he trusted." Harlow thought that Nixon "never got over it and never trusted anybody again." Of Nixon's four brothers, two died as youths. He had an inconstant mother and a father who was at times effusively loving, at times brutish. If not dirt poor, the family was near poor; they worked hard. Yorba Linda and East Whittier were the kind of towns one yearned to hitch a train to escape. Once, Nixon admitted to a reporter from the *Saturday Evening Post* that his past was riddled with a well of missteps that he tried not to dwell on. "I try not to repeat mistakes or to rehash them." As Nixon encouraged Kissinger, "Remember Lot's wife, Henry. Never look back."[21]

The aspect clearly missing from Nixon's accountings was that most desperate of sentimental feeling: loneliness, the absence of human connection. It maintains a deafening silence in Nixon's accounts, a sentimentalist's erasure of sentiment, even as it fills others' recollections of Nixon's early years. Outside Nixon's own retellings, one historian noted, "Nowhere in the several biographies about Richard Nixon is there any mention of a carefree youngster." Quite to the contrary, the young Nixon was a "quiet, little round-faced boy with large, dark eyes," one childhood caretaker remembered. "He was not as outreaching as many children are . . . He lived more within himself." One cousin remembered his se-rious mien. He "didn't strike me that he wanted to be hugged." He did not like to be picked up. Nixon was not a "little puppy dog, one you wanted to cuddle, though he may have longed for it." Not naturally social, and often painfully uncomfortable around company, Nixon withdrew. He smiled and laughed little. At times he had a frightful temper. "That was just Dick Nixon," one schoolmate relayed. He never frolicked with his peers amid the avocado groves and orange blossoms, and he only vis-ited the ocean once or twice in his youth, never hiking in the nearby mountains. "I always think of him in his free time as never one to just goof around. He always had a little spot where he could get off and study," recalled another classmate. One teacher remembered, "He was a very quiet, studious boy and kept mostly to himself." Lacking the easy mantras and homilies he later adopted as an adult, he snuck away to a corner to study, to excel in his studies.[22]

Nixon was a precocious learner. His teacher recalled, "[He] was one of those rare individuals born with knowledge . . . [H]e absorbed knowledge of any kind like a blotter." On his first report card, he re-ceived an *E* for Excellence in all his subjects except for handwriting, for which her received a *U* for Unsatisfactory. He astounded at age six re-citing Shakespeare by heart. Yet "he was a very solemn child," another teacher said. "I have no recollection of him playing with others in the playground." Nixon adored reading, but there, too, the loner Nixon longed for connection. He enjoyed being read to, particularly poems from *Songs O'Cheer*, a collection by James Whitcomb Riley. At once sen-timental, rural and rough, Riley spun quick tales of a small American village. One poem told of Mister Hop-Toad who had not a care in the world except for his warts. Another told of the "hired han'," the Rag-gedy Man who "got skeered" of the rain. For all of Riley's jaunty mirth, there was a sadness to the verses in *O'Cheer*, a village life full of gaiety, but also of melancholic disconnection. One chorus told of the dying days of autumn, "when the frost is on the punkin." In another ballad, the "middlin' fiddler" muses about his fiddle. "I pat her neck, and plink / Her strings with lovin' hands," he sang. "And list'nin' clos't, I sometimes think / She kindo' understands!"[23]

The historian Roger Morris, in his intricately researched biography of Nixon's youth, relates that those who knew Nixon growing up concluded "that they had hardly known him at all." They found it nearly impossible to have imagined his future as a glad-handing politician. When the style for boys was a roughed-up pair of dirty yellow corduroys, Nixon wore standard gray slacks. He abhorred riding the school bus, thinking his schoolmates smelled. He bore a stiffness, a shyness, exhibiting little beyond rigid politeness and good manners. Classmates recalled Nixon in grade school deliberately marching down the halls, head down, arms laden with a pile of books, ignoring or perhaps not noticing those whom he passed. "He had a tendency to downgrade himself," said Ola Florence, his one longtime girlfriend apart from Pat. She liked parties, but "[He was] lonely and so solemn at school . . . He didn't know how to mix. He would never double date. He had no real boy friends. And he didn't like my girlfriends. He would stalk out of the room where they were, his head high." Nixon could be pushy in his attempts to connect. He had a habit, exasperating to many, of finishing others' sentences.[24]

In pictures taken when Nixon attended Fullerton High School, he appeared slender but wide-hipped, sturdy yet slight. He wore a white shirt, a tie tied short. His cheeks, one day to sink into signature jowls, were chubby, the ears small, and his prominent chin still to develop. At most, he gave the camera a piece of a smile, lips folded in as if uncertain. Competing for attention with his face was a mess of kinky hair somehow combed back and contained. The tangle covered a scar. Nixon's earliest memory was of being thrown from a horse-drawn buggy at the age of three. The horse took off. Nixon fell from the carriage, slashing the left side of his scalp. He needed fifteen stitches. From that day on, even

Portrait of Richard Nixon in high school. *Courtesy of the Richard Nixon Presidential Library and Museum.*

when the side part became the fashion, he insisted on combing his mass of hair "straight back to hide" the scar. Most, Nixon recalled running after the carriage, "trying to catch up," "afraid to be left behind." His close aide Monica Crowley came to view the incident as a metaphor for his life, like Lot's wife, needing "to move forward and not look back . . . , to build from ruin."[25]

Yet Nixon resolutely did and resolutely did not look back. He recounted stories of his youth time and again, but nearly always encased them in the patina of the sentimental. The scholar Robert Solomon suggested, "Nostalgia as sentimentality is the ability to focus or remember something pleasant in the midst of what may have been tragedy and horror." Nixon, in evaluating his life, insisted that his early years had not been defined by deprivation. He never conveyed disappointment over how his family could not afford the dues necessary for him to enlist as a Boy Scout or fireworks for the Fourth of July, like his peers, or how they ate chicken instead of turkey on Thanksgiving. Instead, he insisted that his home offered him "unlimited opportunity." He stuck to a sentimental plot of sweet communion over suffering. As he quoted Eisenhower, "We were poor, but the glory of it was, we didn't know it." Nixon admitted, however, to grieving for his two brothers who died young. "There is no doubt that experiencing such an emotional ordeal at such an early age contributed to my sense of fatalism," Nixon attested, only then adding that he resisted such "fatalism." He countered with benevolent life lessons, with light from the darkness, weaving a sentimental yarn from brutal, bad luck. He stressed how, "ironically," his brother Arthur's death "helped me to prepare for and overcome difficult crises in the years ahead."[26]

In particular, Nixon appeared determined to counter the "grotesque caricatures" of his father as a "crude, uneducated oaf." He felt intensely protective of his father. Nixon repeatedly described Francis Anthony Nixon as a "gifted, natural speaker," a talented teacher, the hardest worker he had ever known. According to family lore, Frank was raised in rags. Jeered by his classmates, it was said that he struck back "with a quick tongue and a ready pair of fists." Frank favored the scripture "In the sweat of thy face shalt thou eat bread," and by accounts, he was indeed a hard-laboring man with an adroit mind who pulled his family up from poverty and firmly into the lower middle class. He was political, a noted personality in his small, Quaker community. A "big, old Irish, loud type," he was noisy, a talker, a debater. Neighbors recalled hearing him shouting "all through the neighborhood."[27]

Rather than through sheer brute labor, Frank succeeded with a combination of creativity and determination. He bought the first tractor in Yorba Linda and then hired it out to neighbors still using horses to till their land. Keenly foreseeing the explosion in popularity of automobiles, Frank built a small filling station in 1922, the first one in the area. He outfitted it with a grocery store selling fruits and vegetables, shirts and pants, spools of thread and balls of yarn. He called it Nixon's Market, located three miles outside of Whittier on the El Camino Real to take advantage of the increasing traffic. The store did relatively well through- out the depression. "[The town] became filled with caravans of people coming out of the dustbowl," Nixon's younger brother Edward said. He remembered the bustle of new customers in the store—"Okies and Arkies . . . old jalopy kind of cars, a couple of mattresses on the roof" and "the food pickers, and mules." During Nixon's later childhood, through the toil of the upwardly mobile, through the profitable of Frank's new store, the Nixons moved from Yorba Linda to East Whit- tier, into a white frame house trimmed with green around the bay win- dow and shaded by a pepper tree.[28]

Only on rare retellings would Nixon reveal that most secret of knowledge within the Milhous Nixon home. Only rarely did he say it simply: "Yeah, we got the strap." One story sticks out in particular, re- peated by neighbors but not by Nixon. It was a time when the violence in the Nixon household spilled into public view. The family lived across from a muddy slab of a ditch owned by the Anaheim Union Water Com- pany and used for irrigation; it was three feet deep and ten feet wide. All the neighborhood kids—save for Nixon and his brothers—would "dog paddle or mud paddle" in the brackish ditch. The oft-irritated Frank never allowed them. Catching them disobeying his restriction on one occasion, a furious Frank "yank[ed] them out pretty severely," and dunked them in and out, a cousin recalled. The story of how he almost drowned one of the boys entered the town lore. Yet in Nixon's final mem- oir, he smothered his memories of his father with easy aphorism: "I have never known anyone who worked harder than him," adding that his father was "self-educated but well educated," and more, he was a "man of many talents," a man of "ambition, intelligence, and lively imagination."[29]

Nixon transformed his father's anger into a pitiable state, seeing love in his furies. "He was really very soft-hearted when it came to dealing with . . . punishment to the boys," Nixon insisted. "My father had a pretty loud bark but his bite was far less severe because of the very hard life he had led," he wrote, with not only an ambivalence toward Frank's harsh humor but with a determined empathy. "I imagine that he had received some pretty good lickings when he was a youngster." Nixon's brother Edward also described their father's temper, but noted its erratic quality, not only displaying rage but effusions of care as well. "All of us were kept on edge, concerned that Dad might explode and hurt someone with his tongue," Edward recalled, but then added, "Boy he could castigate us, but he loved us too."[30]

The sentimental favors archetypes—puckish rakes and wenches with hearts of gold—rather than the drawn and detailed characterizations of realism. Frank, in his son's telling, was a Horatio Alger figure, sleeves rolled up, wiping the sweat from his brow, striving and able. Hannah Milhous Nixon was simply a "saint," a "Quaker saint," the very image of sacrifice. She was said, even through the despairing years of the Great Depression, never to have turned a tramp away from the family store. Neighbors never had a bad word for Hannah. By Nixon's account, "[She] never [did] anything but work, work . . . to keep the store going." After moving to East Whittier, he said, his mother woke up at four each morning, mashed the store's overripe fruit—lemon, apple, cherry and mince—and rolled dough to bake fifteen pies for the day's customers. She beat the eggs in the fresh air each morning. Angel food cake was her specialty, each one selling for 25 cents. Nixon saw her not as a woman with her own wants and needs, but as one who "sacrificed everything for her children." Unlike her loud husband, Hannah rarely if ever yelled at her children.[31]

Tragedy struck in Nixon's youth when "baby brother" Arthur died at age seven, in 1925. After a spinal tap, following a diagnosis of extra-pulmonary tuberculosis that had reached his brain, all hope was lost. Nixon remembered his father coming down the stairs, crying uncontrollably and muttering, "They say the little darling's going to die." There was a family story that Arthur had eaten some bad grapes. According to another, the tubercular onset came from raw milk. Nixon's father did not believe in pasteurizing. And still, tragedy hit the Nixons again in 1928. First, they called it "lung fever." Harold, the eldest brother, had also come down with tuberculosis. Much like the eldest Kennedy brother, Joseph, the eldest Nixon son had been deemed the brightest of the brood only to die young. Blond hair, blue eyes, charismatic, Harold was considered the "handsomest and best" within the family—"girls just swooned over him." Harold loved to sit and chat, "always kidding somebody, playing jokes." Brother Edward remembered how Nixon used to follow their eldest brother's lead. Harold fought for five years, coughing, coughing blood. "He withered away," Nixon said.[32]

To help nurse Harold after a relapse of tuberculosis, their mother moved with him to the mountains of Prescott, Arizona. With Hannah gone, Frank and the boys ate canned dinners—chili, beans and spaghetti—except for hamburgers once a week and a pot roast some Sundays. Nixon in his early teens missed his mother terribly. His father fought to keep the family close. "On week ends [sic] my Dad and my brother Donald and I would drive the 400 miles to see them," he remembered. "In our old car it took us 15 hours to make the trip and we used to drive all night to avoid the heat of the desert sun." Nixon recounted that his father "sold half of the acre on which our house was located in order to pay medical bills." To help afford the mounting costs, Hannah took three other tubercular bed patients under her care in Prescott—Larry, Leslie, and the "major," Nixon could still recall decades later. The "major" had been gassed in World War I. She nursed them for two years.

"And then, as each one of them died, she'd get the news. It was as if her own child had died." None survived. Harold would be the last. He was twenty-three.[33]

In Nixon's recollection of how Hannah nursed his tubercular brother, he relayed a view of his mother as saintly. As president, he recounted, "In the five years before [Harold] died, my mother never bought a new dress . . . But the wonder of it was that we didn't know it." In his insistence that Hannah was nothing less than the ideal mother, one senses the intensity of his attachment and the love he bore for her. In his singular retelling, she was clean, her dress literally clean in her son's recollecting eyes. His sentimental gloss makes it difficult to envision a woman who struggled, who possessed flaws as well as strengths. She had been dealt a sometimes-brutal husband, two sons deceased and three more to raise, a life in and out of poverty. Nixon stridently described her selfless works with tubercular patients in the makeshift infirmary—scrubbing floors, replacing one and yet another sputum cup, scouring blood stains from pajamas and robes, giving her young patients bed baths and alcohol rubs, and then hauling groceries from the Piggly-Wiggly. Decades later, Haldeman noted in his diary that Nixon never let his staff "forget that his mother had to scrub bedpans."[34]

Hannah's empathic nature was girdled by propriety. She named each of her sons "properly": Francis Donald after his father, Harold, Edward and Arthur after English kings. She named Richard after Richard the Lion-Hearted, and she wanted her son called Richard, never Dick. Despite the family's meager budget, she made sure her children were clean and freshly dressed, in ironed white shirts each and every day. Hannah instilled in her sons the value of education, teaching Nixon to read before he entered grade school, allowing him to skip a grade. She was a classicist—fluent in Greek, Latin, German and French—but cut her studies short of college to marry Frank. She introduced Nixon to European culture, to Roman and Greek mythology, to Shakespeare, Caesar,

Nixon family portrait when Richard was a three-year-old, 1916. *Left to right*: Harold, Frank, Donald, Hannah, Richard. *Courtesy of the Richard Nixon Presidential Library and Museum.*

Cicero and Demosthenes. In contrast to her husband's periodic eruptions, Hannah offered a model of restraint. "She had a temper too, but controlled," Nixon recalled. She was strategic when dealing with her husband's ill moods. "She knew how to throttle my Dad if he was hurting us intentionally," Nixon added. Indeed, there was a severity to Hannah Milhous Nixon in her faith and in her judgment. She read the Scripture literally. A passage from the Sermon on the Mount states, "[W]hen thou prayest, enter into thy closet," and so, at times, she prayed in a closet.[35]

Nixon hit back at the suggestion of any bitterness or resentment toward his mother for moving to Prescott. At an intimation that Hannah was withholding, he responded with a vehemence. "That's fatuous nonsense. You know, these psychohistorians are psychos," he declared. "I guess it's because perhaps they must have had unhappy childhoods, because basically our family was so close." Nixon expressed an ambivalence on rare occasion and only obscurely. His mother was a quiet disciplinarian "with a look . . . we dreaded far more than my father's hand," Nixon wrote in a college essay. His words were oblique perhaps due to the obliqueness of his mother's reticence, because his pen was still too immature to express such obscurity, such sentiment was still freshly forming in his mind or perhaps because the suggestion bore shame for him. He immediately followed with a qualification. "Not that [my mother's tongue] was very sharp, but she would just sit down and she would talk very, very quietly and when you got through, you had been through an emotional experience." An "emotional experience" would not seem necessarily such a bad thing, but for Nixon, for Hannah, it apparently proved to be. The intensity of the emotional experience proved scary, that is, "very, very quiet," as if illicit, disturbing, and still somehow overwhelming. Whatever the content, her hushed words and silences could, he remembered, elicit "dread." Nixon's first and longtime girlfriend described Hannah as wielding "an iron first in a velvet glove." Of Hannah's reticence, brother Edward finally at one point complained, "I just can't stand it. Tell her to give me a spanking."[36]

One of Nixon's nieces uncomfortably recalled his mother's penchant for the "silent treatment," how Hannah Nixon could keep "at it for days . . . and nobody could talk to her." Here, too, Nixon grew protective, his hackles up, preempting any possible interpretation that might challenge his sentimental view of Hannah as a saint. In one interview, he mentioned that she had never in her life said "I love you" to him. But he quickly followed up, "She didn't have to!" and added, "I feel the same way . . . I don't say 'God bless you, 'I love you,' and the rest . . . That's just the way I was raised." Nixon clung to a singular image of his mother as a hardscrabble, singularly self-depriving angel, "never [one to] turn a tramp away from the door."[37]

The "cult of Sentimentalism" burned out by the end of the eighteenth century. As the rugged and individualistic passions of Romanticism took hold, Sentimentalism was lambasted as a "brand of culpable naivety" for "dupes of a lachrymose sentimentality." Revolted by Sentimentalism's maudlin feelings, an avant-garde underground of intellectuals challenged the centrality of familial bonds and domestic communion. Coffee shops replaced fireside hearths as modish meeting grounds. Romantic, lonely, wandering walks of deep, inward contemplation (through a preferably drizzling rain) became the fashion. Self-actualization, the Romantic pursuit of psychological depth and unique expression of the creative individual, eclipsed communal sentiment and patriotic brotherhood. Only then, as the scholar Michael Bell described it, far from the sentimental, challenging the Romantics, Realism came to dominate, overtaking the subjectivity of feelings, insisting that readers could "only be moved by a tale if [they] think it true." Conservatives damned sentimental feelings as rebellion, a "culpable excess" unrestrained from social norm, a shameful masturbation of emotion. To liberals, those same simple, sentimental feelings inhibited the spirit with canned custom, the puppeteering of emotion, shallow, controlled. So thoroughly indicted, the negative valuations of Sentimentalism became the very definition of "sentimentalism." It was not just that a Sentimental communing of feelings was shallow, but the very word "sentimental" came to mean "shallow feeling."[38]

Oscar Wilde, writing to his lover Lord Alfred Douglas, trashed sentimentalism as "an emotion without paying for it," a pretense, a solipsistic indulgence, even a cooptation. Other critics piled on the derision. As I. A. Richards remarked, "Among the politer terms of abuse, there are few so effective as 'sentimental.'" It is, he concluded, a "lump of putty." The sentimental temperament, scholars have argued, offers a path "reinforcing our satisfying self-image," cheaply "gratifying [an] image of the self as compassionate, righteous." It may energize to great maudlin cause, or threaten to enervate, transforming an "engaged agent" into a jaded and self-satisfied spectator. A pantomime of good feeling may inure from the profoundest joy. It may indulge the easily pitiable in place of the truly pitiful, thus threatening to "desensitize us to the harsher aspects" of life. Sentimentalism's vices—simplification, manipulation, inhibition, triviality—are acts of erasure, erasure of complexity, will, movement, imagination. Sentimentalism is said to be insidious in its tendency to erase all that is not sentimental, to declare the unsentimental impure, cynical, as not worth attending.[39]

Such scorn has been charted as bearing on both the aesthetic and the ethical: that which is shallow of beauty and that which is shallow of character. In this, the sentimental is said not merely to hinder, but to corrupt. On the campaign trail, Nixon's sentimental approach led to him being called a "bad actor," in the aesthetic sense of delivering cloying performances, shallow and unconvincing, too rehearsed. He often reached for truism. He grasped for the simple tale. From his speechwriters, Nixon sought "heart, anecdotes, parables" to vivify his moral argument. He sought "heart, anecdotes, parables" to smooth complex reasoning into easily emotive proselytism like his friend the Rev. Graham—making his messaging easier to digest. The opposition cried cynicism. His opponents razzed Nixon's affecting efforts as "mechanical," "belabored," "trite." In addition to Tanya from Leningrad, Nixon spoke of eight-year-old Karl Jr., who was handicapped; four-year-old Kevin, who "suddenly stood at attention and saluted." He reminisced about the children he encountered at the top of the Ural Mountains while visiting the Soviet Union. As their coterie rode passed, they threw wildflowers and called out to the Americans, "Friendship! Friendship!" The word for "friendship" in Russian is *druzhba*, Nixon remembered.

Far from the difficulties and exigencies of the negotiating table, far from the brimming perils of the Cold War, Nixon delightedly recalled how his host pointed out, "The first word in the English language that Russian children learn is 'friendship.'" The president's writing team scrambled to find such homilies, touching tales, fables, something folksy, something poignant as Nixon aspired to project a sentimental image of the charismatic politician he aimed to be. At a rally in Madison Square Garden, Nixon recounted being moved when he spied a lone teenager holding a placard that read "Bring us together again." The phrase, a simple sentiment, became the theme of his 1968 campaign.[40]

At the Republican convention that year in Miami, Nixon spoke of himself again as a child who "hears the train go by at night and he dreams of faraway places where he'd like to go." His smile locked into place and unlocked a gleaming ramp of teeth. From Oregon, from Iowa, the party faithful from across the nation waved their placards, and "Nixon girls" bobbed in red, white and blue miniskirts. The galleries were draped in red, white, and blue bunting as ceiling netting held an army of orange balloons at bay above the crowd. From the dais, Nixon spoke again of his father, "who had to go to work before he finished the sixth grade" and then of his "gentle, Quaker mother, with a passionate concern for peace." Nixon had scraped his way to the nomination, campaigning tirelessly in the 1966 midterms, collecting chits, fending off a "stop Nixon campaign," fending off the more glamorous Gov. Nelson Rockefeller to his left and the more charismatic Gov. Ronald Reagan to his right. He manufactured the so-called Southern strategy to woo working-class whites by promising to nominate conservative justices to the Supreme Court and to slow-walk school desegregation. But from the stage in Miami, according to Nixon's yarn, the child's climb from poverty to the threshold of the presidency was no feat of political tactics but ordained, a great journey, an adventure. Far from the political compromises that ensured his Republican nomination, Nixon depicted a great sentimental communion as "scores, then hundreds, then thousands, and finally millions worked for [his] success."[41]

Beyond the cloying aesthetic of Nixon's sentimental entreaties, his critics launched a complaint not simply against "bad acting" in the theatrical sense, but against "bad-faith acting" on ethical grounds. His ends, such as détente and the ground-breaking SALT I with the Soviets, could arguably have moral dimensions, but his evocative techniques, like the apocryphal story of Russians' first English words, were seen as emotionally manipulative, cunning lamentations aimed at political persuasion. According to his critics, especially Cold War hawks to his right, his "phony" invocation of the goodness of the Russian spirit belied the on-going enmity between the superpowers. For the left, Nixon's sweet tales of communion, his adopting the role of the grand "peacemaker," belied the bloody tactics he ordered to prolong the Vietnam War and continue the fight against communism across Latin America, the Middle East, Southeast Asia and the Pacific. In Nixon's sentimental screeds, critics saw the aesthetic joined with the ethical—at once crass and devious, stylistically weak yet powerfully dangerous, even cruelly manipulative. As one labor union chief put it, "[Nixon was] the same old double-plated, triple-coated, four-faced and five-ply phony faker."[42]

Some scholars have linked sentimentalism like Nixon's to righteous brutality. The question, much debated, is whether malice is the opposite of sentimentalism or endemic to it. Does one connote the absence of the other, or are the two entwined? After Nixon left office, Nixon-watchers preoccupied themselves with judging his true position as somewhere between what Haldeman called the "light side" and the "dark side," between statesman and war criminal, strategic genius and hatchet man, between, as Haldeman put it, "admiration and disdain." To some, Nixon stood as a sympathetic, tragic figure. He had been a man of his time, one of the "forgotten men," one of his own silent majority, holding steady against the raucous demonstrations of the 1960s.

But, he was also private and plotting. He compromised—slumped in his armchair, racked by paranoia, cutting corners and slinging curses.[43] Did Nixon struggle with the sentimental and the brutal, light and dark? At times, rather than battle against the shadows, the dark could be sublimated, bringing forth the light. Nixon's approach of down and dirty politics threw his sentimental expressions of innocence ever more into relief. Still, alternatively, rather than light from dark, dark could come from light. An antecedent sentimentality, when threatened, could spark a brutal response in Nixon. When he thought himself innocent but cheated, he cheated in turn.

Entwined in Nixon's sentimentality was a developed sense of hurt and its consequences. "What starts the process [of achievement] really are laughs and slights and snubs when you are a kid," Nixon stressed. "Sometimes it's because you're poor or Irish or Jewish or Catholic or ugly or simply that you are skinny." For Nixon, hurt feelings from such treatment provided the basis for the sense that he would, could and deserved to climb. Nixon preached that there was a purpose beneath the pain, a chance for growth, for retribution, a beatified suffering. In his own sentimental telling, he saw himself combating the dark with light. He was Mr. Smith, a simple country lawyer in Washington, determined to do right by the people amid a swamp of corruption. From Nixon's first election to his last, he presented himself as the average Joe, an American Everyman, struggling but deserving to climb. With a righteous indignation, he promised to lift the silent majority by working harder for them than the communists and the intellectuals would. Whether vis-à-vis Hiss, the Kennedys, Jews, or the "Harvards," as he called the professorial elite, Nixon expressed a sense of being deprived of opportunity, of fairness. He wrote and spoke of how "they" played by one set of rules while he was held up to a higher standard. "I knew that I was a target," he asserted. "I had been a target ever since Alger Hiss, because during that case I did the worst thing that you can do to the press: prove that they were wrong." It was a matter, he added, of different "standards"—one for Republicans, one for Democrats. "And then there were standards for me," he lamented. His was a righteousness born of disappointment intertwined with disappointment born of righteousness. Even in success, he suffered jealousies. "Success," Kissinger noted, "seemed to unsettle Nixon more than failure. He seemed obsessed by the fear that he was not receiving adequate credit."[44]

In combating this perceived unfairness, Nixon's sense of ethical right led him to cast himself as the sentimental figure, the hero suffering unjustified slings and arrows, but ever resolute, deserving, good. Grades were earned, jobs and promotions, too. The struggle became an enjoyment, an escape from the bitterness. Nixon found a productive creativity in crisis, in pain. He traded hard fiction for a Horatio Alger tale, neat and moralistic. To fight his "fatalism," he portrayed his lot not as doomed, but adventurous. Those who had tasted battle, he wrote, could never "become adjusted to a more leisurely and orderly pace. They have drunk too deeply of the stuff which really makes life exciting and worth living." Nixon described this titillating drama as an existence lived on tenterhooks, under the watchful gaze of enemies, under the heavy burden of the grandly historic. For one living it, "Only in losing himself does he find himself," he adoringly and paradoxically wrote of such emotional ordeals. Capturing the dualism of the brutal and the sentimental, a young Nixon stressed in his first memoir that only through "exquisite agony" might an event or deed "bear on the fate of mankind for centuries to come." For those who battled could not be "satisfied with the froth" of the uneventful.[45]

Such a saccharine narrative suggests the inoffensive, a soft and easy morality play. But for the "fat-butted" fat cats, as Nixon called his enemies, the hardened politician dreamt of punishment far from inoffensive. For although the weak-minded may be sentimental, the sentimental are not necessarily weak. It's "them/we," Nixon's personal aide attested. It's "light" and "dark," his deputies recalled. The sentimental and the brutal became entwined. When the expectations of easy sentimental morality failed to play out, the brutal burst forth, the need to uncover and combat the cheats and traitors and plots to thwart Nixon's aims. He drew up an enemies lists. From the Kennedys to the press to leakers like Daniel Ellsberg of Pentagon Papers fame, Nixon had his adversaries tailed, their families photographed, their phones tapped. It was us versus them. Nixon's sentiment of innocence cast a dark shadow. He felt swindled and, in turn, felt inclined to cheat. Straying far from the immaculate life of striving and reward he purported to have led, Nixon was "eaten up with resentment," relayed Alexander Butterfield, keeper of the White House tapes. "He hated."[46]

Nixon rarely drank more than a glass of wine. On occasions when he began to indulge, Kissinger noted a change. "Two glasses of wine were quite enough to make him boisterous," his national security adviser recalled, "just one more" glass was enough to cause Nixon "to grow bellicose or sentimental with slurred speech. Alcohol had a way of destroying the defenses he had so carefully constructed to enable him to succeed."[47] From Kissinger's perspective, Nixon's antithetical sides lay just below the surface, the entwined affects not so deeply buried, the brutal and the cloying right beneath his skin. A couple of glasses of wine downed by the mostly abstemious Nixon could bring the sweet and the abrasive to a roil.

In recounting Tanya's shortened life at the 1972 Republican convention, Nixon invoked the contrast between light and dark, the violence of the Germans and her innocence offset. The two, in Nixon's telling, as per the sentimental genre, constituted a dialectic. In late August 1972 outside the convention hall where Nixon spoke to the millions watching, a tent city carnival of counterculture sprang up, in Flamingo Park. Here again was the dualism, the brutal and the sentimental. The aim of the boisterous park festival was to call out the ongoing war in Vietnam, as a biting critique to protest the sentimental goings-on inside the hall. There was a Women's Tent, a Yippies Headquarters and Zippies raising the Vietcong flag. There were streakers and Jesus freaks, a winding path impertinently labeled the Ho Chi Minh Trail, and the smell of marijuana wafting over it all—each group with its own billowing strain. "There's blood on your hands," some jeered at a passing Republican senator. To the delegates in convention attire, they called out, "Murderers, murderers." A large nighttime rally featured the actress Jane Fonda and the radical lawyer William Kunstler. The Black Panther leader Bobby Seale led a chant of "One, two, three, four. We don't want your fucking war." As Nixon took the stage inside, Ellsberg spoke outside.[48]

The protest was a call to expose the brutality of the administration, an attempt to pierce through the patriotic sentiment of the Republican National Convention. Violence spilled over into the street. The crowd yelled at National Guard members, anti-Castro Cubans jostled with anti-war protestors. There was a skirmish involving the American Nazi Party. Windows were smashed along Miami's thoroughfares. The *Washington Post*'s David Broder reported that "police used heavy clouds of tear gas to disperse antiwar demonstrators trying to block the delegates' entry and exit" at the convention center. Protestors threw rocks and bottles at the cops. Hundreds were arrested.[49]

Inside the hall, there stood Nixon in front of his nominators, dressed in blue, his face smoothed with makeup, accepting his nomination—the "Pinnacle of His Career," the *Washington Post* proclaimed. Indeed, the delegates applauded him twenty-five times in eighteen minutes. Nixon denounced quotas, railed against inflation. The veteran of so many election battles ended his speech as he had ended so many before, invoking a sweetly stoic child and a polished mantra or a rugged, old saw. "Let us build a peace that our children and all the children of the world can enjoy for generations," Nixon exhorted. For sentimentalism, for Nixon, was an attempt to influence; and sentimentalism had also influenced his views on life. Children were good; his childhood was good. Tired, his baritone dropped just so. As a near-riot broke out on the streets of Miami, Nixon accepted the nomination with the saccharine tale of the little girl from Leningrad with "brown eyes, a pretty face," the lilting list of her family long dead. "Let us think of Tanya," Nixon urged, capping his performance with a slow and practiced bow.[50]

Interlude One

AS THE WIND BLEW, Pat Nixon's hair did not. Her famous hairdo crested in a high puff of strawberry blond. Thin as a bird, spine straight, the first lady gazed up at her husband on the dais as he campaigned for reelection in 1972. One reporter described Pat's elongated back appearing as stiff as the "figure of a young asparagus." Observers noted a "relentless vigil," an "almost frozen attention." From one stop to the next—Topeka, Nashua, Flint—her head tilted as she watched, rapt, listening to the same speech she had heard countless times before. *Time* magazine described how Pat, with an air so far from her husband's awkwardness, "tackle[d] a crowd of strangers like a bee that has spotted a new clover field." Through 100-degree heat and through pelting sleet, through protestors ripping down her supporters' signs, cameras followed the first lady from the high seat of the Kremlin to the earthquake-ravaged streets of Peru. Junket after junket, meeting and greeting, "she does not simply shake a hand," *Time* marveled, "she cuddles it in both of hers."[1]

Pat lacked the eloquence of an Eleanor Roosevelt; she was neither the spectacularly photographed Jackie Kennedy nor Lady Bird Johnson, whose words rang with purpose. Pat was instead praised for her efforts as a wife and a mother, with news outlets quite literally naming her the "outstanding Home-maker of the Year" in 1953, "Mother of the Year" in 1955 and the "Nation's Ideal Housewife" in 1957. The Nixon family friend and popular, conservative evangelist Norman Vincent Peale commended Pat as "the prototype of the finest type of American woman . . . [who] could be president of an association of good mothers and housewives." When she spoke, she painted a picture of a pristine marriage, never "shivers or sweats."[2] In sentimental fashion, she presented a portrait of dearness and fondness unruffled by the angst of her era, the ire of her husband, or the messiness of sex.

Mrs. Richard Nixon, as she was often referred to in newspapers, "prunes her thoughts to a single sentence," one reporter remarked. "You'll have to ask Dick about that," she regularly demurred, or "That isn't for me to say." She told *Time*, "I try to help him along by doing the best I can as a listener." One writer described Pat as "one of the greatest question-parriers in the world." Just as journalists looked for the "real Nixon" for decades, they searched for the "real Pat." She became a muse for *Time*, *Ladies Home Journal*, and *Good Housekeeping*. Headlines promised insight into "The Silent Partner," "The Other Campaigner," "The Real Pat Nixon." Yet as her curt posturing proved insufficient, interviewers grew impatient, determined to pierce the fixed visage. "We feel cheated," Nixon's cousin, the novelist Jessamyn West proclaimed. "We want to know." She further said, "If not told, we speculate." Did Pat's reticence come from a quiet temperament, from cold calculation, or simply from having nothing to say? Perhaps her silences arose from the punishing years of politics, out of a punishing childhood, out of a fear of being punished. "She is a lady who plays it safe," the *Today Show*'s Barbara Walters commented. "But on the other hand, she doesn't make mistakes."[3]

With not a smudge in her makeup or a run in her stockings, in apparent perfection, Pat attracted detractors. Amid the raging culture wars of the 1960s and 1970s, Pat became a symbol of the prototypical 1950s wife, a Donna Reed, a good sport, made-up, always contained, stuck in time. As the historian Gil Troy wrote, "The wifely loyalty that made her popular . . . as the vice president's wife became controversial a decade later." For cultural conservatives like Peale, Pat carried the torch for a lost wifely ideal, whereas feminists considered her cheery charms an affront to the progress of women and feminism. She was thought to be a puppet, the reined in wife of Dick Nixon, trailing a foot behind, ever willing to hawk his wares. The press that had celebrated her unflagging demeanor earlier in Nixon's career turned on her. *Time* dismissed the first lady as "little more than a speaker's platform mannequin." *Newsweek* sarcastically described a wife like Pat as a perfect domestic accessory, a "public man's dream," no more than "a seemingly selfless, super-efficient helpmate."[4]

Like the sentimental, Pat's affect was deemed at once too much and yet too little, sweetly effusive yet cold. She was dubbed "Plastic Pat," her indefatigable smile disparaged as insincere. Far from fur or diamonds, the plastic moniker suggested a lower class status, that she lacked sophistication in the brightly colored clothes she preferred, that she and her adoring gaze were cheap. Out of step with the ironic and skeptically chic, Pat could never be acceptable to the cool counterculture. The novelist Ann Beattie, who would go on to write a fictional biography of the first lady, considered Pat a "person I would have done anything to avoid—to the extent she was even part of my consciousness." Worse than scandalous, Beattie deemed Pat boring. She was spoken of as frivolous, as a Watergate footnote, unworthy of inquiry or attention.[5]

From the harsh judgment of her detractors in the 1960s, Pat's reputation began to shift again in the wake of her husband's resignation in 1974. That fall *Time* made amends in "The Relentless Ordeal of Political Wives." First ladies like Pat had become "public property, . . . subject to unending scrutiny, . . . accolades and criticism," the magazine wrote. They have been "used and then abandoned or ignored or forced to turn the other way as 'power groupies' cluster around the Big Man." In place of portrayals of Pat as either pristinely domestic or callously apolitical, subsequent assessments tended to focus on her as a casualty of cruel and unfair treatment. The narratives countered her critics by trying to rescue her from the plastic image. Her daughter Julie Eisenhower wrote a glowing and largely uncritical account of her mother's life that emphasized Pat's warmth and fortitude through harsh times. The extended academic treatments by Lester David, *The Lonely Lady of San Clemente*, and Mary Brennan, *Embattled First Lady*, portrayed Pat as a woman "of the people," one of the sidelined silent majority that Nixon so effectively courted. She became a portrait of suffering, a victim cast aside. She had lifted herself out of terrible poverty only to be ignored by her husband and lambasted by critics for taking on a role in which women of her time were cast. Troy describes how the public view of Pat was limited, her subjectivity lost as she became objectified in a political culture that focused "less on what Pat Nixon did than on what different people expected her to do, . . . less on who she was than on to whom she was married."[6]

Pat's patina of sweet but curt sentiment, however, was not simply the product of her objectification by supporters or a fabrication by her detractors. To a great degree, it was a role she adopted, a performance like so many of her husband's. And like her husband, Pat felt that she had to be in control of her emotions, as close friends described, to keep a "rein on herself." Julie attested, "Mother always . . . scorned complainers." Pat told her daughter, "I detest scenes. I just can't be that way." She hated interviews, and when granted, no tape recorders, too invasive. Feelings—so central to sentimentalists like the Nixons, so effusive yet potentially complicating—needed to be contained lest they overwhelm. About her instilled composure, Pat remarked, "I keep everything in. I never scream or do those things . . . If I have a headache no one knows it." Not a cough, a cold or the flu. "I don't get ill . . . I just don't." Furthermore, of acts of anger, she swore, "I may be dying, but I certainly would never say anything about it. I never have tantrums. If anything makes me mad, I'm silent."[7]

Along the lines of David Hume and Adam Smith's Sentimentalist thinking, the historian Donald T. Critchlow writes, conservative women of Pat's day embraced the notion of "the hierarchical family in which the wife and mother was the cornerstone." Women were seen as "the primary conveyer of tradition and custom, morals, and civil habits and manner," whereas men were deemed the conveyors of progress and individualism, battling in the grime of politics and hard labor.[8] Nixon on the public stage, Pat in a domestic setting, each sought to thrive in their separate spheres. Pat was determined not to compete with Nixon, but to complement her husband's strengths and shortcomings.

As the wife of a national figure, however, Pat had to straddle the public and the private by putting the comportment of her domestic life on display. William Safire captured both Pat's wiling sensibilities and the confinement of her position, noting, "[She] must be unfailingly supportive in public and constructively critical in private. She must see all to avert trouble and say nothing to get into trouble." Nixon heaped praise on his wife: "She had the characteristics of a great actress . . . at her best when on stage." Far from simple and straightforward, Pat was malleable, an actorly figure navigating through contradictory and competing roles. She was a woman who expressed tremendous care even as she muffled her own suffering. She campaigned for the importance of community even as she insisted on a strict need for self-sufficiency. She was a feminist, but without publicly demonstrating, a progressive favoring much of the left's agenda while harboring a conservative aversion to expressing so much. When challenged, Pat's mood, like her husband's, could turn ornery and defensive. They both attained impressive success while sharing a sense of deprivation, even resentment. Yet in place of Nixon's outbursts, as her biographer Brennan noted, "Pat chose more passive-aggressive methods—venting to friends or making snide remarks to her husband."[9]

Nixon aided in constructing the pristine image of his wife as the sensible woman and their home as a conservative household. He painted a portrait of Pat and their children as ideal, never anything but loving and loyal, contained, never a hair out of place. Nixon erased the unruliness of family drama with simple expressions of fondness. He filled his campaign literature with Norman Rockefelleresque portraits. Troy wrote how Nixon battled "Communism with an arsenal of postwar American domestic artifacts: attractive children, slim wives, suburban décor, television sets, toy cowboys, and lawn furniture." The girls called him "Daddy." Pat was Pat. They always had dogs. Nixon's daughters, Tricia and Julie, expressed a lot of affection for their parents, especially their father. "No man has ever had a stronger family than I have had," Nixon contended. He insisted, in sentimental fashion, that the family was nothing but supportive—and enthusiastically so.[10]

Nixon spun his wife's life into a life lesson as he had spun his own. He championed Pat's biography as a "classic example of triumph over adversity," judging her a "strong character who is at her best when the going gets rough." Even poorer than Nixon in his youth, she was born in a raucous tent town, a ten-acre truck farm with no electricity and little plumbing, in Ely, Nevada. "Primitive," she recalled. There were few pleasures—contests for the prized sow, bareback riding on the family's plow horse. She remembered sitting in a

The Nixons celebrated
daughter Tricia's marriage to
Edward Cox with a wedding
at the White House in
June 1971. *Courtesy of the
Richard Nixon Presidential
Library and Museum.*

family buggy at the age of four, waiting outside the grocer as her father,
William M. Ryan, Sr., shopped. "I'd watch the corner to see if he came back
carrying a strawberry cone," she recalled. But there was no money; there was
no cone. Pat remembered feeling deprived. "I just waited and hoped." As she
added, "In our family, we held our disappointment." In another early
memory, she recalled her father, a big tease, taking her to town to run
errands. While he shopped, his friends, also fond of ribbing, gathered around
and began bartering. The prize was Pat, going for a week's worth of groceries. "Amid much laughter, the men would bid," Julie wrote, relating her
mother's recollection. "[S]itting very straight, her red cape spread around her
like a fan, her eyes straight ahead, [she] never revealed even to her father that
she was terrified he would sell her."[11]

"When my mother died I just took responsibility of my life," Pat told Julie. She was thirteen, keeping up a home (at times a tent) for her father and brothers. It was a life of cooking, laundry, her house to scrub clean. Her father, a drinker, had a great drooping moustache, a quick humor, always searching for the next gold mine. Yet with his family, he was "quite strict." Pat learned to avoid confrontation and not to cry as a child. Friends growing up thought of Pat as a "tremendously disciplined person," one who bore "deep scars." She was "*very* ambitious," a high school friend recalled. "She was the type of person that would push to get where she wanted to go." Pat nursed her father through silicosis, contracted from working in copper mines. Yet ever the sentimentalist, when he died, she tried to muffle the suffering with sweet sentiment. She recounted, "Life was sort of sad, so I tried to cheer everybody up. I learned to be that kind of person."[12]

Pat excelled, like her future husband, at school, in student government, on stage. Also like Nixon, she worked. Alone as the Great Depression hit, she labored at various jobs to pay her way through the University of Southern California in pursuit of a merchandising degree. As one professor recalled, "If you went into the cafeteria, there was Pat Ryan at the serving counter. An hour later, if you went to the library, there was Pat Ryan, checking out books." She had not yet developed her cheerful visage, the plastic sheen. The professor noted, "It always used to disturb me how tired her face was in repose." Pat remembered how her college classmates snickered as she worked as a janitor. She became a telephone switchboard operator. She worked in a dentist's office as an x-ray technician. She cared for tubercular patients in a sanatorium.[13]

Pat also had not yet adopted her future husband's ascetism. When she worked as a typing teacher at Whittier College, she kept a full dance card. The "American working girl," one friend pegged her. "She had gaiety and a love for life and a sparkle in her eye," her friend disclosed. She acted in bit parts in Hollywood movies and modeled for a well-known Los Angeles department store. One of her typing students from Whittier recounted how young and pretty she was "in the latest fashions" and bright colors. She had an "air of mystery," high cheekbones, lavender perfume. On test days, as her pupil remembered, "She stood by the window and we could see her silhouetted against the sunlight. I was always fascinated by her marvelous posture."[14]

However adventurous she was at socializing, Pat set strict standards for her typing students. She taught them manners, the need for an armor of propriety in order to be taken seriously. Her students were to behave like young ladies: no liberal leniency, no excuses, no curves, "no compromises, no errors, no second-rate job." She had firm ideas on how a woman should act, how a woman needed to present herself to get ahead: hair combed, shoelaces tied, skirts straight, spines stiff—"needles" not "noodles"—and no chewing gum. Both the typing student and the letters typed were to be "pleasing to the eye." Pat became known for her inhuman output, returning the assignments of all thirty-five students the day after their submission, every incorrect *a* for an *e* marked. She was determined to pass along the need for self-sufficiency to her female charges. One student recalled how she "insisted *we* learn how to change ribbons, clean our typewriters, repair them if they stuck."[15]

After meeting in California as actors in community theater, after a period of long, unrequited doting, during which Nixon offered and chauffeured Pat to dates with other men, as the story goes, she eventually gave in to his determined pursuit. Pat was drawn to Nixon's drive; they married. He went off to war in the Pacific, and upon his return was soon recruited to run for Congress, at which point the Nixons embarked on the adventure of a political life together. They were the "Pat and Dick team," Julie wrote. They were "going places." Pat typed the fliers, he hung them. At house teas across California's Twelfth Congressional District, he spoke as she hosted. She had an excellent memory for faces and names, far better than his. He excelled on the stage, she one-on-one. They each thrived in their spheres. As Pat described, "I go around with him and talk to the women . . . I never discuss politics, but answer any other questions I can."[16]

Most women made Richard Nixon nervous. A college friend remembered how an awkward Nixon would try to coax his dates into debates, asking questions like "What would have happened if Persia had conquered

Greece?" In his first campaigns, Nixon suffered through endless teas and house parties, struggling to look women in the eye. A cousin described the Nixon brood's relationship to sexuality as "maiming inhibitions." There were three rules: "don't talk about it . . . don't play with it . . . keep it covered up." Nixon was mortified when, in front of his secretary at his law firm, he had to question a couple about their sexual encounter in a public park. Tax cases were comfortable, farm deeds a snap, but personal matters . . . Not so much. "I had a divorce case to handle, and this good looking woman . . . began talking to me about her problem of sexual incompatibility with her husband." Nixon recalled, "I turned fifteen colors of the rainbow."[17]

Nixon interpreted the complexities of gender and gender differences in broad brushstrokes. He judged, "Girls that are beautiful . . . don't have much upstairs, and those that have brains are not very pretty." He essentialized women, as well as men, in a few characteristics. Women "bear grudges," he felt. "They're highly idealistic . . . [And] they're very, very hard losers."[18] The two women closest to Nixon—his mother and his wife—he insistently beatified in a soft, saintly light. They struggled, suffered, worked hard, but beautifully. Pat offered Nixon an alternative to the women in his day agitating for feminist change, equal rights and liberation. She, too, possessed those traits key to Nixon's character: his sentimentalism, strong work ethic, sense of aggrievement and need for emotional control.

In many areas, Nixon's personal peccadillos could take a turn toward the pragmatic, if not progressive, when transferred to the political sphere. In his public life, he professed attitudes far more liberal toward women than he sought in his domestic relations. From a distance, he in theory supported individual striving by women. He supported the Equal Rights Amendment in his 1968 presidential campaign. Once in office, he went on to quadruple the number of women in high-level federal jobs. He appointed Anne Armstrong to his cabinet as counselor to the president. He expanded Title IX of the Civil Rights Act of 1964 to prevent discrimination against women in federally funded assistance. Yet in his own domain, Nixon surrounded himself with men.

"Politics was a harsh, even hurtful battle, a man's world, and he had difficult thinking of women making political strategy and decisions," Julie wrote. After the disillusioning Checkers scandal in 1952 and Nixon's climb to the vice presidency, "Pat still had advice and criticisms, but her recommendations were no longer a matter exclusively between her and her husband," their daughter judged. Rather, her mother's ideas "were weighed along with the seasoned views of an entourage. And her advice was not always taken." Nixon preferred instead to confer with a small cadre of male confidants. Although he supported the advancement of women in the workplace, it was men whose judgment he trusted. It was with men that Nixon developed a cult of toughness. Theirs was an admixture of machismo and aggrievement. Summoning H. R. Haldeman, Bebo Rebozo or Charles Colson, Nixon would huddle for rough talk and ambitious political plotting for hours on end, well into the night. The singular exception to his all-male rule was Pat. In his diary Nixon wrote, "Her criticisms . . . are not intended to hurt, and she usually does understand the problems we have." His words suggested a mix of trying to downplay his hurt while showing respect, hinting at his vulnerability to her thinking. He valued her "sensitivity about people," a sensitivity he felt he lacked.[19]

Pat, too, supported the tenets of the women's movement. She urged her husband to appoint a woman to the Supreme Court. After *Roe v. Wade*, she announced that she was pro-choice. "I am for equal rights and equal pay for equal work . . . But I don't believe in parades," she maintained. Like her demeanor, her politics were a vigil to temperament control. "I don't think women gain anything when they use loud techniques. The smarter thing would be to work quietly, to write your Congressman." As for the demonstrators at universities, she deemed them to be "SDS goons," lumping them all in with the left-wing Students for a Democratic Society. Pat, spine stiffened, smile in place, stood in the ramparts defending a previous age, her husband, a sentimental space of their own. Just as she had taught her typing students, she aimed to forward women's greater opportunity while maintaining a reserved comportment of character. Talking with the noted feminist leader Gloria Steinem, Pat took a swipe at the burgeoning women's movement, "I just want to go down in history as the wife of the President."[20] Her goal was not independence but a perfect fellowship with her husband, with her daughters, with her country. She imagined a world in which women could excel as women in their discrete role as supporters and nurturers, appreciated but not threatening, not competing with the status of their male counterparts.

In salute to that combination of self-sufficiency and domesticity, Pat attested that even as first lady she dressed in five minutes and ate in ten. Hers was an insistence that she was a woman "of the people," that she ironed her own clothes and darned her own socks. Antithetical to her plastic image, Pat maintained that what you saw was what you got. Hard work remained central to her sense of self and purpose. She had volumes of mail to answer, sometimes up to four hours a day. Among her first lady duties, she chose to renovate the White House, overseeing painting, furniture repair, recarpeting, acquiring a gallery of Americana, 600 paintings and antiquities, a Monet, far more than the much-more publicized beautification efforts of Jacqueline Kennedy. She hung portraits of each first lady. "We'll beat Versailles yet," Pat promised.[21] It was a sensible venture that enabled Pat to thrive within the delineated domestic sphere.

Women of Pat's sensibility were not those poor individuals needing a helping hand; they displayed not a "smudge or a spot or a wrinkle" and conspicuously so. No longer poor as in her youth, Pat became the one providing alms. The sensible woman felt responsively and then acted responsibly. Through Pat's rapt attention, according to the centuries' old tradition of sentimentalism, she could absorb the goodness in the world, and through imbibing, become good for herself, for her self-development, and for social cohesion, for social progress in a time of riots on campus and turmoil in American cities. The sensible types defined themselves by how genuinely they commiserated, feeling truly compelled to give, as the historian Sarah Knott suggested, to turn commerce into communion. Drawing on her own experience of upward mobility, Pat developed a classically liberal view. "I really believe that in this country you don't have to inherit anything," Pat insisted to *Vogue*. "Just work hard and you're bound to get ahead." Pat's devotion to charity, mixed with this classic liberalism, developed into a commitment to volunteerism rather than public policy or reform. She pressed each American to donate 20 minutes a day. "It is your heart that is speaking," she maintained. Still, in her mission, she was caught between the adventurous and the sensible, the dancing Irish gypsy and the exacting typing teacher. As Helen Thomas, the one-time dean of White House correspondents, put it, "She wants to make a bold appeal to our selfless, charitable instincts . . . but boldness might be equated with loudness, and we have been told to lower our voices."[22]

As much as Pat attempted to sustain her steady commitment and cheer, it was during those years in politics that the constant politicking became a long-enduring sacrifice. She came to hate the campaign. She pressed Nixon not to run after the humiliation of the secret fund affair in 1952. On stage during the televised Checkers speech, she described becoming the plastic mannequin she would so insidiously be accused of being. She recalled, "The *best* I was able to do was sit like a wax figure, afraid if I made one move and I might show too much emotion, my control might give way on the screen." Her best friend Helene Drowns recounted, "It almost killed me to look at her—she was like a bruised little kitten." Just as Nixon protested, it was the "unfairness" of it all that tortured Pat—the investigation into her husband's small fund while Stevenson's much larger secret campaign donations barely caused a stir. "It makes me so exasperated, so tired," she related, judging that it was then that she "lost the zest" for politics. Later, with the defeat to Kennedy in 1960, Julie remembered her mother "disillusioned beyond redemption" as she saw the election as stolen and could not fathom so many people's indifference.[23]

As much as defeat, however, Nixon's political success put a strain on his and Pat's marriage as he became more unavailable and remote. On the most-momentous election nights, Nixon took his own suite to watch returns while Pat and the girls viewed them in another. On weekend getaways in Key Biscayne, the family rented one house for the president and another for the family. The Nixons were often apart—Nixon at Camp David, on Montauk, in the Bahamas. For all the closeness he boasted, Nixon needed space. Nixon's aide Frank Gannon described the high, but remote drama among the family, "like actors in a Tolstoy saga—slipping notes under doors or leaving them on pillows, or having intermediators convey awkward news." *USA Today* gathered that the couple exchanged "little affection, and [the president] sometimes seemed to ignore her completely." Pat craved compliments from her husband, what she called a "pleasant crumb." The candidate's media consultant, a young Roger Ailes, even sent out an urgent memo to Haldeman: "President to show a little more concern for Mrs. Nixon as moves through the crowd." Unsatisfied with the Nixons' performance as a family, Ailes began to stage direct their marriage. "From time to time [Nixon] should talk to her and smile at her. Women voters are particularly sensitive to how a man treats his wife in public. The more attention she gets, the happier they are."[24]

While flying, Nixon most often nattered on in the front cabin with a chief aide, with Pat relegated to the middle cabin with the staff. The children sat and played in the back. After landing, they assumed their genial roles. At the front of the plane, they lined up behind the president, in parade formation. Nixon would greet them each in turn. The stage was set. "The airplane door would open and they would walk out to stand as a family, waving and smiling to the airport crowd," chief domestic advisor John Ehrlichman recalled. Nixon gave his firm, one-armed-wave, and at once they seemed the perfect first family. During the 1968 campaign, Ehrlichman recounted, "Day after day, four, five, or six times a day, the family would be assembled and disassembled, along with the camera tripods and loudspeakers." It was a sentimental tableau on the tarmac: the familial bond, the loving portrait, a greeting card, a yearbook photo, simple, clean.[25]

It was on trips to foreign lands, when on tours beyond the confines of Washington, that reporters observed Pat truly "emerge from her shell." In 1953, along with her husband, then vice president, Pat traveled for seventy-two days around the world. For events, she did her own makeup, used rollers and an ordinary electric curler to do her hair, sometimes adding a hairpiece or preferring a wig. She was proud of her humble efforts. No maid was needed; she packed herself. As she made a point of disclosing to trailing reporters, she folded each dress once at the waistline. She would wear six evening gowns twelve times each. The former Pat Ryan became a world-traveling volunteer ministering aid to the poor and then dining with kings.

Pat Nixon as international
ambassador, visiting a
Polynesian village in Janu-
ary 1972. *Courtesy of the Richard
Nixon Presidential Library and
Museum.*

She rubbed noses (literally) in a Māori village in New Zealand. She ate K
rations in her unair-conditioned room when the food at official banquets
proved too exotic or inedible.[26]

Traveling alone as first lady, Pat greeted the powers that be in thirty-two
countries. She became the first first lady to act as an official representative of
the United States. She was the first to visit a combat zone, in South Vietnam.
Far away from her husband, she earned rave reviews back home. With a
retinue of forty, Pat toured the West African coast, covering 10,000 miles in
eight days and greeted with all the "ruffles and flourishes and 19-gun salutes"
rolled out for heads of state. She reviewed honor guards. Villagers swarmed
her open-car motorcade on her stop in Monrovia. She was cheered and
greeted by Liberians under canopies of intertwined banana trees. Her hosts
feted her to beats of hollowed-out logs and tightly bound drums. The

traveling correspondent for *Time* described the "sinuous writhing of bare-breasted women within inches of her chair," a far cry from the girdled propriety expected of the American first lady stateside. Pat declared in Accra, "I wanted to show that we are good neighbors, good friends." Charmed, Ghanaian chieftains praised her with the commendation that "not even a lion could destroy" the American first lady.[27]

Back in Washington, however, Pat missed the camaraderie of the early years of her marriage, and at rare moments, she let the veneer slip. She confided to one reporter about the loneliness of raising two young daughters with a politician husband. If not resentment, she expressed disappointment. He displayed few if any affections, rarely a hand held, often ignoring her in public. She admitted feeling at times like a widow. She maintained two houses neither of them satisfactory as a home. Of the White House, she said, "We love this house," but then, "We are shut in this house . . . There is no place to walk on the White House grounds without people watching—no . . . fresh air." Pat, like her husband, felt walls of distrust closing in. She endured being a fascinating object, obliged to sign autographs whenever she dared run an errand. She complained how the "prying press" and campaign rallies distorted family life. "You'd think I was one of the inmates . . . just a fish in a bowl." Pat remained stoic as protestors at a daycare center she was visiting held signs reading "How many of these little kids are going to be soldiers?" and "Killing for peace is like raping for chastity." As Nixon's presidency tumbled into scandal, Julie's classmates at Sidwell Friends, an elite private Quaker school in Washington, waved newspapers and cartoons accusing her father of being a bigot, in league with the Ku Klux Klan.[28]

Pat hoped that her daughters would avoid following her path. She foresaw little good fortune for Julie and Tricia if they chose to marry politicians. "I had expressed these doubts to our daughters, but not to him," she said. "A man has a right to make his own decision about his career. A woman should support that decision." Yet to one friend, Pat confessed, "I've given up everything I ever loved"—dancing, family vacations, going to musicals and art exhibits, all the activities she and Dick had taken up as a young couple. She enjoyed grocery shopping at Gristedes and the A&P. She liked sewing her daughters' curtains, she explained. Then muffling herself again, she recovered. "The people who lose out are the children," she insisted.[29]

Beyond the cultural cleavage between conservatives and feminists that so polarized Pat's standing, she elicited strong reactions from those who knew her personally. Given her husband's reputation, judgment of Pat pivoted on the question of her genuineness and veracity, and as for Nixon, reactions ranged from fealty to disgust. One White House aide proclaimed her "the most compassionate, accessible first lady in history." Alice Roosevelt Longworth, the eldest daughter of Theodore Roosevelt and known far and wide for her "acid tongue," simply stated, "I have nothing unkind to say . . . She's [a] warm, thoughtful, selfless woman." Helen Thomas, whose reporting eventually dated from Mamie Eisenhower through Laura Bush, called Pat the first lady "who loved people the most." Yet for some in her husband's retinue, that same warmth ran thin. Vice President Gerald Ford was wary. He described the first lady as ever "in the background . . . always under total self-control." He sensed a range of feeling to which he was not privy. "She seemed to be getting in her mind and cataloguing it. What she did with it, I don't know," Ford attested. "Very seldom did she offer an opinion," but there was a sense she was keeping score.[30]

Pat was not so much valued in the West Wing as endured. "Next to her, RN looks like Mary Poppins," one aide groused. Nixon's staff thought she carped, that she pecked. The first lady's "suggestions and complaints were tolerated without being much heeded," Ehrlichman recalled. Pat's ideas were often not appreciated as "she could become very much upset over small details," he wrote. One family friend spoke of how Pat could be "waspy and stung [her husband] a lot." Haldeman was said to have "bore the brunt," as the chief handler of the first lady, when she wanted the president's attention. Pat's lead secretary found the president's aides stifling, "chauvistic [sic]." Nixon could be condescending to Pat in front of the staff. He did not want her to be an opinionated Eleanor Roosevelt or steal the spotlight like Jacqueline Kennedy. "She wasn't allowed to express an opinion," according to one television reporter. "Would she say something wrong? . . . Would they scream and yell?" When she did speak up, Pat was largely ignored. "I never heard any wife cut off in public so curtly with out [sic] a rejoinder, not even a dirty look," a one-time close campaign advisor recounted. He came to believe that Nixon would have "made it very miserable for her if she hadn't [remained silent] . . . She was gracious and honorable, but weak with him." Diane Sawyer, at the time a speech-writing aide, determined the marriage had become "a dance of unhappiness."[31]

Friends dismissed the tensions between Pat and Dick. They simply were not "show people" like the Reagans. Alexander Haig swore that Nixon "worshiped Pat," and she swore to the press, "I have the best man in the world. I love him dearly." The biographer Will Swift portrayed their marriage as a source of vital support for both of them, a loving partnership necessary for their individual equanimity, if at a healthy distance. In later years, away from the staged performances and in the privacy of their own space, Nixon's foreign policy assistant Monica Crowley saw real affection between the two. "He fluffed her pillows when he knew she was preparing to rest," Crowley wrote. "She chilled his favorite drink, white grape juice." They shared a "silent language" in their retirement, Crowley observed, describing how they watched the evening news together, gently teasing.[32]

Gloria Steinem scored an interview with Pat for *New York Magazine* in fall 1968 on a flight from a campaign rally in Denver to another one in St. Louis. The emblem of conservative domesticity and the standard-bearer of leftist feminism met at the front of the airplane flanked by a "sleek young staff man." Steinem made note of Pat's "freckled hands neatly folded," her "ankles neatly crossed," her smile a "public smile." Like so many interlocutors, journalists and historians to come, she wanted to take a measure of the "real Pat" beyond what she saw as the canned affectations. Steinem wrote that she was determined to avoid Pat's bland pronouncements, like "I just think he'd make a wonderful President" and "You'll have to ask Dick about that." Steinem thought she might have more luck with questions about Pat, rather than politics. The pair began to chitchat. Pat disclosed that like her husband, she enjoyed musicals, such as *My Fair Lady* and *Hello Dolly!* She preferred historical novels, in particular about Queen Victoria and Mary Todd Lincoln, and she liked fashion shows, going to museums and parks. She insisted that she enjoyed every campaign rally, that each one was so different—some inside, some outside, "some have old people; some have young."[33]

As the interview stretched on, Steinem began laying bait and probing. As was Steinem's want, she was in a mood to tussle. She asked whether there were "any persistent mistakes in the press" that needed correction. Steinem had heard about Pat's being irritated by a story in a Seattle newspaper that painted her as "a catatonic smiler." Pat assured Steinem, "No, no . . . You ladies of the press do a fine job." Steinem nudged a bit, saying that she had never met a person who approved of all the press's coverage. And to that, Steinem thought she saw a "flicker of annoyance behind the hazel eyes." In contrast to Pat's cheery effusions, Steinem equated the glint of anger as "the first sign of life," albeit a momentary one. She soon grew frustrated again with Pat's continued pleasantries, the achingly slow pace of questions parried and parried again. Steinem found herself repeating her queries. She finally took objection when the soon-to-be first lady declared Mamie Eisenhower the woman in history whom she admired the most "because she meant so much to young people." "I was in college during the Eisenhower years . . . and I didn't think Mrs. Eisenhower had any special influence on youth," Steinem shot back. "You didn't?," Pat responded and then paused. "Well, I do . . . Young people looked up to her because she was so brave all the time her husband was away at war."[34]

It was then that the acrimony brimmed over according to Steinem's retelling. She wrote as if she had finally hit her mark. Pat simmered as she so rarely simmered on the public stage. "The whirlwind of feeling was not out of control," Steinem qualified, describing how Pat's steadied, low voice began rolling out a long-held accusation over entitlement, free reward, easy living. "I never had time to dream about being anyone else," Pat said. "I had to work." She defended herself with her sad biography: Her parents had died; she worked through college and while Nixon was overseas in the Navy. "I haven't just sat back and thought of myself or my ideas or what I wanted to do . . . I've kept working. Right here in the plane I keep this case with me, and the minute I sit down, I write my thank you notes." As the plane had landed and was approaching the ramp, the aide flanking them had begun signaling an end to the interview, but Pat was not finished. She was bothered by the notion of a woman like Steinem—one who had the luxury of time to think about such abstractions as the woman Pat held in most esteem—and irritated by the insinuation that she was thoughtless and shallow. Pat told Steinem, "I don't have time to worry about who I admire or who I identify with. I've never had it easy. I'm not like all of you . . . all those people who had it easy."[35]

A sentimentalism such as Pat's would seem a genre antithetical to feminists' embrace—so classically pictured as Samuel Richardson's Clarissa, as a bird caged in a small room only to end up in a coffin. The sentimental affectations of dearness and fondness like Pat's have been historically and pejoratively trashed as weak, as shallow. Sweetly affecting heroines in Sentimental literature, the scholar Claudia Johnson argued, "reinforce established social arrangements"; sullied women get their due while their men and relations get their freedom and the bounty of happy endings.[36] Pat was supposed to shimmer, rapt, her head tilted, hair impervious to wind, only then to be abandoned by her husband to the campaign bunkers. She was left alone even as she was expected to embody him. The press painted Pat as deferential to conservative mores and, indeed, to her husband. At times, she seemed even to erase herself for him. Pat frustrated feminists. She appeared to have choices though she seemed not to make them; she seemed a bird in a cage with the door sprung wide open, nonetheless remaining inside to sing an old tune, exquisitely practiced, but not her own.

In literary theory from the 1990s, however, feminist scholars attempted to recast sentimental figures like Pat as far richer characters than the derision standard views suggested. Reorienting the critique, Janet Todd described how the sentimental "gave centrality to women . . . and brought female consciousness under investigation." Sentimentalism for a woman like Pat offered a female space "of their own," a "culture of their own," their own books to read, their own books to write, a language to challenge, to master, to embody emotion apart from men's dominating grip. This feminist scholarship reconsidered sentimentalism as a performance challenging the bonds of a coercive patriarchy of confinement and punishment. The historian Elaine Tyler May described the "liberating arena of fulfillment through professionalized homemaking, meaningful childrearing, and satisfying sexuality." Before the revolts of the late 1960s, sentimentalism offered women like Pat a space to develop, to excel. As feminists had so dearly sought, Pat, too, had labored for a space "of her own," even though hers was not the feminist "culture of their own."[37]

Pat climbed to the greatest of heights by projecting sentimentalism. Conservatives celebrated her as a symbol of a lost womanhood. For her advocacy of domesticity, for standing by her man, as a sensible woman far removed from the protesting feminist herd, spine straight, rapt and vigilant, Pat became the first nominee's wife ever to speak at a major political party's national convention. She received a ten-minute ovation from Republican loyalists in the Miami Beach before her husband's nomination in late August 1972.[38] The sentimental sheen glowed, for Pat's was a conservative sensibility, not one of perfuse emotion but a cornerstone of containment, an abundant affective manifestation of others' trials and ordeals. Her sensibility was poised, radiating a goodness of feeling to the world, a city standing poised on a hill.

By the end of their conversation, as their plane taxied on the runway, as the Nixon aide grimly called for a halt to the interview, Steinem had got her story. She had riled up the soon-to-be first lady. She dismissed Pat's smiles and cheer as deflections and unserious, while judging Pat's annoyances, her jealousies and drive as genuine and substantive. Steinem reported how she had pierced the plastic sheen in discovering in the Nixons a shared "great drive" and a shared "deep suspicion." She added a note of sympathy, remarking how hard "running against the Kennedys . . . must have been a very special hell for them . . . as if all their deepest suspicions had been proved true." Then, Steinem described how the sentimental shield was raised, how the smile returned to its place. Pat adjusted her diamond ring. She patted Steinem's arm as if the two were old friends. "Now I hope we see you again soon," Pat offered, followed by a string of peppy farewells. "I really do," she said. "Bye now; take care . . . I've really enjoyed our talk."[39]

3 | The Working Life of Richard Nixon

IN A SUITE on the thirty-ninth floor of the Pierre Hotel in Manhattan, the two men sat overlooking Central Park and Fifth Avenue. It was November 25, 1968, three days before Thanksgiving. Nixon reclined on a sofa, sipping cup after cup of endlessly refilled coffee. The newly elected president was holding interviews to staff his incoming administration. The two had met only once before, a year earlier, for a perfunctory discussion of perhaps five minutes when Henry Kissinger served as an advisor to Nelson Rockefeller, the liberal and long-serving governor of New York and Nixon's vanquished competitor for the Republican nomination. Kissinger remembered "not knowing what to expect" of the already hallowed but controversial figure. The State Department, Foreign Service, and Central Intelligence Agency were disorganized, Nixon told Kissinger. The Kennedy and Johnson administrations had made a mess of bureaucratic order and efficiency. More worrisome, he thought, after decades of Democratic rule and years of hiring liberals for government positions the entrenched bureaucracy would be disloyal. To counter the plotting that he expected against his agenda, the president-elect planned to centralize foreign policy in the White House. He wanted Kissinger to helm the effort as his national security advisor. Kissinger liked what he heard, but as Nixon spoke, in just their first real meeting, the soon-to-be national security advisor could not help but notice a disconnect in Nixon's delivery: "[His] movements were slightly vague and unrelated to what he was saying," Kissinger later wrote. He recalled that it was "as if two different impulses were behind [Nixon's] speech and gesture."[1]

Kissinger was far from alone in detecting this incongruence. While covering Nixon's first inauguration, the journalist and historian Garry Wills discerned a similar stuttering eccentricity in between the new president's calls in his address for the "majesty of the moment" and "man's deepest aspirations." The "features do not quite work together." There was a "disjointedness," Wills wrote. The journalist Edwin Black noted that his "smile is a tiny bit too late."[2] Just as Kissinger described, the two journalists detected from Nixon's crown to his heels a discernible, slight delay, as if when he spoke he needed to monitor himself, to consider his each movement or action. It was as if Nixon had never quite mastered the role of Richard Nixon.

However hard Nixon tried, he often failed at the affective communing central to the sentimentalist's aim. When in the company of others, he felt uncomfortable. He detested meeting strangers and almost never spoke to a fellow passenger on an elevator. He simply was not the glad-handing type. Nixon's subordinates found him tense, repeatedly remarking that Nixon was shy and self-conscious, that he was not a "man of relaxation." Quick pleasure, ease, eluded him. Putting his feet up? That was difficult. Drinking, dancing, letting loose? That was hard. He was fussy: Steaks were cut too thick; ice should have no holes. "Before putting his legs up on a silk-covered stool or ottoman, [he] goes into the bathroom and gets a towel to put under his legs," observed the liberal raconteur Stewart Alsop, joking, "He is not just square—he is *totally* square." It is this inhibited, fidgety side of Nixon that presents yet another angle for understanding his incessant need to assume various roles in public. By this measure, his dogged secretiveness was not mere political strategy, or as he so often invoked, a matter of national security. Nixon struggled to play his parts, and in part, his need to perform was itself a tool to manage the uncomfortable act of being Nixon.[3]

As Nixon traded role for role, he pursued what the biographer Roger Morris called a "politics not of wing or doctrine so much as ceaseless self-advancement." Nixon's was a walking Gospel of Achievement. Hard work, the awkward and brooding Nixon hoped, could set him free. Hard work—not brains or brawn or luck or love—could put him on the path out of loneliness, disappointment, and what he called his "fatalism." A devoted striver from a young age, Nixon became president of the eighth grade, his high school, his college classes and his college social club, which he had helped found. "I won my share of scholarships, and of speaking and debating prizes in school not because I was smarter but because I worked longer and harder than some of my more gifted colleagues," Nixon maintained. He told of how, at age thirteen, his maternal grandmother, Alma Milhous, gave him a framed inscription of a Longfellow poem:

> Lives of great men all remind us
> We can make our lives sublime,
> And, departing, leave behind us
> Footprints on the sands of time;

Nixon hung the ode to ventures of solitary greatness over his bed. Forty years later, he wrote in his final memoir, "To this day, it is one of my fondest possessions."[4]

In place of failed sentimental connection, Nixon slid into a Romantic mood in the mode of Longfellow, of the rugged and striving individual. "In the arena," as Nixon often remarked, channeling Theodore Roosevelt, a man became great through effort, through independence, through drive. The historian K. A. Cuordileone wrote of how Roosevelt's and then Nixon's message of self-reliance evoked the nineteenth-century Yale sociologist William Graham Sumner's notion of the "forgotten man." In the years following the Civil War, Sumner had argued that the "forgotten man" struggled, destitute, emasculated and dependent on the largesse of a ruling class. The expanded federal government and increasingly powerful big business were said to have sapped Americans' vigor. To counter, Sumner preached a heroic, revanchist individualism. In a revival of Sumner in the years following World War II, the refrain of the decline of the American male regained currency. The expansive measures of the New Deal came under attack as had the governing federal powers under Reconstruction. What had been Sumner's fear of the ruling class evolved into a fear of communist domination, a nation of dependents, of handouts and centralized rule. American men of Nixon's generation and class worried about becoming "victims of a smothering, overpowering, suspiciously collectivist mass society."[5]

Cuordileone described the anxiety as translated along gender lines, writing, "A society that had smashed the once-autonomous male self, elevated women to a position of power in the home, and doomed men to a slavish conformity."[6] As women gained sway in the domestic realm, they allegedly sapped the strength of society through their imposition of etiquette, education and shallow communion. In this way, the sentimental mode that had been a salve for conservatives also became a threat. A rugged Romanticism offered an alternative, a model of how men were made not through education, nourishment and good feeling, but through battle "in the arena," through the strenuous life.

Nixon's tendency to identify with hard-striving pursuit led Wills to dub Nixon's path a "spirituality of improvement," a "cult of crisis." A crisis, as Roosevelt and then Nixon defined it, was not a collective trauma but a test of an individual and his moral fortitude. Life was a series of tests, and only the tested could demonstrate their mettle. It was another conception Nixon shared with John Kennedy (and even emulated). As the latter proclaimed in his Pulitzer Prize–winning *Profiles in Courage*, "Great crises produce great men, and great deeds of courage," a "grace under pressure as Ernest Hemingway defined it." Nixon espoused that a politician needed to be a "tough son of a bitch" with "real guts," "having to scrape for everything [that] makes you stronger." The men Nixon idolized projected such hard-edged Romantic images. As the historian Kevin Mattson noted, they were the rugged and lonely types from pulp fiction, the steely eyed cowboy likes of Gary Cooper and John Wayne and Micky Spillane's case-cracking private eye Mike Hammer.[7]

Nixon's relationship to the laboring life translated into a classic liberalism undergirded by a progressive pragmatism. Thus, striving matched with self-regulation became the framework Nixon advocated for rescuing the forgotten man. Nixon argued in his memoirs that for the founders of the United States, "The lodestar of their idealism was the concept of liberty." Capitalism was not immoral but amoral, "generat[ing] wealth with ruthless efficiency." In short, every man became a commodity "spiritually *priced*" to thrive or sink in the open market of money and ideas. For Nixon, limited government could promote equality of opportunity by limiting discrimination against those born less fortunate. Such equality served to maximize a society's efficiency through the broader distribution of capital. Yet, if laws sought to ensure equality of ends rather than opportunity, Nixon foresaw a government that would impose leveling for leveling's sake, rewarding strivers and the indolent alike, "destroy[ing] the incentives for producing wealth." Nixon associated government-mandated equality, great wealth redistribution and nationalization with soul-sapping authoritarianism. Throughout his political career, he ran on a message of getting people off the government dole and to work. As president, he pushed for "workfare not welfare" in his broad-ranging Family Assistance Plan (FAP) and his affirmative action program.[8]

Indeed, Nixon further applied his hard-laboring ethos to international affairs and economic development. "Both the defeated countries in World War II, Germany and Japan, received U.S. aid," he told Chinese prime minister Zhou Enlai on his historic visit to Beijing in February 1971. Many other countries had received aid as well, he noted, yet he qualified, "If we analyze why Germany and Japan have done so well, it is because they have qualities of drive and are willing to work hard." Aid to India had been wasted, as its people lacked the "the spirit of determination." It was not, he proselytized, "the help that is provided a country that counts," it was "whether the people of that country have the will to use this help. If they don't have that, the money just goes down a rathole." For American cold warriors like Nixon, the ideological competition between the superpowers and their dueling modes of economic development came to be judged along the lines of hard work, like Sumner's notion of the striving but forgotten man, and further, in terms of gender. In his broadly popular treatise, *The Vital Center*, the liberal social critic Arthur Schlesinger, Jr., wrote of the "hard" and the "soft" of U.S. foreign policy, of the anti-communist venture as male, proactive and "vital" and of the communist cause as overly maternal, indolent and degenerative.[9]

So "what did the [Nixon] boys do?" one neighbor from his hometown asked and answered. "They worked." Nixon and his brothers were pressed into service from a young age. An early stint at the butcher's station in the family market proved too bloody, with Nixon almost chopping off the tip of his finger with a meat cleaver. Too clumsy to work the slicing station in the family store, the awkward Nixon became responsible for produce. He woke up at four each morning and drove to the Seventh Street market in Los Angeles to buy fresh fruit and vegetables wholesale—apples, grapes, corn, cucumbers. He washed and primped the produce. Only then did he shower and leave for school. "You're lucky, Dick, to get such good grades so easily," one high school classmate remarked. "It isn't luck," Nixon retorted. He had to work, he was convinced. "You've got to dig for them."[10]

Similarly to his hard-laboring father, Nixon relied on a rigid determination to muscle through the "Roaring Twenties," the son's adolescent years, and then the Great Depression, as a young adult. His striving was as relentless as it was impressive, constant if unsatisfying. He returned time and again to certain through lines. In one well-worn tale, he spoke of his athletic career. At five-foot-eleven, one hundred fifty pounds, he was a clumsy third-string substitute on his high school football team, but Nixon would remember practice with an enthusiasm for the struggle, as "the most exciting kind of combat imaginable." As he recalled, "Mostly I took it [to gain] discipline for myself and to show others that here was a guy who could dish it out." As one teammate, weighing in at 211 pounds, recounted, "We couldn't let up or the coach would be on us. So I'd have to knock the little guy for a loop. Oh, my gosh, . . . The harder you hit him the more he came back at you."[11]

Nixon went on to earn a partial undergraduate scholarship to Harvard that he could not afford to accept and later a $250 full-tuition scholarship to Duke law school that he did. And there, too, at Duke, he rose, becoming president of the Student Bar Association. "He never expected anything good to happen to him or to anyone close to him which wasn't earned," a classmate recalled of Nixon's stubborn drive. After excelling in law school, he failed to land a top-flight job at a Wall Street firm. The Federal Bureau of Investigation turned him down as well, so he returned home to Whittier. Nixon's hard work had landed him behind a plywood desk advising clients for $5, living in an apartment over a garage.

Hannah described her son as stoic in his fate, dried eyed in the face of such suffering; he was a lamentable creature, "undemonstrative," as "he was always to face tragedy." Nixon, however, was rarely, if ever, so impossibly well-tempered. He experienced devastating pangs of disappointment over the loss of the spot at Harvard, the white-shoe jobs on Wall Street and a position with the FBI. The losses could at times be "shattering." He experienced stretches of abject collapse. "He wrote these sad letters," his girlfriend Ola Florence remembered of his time in the small California law firm. "I've almost decided that I don't like this law business. No fooling. I'm getting almost disgusted," he despaired. Nevertheless, Nixon returned to his Horatio Alger ethos. He clung to the faith that hard work could set him on his path, and in slightly more than two years, at just twenty-seven years of age, became full partner in his Whittier firm. Nixon quickly amassed accolades, taking seats on the board of the Kiwanis and the La Habra Chamber of Commerce and not long thereafter becoming a full trustee of his alma mater Whittier College.[12]

Nixon's climb was single-minded. After his Navy deployment during World War II, he jumped at the first opportunity to run for Congress. While campaigning in 1946 for the House of Representatives, Nixon did not own a house or a car. He had never even met a member of Congress. California senator William Knowland remembered the young Nixon as "a little man in a big hurry," already known for his "mean streak." Not long after his first reelection to the House in 1948, and despite being told by his friends across the board that it would be "political suicide," Nixon still had greater heights in mind. Along with Thomas Dewey's defeat by Harry Truman in that year's presidential elections, Republicans had lost the House. Disempowered as a minority congressman, but determined to capitalize on the national prestige he had recently won by his very public takedown of the diplomat Alger Hiss, Nixon looked to climb farther up the political ladder. After a "fighting, rocking, socking campaign," he won big in his 1950 Senate race. He never tired of recounting how he labored for his success, how in that first senatorial campaign he attached loud speakers and "NIXON FOR SENATE" and "I LIKE NIXON" signs to a wood-paneled Mercury station wagon crammed full of campaign literature. Traveling up and down the state over two months and 15,000 miles with Pat, he made street corner appearances from atop the back bumper.[13]

Two years after Nixon's election to the Senate, he was elected vice president on Dwight Eisenhower's ticket, and only months after losing the presidency to Kennedy in 1960, he pivoted to seek, ultimately unsuccessfully, the California governorship in 1962. The ultimate prize shifted—starter on the football team, attorney in Manhattan, leader of the free world. It was an interminable climb, with victory never satiating,

Nixon delivering a speech from the back of his wood-paneled Mercury station wagon during his successful 1950 Senate campaign. *Courtesy of the Richard Nixon Presidential Library and Museum.*

Nixon adopted an average Joe persona while campaigning in 1962 for California governor, a race he would lose to Pat Brown. *Courtesy of the National Archives.*

never quite fulfilling. "Where everybody else would say, 'Let's have a party now,'" H. R. Haldeman noted, "Nixon would say, 'Let's get to work now . . . We've won, now it's our burden.'" Even after winning the presidency in 1968, he looked for a higher prize. To great applause during his first inaugural address, as the cold snapped at the dais and some seventy people huddled on the steps of the Capitol, Nixon spoke of space flight to the moon, "throwing wide the horizons of space." Only then he charted a grander cause for himself, beyond a role model, chief executive, president or astronaut. Nixon asserted to the nation on that first day of his first term, "The greatest honor history can bestow is the title of peacemaker."[14]

For a man who so desperately sought control, perhaps ironically, perhaps tragically, it seemed as if Nixon lacked control even of his own fingers. Nixon struggled to snap open pill bottles. When pinning on military medals, he at times poked recipients. According to Pat, he had trouble hammering a nail. His biographer Jonathan Aitken, who interviewed Nixon for more than sixty hours, recalled him as magnificently adroit at talking about foreign affairs. Yet, Aitken noted, the *tour d'horizon* was undercut as he was "ludicrously clumsy when it came to putting sugar lumps into his tea with a pair of silver tongs." Jeb Magruder, a onetime high-level aide to Haldeman, recalled a classic Keystone Cops routine: A pen had been placed on Nixon's Oval Office desk. "[He] picked it up, put its top on, and tried to sign the bill with the top on," Magruder recalled. Seeing his error, Nixon removed the cap and began to sign, only to stick himself in the left hand, fumbling the cap and dropping it on the floor. Magruder remembered how "total chaos ensued" among the solicitous group gathered, "as half the Cabinet dropped to its knees trying to find the top." To counter Nixon's confusion and clumsiness with switches, it was Haldeman's fateful idea for the Oval Office taping system to be voice activated. No futzing necessary to begin the recording,

Nixon needed only wear a pager-like gadget, a tape locator, in the proximity of one of the machines. It would record his every word.[15]

Nixon's critics made light of his discomfort. With each cartoon, his jowls sagged, his eyebrows thickened, his ski-jump nose grew more buffoonish, growing like Pinocchio's with every lie. With each comedic impression, Nixon's head shook with a palsy, his baritone growing ever more graveled as if, despite his greatest restraint, a pent-up anger could not but quake from his body. "All I had to do was mention Nixon's name," the comic Steve Martin recalled, and his college audiences guffawed. Nixon so lacked in humor, he reminded Norman Mailer of a "church usher . . . who would twist a boy's ear." Hunter S. Thompson could not picture Nixon "laughing at anything except maybe a paraplegic who wanted to vote Democratic but couldn't quite reach the lever." Indeed, few recounted instances of Nixon joking, but Pat recalled a costume party once, early in their marriage. For the festive gathering, a friend of theirs went as Beauty. Nixon was the Beast.[16]

As Nixon felt rejected, he in turn rejected the Washington social set. He railed to his staff about the Georgetown crowd, with their "boring and time-wasting tea parties." Tish Alsop, the wife of Stewart Alsop and a pillar among the Georgetown set, returned the slight. "Nixon danced one dance, with me," she recalled about one of the exclusive evenings she hosted. "He's a terrible dancer. Pat didn't dance at all. They stayed only half an hour. It was as if the high school monitor had suddenly appeared. I couldn't wait for him to go." One dear friend of the Brahmin Adlai Stevenson explained that it was not a matter of substance. The Washington elite "winced" at the very "style of Nixon or to be more painfully exact, the lack of one—that pervasive and alchemic falsity." The Alsops and their socialite friends found Nixon fake, fidgety. In their class's judgment, he came up short; he was cheap, "ersatz." He was not worth their time.[17]

Rather than balls and social galas, "Dick and I prefer more worthwhile things," Pat later quipped although she always loved to dance.

William Rogers, Nixon's close and rare confidant and secretary of state, believed that Nixon held on to the sense that others did not like him. He felt the Alsop set ever laughing at him. As president, Nixon stole away from the crowded West Wing at every chance to his "hideaway" in the Executive Office Building (EOB). "He's like a polite but distant hermit," one aide commented. "He emerges every once in a while from his cave, blinks in the light, and then goes back again." As William Safire noted, "[He] simply could not relax with people." It was puzzling. "I can make a speech on television to millions," Nixon remarked, "but I can no more go up to a single individual and ask for a ten-dollar political contribution than I can fly." For all his reputation as the grand negotiator, as master of the deal, Nixon was never comfortable with personal negotiations. He talked menacingly of getting tough on his staff, but he recoiled from direct confrontation. He hated the face-to-face. He would not fire a secretary, aides recalled. In contrast to Kissinger's raring ire, when Nixon spoke harshly of someone, he did so behind their back. "[The] problem is that [the president] is not willing to stand tight on unpleasant personal situations and won't back us if we do," complained Haldeman, onto whose shoulders such conflict fell.[18]

What was more, Nixon proved to be a poor administrator, quicker in thought than organization. He struggled to manage people and the sprawling government bureaucracy. Prior to the presidency, his largest administrative challenge had been running a small platoon in the South Pacific during the World War II. "In his wilderness years," as Aitken noted, "[Nixon] had even found it difficult to manage his personal and business routines with staff assistance." To combat confrontation and clutter, to sidestep awkward interactions, as Nixon insisted to his chief of staff, "I must build a wall around me." And so he did. The Oval Office was secured against all but those whom Nixon deemed most essential. The paper flow was tightly and efficiently directed. Nixon preferred a memo to a face-to-face. He avoided what he called "the laying on of

(*Background, left to right*) The "Three Germans"—chief of staff H. R. Haldeman, domestic advisor John Ehrlichman, and national security advisor Henry Kissinger— along with Secretary of State William Rogers in attendance in 1969 when (*foreground*) Nixon met with his idol Charles de Gaulle, the former French president. *Courtesy of the Richard Nixon Presidential Library and Museum.*

tongues." As the *Washington Post's* Bob Woodward observed, "Compare his schedule with the schedule of somebody like Bill Clinton. Clinton is all over the place: talking to everyone. Nixon was almost born in a bunker." LBJ had thirty-two direct lines on his telephone in the Oval Office. Nixon had five—one to his lead secretary Rose Mary Woods and one White House outside line. The other three buttons buzzed Haldeman, Kissinger and John Ehrlichman—the inner circle known as the "Three Germans," due to their shared heritage.[19]

H. R. "Bob" Haldeman became head of the White House's memo-driven apparatus. The Bob came from Robbins, as in Harry Robbins, not Robert, as many if not most assumed. In a time of hippie shag, he sported a Marine crewcut, buzzed square. Haldeman described himself as the "rah-rah college type," a one-time Eagle Scout. He had been an enthusiastic homecoming chairman at UCLA, roaming about "in saddle shoes and a cashmere sweater." He became a member of Mensa. He was sturdy. In photographs, he always seemed to be leaning in. To his own aides—seen by many as a pack of Haldeman clones, a gang of men in their twenties and thirties largely drawn from the advertising world— he could be "cruel" and "humiliating." Each morning, Haldeman sat with his back to his desk as his staff gathered around in a semicircle. With a flair for the dramatic, at exactly ten o'clock, he would spin around in his chair to face his aides and command the first staffer to his right, "Begin."[20]

Haldeman has been credited with institutionalizing the chief of staff as the bureaucratic hub running the West Wing. He thought of himself not as an "impediment," but an "accelerator." One deputy recalled how Haldeman "regularly emerged from the Oval Office with his yellow legal pad, reading directives . . . or going to his dictating machine [to] spit out instructions to the staff." It was his responsibility to make sure the boss's decisions were carried out, absent a few he judged as simply unwise. It was also his responsibility to play the heavy, as it fell to the chief of staff to tell the likes of Nixon's wife and daughters that the president was too busy for whatever they had in mind. Haldeman's philosophy: better for him to be the "S.O.B." guarding the door than a visitor thinking his boss was the "S.O.B." who turned away the caller. Ehrlichman, Nixon's domestic policy advisor, teased that it was Nixon and Haldeman's relationship that was the president's "true marriage." Safire found a similarity in the duo to "Cathy and Heathcliff in *Wuthering Heights*—Cathy [Haldeman] insisted she was not so much in love with Heathcliff [Nixon], as she *was* Heathcliff."[21]

Ehrlichman, a straight-shooting Christian Scientist, was by many measures Nixon's other close aide. In the 1960 presidential election campaign, Haldeman had been Nixon's chief advance man, but in 1968 Ehrlichman filled that role. Ehrlichman and Haldeman had been classmates at UCLA, "not close but friends." They became more familiar with each other through their wives. Their families socialized when they had a chance, but the pair were also rivals for the king's ear. Ehrlichman favored more progressive domestic programs and reductions in defense; Haldeman favored implementing nearly everything the boss wanted. Where Haldeman antagonized staff, the bald and hulking Ehrlichman was said to be "a scholar and a gentleman," a "wonderful, loving, teddy bear."[22]

Despite Nixon's own lack of experience in big business and finance, as president, he chose what he called a "corporate" model to reorganize the public sector along the lines of the private. Despite his personal fumblings, he wanted the executive branch to run smoothly, efficiently and under his control. As Ehrlichman counseled, "[It] should be like a corporation where the executive vice presidents (the cabinet officers) are tied closely to the chief executive . . . [, and] when he says jump they only ask how high." Just as Nixon had spoken about centralizing control of foreign policy in his meeting with Kissinger at the Pierre Hotel, so, too, the president wanted Ehrlichman to centralize control in the domestic sphere. Nixon appointed him as head of the Domestic Policy Council, an innovation meant to mirror the National Security Council, to forecast and rapidly adopt policy options. In another move toward both "centralization" and "politicization," as the scholar Karen Hult describes, Nixon looked to place high-level administrators closer to him physically, bureaucratically and ideologically. Although in theory Nixon advocated a smaller government footprint, in reality he expanded the White House and Executive Office staff by nearly a third between 1969 and 1971 through a flood of new positions. He viewed appointments to the bureaucracy as akin to filling seats on the Supreme Court. "If he could change its makeup, he could affect the generation beyond his own occupancy of the White House," Safire explained, transforming government machinery entrenched with Roosevelt and Truman holdovers to a bureaucracy of Nixonites to rule far beyond his tenure.[23]

The New Federalism, as Nixon called his plan for government restructuring, aimed at streamlining the power and operations of Washington by lessening the federal bureaucracy's involvement with the American people. He hoped to cut service programs overseen by Congress and Washington agencies by sending funding in the form of block grants directly to localities to implement and supervise programs as they saw fit. To establish clear lines of authority and accountability, Nixon further attempted to centralize control of the purse strings in the executive branch under the auspices of the newly created Office of Management and Budget (OMB). The OMB was charged with evaluating all budgets before they were passed on to Congress for approval. Nixon's critics decried his restaffing and restructuring as an "imperial" power grab, an effort to form a "counter-bureaucracy." Nixon insisted that "bringing power to the White House" was necessary "in order to dish it out."[24]

In foreign policy, Kissinger, the third and final member of the German troika of gatekeepers, had been a prized scalp for Nixon, having served as a chief advisor to Nelson Rockefeller. "Nixon coveted him," Haldeman recounted. He had assumed that Kissinger was "good because he belonged to someone who could buy whatever he wanted." As national security advisor, dashing from Washington to Paris to Hanoi, Kissinger based his "shuttle diplomacy" on clandestine action and magnetic performance. At once withdrawn and sycophantic, at once frenetic and insulting, Kissinger presented a moving and moody target for the president to try to control. Nixon worried that his national security advisor had acquired a massively inflated reputation and a clutch of admirers apart from the president's own. Indeed, Kissinger had become a national icon by 1973, the beginning of Nixon's second term in office. "Henry Alfred Kissinger has . . . become a legend, and the word is not lightly used," the *Chicago Sun-Times* proclaimed. "As a reputed ladies' man, he undoubtedly has given aid to every squat, owl-eyed, overweight and middle-aged bachelor in the land." To confidants like Haldeman and Alexander Haig, Kissinger's deputy, Nixon groused that the press was giving his foreign policy advisor too much credit. He simmered when he had to share *Time*'s 1972 Man-of-the-Year with his chief foreign policy aide.[25]

Kissinger, although far more affable and charming than his boss, still had much in common with the president. While Kissinger favored the wry remark and Nixon preferred the heart-felt overstatement, while one descended from German Jews and the other California Quakers, both felt like outsiders in Washington. The two saw themselves as Romantic strivers, "lone cowboys" suffering silently in their rugged and often-lonely climbs. In a description not far than one characterizing Nixon, Kissinger's peers saw the national security advisor as a malleable type. The political scientist Hans Morgenthau would remark, "[Kissinger was] a good actor who does not *play* the role of Hamlet today, of Caesar tomorrow, but who *is* Hamlet today and Caesar tomorrow." Through their shifting guises, both Nixon and Kissinger sought to consolidate power and control under their own auspices. They were "tough on people," "motivating people by fear." Like Nixon, "Henry saw a lot of ghosts in the dark out to get him," Haldeman wrote. Lawrence Eagleburger, a long-time aide to Kissinger and later secretary of state, noted, "Both had degrees of paranoia. It led them to worry about each other, but it also led them to make common cause on perceived mutual enemies." Kissinger was thought of by many, perhaps by most, as Nixon's Rasputin. Nixon relished the back and forth in their seminars-for-two as they moved from historical topic to philosophical conjecture across the world map, only to stumble over grudges, ruminating, circling over grievance. For all of Nixon's complaining against Kissinger, he enjoyed the rare comradery of a mind at once expansive, at once keen and cutting.[26]

Each morning, as the Three Germans arrived in the Oval Office for a 7:30 group meeting, Kissinger greeted the chief of staff with "Guten Morgen, Herr Haldeman," who then shot back, "And a guten Morgen to you, Heinz." They were "All the King's Krauts." The so-called Teutonic trio was said to have constructed a "Berlin Wall" around the president. By contrast to the stories of the sprawling National Security Councils of Kennedy and Johnson, of reported tales of commands lost and directives not followed, Nixon insisted on order and efficiency, operating through memos, an atmosphere shorn of the niceties of niceties. Haldeman became well aware of his boss's "petty, vindictive orders," his always wanting "to go for the jugular," so along with the softer Ehrlichman and the smoother Kissinger, he helped build a still higher wall. The Three Germans not only organized Nixon's time, they also organized the diffusion of Nixon's ideas and the implementation of his orders. The wall, Haldeman judged, was as much a barricade to protect Nixon from others, others from Nixon and, as the chief of staff noted, for "*this* President to be protected from himself."[27]

A creature of habit, within the wall Nixon required guard rails to work. He needed a routine. Breakfast at 6:30 or 7:00 a.m., preferably eaten quickly. Avoid lunches for time's sake. "I hate staff parties," Nixon complained. "The business or political lunch is for the birds. I can eat in ten minutes. Why waste an hour or two on eating?" He showered at the EOB, shaved and then returned to work. Aides would find Nixon leaning back in his brown club chair, his ashtray and pipe perched on a little table at his side, dictating for hours to Woods or scribbling on a yellow pad on his knee, marking up bits and pieces and rereading. He ate dinner at the EOB four to five times a week, perhaps had a glass of wine, maybe a round of bowling and then back to work. He often took a briefing book to the White House residence to mull over in his bedroom. He thought of it as "homework."[28]

Nixon balanced long stretches of "thinking time" with long stretches of "staff time"—one-on-one sessions with one or another of his favorites. He maintained a tight retinue of confidants even as his inner circle shifted during his time in office. He preferred only a few men's attention, those he felt most comfortable with, those he thought he could trust, who could put him at ease. At the same time, Nixon valued a marketplace of ideas in the classical liberal sense, and it was in this closed atmosphere of debate, jockeying and rumination that Nixon as a social creature became most at ease. It was a company of men. He balanced gray-flannel insiders with free-wheeling outsiders. He depended on the straight-shooting, rule-sticklers Haldeman and Ehrlichman but eagerly parried and spit-balled with the fashionably grandiose Daniel Patrick Moynihan and Kissinger. At times, he strategized regularly with press aides and speechwriters like Raymond Price, Jr., and Ron Ziegler who tossed around the "hip" notions of image and representation. At other times, he cloistered furtively with late-night confidants like his "hatchet man," Charles Colson, best friend Bebe Rebozo or his lawyer Leonard Garment.[29]

There were additional guard rails. From the first day Nixon stepped into the Oval Office as president, he strictly limited his intake of the press he so detested. Every morning, two staffers prepared a summary memo of the previous day's news to be on his desk by 8:10 a.m. The briefing book contained clippings of the good and the bad from the nightly networks, the talk shows, fifty newspapers and thirty magazines, from the *New York Times* to the *Honolulu Advertiser*, *Newsweek* to *Jet*. Nixon digested the latest news every morning for half an hour alone in his office. He drew up instructions and questions for his staff, making notes in the margins. "Why did this happen?" Or to Kissinger, "K, let's get on this one right away." An aide then transcribed his scribblings for the elaborately funneled, memo-driven White House. In this way, communication remained impersonal and aloof. The president could keep his guard down, his office quiet. With the written summaries of the day's news, Nixon could pore over the latest reports while maintaining a strictly controlled regimen in his media diet.[30]

Rather than enlightening the president, however, the written summaries, his "window on the press," all too often reinforced Nixon's combative inclination. They served to cloister the president ever more, drawing him deeper into a well of right-wing paranoia. The political scientist Christopher Karpowitz found that like Pat Buchanan, one of the two aides who prepared the news summaries, the reports "tended to be intensely ideological and partisan." They depicted conservatives "as beleaguered by Democrats (especially members of the Kennedy family)." It was a familiar, worrying narrative to Nixon. After receiving exclusive, contemporaneous access, Don Oberdorfer of the *Washington Post* reported that the president's daily news intake reinscribed a simple "we versus them" narrative. Haldeman noted that the news could leave the president "anxious," "preoccupied," in a "strange mood." Yet, Nixon never stopped reading, compelled to know what the press and the public were saying about him. In this way, each morning, he looked out of the bubble while hiding within it.[31]

Nixon's messaging had been starkly consistent as he climbed. In his first speech in seeking the nomination for his first congressional run, Nixon espoused a mantra of "individual freedom" over "government control" and, specifically, the desire of veterans like him wanting "respectable jobs," not the "government dole." Nixon had been turned off by his World War II experience working at the Office of Price Administration. He grew cynical over the mesh of red tape that developed through the New Deal years. As a congressional representative, Nixon joined a tide of Republicans, from the moderate California governor Earl Warren to the staunchly conservative Ohio senator Robert Taft, in warning of their opponents' affinity to New Deal big government, "left-ist organizations" and, most especially, labor unions, considered an anathema to the individualists' working ethos. They red-baited, raising the specter of communist Democrats. In running against Helen Gaha-gan Douglas for Senate in 1950, Nixon's central campaign tenet was "sim-ply the choice between freedom and state socialism," touting himself the candidate for freedom, liberty and against the un-American way.[32]

The abiding puzzle for scholars and Nixon-watchers has been that once elected chief executive, the hard-scrambling Nixon seemed to change roles. He had been a critic, but now he held responsibility. Sud-denly, he was in charge of the big government against which he had railed for a lifetime. In hindsight, noting the difference between Nixon's con-servative reputation and his presidential record, the historian Alex Wad-den dubbed Nixon a "liberal in wolf's clothing." The political scientist Richard Nathan memorably wrote that Nixon was a "liberal on domestic affairs, even though he tried to make us forget that." He nearly dou-bled the budget for food stamps and doubled spending on government-subsidized housing, building twice as many units as had been built since the 1930s. He budgeted $60 million to help minority businesses and an-other $100 million on the "war on cancer." Herb Stein, chair of Nixon's Council of Economic Advisors, recounted, "Nixon felt he ought to be for traditional virtues. He regarded himself a champion of the silent ma-jority. But he wanted to be a 'modern man' and recognized as such by intellectuals and liberals." He seemed unable to restrain himself from playing to the Alsop and Schlesinger crowd. Stein further described how his boss had been "impatient with the dull, pedestrian and painful eco-nomics of conventional conservatism . . . [H]e yearned for the long bomb."[33]

Moynihan, Nixon's liberal domestic advisor, a Harvard professor, one of those in the intellectual set, crowed, "We may well have been the most progressive administration on domestic issues that had ever been formed." Yet, scholars subsequently split over whether Nixon's agenda drove his politics or vice versa—that is, whether Nixon was a pragmatic progressive or a progressive pragmatist. On a purely practical level, if Nixon wanted a lasting record to tout, he had few options but to compromise. After eking out a victory with less than 1 percent of the popular vote in 1968, he could claim little to no mandate for a conservative agenda. His presidency was the first since 1853 during which the opposition party controlled both the House and the Senate. He cursed the Democratic Congress as "cumbersome, undisciplined, isolationist, fiscally irresponsible, overly vulnerable to pressures from organized minorities, and too dominated by the media." Yet he had to hew to a generally progressive course of legislation in his pursuit of significant accomplishments, the "long bombs" that could make his presidency historic. Working within the bounds of the politically possible, reading the public's desire to retreat from foreign ventures and attend to concerns at home, the politically expedient route meant reducing spending on the military while sharply raising the domestic budget—so much so that Nixon became the first president since World War II to spend more money on domestic programs than on defense.[34]

Still, Nixon's motives remained elusive as his moods shifted within the confines of the politically expedient. Vacillation and rumination clouded his strategic vision: courting union support then attacking the unions, advancing civil rights for African Americans then backing away, passing liberal legislation then ruing overspending and government corruption. He slurred gays and then predicted that gay marriage would be legal by the year 2000. Most often, Nixon's ambivalence took the form of regret, his looking back and lamenting a past decision that had gone south. After increasing spending, he grumbled that "too much money sticks to the fingers of the bureaucrats and doesn't get through to the poor." Nixon doubled the budget for environmental protection and created the Environmental Protection Agency and the National

Oceanic and Atmospheric Administration. He preserved 82,000 acres across the fifty states for 642 parks. He then privately complained to a circle of established conservatives, "We made the mistake of going overboard on the environment." He expanded funding for food stamps and social security benefits only to cavil against handouts. Nixon was the first to index Social Security to increases in the cost of living, only then he claimed that he had pushed the measure merely to preempt liberals running on Social Security hikes in the next election. Nixon ensured guarantees for greater support for the aged and the disabled but then attempted to undercut Johnson's Great Society programs, pushing for reductions if not elimination of the Jobs Corps, the Office of Economic Opportunity and daycare funding.[35]

At times, Nixon baldly boasted to his staff of the political games he was playing. Nixon sometimes pontificated about the pointlessness of the president in domestic affairs. He told the popular journalist Theodore White, "I've always thought the country could run itself domestically without a President. All you need is a competent Cabinet to run the country at home." Foreign policy seemed to dominate the president's focus, as he professed that domestic concerns added up to little more than "building outhouses in Peoria." A discouraged Buchanan complained that the administration's record was a "hybrid, whose zigging and zagging has succeeded in winning the enthusiasm and loyalty of neither left nor right, but the suspicion and distrust of both." Herb Stein called the agenda "general schizophrenia."[36]

Yet, for all Nixon's ambivalence, scheming and disinterest, one can still decipher the ideal of work as a consistent through line in his philosophy. The historian Herbert Parmet called his agenda a mix of "practical liberalism" and "conservative populism," applying big government solutions to foster free and fair entrepreneurial opportunity for the average American. Politics could all too often trump ideals, but Nixon had a line. He could cast aside some values as unnecessary, but the opportunity to work remained key. Most demoralizing, in Nixon's estimation, was the circumstances in which government programs paid more for those who did not hold a job than for those who did. He recoiled at the idea of encouraging indolence.[37]

Nixon most directly advanced his get-to-work ethos in 1970 in trying to pass his far-reaching Family Assistance Plan (FAP). The battle over welfare reform had become pitched. The New Deal consensus teetered under Johnson's unpopular tenure as failure in Vietnam tore the Democratic coalition asunder. The civil rights movements champed impatiently at halted reform, with an outbreak of urban riots blamed on deepening inequity and a failing state. Liberals argued the need for a bigger public safety net, whereas conservatives blamed crime and poverty on a failure of personal responsibility. The latter rankled against "coddling welfare mothers" who purportedly refused to work while bearing illegitimate child after child. Nixon complained that Americans had been spoiled in the 1960s by what the social critic Henry Fairlie was calling the "politics of expectation." He maintained that overpromising politicians had stifled society "by raising hopes they proved unable to fulfill" in the economy, education and social relations.[38]

The Harvard professor and one-time Johnson advisor Moynihan, who guided much of Nixon's FAP bill, argued controversially and quite prominently that a "tangle of pathology" had grown among the ranks of urban African American poor. In a 1965 report he titled *The Negro Family: The Case for National Action*, Moynihan warned of "virulent . . . anti-white feeling[s]" and the "social alienation" of militant minority groups. The report made Moynihan a household name as he contended that black women "dominated" their families because black men could not consistently earn a family wage. Echoing Sumner's vision of the forgotten man, Moynihan argued that joblessness and reliance on female advancement for family support further emasculated black men by not allowing them to fulfill their central familial role. They abandoned their children, setting in motion patterns of teen pregnancy, single mother-hood, underachievement and delinquency. "[The] breakdown of the Negro family led to a startling increase in welfare dependency," Moyni-han wrote, calling for a "national effort to strengthen the Negro family" to help address "civil disorder" by alleviating domestic disorder. As the scholar Susan D. Greenbaum noted, Moynihan's ideas about a "black pa-thology" and a "culture of poverty" were not confined to conservative circles but were further popularized by the Marxist anthropologist Oscar Lewis and the then best-selling socialist and theorist Michael Harrington. In particular, the analysis spawned de rigueur Freudian analysis advanced by the likes of the developmental psychologist Erik Erikson, who made the figure of the strong and stable father central to healthy childhood development.[39]

To combat the nation's "black pathology," Moynihan and Nixon's FAP legislation aimed to aid those working within the system and pun-ish those protesting against it. The greatest innovation was that the plan covered not only the unemployed, but the working poor as well. The pro-posed plan's sweeping reform guaranteed $1,600 annually to each family of four. The key to the program was that recipients would be re-quired to take available jobs. Derived from the University of Chicago economist Milton Friedman's idea of a negative income tax, the plan re-warded work. The first $60 of each paycheck each month would not be taxed, and FAP recipients would be allowed to deduct 50 cents from monthly welfare checks for each dollar earned. Families earning up to $3,920 per month would receive governmental assistance. In a 1969 ad-dress to Congress on welfare, Nixon had demanded that the "task of Government is to enable you to make decisions for yourselves." The key, he told Safire, was to "get people off welfare rolls and onto payrolls." He uttered a familiar chorus to Haldeman: "Work requirement, work re-quirement, work requirement." Nixon's "workfare" program centered around self-sufficiency rather than communal aid, cash assistance instead of social services. He looked to empower the family by promoting responsibility through an income approach that favored choice. Indeed, the path the president imagined for saving poor Americans mirrored his own experience and arduous climb. FAP's get-off-the-dole message spoke deeply to the ever toiling Nixon. As the *New York Times* wrote, Nixon "stressed work as an antidote to poverty." It was a refrain he had learned from his father: "no work, no welfare."[40]

From Bayard Rustin to Martin Luther King, Jr., prominent liberals and civil rights advocates recoiled at the notion that FAP "blamed the victim." The program shifted focus away from the failures of the system to the failure of individuals' will and moral standing, pointing to poor decisions families made as opposed to the rigged game in which they were caught. The idea of a "pathology" made a lack of privilege out to be a disease. Further, the scholar Jill Quadagno argued, gender bias undergirded the structure of Nixon and Moynihan's welfare reform. The bill favored the conception of family structure common to conservatives of Nixon's generation and class. FAP incentivized two-headed households over the female-headed homes regularly found in African American communities. Although childbearing was subsidized, daycare support remained meager, a combination that required women to remain outside the workforce and dependent on a male breadwinner.[41]

Moreover, Nixon's conception of FAP was laced with a racial affinity to ethnic whites. He wanted to appeal to "old-time ethnics," he told Haldeman, "Poles, Italians, Irish." By promoting a "workfare" approach, he sought to expand the reach of government assistance from welfare's focus on unemployed racial minorities to the concerns of blue-collar white workers. In that vein, Secretary of Labor George Shultz dashed off a memo declaring that blue-collar whites had suffered too long from "living in close proximity to the poor and the near-poor . . . They feel the relentless pressures of the minorities in their immediate neighborhoods, at the job site, in the schools, and in the community. Observing the welfare programs for the poor, they feel excluded and forgotten." Shultz added the common slur that those on welfare were "free riders," simply lazy. The administration judged that the climate might be ripe for racial division rather than unity among the working poor. FAP could play off such resentments by pitting those on workfare against those on welfare.[42]

Nixon's attitudes toward race were, like his domestic agenda, inconsistent and elusive, appearing at once politically opportunistic and at times progressive. In his first campaign for a seat in the House, Nixon had called Southern racists "just as dangerous on the right as the Communists . . . on the left." During the campaign, in 1946, the local chapter of the National Association for the Advancement of Colored People (NAACP) presented him with an honorary membership. As vice president under Eisenhower, he pushed for more minority executives in the automobile industry. He spoke to more and more black audiences, including the National Association of Colored Women and the youth group of Metropolitan Baptist Church, in Washington, DC, despite being warned that "many left-wingers" in attendance would be clamoring for "all out integration with no holds barred." To the congregated, he spoke of sharing their purpose, "as Americans, want our country to be one in which opportunity for ourselves and our children are equal." Nixon became the tip of the spear for civil rights in the Eisenhower administration. In his vice presidential acceptance speech in 1952, he pushed for African Americans to "receive first class citizenship," adding a progressive social agenda to his ethical aims as he asserted that Americans "should not and we will not rest until every Negro has an opportunity to obtain proper housing, prospering medical care and the unlimited ability to live as every American should live." He lent his support to the 1957 Civil Rights Act, which established the Civil Rights Division of the Justice Department.[43]

During the wilderness years following the vice presidency, Nixon quite prominently supported the 1964 and 1965 Civil Rights Acts. He was drawn in at that time not by the issue of racial inequality, but by the idea of creating a class-based, color-blind, workers' alliance in coalition with the Republican Party. "In a time when the national focus is concentrated upon the unemployed, the impoverished and the dispossessed, the working Americans have become the forgotten Americans," he preached. Nixon's goal for "working Americans" looked to unite North and South, urban and rural, black and white.[44]

Nixon stumped for the presidency with African Americans icons— Jackie Robinson in 1960, Wilt Chamberlain in 1968 and Sammy Davis, Jr. in 1972. During the latter two campaigns, however, Nixon abandoned his focus on a coalition of the working poor. Instead, he developed the so-called Southern strategy to siphon social conservatives from the far-right Goldwater and Wallace camps. NAACP leader Roy Wilkins warned that Nixon would "turn the clock back on everything." Nixon dog-whistled to the hard-hatted white "middle" of the Old Confederacy and then to his silent majority, which opposed the counterculture, the anti-war movement and the advancing promotion of civil rights. He campaigned against crime-ridden cities, mothers on the government dole, and pushed the urgency for law and order. Nixon promised Sen. Strom Thurmond, the leading segregationist from South Carolina, that he would put a halt to court-mandated desegregation. He would appoint Supreme Court justices who would "respect the Constitution rather than rewrite it." In a further nod to whites, as his vice presidential running mate he selected Maryland governor Spiro T. Agnew, who had fiercely scolded black activists after the riots that erupted following King's assassination in 1968.[45]

In a subtle reading of Nixon's policies on race, the historian Dean J. Kotlowski identified a troika of shifting exigencies: "politics (appeasing white voters), principle (opposing overt discrimination), and practicality (an effort to stay ahead of the courts)." Although the valence of Nixon's reforms pointed to a furthering of equal opportunity for African Americans, on balance he never put his political capital behind an overt and spirited campaign. As Kotlowski tellingly points out, Nixon spent only 10 of the 1,100 pages in his memoir *RN* on the issue. Safire recalled Nixon's dictum for civil rights as "make-it-happen, but don't make it seem like Appomattox," what the sociologist John David Skrentny has called a "whispered 'We Shall Overcome.'" Nixon took a middle path by advocating the overturning of segregation laws in the South while at the same time not promoting laws in the North mandating integration. He expanded assistance to minority-owned businesses and funding for civil rights agencies. His daughters Tricia and Julie attended integrated schools. At the same time, the Nixon administration pursued illiberal law-and-order tactics. Attorney General John Mitchell gave the go-ahead to J. Edgar Hoover's FBI to surveil and crack down on black civil rights and black nationalist movements with the Counterintelligence Program (COININTELPRO), imprisoning nearly a thousand Black Panther members during Nixon's first term. Under Nixon's stewardship, the proportion of blacks attending all-black schools plummeted, from 68 percent in the South to only 8 percent. Yet even that seemingly definitive data point can be attributed more to judicial rather than executive branch decisions. During the same period, black unemployment rose from a low of 6.4 percent in 1969 to 10 percent by 1972 and to 14.8 percent in 1975, suggesting a systemic racism persisted that Nixon's limited and ambivalent reforms did not address.[46]

FAP passed in the House of Representatives in April 1970 even as it attracted a cross-section of critics. Liberals complained that $1,600 provided half a livable income when the poverty line stood at $3,200. Social workers saw FAP as a challenge to their expertise and their approach of helping the poor through services rather than cash infusion. Labor leaders worried that with more incentive to work, the competition from welfare earners would drive down wages. Farther left, House representative Shirley Chisholm from New York compared the legislation to "involuntary servitude" due to its work requirement. On the right, the Chamber of Commerce purchased full-page newspaper advertisements alleging, "FAP would triple our welfare rolls. Double our welfare costs." Southern conservatives balked. Russell Long of Louisiana, chair of the Senate Finance Committee, slandered poor black single women with large families as "brood mares." To Haldeman, the president railed as the pressure mounted in response to the bill's passage. "Seventy-five percent of the people are against giving more money to people on welfare," he complained, railing, turning his anger on African Americans with whom he had for much of his early career sought coalition. "This looks like Nixon supports giving more welfare to black bastards." At the time, Nixon's primary focus had been shifting more to the quagmire of the Vietnam War. In late 1972, FAP died in the Senate Finance Committee, never reaching the Senate floor.[47]

Nixon was far more comfortable supporting racial integration in the adult workplace than forcing the integration of schools. It was in the workplace where Nixon made his major civil rights breakthrough. He pushed for affirmative action in his Philadelphia Plan. Shultz promoted the legislative drive that pressed for "fair employment" in public sector, construction union jobs to ensure that companies lived up to fair-hiring standards. In 1970 Nixon's Labor Department issued Order no. 4, mandating affirmative action for government jobs paying more than $50,000; it was revised a year later to specifically include women. The aim was to pursue "good-faith efforts" to achieve the goal of offering jobs to minorities with qualifications equal to white applicants. At the time, blacks constituted only 1 percent of construction union members, such as pipefitters, plumbers and iron workers. Affirmative action added a timetable to civil rights reform, from a starting point in 1969 of 5 percent of skilled, public sector jobs openings being filled by minorities to a goal of 9 percent by the end of Nixon's first year in office, incrementally increasing to 26 percent by the end of his first term in 1972. "The name of the game," Shultz said, "is to put economic flesh and bones to Dr. King's dream."[48]

Opponents called the approach "reverse racism" and in violation of the Civil Rights Act of 1964, which legislated color-blind treatment. AFL-CIO president George Meany called affirmative action cheap politicking meant to score "Brownie points" with minorities. Critical voices on the left attacked the plan on the grounds of political expediency, "racial pork barrel" fare. Regardless, Nixon pressed forward with his particular idiosyncratic philosophy. He bolstered "black capitalism" through the creation of the Office of Minority Business Enterprise. The president aimed to go beyond the negative approach of prohibiting discrimination to the proactive endeavor of closing the gap in racial hiring. Affirmative action was not a matter of equal ends, but equal opportunity. He opposed quotas and expansive service programs. As with FAP, he did not want to reward the purportedly lazy and undeserving. He wanted to reward work.[49]

In Nixon's 1974 farewell speech to White House staff, delivered under the pall of the Watergate scandal that had driven his resignation, he once again turned to the centrality of work, returning to the story he told of his father's life. "I think that they would have called [my father] sort of a little man, a common man," he began, again echoing Sumner's somber treatises. "But he was a great man because he did his job, and every job counts up to the hilt, regardless of what happens." Nixon continued, "My success meant to him that everything he had worked for and believed in was true: that in America, with hard work and determination a man can achieve anything." In Nixon's tale of his father, there was a message that rang both truly and tragically. For all his sentimental gloss, in his retellings, in his insistence on the Romantic drive of the individual, there was a bitterness in the tale that Nixon was determined not to acknowledge. In his own unquestioning devotion to work, there was a lesson Nixon seemed not to learn: that is, despite all of his protestations to the contrary, hard work did not always allow a "man to achieve anything." For, yes, on the one hand, Nixon's outsized success attested to the limitless opportunity that hard work could bring, but hard work had not been enough to realize his father's ambitions.[50]

By accounts, despite a masterful mind and a lifetime of unwavering labor, Frank managed to scrap together a life disappointed. For all his upward mobility, perhaps, above all, Nixon's father was a man of dissatisfaction. He suffered from ulcers and "nervous headaches" throughout his adulthood. Nixon recalled that his father bitterly regretted his lack of education. By Frank's estimation, his lack of schooling determined the course of the rest of his days. Nixon recounted the chorus of lament: "Never a day went by when [my father] did not tell me and my four brothers how fortunate we were to be able to go to school." It was no doubt a challenge and a burden. As Nixon wrote, "I was determined not to let him down."[51]

Nixon overcame his shy and clumsy nature as he climbed from near poverty to the highest of office. Hard work proved to be Nixon's comfort and constant companion; he played the role of the striver with most ease. In work he could retreat from social discomfort to a place where he could excel individually. He projected this ethos onto the nation. Nixon spent a career carping against FDR's expansion of government as anathema to the laboring life. Of Johnson's Great Society reforms, he complained that "instead of inspiring people to work hard," welfare "programs spawned a new constituency of government dependents." Nixon's "passion issue," as Ehrlichman had called it, was to bolster those who earned their way, who worked equally hard regardless of race.[52] From FAP to affirmative action, he advocated empowering Americans to work, to wean themselves from the government dole.

"My impression of Nixon," his Republican rival George Romney said, "is that he is the brightest and ablest man we've had in the White House since World War II." He employed his strengths—a quick intellect, creativity of thought, ability to manipulate a room, industriousness, resilience and determination—to fashion his various masks. Around his command post, he ably built guard rails as well as a wall, behind which to withdraw. He depended on a memo-driven office and a hierarchy among his staff in the White House that his confidant and lawyer Garment called the "walled garden of Nixon's soul." Nixon's was an eerie act with a distinctive incongruence that Kissinger noticed at their first get together in the Pierre Hotel. Mary McGrory of the *Los Angeles Times* wrote about "the switchblade smile that never reached the eyes, the gestures that never matched the words." Tom Wicker at the *New York Times* described Nixon's movements "as if a sound track were running a little ahead of or behind its film."[53]

For all his time in public roles, Nixon was a man of distance. Indeed, Haldeman could recall only one time "in my entire relationship with him" being invited to dine informally with him and their wives, and that had been in 1962. "I was his closest professional associate, [but] to this day he doesn't know how many children I have," Haldeman remarked. Despite his years of service to the man, Haldeman concluded with a note of sorrow or perhaps anger, "I'm not Nixon's friend . . . Nixon treat[ed] us like employees." Their first handshake, Haldeman noted in his diary, was on April 29, 1973, amid discussing Nixon's resignation with his aides. Ehrlichman added that the boss "never mastered the spelling of my name."[54]

Part II: On Madness

4 | Madness in the Act

The First Campaign

IMPRESSIVE WAS A GOOD way to describe Horace Jeremiah "Jerry" Voorhis. Graduating Phi Beta Kappa from Yale, he worked as a cowboy in Wyoming and assembled Fords in a North Carolina plant. He had the resumé of a venturous philanthropist. He volunteered to fight poverty for the radical Upton Sinclair, and, between the world wars, did missionary work for the YMCA in the slums of Germany. He even invested most of his million-dollar inheritance to found a home for runaways. His colleagues in the U.S. House of Representatives voted the Democrat Voorhis among its top ten members for rectitude and studiousness. The Washington press corps ranked him "first in integrity," a "political saint." In 1946 Voorhis ran for a sixth term in California's Twelfth Congressional District, which extended from Pomona west to Whittier, inching up to the southern border of Los Angeles, and stretching northeast to the San Gabriel mountains. A number of senior Republicans declined to run against Voorhis as his seat was deemed the third most secure in the country. Voorhis could not have imagined that he would be smeared in what was his sixth run for Congress— called a traitor—that his political career would end just as his opponent's began. The impressive Voorhis could not have known that the first line of his obituary would be that he lost to Richard Nixon.[1]

On September 13, 1946, hundreds crowded into the auditorium at South Pasadena Junior High School for the first debate in the contest, Nixon's first congressional campaign. It was a sweaty Friday night. The event began with the pledge of allegiance, then each candidate had fifteen minutes to speak. Voorhis went first. Perhaps overconfident, perhaps distracted, the incumbent rambled, digressing, his message disjointed. The political saint Voorhis was known to lapse into moralizing, what one right-leaning local newspaper called his "visionary mental meanderings." Nixon looked lean, even a little gaunt, in his baggy suit. "Dark, lank," *Time* reported. His impressive five-o'clock shadow was growing back. Some called the thirty-two-year-old Nixon handsome. He charged. Before the crowd of nearly 1,000, Nixon took direct aim at the digressing Voorhis, at the New Deal, at shortages in a time of promised postwar abundance. Some in the audience cheered. Nixon tried to tie the Democrat to the unpopular president, Harry Truman. He accused Voorhis of pushing to ration gas, meat and grain.[2]

By 1946 the ground was fertile for a raring populist like Nixon, a candidate who promised to take on the wealthy and elite in the name of the common man. He aimed to capitalize on the unpopular excesses of a sputtering New Deal. A postwar economic slump and strikes, rationing, fears of another war, of an expansive, corrupt government festered. Worry began to grow over conversion from the demands of military emergency to a peacetime economy as 10 million Americans returned home from foreign campaigns. "Why," Nixon asked voters, "is a Nation which produced to capacity for war failing to meet the desperate need of millions of Americans for housing?" Confusion swirled as stores' stocks emptied, and costs for goods rose. Truman announced another year of price controls. Labor demanded higher wages and better working conditions, emboldening a wave of strikes to a level no one could remember. Tent cities sprang up to house veterans and their families. The wanting rued the shortages, the dashed dreams of a postwar abundance, the specter of an insurgent socialism.[3]

That autumn night in the South Pasadena gym, the true turn of the first debate came during the question-and-answer with a mix of populist accusation and whispering. A Democrat in the audience asked about the Congress of Industrial Organizations' Political Action Committee

(CIO-PAC), the PAC being the labor organization's political wing. The questioner repeated a charge that the much-respected Voorhis was supported by, and even underwritten by, the "Communist-dominated forces" of the CIO-PAC. As a friend of Voorhis's said in rehashing the accusations, many think "you are a wild-eyed radical," a supporter of the doctrine of collectivism sweeping the world. The reality was that Voorhis had not been endorsed by the CIO-PAC; he had won the endorsement of the National Citizens Political Action Committee (NCPAC), a non-union labor rights group, completely independent of the immense and certainly communist-influenced CIO-PAC. In fact, the leftist CIO-PAC had specifically decided against supporting Voorhis precisely because of his measured stance toward big labor and his hostility toward the Soviet Union.[4]

The incumbent Voorhis denied the red-baiting accusation. He demanded evidence. "Here is the proof!" Nixon declared. For even before Joseph McCarthy introduced his infamous lists of alleged communists, Nixon had brought his own prop to the South Pasadena auditorium, his own dark material. He waved around the evidence, the secret, detailed knowledge that would unmask his accused, red-conspiring foe. The mood turned pugilistic as Nixon thrust the document at Voorhis, challenging his opponent to read the bulletin. As one observer recounted, "The crowds caught the smell of blood—the drama of the Old Champ who was in for a beating at the hands of an appealing youngster." Voorhis hesitated and then demurred. From the mimeographed copy of Bulletin no. 9, Nixon, himself, read, "The Los Angeles chapter of the NCPAC announced the group's endorsement of Voorhis." He listed the names of the members who sat on the boards of both the NCPAC and the communist-leaning CIO from the sheets in hand. He aimed to conflate the two PACs in the minds of the voters. Finding names on each page that matched, Nixon announced, "It's the same thing, virtually, when they have the same directors."[5]

One Nixon supporter was particularly impressed by the young Nixon's fierce performance, speaking of how he "proceeded to take Voorhis apart piece by piece, and toss him around the audience." Kyle Palmer, political editor of the conservative *Los Angeles Times*, reported his first impression of Nixon as a "somewhat gawky young fellow who was out on a sort of giant-killer operation." In the words of one Voorhis friend, "Jerry, he murdered you."[6]

As the historian Irwin Gellman has observed, the flaws in Voorhis's reelection campaign extended well beyond the communist accusations. Even after five terms in office, Voorhis had developed neither deep political roots nor an electoral apparatus in his home district. The Democratic incumbent relied on a small group of advisors including his rich father, while in contrast, the upstart Nixon built broad support among small business owners in the Twelfth District. Having run previously successful campaigns, and presumed by even senior Republicans as unbeatable, Voorhis overestimated his acumen and underestimated Nixon's prowess. In his political messaging, he walked a line that proved to be too narrow a distinction by accepting NCPAC's endorsement, which could be readily confused with one from the CIO-PAC. He further failed to appreciate the national turn in the tumultuous year following the end of World War II, the discontent among Democrats and revolt against the New Deal domestic order.[7]

Ahead of the debate, there had been rumors about the CIO-PAC supporting Voorhis. Sensing an opportunity, Nixon introduced the issue at his campaign's kickoff rally in Whittier on Labor Day. "I have no support from any special interest or pressure group," Nixon decried and insinuated. With less subtlety, he added, "I welcome the opposition of the PAC, with its Communist principles and its huge slush fund." Nixon's campaign chair floated the accusation that the Voorhis operation was underwritten by communists, and Nixon repeated the charge in his stump speech. In its choreographed attack, the Nixon campaign promised to "offer the proof at the proper time." In local newspaper advertisements, they framed Nixon's ideological battle as against the "radical" leanings of his opponent. The local Alhambra *Post-Advocate* picked up the accusation as did the *South Pasadena Review* and the *Monrovia News Post*. The *Los Angeles Times* declared that Voorhis bore a pro-Russian taint. On street corners, the Nixon campaign passed out red thimbles championing "NIXON FOR CONGRESS—PUT THE NEEDLE IN THE P.A.C." Which PAC was not specified.[8]

Franklin D. Roosevelt had proposed, "If a leader didn't have enemies, he had better create them." Nixon took the seemingly off-handed comment by the often flip FDR to heart. Nixon extemporized, "If a loyal supporter will fight hard for you, he will fight twice as hard against your enemies." In Nixon's historical reading of Roosevelt, New Deal populism was merely a canny political strategy to wage the war of the many against the rich few. The New Deal was a cynical ploy. FDR had harangued against a shadowy cabal, against the "princes of privilege" and "economic royalists," to manufacture a coalition of discontents, according to Nixon. Roosevelt's scheme aimed to single out easily hateable adversaries. Nixon called them "useful enemies."[9]

To defeat the impressive likes of Voorhis, Nixon adopted his own brand of grievance, orchestrating a public trial steeped in patriotism and conspiracy. Crucial to the scheme was riling up the populist resentments of the vaguely defined common man against a vaguely defined traitorous elite. The narrative need not be logical. Voorhis was simultaneously cast as the ultimate insider—the rich and corrupt, living off the largesse of Roosevelt's expansive state—and as the outsider communist— plotting to hand the country over to the Reds, who had infiltrated the ranks of America's unions, PACs and the Democratic Party. The charge painted Voorhis not only as a partisan opponent, but also as an enemy of the state, calling for an excommunication of the un-American Democrat. The young Nixon made a point to regularly remind audiences that his political opponent, a veteran of Washington, had not served his country in World War II. In Voorhis, Nixon had found his first useful enemy.

Nixon had not yet developed his "madman theory," but the anti-CIO-PAC strategy bore early components of the ploy. Nixon displayed an early understanding of instrumentalizing the potentially explosive paranoia of voters, rather than courting their reason. Painting Voorhis as a pawn to the CIO-PAC played on his supporters' concern that a band of communists or the wealthy lay somewhere in wait, an allegation that he neither proved and would later deny ever believing. Instead, he insinuated against Voorhis by pointing to the NCPAC endorsement and asserted, "If the people want bureaucratic control and domination . . . , then they should not vote for me, but for my opponent." As with the nuclear blackmail Nixon would later employ, it was a shell game that shifted from accusation to accusation—from threat to threat—promising an ultimate, explosive revelation. The tête-à-tête with Voorhis, as with the madman theory, was existential in its ramifications. If the voters failed to elect him, Nixon cautioned, Voorhis would rob the people of their due in the economic and social spheres. The New Deal order, if left unchecked, would stifle the individual, consuming the people in its socialist aims. "The basic issue facing the nation today is whether America is to be a nation in which the govt tells us what we can do and how we can do it in every phase of our lives," Nixon warned on the campaign trail.[10]

As the scholar Dieter Groh has written, the key to such conspiracism is not to concede that a constituencies' distress is unbearable, but instead to make a group's suffering conceivable, even manageable, by pinpointing a culpable "injustice, a wrong, an evil, bad luck, a catastrophe." The unearthing of conspiracy can serve as a tool to delegitimize the hidden but omnipotent foe, to disempower the overwhelming force by revealing its form. The allegation of collusion becomes the method. The fix is the great unmasking of the enemy's plans. Even as Nixon's target voters felt they lived correctly, even valiantly during the world war, they nonetheless found themselves confronted subsequently with what they deemed to be undeserved hardship. A populist conspiracism like Nixon's allowed dispossessed constituents to dispel their sense of sheer devastation, hopelessness and confusion in the early aftermath of the war, to commandeer the plot, recasting themselves from victims to accusers, from casualties of history, to makers of it. The conspiracy theory afforded an explanation to turn disappointment and anguish into legible form, even purpose, as it offered an avenue for converting suffering into a rational design, a refuge from the even more hellish thought that there was no conspiracy, that there was no rhyme or reason for their pain and life's unfairness. From conspired against to conspiracist, Nixon's farmers, clerks and veterans, all suffering, could become heroic agents unmasking rampant corruption in the state's misdeeds, and a first-run candidate could unseat Voorhis as their newly ordained, virtuous crusader.[11]

In Middle River, Maryland, in the summer of 1945, Nixon was finishing his service to the Navy as Gen. Douglas MacArthur approached the outskirts of Tokyo. It was then that he received an unsolicited letter from an old mentor, a high-up at the Bank of America back in California. The inquirer was a senior member of the Committee of 100, a local clique of Republican patrons. His cross-country missive asked if Nixon might consider running for Congress. After all, Nixon was a family man, a churchgoer. He had military service and two medals to show for it, came from good Quaker stock and was a Duke law school alum. The committee was looking for a fresh face like his, the letter emphasized, a "candidate with no previous experience." The moneyed Republicans of the Twelfth District, in particular bankers, lawyers, businessmen, had been chafing at Voorhis' liberal agenda whatever his beatified reputation. The Democrat's support for labor irked the manufacturers and agriculturists, and his backing of a strong Federal Reserve bothered bankers; his antitrust stance upset insurers. Voorhis was often the lone dissenter on congressional votes. He was a crusader whom the Committee of 100 was eager to unseat as the Whittier-well-to-do looked to "unshackle" business from New Deal regulation.[12]

Dick and Pat spent two days in in their tiny apartment weighing his opportunity to serve in Congress. The breakdown of registered Republicans and Democrats stood at nearly 50–50 in the district as the country chafed against shortages and rationing of coffee, flour, nylons. Voters pushed for change. For a young lawyer, even losing would raise his public stature, Nixon reasoned. But then again, Dick and Pat had $10,000 of personal savings and were looking to put a down payment on their first home. Further, Pat was pregnant. Given the expenditures of a campaign, they thought they would have to move back in with Nixon's parents. Conversely, Nixon was a striver, and he liked a bet. "You made your money by gambling," one friend reminded him about his favored recreation when stationed in the South Pacific. "You should be ready to risk it again to win a bigger pot." By some accounts Pat thought the idea an adventure. Later she expressed a more tempered view to a *Time* reporter. "I felt that a man had to make up his mind," she recounted. "I told him that it was his decision and I would do what he liked."[13]

Nixon liked the idea of running. He exhaustively prepared for his interview, as per his routine. Flying back from Baltimore to his hometown to meet the Committee of 100, he wore his Navy uniform; he had sold his civilian suit during the war to help Pat pay bills back home. He took a limousine from the Los Angeles airport. On the morning of November 2, 1945, the dining room of the William Penn Hotel was full for the $1.50-a-plate gathering. Nixon delivered a speech inveighing against an overreaching government and the plight of returning veterans. The audition lasted ten minutes. He impressed. Those gathered found Nixon an "electrifying personality," willing to put up a fight. The committee members sensed that the precocious Nixon had a willing style—"very aggressive" and yet guarded, authentic and yet malleable. He was a "political animal," a prominent advertising salesman concluded. By one account, the first ballot was 55 for, 22 against, but by another account 63 for, 14 against. On the second ballot, the vote was unanimous in Nixon's favor. The committee boosters thought Nixon a "natural." They had "never seen such favorable comment on any candidate," a member and former law partner wrote to Nixon.[14]

Far from assuming a role as a puppet to his backers or simply riding with the desperate times of the country, Nixon moved to take control of the battle against Voorhis, throwing himself into the campaign. Pat addressed envelopes from their sparsely furnished headquarters with its two chairs, a sofa and a borrowed typewriter. She took to the streets to pass out literature. As the biographer Roger Morris found, "The candidate himself even decided the precise telephone poles . . . where campaign posters should be place[d]." Nixon's energy, like his ambition, proved relentless. He game-planned in daily strategy sessions with advisers. Through nearly a year of primaries until the general election, Nixon hit the community forum circuit. He judged that personal contact was key, filling his calendar with small meetings of less than fifty people and handing out fliers. He planted loyalists in his crowds to ask him questions. He studied his opponent, ducking into the back of Voorhis rallies. He rehearsed arguments and replies from the media, never turning down a chance to speak to one and then another reporter. The campaign unleashed 100,000 postcards on the district, mailed thousands of endorsement letters from insurers, automobile dealers, doctors and dentists, the wealthy middle class of Nixon's district. His work ethic, as would prove true throughout his political career, was unstinting, shaking hands, arguing his case, drafting more leaflets, sometimes clocking in twenty-hour days. He was out campaigning when his first daughter, Tricia, was born.[15]

Nixon's campaign message resembled the one adopted by a wave of Republicans in the presidential midterm year as the party tried to marry big business and white working-class constituencies. Across the country, "Had enough?" became the indignant slogan of Republican campaigns. It was a grievance, a rallying cry and, implicitly, a populist accusation against the New Deal order. The charge was not merely that the Truman administration was filled with incompetents, but with thieves, war profiteers, and hoarders. Republicans rallied their constituency of "Middle Americans" not only with an anti-statist, political tune, but also by fomenting class rankling. They offered to turn the status quo upside down, empowering the powerless and dethroning the enthroned. This conservatism built on populist rallying of the "forgotten man" as theorized by the Reconstruction-era sociologist William Sumner and later employed by FDR. Yet where Roosevelt turned to an expanded state for the answer to the commoner's woe, the Republicans' creed looked to libertarianism. They warned that the New Deal order would stifle the individual, consuming the people with its socialist aims. Republicans like Nixon blended a late nineteenth-century progressivism calling for an efficient, technocratic government with a conservative's desire for lean, little-regulated business. The mix of doctrine amounted to a call for capable, but fewer, Washington bureaucrats—meaning appropriate, but little, government control—what Nixon called a "progressive but practical" political platform.[16]

In this progressive pragmatism, Nixon wove together the interests of his wealthy donors with the antigovernment grievance of the working-class voter. He acted the little man even as he concealed his backers behind the curtain. He promised to throw the bums out, speaking the working man's patois. "Remember, the bootblack on the curb carries as much weight with a ballot as a bank president," his pamphlets reminded. Nixon vowed to cut through the red tape of Washington bureaucrats who impeded homes from being built and aid to veterans being spent. He promised to hunt down the excess war material used in graft. He erected billboards with the familiar populist slogans "Time for Change" and "Don't Be Fooled Again!"[17]

Nixon favored a throaty Americanism, a nostalgic nationalism, folksy stories of his naval days, the alert that he, too, was taking up arms to save the nation from foreign infiltration. He reminisced about his time in the military, that "typical American melting pot," where one of his naval brethren came from the "slums of New York," another from a "well-educated" family to mix with a Texan, a Mexican and a Native American. In the feverish heat of the Pacific, in the grime of Guadalcanal or Bougainville, they washed themselves in tidepools that stank from bacteria, Nixon recounted. He voiced their grievances: Now back home, one of his fellow veterans could not afford school, another needed a truck, another was caught in government regulations that prevented him from building a home. Patriotic veterans were returning to the country to suffer through an economy bungled by Washington bureaucrats and corrupted by fat cat insiders. At the same time, he warned hazily of a conspiracy beyond the nation's borders. As he made the local rounds of coffee klatches and barbeques, Nixon's campaign pamphlets pledged with nationalist affront "to resist with all my powers the encroachment of foreign isms upon the American way of life."[18]

Some of the campaign's advertisements directly posed the question "Who Is Richard M. Nixon?" Like the cowboy-philanthropist-congressman Voorhis, Nixon's literature touted a list of identities: Public servant. Veteran. Sports enthusiast. "Experienced Attorney." A "Fine Young Christian Gentleman." At once a "Natural Leader" and a "trained scholar," but then, too, an "EVERYMAN." His pamphlets described a man for all constituencies. It was a foreshadowing of the career of Nixon, the "new Nixon" and the new "new Nixon," ever the performer, forever reinventing himself for a different electorate. Yet instead of sketching a portrait of swashbuckling success like Voorhis's, the clipped biography in Nixon's campaign literature presented Nixon as the common man, as once a "service station operator," a "fruit grader in a packing house," someone who "knows what it means to sleep in a foxhole—exist on K rations—'sweat out' an air raid."[19]

Each claim in his pamphlets bore truth, but then again subtly exaggerated Nixon's record, cloaking the upwardly mobile lawyer in the dress of the most plain. It was true that he had packed fruit, but when he was eight. He had helped the family operate its service station while a teenager. He had served on naval bases bombed by nearby Japanese but without foxholes. It was not his immense talents but his "practical knowledge of business" that Nixon emphasized on the trail, in advertisements and fliers. What counted was, as his pamphlets stated, "Nixon knows how it feels to wear a uniform." With the relish of the nationalist, populist and the nation's founders, Nixon pledged "to preserve our sacred heritages, in the name of my buddies and your loved ones, who died that these might endure." He preached "sincerity" and "common sense," a conservative patriotism that set him apart from the elite, liberal and allegedly un-American Voorhis.[20]

It was in March 1946, just months into Nixon's first campaign, that Winston Churchill proclaimed that the communist menace had divided the world in two with an Iron Curtain. None could yet assume that the conflict and competition against the Soviet Union would run cold; after all, one world war had followed another, and in the wake of the carpet bombing of European and Japanese cities and the afterglow of Hiroshima and Nagasaki, the very magnitude of destruction had exploded qualitatively. "The War Is Not Over" the *New Republic* headlined. Europe remained a bed of tinder as the Soviets threatened to spark revolution in Greece and Turkey. The question of Germany's allegiance festered. The fear of a resurgent Germany loomed.[21]

Would the sputtering American experiment fail? To redress economic woes, would Americans turn even further toward socialism than FDR's great works had, perhaps to communism even? Could the American people be tricked by the promises of a workers' paradise? "To err is Truman" went one jibe. "Russia abroad and labor at home" warned another. The twin terrors of oncoming recession and Red infiltration outpaced the anticommunist fervor that had followed World War I. The Red Scare took on the shape not only of a pitched battle to come, but also of imminent conspiracy behind what the California Un-American Activities Committee dubbed a "cloak of secrecy . . . as impenetrable as human ingenuity will permit." Amid the gathering populist storm, accusations flew about liberal elites in the government, unions, the media and Hollywood. This vague amalgam of the presumed powers that be were blamed not just for failing, but in conspiratorial fashion, were also said to be subverting their country from within. The enemy was no longer at the gates, but inside the castle. The archconservative Chamber of Commerce capitalized on this hydra of ideological-nationalist-populist upheaval by wielding a new tool: guilt-by-association between communists, leftist PACs and unions. More benign allegations accused big business conglomerates of hoarding finances and resources, but in harsher pique, the Chamber of Commerce leader commanded, "We will have to set up some firing squads in every good-sized city and town in the country and . . . liquidate the Reds and Pink Benedict Arnolds."[22]

Republican candidates fanned the conceit, charging that the welfare state had led to a police state. For them and for the upstart Nixon—this antisubversive fare served as a method for locating weak links in the still prevailing New Deal. It supplied a store of useful enemies as the upside-down logic of conspiracism took shape. The organizing principle in Nixon's red-baiting accusations relied on what Jon W. Anderson has called "premature entextualization"—trading a larger context for a specific story. Hypothesis becomes thesis. *Post hoc ergo propter hoc.* Motives are derived from consequences. Facts are filtered for evidence. Convenient details become significant while inconvenient ones become extraneous.

In 1946 only the pertinent was retained, "leaving only a purified text" of guilt, wrongdoing and, above all, purpose as evidence was sifted, as two PACs became one, as a long-serving, anticommunist congressman was deemed a Red, as the swiftly climbing newcomer cloaked himself as the victim of the system, as scaremongering became righteous rage. The aggressive Nixon accused Voorhis of trumping up accusations, of "RABBLE-ROUSING, SLANDEROUS ATTACKS ON HIS WAR VETERAN OPPONENT, RICHARD M. NIXON." With feigned, full-bore pathos, Nixon carped, "Who is he to make scurrilous statements about an honest, clean, forthright young American who fought in defense of his country in the stinking mud and jungle of the Solomons? Coming from a man like Voorhis who stayed safely behind the front in Washington." Voorhis recounted that at speech after speech, as he made the rounds of the district, he was met with a crew of young men in the front row, laughing, booing and shouting. Voorhis was convinced they were Nixon goons.[23]

Fortunately for Nixon, Voorhis had been a registered socialist in the early 1930s, adding yet another chink in his opponent's armor. With that, if unable to quite peg Voorhis as a Red, he could at least paint his opponent as pink. Nixon publicized that in the previous four years, Voorhis had voted for forty-three out of forty-six pieces of congressional legislation endorsed by the CIO-PAC. Nixon called them the "46 mysterious votes." All the while, Nixon elided the content of the forty-six votes, which included prohibiting a poll tax, expanding school lunch assistance, approving a loan to Great Britain to fend off the Soviet Union, and opposing making permanent the House Un-American Activities Committee (HUAC). The attacks ignored that Voorhis had combatted communism and heartily. The only legislation to bear his name—the Voorhis Act, Public Law 879—was an antisubversive bill that required communists and any other organizations controlled by foreign entities to register with the Justice Department. Earl Browder, leader of the

PAGE TWENTY
POLITICAL ANNOUNCEMENT
THE MONROVIA JOURNAL
POLITICAL ANNOUNCEMENT
THURSDAY, OCTOBER 31, 1946
POLITICAL ANNOUNCEMENT

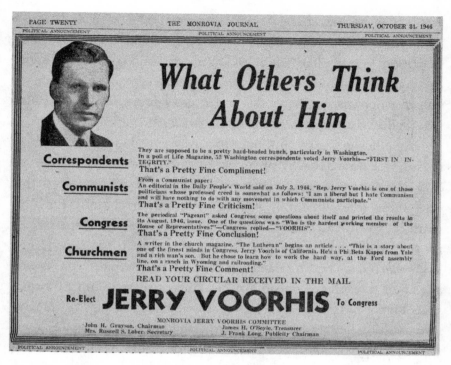

What Others Think About Him

Correspondents

They are supposed to be a pretty hard-headed bunch, particularly in Washington. In a poll of Life Magazine, 53 Washington correspondents voted Jerry Voorhis—"FIRST IN IN-TEGRITY."
That's a Pretty Fine Compliment!

Communists

From a Communist paper:
An editorial in the Daily People's World said on July 3, 1946, "Rep. Jerry Voorhis is one of those politicians whose professed creed is somewhat as follows: "I am a liberal but I hate Communism and will have nothing to do with any movement in which Communists participate."
That's a Pretty Fine Criticism!

Congress

The periodical "Pageant" asked Congress some questions about itself and printed the results in its August, 1946, issue. One of the questions was "Who is the hardest working member of the House of Representatives?"—Congress replied—"VOORHIS".
That's a Pretty Fine Conclusion!

Churchmen

A writer in the church magazine, "The Lutheran" begins an article . . . "This is a story about one of the finest minds in Congress, Jerry Voorhis of California. He's a Phi Beta Kappa from Yale and a rich man's son. But he chose to learn how to work the hard way, at the Ford assembly line, on a ranch in Wyoming and railroading."
That's a Pretty Fine Comment!

READ YOUR CIRCULAR RECEIVED IN THE MAIL

Re-Elect **JERRY VOORHIS** To Congress

MONROVIA JERRY VOORHIS COMMITTEE
John H. Grayson, Chairman James H. O'Boyle, Treasurer
Mrs. Russell S. Lober, Secretary J. Frank Long, Publicity Chairman

A 1946 advertisement to combat Nixon's red-baiting of Jerry Voorhis, U.S. House of Representatives incumbent from California's Twelfth Congressional District, during Nixon's first, and successful, run for public office. *Courtesy of the Claremont College Library.*

American Communist Party, had denounced Voorhis' eponymous bill as a measure of the "sweep of fascization [*sic*] over the capitalist world."[24]

Far from Nixon's pinko caricature of his opponent, Voorhis had cross-examined alleged communists while he served on HUAC and continued to level charges against Soviet efforts to control "puppet governments." The *People's World*, a California communist daily, declared Voorhis a "red-baiter" and a "false liberal." The Communist Party in the Twelfth District said that Voorhis had fallen under the wiles of HUAC, kowtowing to "his un-American fellow-Fascists." With a fervor reserved for the apostate, they charged Voorhis as no longer being an idealist but a "stool pigeon" imperialist and a warmonger. To the communists' consternation, Voorhis, like Nixon, endorsed containing the Soviet Union. In equal parts, both candidates railed against the idea of great spheres of influence dominating the world's order, proclaiming their support for independent nations as "free and equal partners."[25]

Nonetheless, Nixon continued to play fast and loose with Voorhis's record. He claimed that his opponent had brought paltry returns to the district, being the primary sponsor of only one of 132 bills passed. In this way, Nixon accused Voorhis of being both a powerful tool of the communists as well as an ineffectual loser. Voorhis remained nonplussed by the suggestion that he was a do-nothing. He pointed to a ream of legislation that did not bear his name but in which, he asserted, he had played a leading role: the expansion of disability insurance in California, school-lunch programs, control over atomic energy and agricultural reform. Voorhis had spearheaded the proclamation of a National Employ the Physically Handicapped Week, a key focus for veterans returning from the battlefield.[26]

Voorhis and Nixon faced off in front of more than 7,000 constituents in five debates, during which Nixon continued to rail against the liberal governing elite, the New Deal and communists. In the apocalyptic fashion of the conspiracist, he warned that his countrymen had reached a "day of reckoning." His was an allegation of guilty association that purported that Nixon and only Nixon could pierce the conspiracy. He wielded a paranoia to intimidate his foe as he coopted the panic of the Red Scare for political purpose. He won a convincing 57 percent of the electorate, or around 15,000 votes, in a wave that saw seven more Republicans in California defeat incumbent House Democrats.[27]

In a postelection roundup, *Time* helped mythologize the Nixon victory as a "grass-roots" effort. The *Washington Times Herald* touted Nixon as "typically American as Thanksgiving." Nixon later called his knocking horns with Voorhis a "very honest debate." He insisted to the press, "Voorhis lost because that district was not a New Deal district," and "I have no personal quarrel with my opponent." Nixon's subsequent campaigns would adopt a narrative similar to that in 1946. "Above all," his 1950 Senatorial campaign literature espoused, "Dick Nixon is human. He came from the people, and is still of the people, a regular guy." Far from the chicanery that would later become synonymous with his name, Nixon projected an image of himself as the clean candidate, the average Joe. It was the Nixon he made famous with his Checkers speech against accusations of a secret fund, the Nixon who insisted in his campaign literature that he "may make a mistake, but he will always stand on principle, and act with sincerity and forthrightness."[28]

At the same time, throughout those campaigns, Nixon accused his opponents of corruption. As he himself struck a patriotic tone, he targeted his opponents for excommunication from the body politic by tagging them un-American. It was the same searing theme that he had begun developing during his first run for office and that he would rehash, in variation, his entire career—that is, send small-town Dick Nixon to infiltrate Washington to throw the leftist infiltrators out. America had been stolen from the true Americans, he exhorted, as he whipped his electorate's fears into a panic. The accusation of conspiracy lay at the heart of Nixon's politics. His mission was, in Nixon's framing, a populist countercoup against the reigning (and secretively) powerful.

In 1950 Nixon jeered the liberal and elegant Helen Gahagan Douglas in their race for a California Senate seat, adopting the line that she was "pink right down to her underwear." Unlike Voorhis, she actually had accepted money from the CIO-PAC. Unlike him, she had applauded the post–World War II accords reached with Joseph Stalin at the Yalta conference. Nixon circulated literal "pink sheets" recording the number of times Douglas had voted with the Republican Vito Marcantonio, a New York congressional representative with well-known communist leanings. Then again, as a vice presidential candidate in 1952, Nixon claimed that his opponent, the Brahmin Democratic candidate Adlai Stevenson, had a "form of color blindness—a form of pink eye—toward the Communist threat." During the 1954 midterms, he continued his anti-communist cant. As vice president, Nixon boasted, "When the Eisenhower administration reached Washington . . . it found in the files a blue print for socializing America." From Voorhis to Alger Hiss to the Kennedys, the elite, as the populist Nixon portrayed them, were a closed cell of decision makers, of string pullers and kingmakers. In his race for president in 1968, he inveighed against his Democratic opponent, Hubert Humphrey, as being in league with communists, appeasing the North Vietnamese, raring to sell out the United States. By 1972 he was courting the silent majority—those "non-shouters and non-demonstrators" whose lives and livelihoods had been undercut by a clique of intellectuals and counterculturists more keen on quoting Marx than taking showers.[29]

Voorhis by then had moved halfway across the country to Winnetka, Illinois, just outside Chicago. He exited politics quietly, returning to charity work. "Hardly a quarter-year has passed in all the nine (9) years since Mr. Nixon defeated me that there has not come from the Nixon publicity mill another version of the campaign of 1946," Voorhis finally complained, in March 1956, to a journalist from the *Reporter*, a New York–based magazine that, like him, espoused an anti-communist doctrine with broad, leftist advocacy. Voorhis had not uttered a public word on the record about Nixon for nearly a decade, but he was haunted by the notion that Nixon's characterization of his political career had become the one for the records. "Always, of course, he has been the knight in shining armour and I have necessarily been some sort of being sufficiently unworthy, so the knight was justified in the use of any sort of tactics or weapons in doing away with me." Voorhis defended himself against the charge of communism by pointing again to his anticommunist credentials. He pointed again to how the *People's Daily* had attacked him time and again, how he had sponsored the Voorhis Act against subversives.[30]

In a book Voorhis published in 1972, nearly twenty-five years after the standoff against Nixon, he returned once again to his long-passed and fateful last campaign, writing, "To one practice Richard Milhous Nixon has been faithful. He has done whatever . . . would advance his political fortunes." Titled *The Strange Case of Richard Milhous Nixon*, the book was a prosecution, not a narrative, a dissection of Nixon akin to Voorhis's interrogations of communists when serving on HUAC. Each chapter laid out evidence of cheating, lying and graft. Voorhis presented a case for how, with "wondrous flexibility," everyone "[Nixon] has ever campaigned against has turned out, on his investigation, to be linked to something sinister."[31]

Voorhis explained how he had been "Richard Nixon's first victim," sitting atop Nixon's long list of useful enemies. Indeed, Nixon in that very first political campaign had already begun developing and honing his political skills, deftly stoking his constituents' paranoia. Nixon, once the president of the Student Bar Association of his Duke law class, taunted Voorhis, casting him as suspect with his overly schooled, "high-sounding phrases." Nixon's message mixed the populist anti-elite and ideologically anti-communist elements of the Red Scare with logical inconsistency, which, nonetheless, with a shrewd touch, proved convincing. With the machinations of the contradictory conspiracist, he disparaged his opponent as an insider, born with silver spoon in his mouth, and a Red outsider. He warned that the New Deal was a puppet program for fat-cat industrialists and, at the same time, a tool of socialist design. It was the beginnings of a mad style as the fresh-faced Nixon stoked his constituents' fears, began feigning outrage, threatening catastrophe as he played with fire. It was "folly for one who happened to stand in the way of Richard Nixon," said a resigned Voorhis. "I would like very much to forget the campaign of 1946." For the rest of his life, the pipe-smoking, one-time-cowboy-turned-philanthropist Voorhis rued the loss. "[I] let the country down by not getting elected," he lamented. Voorhis's failure at the polls, he felt, had spawned the "ruthless" future president. "If he hadn't defeated me then, he'd never have received another chance to run for political office," Voorhis said. "I'm sorry and repent about it."[32]

Interlude Two

POLITICAL SCIENTISTS HAVE typically considered madness as synonymous with risk-taking, suicidality, and the self-defeating. For game theorists, irrationality and insanity traditionally became one and the same; the mad strategist was defined by his propensity to play Russian roulette all too eagerly. Certainly, Richard Nixon was not thinking in terms of present-day understandings of mental illness in developing his "madman theory." He thought not of "the more or less touched" as Lord Byron described, as Kay Redfield-Jamison, a leading professor of psychiatry at Johns Hopkins Medical School, has described mood and personality disorders.[1] Nixon thought not of the schizophrenic conversing with phantom companions, the manic's hyper grandiosity or the depressive's catatonic despair. He thought not of the sociopath threatening neighbors and kin in disregard, not of the narcissist or the traumatized reliving defeat over and again.

Madness has historically proven stubbornly difficult to define. The traditional descriptions of madness—a loss of thoughtfulness, rise of unpredictability, predominance of the emotional, of the illogical—tend to leave a void due to the elusive nature of such classically accepted and indeterminate traits. The condition is chaotic, dark, shapeless. "A patient starts to sing in the middle of the night," the esteemed twentieth-century psychiatrist Karl Jaspers wrote, "he attempts suicide, . . . a key on the table excites him so much, all this will seem the most natural thing in the world to the patient but he cannot make us understand it." Jaspers called mental illness "unununderstandable."[2] Indeed, the complexity of the symptoms of the mentally disordered has defied the rational/irrational dyad in political science and the triad of the id, ego and superego of Sigmund Freud and his acolytes in psychology. Madness resists clean, clinical classification as patients trade in irregular combinations of the dangerous, exciting, desperate, compulsive and, too often tragically, of the meaningless. The *Diagnostic and Statistical Manual of Mental Disorders* (DSM) continually grows in length with each new edition, undergoing restructuring and revision as categorical schemes are developed to define newly recognized and revisited psychiatric disorders.

Confusion over what is madness is as old as madness itself. The ancients, including the likes of Virgil, Ovid and Lucan, asked *Quis furor?* What is this madness? At times when inclined toward the biological, they noted an abundance of black bile or perhaps a "floating womb." Looking to the mind, Plato likened madness to the "condition of slavery," as a person was enslaved by his thoughts, as if bound to serve mad predilection. Yet Plato also saw creativity in madness, a burst of new ideas, inexplicable strength, and from there sprang a nagging sense that within that *furor*, there grew a power, that there was utility in madness. In Plato one finds already a need to rationalize the irrational, to define what Byron called his strange "*mélange*," to contain the *furor*, but also to map out the power wrought by madness. The historian Debra Hershkowitz adopted the term *discours furieux* to describe categories of chaotic temper. Plato delineated four categories of madness, associating them with divine power: mystic vision (of Dionysus), creative ecstasy (the Muses), supreme sight (Apollo), and love-struck folly (Aphrodite and Eros). Over time, a rich history developed of such avowedly useful and even benevolent madness played out in fits of strength, acts of superior sight, foresight, sharp self-reflection and in creative piques of beauty.[3]

In Nixon's own discours furieux, the type of madness he suggested feigning was a crude one. Simply put, it corresponded to a literal definition of "*mad*-ness," as being too angry, the state of becoming one's temper. Nixon's conception crystallized into a portrait of a ruler let loose—not by glee or lust or grief—but by a wrath unmoored and unreasoned. He intimated that his theory's madness was to appear as a tempestuous impulsivity catalyzed by suicidal (i.e., nuclear) abandon and, of course, replete with rage. He was to act the stymied player, at peak pique, clearing the board of game pieces with one mean sweep of his arm. He imagined the role of a latter-day ogre, a bully, in his own words, "obsessed," "angry," not able to be restrained. It was a madness that, he warned, "may get out of control."[4]

Nixon's idea of madness harkened back to ancient conceit, classical thinking and the musings of the Romantics. To the Greeks, madness was *thymos* (passion), disrespected and unbound. It was dark humor unbalanced by vindictiveness, foaming with bilious spite. It was an undefined base anger imagined and reimagined time and again as the most authentic of emotions: the mark of Cain's cruelty, those damned to "drown again and again, choking on their own venom" in Dante's Fifth Circle, the "nasty, brutish" temper of Thomas Hobbes's natural man. Such madness has been hailed as the core of human nature, the truest of feelings if allowed to be released: Freud's unrestrained *id*, Joseph Conrad's heart of darkness, William Golding's lord of the flies, the Hulk. Classically, the notion of such a raging madness, a mad-ness that brings a loss of wit, a vengeful wrath inhuman in force and savagery, incapable of control, was thought bestowed by gods unto man. As the scholar Andrew Scull wrote of Homer's epics, madness was most commonly wrought "in the heat of battle, where men become frenzied, lose control" and were "possessed" by divine force. In the *Iliad*, Achilles seethed over the vanquished but still pleading Trojan prince Hector. With punitive and unearthly temper, drained of mercy, the great Greek warrior raved, berserk: "Beg no more, you fawning dog . . . / . . . Would to god my rage, my fury would drive me now to hack your flesh away and eat you raw—such agonies you have caused me!"[5]

Through passion came a vicious strength for the Greek avatar, but, so too, the abandonment of Logos. This deviation from rational thought at times became conflated with a breaking of social boundaries. In myth or story or understanding, transgressing bounds of respectable thought became manifest as the breaking of literal bonds. In the biblical tradition, the sheered and blinded Samson—with suicidal abandon, possessed by wrath and vengeance, crying to the Lord for strength—pulled down the two central pillars of Dagon's temple in Gaza, crushing himself and more than 3,000 Philistines. He killed soldiers and innocents alike. Such was considered the gruesome carnage wrought by mad possession. Turning on its head the idea of madness as crippling, Samson's story suggested that a loss of wits could bring godly strength.

Yet rather than the supremely strong, perhaps the most consistently esteemed of the mentally ill are found in the Apollonian tradition, the long history of mad prophets, unsoothing sybils and oracular eccentrics, weird, weïrd, wyrd and weyard sisters, cross-eyed fanatics and bare-footed buskers. Some such infirm minds were believed to reveal special avenues of perception. Possessed, haunted, cursed, blessed or prey to sin, they traded sanity's clarity of vision for access to magical planes of spectral sight. It was an ironic gift: the mindless leading the mindful. This mad tradition evolved into the secular but no less far-seeing court Fool, whose gift of insight outstripped that of his sane but blind master. The Fool's loose play with words and mores, his seeming loose grip on reality, like a carnival, like his festival garb worn daily, turned the everyday upside down. For centuries, over and again, the turn of sense into a state of madness was thought mysteriously to reveal a deeper truth, one hidden by mundane thought, the strictures of the rational mind and the tyranny of reason.

In this ironic fashion, as Scull wrote, "Folly was mobilized to hold up a mirror to the moral failings of all humanity." Such was the windmill-tilting wisdom found in Don Quixote's transgressive madness. Such was King Lear's Fool, whose "wild babblings, and inspired idiocy" Samuel Taylor Coleridge remarked, could "articulate and gauge the horrors of the scene." Such madness echoed throughout Shakespeare's cannon. The Bard's mad players could be supremely insightful, compelling, quick in wit, sexy, curious and sweet, smart but unwise, odd, confused, star-crossed, inappropriate or cruel. He made madness central to his quartos. The grossly infirm of mind— Lear, Macbeth, Falstaff, Prospero—became the most celebrated stalwarts of high drama.[6]

Nixon's idea of wielding madness, his madman theory, was the strategy adopted by the most famous character in all of theater, probably in all of literature, Shakespeare's Hamlet. With an "antic disposition," the forlorn prince fashioned an insanity. By performing madness, Hamlet attempted to out the truth of his uncle / step-father's fratricide. Such were the intemperate "mouse traps" he gamely laid for his mother, uncle / step-father and the court of Elsinore. Indeed, it is from the words of Polonius, the Danish courtier, that one draws the phrase a "method in his madness." The crux of the play—the plot even more central than the prince's revenge fantasy—was the enticing issue of the madman theory: was Hamlet playing mad or had he already been driven insane? Are we watching a crafty young man take the rightful control of his father's fief or is he losing it? The question of the play became one of volition, that is, whether the prince acted strategically or compulsively, whether his was a "positive deviance" or a destructive one.

The potential for not only strength or sight but also strategic creativity in the insane spans the Western canon. Indeed, to locate the underlying logic of the madman theory, Nixon need only have opened a copy of *Discourses of Livy*. Machiavelli was quite clear: "It is very wise to simulate madness at the right time." He particularly praised the mad form of feigned "idiocy" or stupidity (*stultizia*), what we would call "playing dumb," an iteration of the clever Fool. As Machiavelli wrote with arch irony, "There has never been anyone so prudent nor so much esteemed wise . . . [as] Junius Brutus for his simulation of stupidity." The Roman upstart's ability to act mad was a necessary play of obsequiousness to pursue reform of the state even though, in fact because, a man like Brutus lacked the military credentials for such influence. Machiavelli concluded quite clearly, "One needs to play the madman [*pazzo*], like Brutus, and make oneself crazy [*matto*], praising, speaking, seeing, doing things *against your mind* . . . so as to please the prince." If such madness is played well, Machiavelli intimated, an also-ran like Brutus, and by extension a malcontent like Nixon, could capture the power behind the throne.[7]

Further, there has been a long albeit inconsistent linkage of mental illness, especially of "melancholy"—today diagnosed as depression or bipolar disorder—with an elusive creativity. It has been postulated that rather than a distortion of reality, flights into the depths of despair and regret can bring about deeper wisdom. The Renaissance glorified melancholic genius. Misery, ingenuity and penetrating vision were an artist's gift and burden. John Milton canonized the "divinest Melancholy." As the writer Andrew Solomon noted, in the 1630s the depressives' conduct, shorn of anguish, was mimicked for enjoyment, "lounging for hours on long sofas, staring at the moon, asking existential questions." The hope lingered, as Solomon suggested, that some "psychosis contains imagination."[8]

The mad melancholic won even greater laurels amid the boom of Romantic thought in the late eighteenth century and into the nineteenth. Madness came to be thought of as a strategy not only for the play of Machiavellian politics, but for self-awakening. Genius might elapse the frontier of Reason. The Romantics did not simply suffer the onset of madness; they encouraged it. As the novelist J. M. Coetzee described, "Poets deranged themselves with opium or alcohol so that from the brink of madness they could issue reports on their visionary experiences." Wordsworth, Shelley, Blake, one poet after another, wallowed in the loss of wits brought on by misery. As Byron opined of his lot, "We of the craft are all crazy, . . . from woe wrung overwhelming eloquence." In "Ode on Melancholy," John Keats wrote that "in the very temple of Delight/Veil'd Melancholy has her Sovran shrine." Intellectuals and a generation of their admiring acolytes fetishized insanity. Goethe's young Werther became, almost instantly, the ideal of beatified anguish. The slim *Sorrows of Young Werther*—a fictive collection of sorrowful letters—sold out as soon as it appeared in bookstores in the fall of 1774. As the German scholar Peter Boerner relates, "Reprints followed, then pirated editions. Young people devoured it with tears in their eyes. Some dressed like the novel's protagonists . . . Cases of suicide were associated with it. There was talk of a 'Werther fever.'"[9]

Gifted masters like Fyodor Dostoyevsky and Vincent van Gogh were, themselves, like their agonized subjects, transformed into venerated symbols of ecstatic creativity inspired by their unremitting misery. The poet Rimbaud was the *suprême savant* for such regression into the irrational. He became an "icon . . . in revolt against rationality," wrote the scholar Alan Thiher, a bridge between the "belated utopian romantic" and the precocious "flower child." Arthur Rimbaud crystallized the notion of a power in madness when he proclaimed, "The Poet becomes a seer by a . . . disordering of all the senses." He inspired the notion of delusion as ecstasy. His was a liberation theology of madness, freed from the vassalage of rationality, from the "new nobility" of science and modernity that overtook his age. For Rimbaud and his followers, in ironic fashion, illness wrought experience. Infirmity brought knowledge. Madness was useful.[10]

Romantics so aestheticized the mad that insanity was thought to bring forth not only strength, insight or creativity but beauty itself. *Ophelia* (1851–52), John Everett Millais' famous painting of Hamlet's drowned lover, became (and largely remains) the standard portrait of her mad demise, if not the common vision of female madness itself. Millais chose to depict Ophelia not struggling amid broken garland, not fiercely heaving up streams of muddied water or dead and rotting, afloat, blistered and bloated, a marbleized hue of whites and purples. Instead, Ophelia's deathbed suggested the Edenic, a peaceful refuge, free of her witless spells and mad garble, her torn garb, her frenzied woe. For Millais, the suicide of the young Danish girl raised her to the pinnacle of feminine beauty. Through suicide, her soiled wits returned her to nature's habitat. The damsel *through* distress became, as Queen Gertrude claimed, "as one incapable of her own distress, / Or like a creature native and indued / Unto that element."[11] By Millais' brush, Ophelia retained a beauty in the liminality of her madness; near awake and cleverly alluring.

A related madman theory arose according to which some women feign madness as a shield against the danger of sexuality. So went Ophelia, that "document in madness."[12] So, too, many have argued, went Salem and her teenage witches. This notion peaked in a literal pique of fit with the Victorian notion that "hysterical" women were unconsciously retreating from sexual danger by immobilizing parts of their bodies. Their hysteria was thought a mad strategic refuge from violent men—unless, of course, like Lot's wife, they were frozen by force of their own sinful curiosities. As for Hamlet, the question of performance and volition lay at the center of such accusations. Was the hysterical woman a prude? Was she a tart? Was she longing for male attention? Or was she soiled and stuck in a repressed state due to formative abuse, as Freud theorized? Did she use her madness only for it to overpower and trap her? In this, Victorian clinicians turned to a central preoccupation of this book: Is madness an affliction or a ruse?

On rereading the literature on hysterical, Victorian women, feminist scholars have suggested that such a touch of madness could be a useful ploy. Such a purportedly mad woman as Rochester's wife in *Jane Eyre* was kept in the attic by her husband, yet, as the scholars Sandra M. Gilbert and Susan Gruber describe, "inconvenient" women trapped in their own space found a power. Madness provided women with a space—untouched by the silencing of male abuse—to create a "literature of their own." Even and quite because they were thought mad, even while confined by the strictures of a patriarchal code, they can be said to have found a freedom in their liminal space.[13]

The mid-1900s, a century after the Victorians, brought renewed veneration of the power of madness and the utility of the unreasoning. Among the Beats, then the hippies and the yippies, drug-induced madness was thought to bring enlightenment, insight-by-hallucinogen, if not the "best sex ever," an preoccupation of the era. It was Richard Nixon's nightmare come to life. Allen Ginsberg and William S. Burroughs rhapsodized about the quixotic charms of psychosis. Jack Kerouac beat out a whirling anthem: "The only people for me are the mad ones, the ones who are mad to live, mad to talk, mad to be saved, . . . who never yawn or say a commonplace thing, but burn, burn, burn." In a latter-day Romanticism, musical genius, poetry and pop art became dependent on drugs, the loss of one's wits, the pursuit of the "pure, spontaneous Self," the worship of a higher consciousness, freedom from conventional thought and, more specifically, Western civilization's rational grip. Even as industrialization boomed, as postwar abundance and mass culture flourished, the ascetic became the aesthetic. The bare-footed became the bard. Poetry steeped in the unsweetened sorrows of the likes of Sylvia Plath, Anne Sexton and Robert Lowell. The Janis Joplins, the Jimi Hendrixes, the "hypnotically erotic" Jim Morrison burned bright and then unleashed a crescendo of public anguish, dying young, thought of as sacrifices on the tragically empowering altar of the day's madness. Even the once-boyish Beatles dabbled in the dope-filled haze in a show of their artistic maturity.[14]

Of Michel Foucault's anti-psychiatric *Madness and Civilization* (1961), the psychiatrist David Cooper wrote, "Madness has in our age become some sort of lost truth." Foucault and his acolytes argued that the mad were prisoners of an over-reasoning and punitive authority, pill-baited and trapped in a Keseyian cuckoo's nest. Foucault reinterpreted the long history of abusive asylums as an attack against the special, the different, the silenced creatives. The maltreatment of the mentally ill—the overcrowding and unsanitary conditions, the tranquillizing drugs, the baths of extreme cold, heated closets, shock boxes, lobotomies—was, to a Foucault disciple like Cooper, nothing less than the "crucifixion of our age."[15]

Not far from Plato's "divine madness" or Milton's "divinest Melancholy," Foucault's madman theory exalted madness in the name of religious ecstasy. Anti-psychiatric contemporaries of Foucault helped popularize the centuries-old tradition. They venerated latter-day mystics, witches and Fools. Madness, they argued, was a tool to wield, with which to see, to make life beautiful. Scholars like the psychoanalyst Thomas Szasz suggested that the mad knew truths about family and society so dangerous as to be pathologized, ostracized, dismissed if not locked up. In the "socialization" process, the mentally ill lost their individual will, creativity, even sublime thought. For the psychiatrist R. D. Laing, schizophrenics' challenge to social order threatened society's framework. Schizophrenia, he argued, was not a chaotic mind gone awry but a "rational strategy of withdrawal from an all-too threatening world." The sociologist Howard Becker wrote that the label of "deviance" served to cut the mad down, to quell their threats. He proffered that insanity arose not from too little but too much "socialization" by a domineering family or an oppressive society.[16]

Flirting with New Age thinking, these notions became popular fanfare for the mystic and intellectual counterculture, those "deviants" Nixon so despised. "Everyone in our 'helter-skelter' days is now talking of Laing," one devotee put it. "It is not the case that God first makes mad those whom He would destroy; He first . . . allows dementing societies to make mad the very ones whom He wishes to be prophets." Yet the critic Lionel Trilling decried scholars like Foucault and Laing who preached a "doctrine that madness is health." They denied the "pain of . . . bewilderment and solitude" in psychosis by aggrandizing suffering as a liberation from an alienating society, Trilling critiqued. After all, such preachers of a Romanticized insanity did not in the least "have it in mind to go mad" themselves.[17]

Nixon, too, was incensed by the mad revolutionaries of the 1960s. He felt threatened not only by the youth movements protesting the Vietnam War, the activists impatient over stalled civil rights, but also by the counterculture itself. His sharp-tongued vice president, Spiro Agnew, once dubbed the "Robespierre of the Great Silent Majority," taunted demonstrators as "ideological eunuchs." Gen. Earle Wheeler, chairman of the Joint Chiefs of Staff, belittled the new madness as a cult of "interminably vocal youngsters, strangers alike to soap and reason." Nixon raged against the "bums" as the aestheticization of madness peaked in popularity within the counterculture he so deplored—and that so deplored him. Thus, it is ironic that at the same time Nixon was barricading himself against the raging, mad sixties, he was also dabbling in the mad arts himself, in formulating his risky grand nuclear theory. He joined in a generation's proposition that the irrational could be useful.[18]

From the Greeks to Shakespeare to today, the theater has remained a central arena for feigning madness, now joined by film, video and YouTube channels. Like walking the stations of the cross, particular affectations have through their performance grown into recognizable, stock gestures associated with those acting crazy: fidgeting, hair pulling, eyes bulging in fear or fascination. For Shakespeare, the mad were known to riddle and to rhyme nonsense. On the stage, fictive madmen and women mutter bitter nothings or speaks in tongues. They self-interrupt, spit, shake, scream, strip, shit and dance in frenzied revelry to no audible tune. Feigned theatrical madness is a costume, worn for a night or regularly at a particular hour on particular days of the week, until the curtain falls. It is contained within each play's performance. Aestheticized insanity has a routine in its tics, a fixed dialect underlying its chaotic sense, as fixed as Plato's four categories of Dionysus, Apollo, the Muses, and Aphrodite and Eros. With great courtesy, at the end of the play, the actors return to the stage to bow and present themselves to the audience assuredly unharmed and no longer infirm. As the British psychoanalyst Adam Philips noted, "If we began to have the feeling that the people playing the Lears and the Macbeths were really as mad as they seem to be in their plays, being a member of the audience would become much more disturbing."[19]

The truly mentally infirm, the unedited, walk uncomfortably off the familiar path. From Nixon's perspective, the key to his pursuit of madness was, as Philips argued, capturing those aspects that "terrorize" and compel us about the madman. In Nixon, it was not the recognizable tics, but the extremity of his disposition, his ingenuity and his impulsiveness. He presented the dangerous, creative and uncertain contradictions of madness distinct from the canned crazy distinguished by the greatest actors in maddeningly convincing performances—the Hannibal Lecters, the Jokers, the Patrick Batemans, the Annie Wilkeses. It was Nixon's ability to make madness both dogged and uncertain, sincere and utterly untrustworthy. For he was, at once, stiff but nimble, rigid but resourceful, restrained but tricky, an ideologue and a realist. He was, Haldeman found, the "strangest man I ever met."[20]

The roots of Nixon's wielding madness bore signs of old roots, a long lineage from the Greeks to Shakespeare to Rimbaud to the hippies. It was an insistence on the limits of the rational, an idealization of the peculiar genius and of madness, a belief that madness can be wielded for great thought, creativity, strength, purpose. The ironic contention, as passed down for centuries, rests on a series of inversions: that out of blindness could come special sight, out of confusion could come clarity, from foolishness could come focus, from melancholic despair could arise the heights of beauty. Plato maintained that "the greatest of blessings come to us through madness, when it is sent as a gift of the gods." This "divine madness" was an ironic inversion transforming a burden to a boon, a disability to a capability. It tantalized Nixon with the idea that from bluster could come amity, that from rage could come accord, that from war could come peace.[21]

5 | Madness in the Mind

Rage and Conspiracism in the Presidency

IN THE SUMMER OF 1969, in the first year of his presidency, Nixon became absorbed by the incident at Chappaquiddick. The questionable circumstances surrounding the death of Sen. Edward "Ted" Kennedy's companion in a car accident offered immediate political fodder for Kennedy detractors. The youngest of the clan had failed to inform the police of his late-night car crash off Chappaquiddick, on the eastern end of Martha's Vineyard, Massachusetts, until nine o'clock the following morning. There was word of "heavy drinking." Some observers were calling the accident "politically fatal." Others saw a cover-up. Kennedy's hometown paper, the *Boston Globe*, dubbed the accident "the most famous traffic fatality of the century." With Chappaquiddick, the previously untouchable Kennedys appeared suddenly vulnerable, tainted. Nixon was, as Haldeman noted, "fascinated."[1]

On July 18, the married Kennedy had left a family steak cookout at 11:15 p.m. with Mary Jo Kopechne, a twenty-eight-year-old former secretary of his brother Robert. Kennedy tried to explain: The dirt road . . . the wooden bridge . . . the salt-water inlet. "I remember thinking, as the cold water rushed in around my head, that I was for certain drowning," he reported amid the clicks and clatter of the ensuing press conference. "Then water entered my lungs, and I actually felt the sensation of drowning. But somehow I struggled to the surface alive," Kennedy said. "I have no recollection of how I got out of the car." Then thirty-seven, husky, with a wave of still dark thick locks, he swore, "I came to the surface and then repeatedly dove down . . . in an attempt to see if the passenger was still in the car. I was unsuccessful."[2]

Nixon had believed that Kennedy would be his strongest competitor in the 1972 presidential election. But with revelations of how the junior senator from Massachusetts had abandoned his black Oldsmobile Delmont in Poucha Pond, how Kopechne drowned late that July night, Kennedy's misdeed all but disqualified him from the race. "What if he were President and the Russians phoned on that hot line and said they were going to bomb us within the hour and he forgot to report it to the Pentagon?," groused one New Orleans cab driver. "I think his nine-hour period of confusion stemmed from just too many tragedies," a housewife from Seattle empathized. "Teddy," another star-crossed Kennedy, appealed to the "fancies and fantasies of the public" wrote a Nixon aide.[3] He was all that Nixon was not—a mix of glamor, ease, largesse. Nixon could rejoice in his unexpectedly swift disarmament, basking in the revelation of a salacious crime, the unmasking of a foe, yet the president did not—or at least not entirely.

During an otherwise uneventful visit to the White House by a clutch of senators less than two weeks after the accident, Nixon took Kennedy aside. He comforted him. He identified with the tragedy of the situation. Indeed, with Kennedy he traded one hated foe for another, commiserating with the Massachusetts senator about the highfalutin media's harsh treatment of him in the wake of the accident; how quickly they had soured on the once princely Kennedy after such favorable coverage up until the morning following the accident. Nixon schooled him on the essential dynamic he needed to understand about the press: "[They] are your enemy at heart even if they *do* like you, because their prime motivation is the story."[4]

Nixon's speechwriter William Safire sat across the room out of earshot, watching the two. "Nixon, who had experienced premature political burial himself, was talking gently and reassuringly, and Kennedy was listening," he recalled. For ten minutes, the two maligned figures huddled and spoke too softly to hear. Missing was the president's bile.

Gone was his ire toward the heirs of Camelot. Nixon's sympathy lied not with the young Kopechne or in some long-enduring fondness for the youngest Kennedy. Rather, he identified with the up-and-comer unceremoniously cast aside as the tragic knave, the banished political princeling, suddenly an outsider. In the president's estimation, Kennedy's fall from grace swiftly elevated him as a sympathetic figure.[5]

After huddling with Kennedy, Nixon gathered his thoughts. Scribbling a note to himself in case he was asked a related question at the next press conference. He felt inspired. He wrote a Longfellowian anthem for the defiant losers, for those who came back, for those feats with which his own name had become synonymous:

> Defeat—doesn't
> finish a man—
>
> Quit—does—
>
> A man is not finished
> when he's defeated
>
> He's finished
> when he
> quits.

For Nixon, disaffection was a badge of honor. Marginality had its own status, as Nixon hoped that a counter-establishment of outsiders such as himself could replace the current establishment. He envisioned the silent majority becoming the new radical chic. As he had consoled the young Kennedy, "[Journalists] are your enemy at heart." Their story was not his story. The press's account was the insiders' rendering, that of the old guard, which, Nixon was convinced, threatened his outsider logic, ridiculed and laughed at him, conspired against him.[6]

To combat the apparent unfairness of the powers that be, Nixon, in the tradition of the mad Fool, envisioned turning power on its head. In the abiding topsy-turvy of Nixon's experience of injustice, fair was foul, so he intended to turn foul into fair. Those colluded against were justified in becoming colluders, as he judged that his enemies' misdeeds countenanced his own; he felt entitled to level the playing field, to play fast and furious, to hoodwink. His strategy contained both poles of the "madman theory": the madness and the play. Among his fraternity of aides and deputies, the young Donald Segretti, a "secret recruiter" of potential fellow dirty tricksters for Nixon, liked to stress, "What fun we could have." The Nixonites liked to call their tactics "rat-fucking." For even if Nixon lacked a developed sense of humor, he certainly reveled in a certain style of political gamesmanship. He was Slippery Dick Nixon, Tricky Dick or, as the novelist Philip Roth imagined, Trick E. Dixon.[7]

Nixon's sympathy for Ted Kennedy and the brief détente over Chappaquiddick did not last long. The plot moved on in Nixon's mind, from one enemy to the next. After berating the conspiratorial press, Nixon returned to targeting what his aides liked to call the "super swinger jet set types"—the rich like Kennedy, the privileged few who could leave a woman drowned and get off with parole, found guilty only of leaving the scene of an accident. Soon Nixon pressed his aides to find "more Chappaquiddicks." As the historian Luke Nichter has suggested, "Nixon did not intend to simply win in 1972; he wanted to destroy his opponent." Wanting a "little persecuting," he ordered a "dirty tricks approach." H. R. Haldeman, Nixon's chief of staff, recommended circulating posters at Kennedy rallies that read "Would you ride in a car with Ted Kennedy?" Nixon hired private detectives to follow Kennedy on vacation in Hawaii and then back in Martha's Vineyard. They needed "to watch him," Nixon told Haldeman, not "on and off," but constant tailing. Further, electronic surveillance would be "better than . . . hiring 18 more researchers, you know, little boys to go over there and try to figure out what the PR line should be." Nixon ordered wiretapping on the other leading Democratic contenders—Maine senator Edmund Muskie and South Dakota senator George McGovern. "Maybe we can get a scandal on any one of them," Nixon said. Then, countenancing his own chicanery by leveling charges of his experience of unfairness, he reminded Haldeman of his suspicions about Democratic duplicity during his failed gubernatorial campaign in 1962. "How'd I lose?" he groused. "They had access to every goddamned thing you imagine . . . My house! Where they had every goddamned thing!"[8]

A buttoned-up Nixon was careful to control his temper in his three memoirs. He rarely ever carped directly, yet he griped implicitly throughout. Even in his first memoir, written while still a young man, Nixon presented himself, his persistent part, as ever the whipping boy of liberals, political opponents and the media. As his career advanced, and his roles changed, he felt constantly vulnerable. The press mistreated him for being unwilling to give up the family dog Checkers. Protestors hunted him on the streets of Venezuela. Even after major victories, as in the espionage case against Alger Hiss, he complained of being hounded by a liberal press out to get Richard Nixon. For the story he told of his life was born not only from striving, but from complaint. Ever donning the role of the victim, if he was egregious, he insisted, it was because he was aggrieved.

Through much of his career, Nixon's political opponents were drawn from the elite of the elite. First, he ran in 1946 as a dogged underdog for the House of Representatives against Voorhis, the son of a millionaire-automobile executive. Once in Congress, as a member of the House Un-American Activities Committee and in front of seemingly the nation's entire press corps, Nixon faced down the dapper Hiss, a member of the Harvard crowd who directed the lofty ranks of the State Department. Nixon's competitor for a California Senate seat in 1950, Helen Gahagan Douglas, was not only a famed actress, but also married to a

Hollywood executive. When Nixon ran for vice president on Dwight D. Eisenhower's ticket, at the top of the opposing ticket sat Adlai Stevenson, the very definition of refined cosmopolitanism. A Choate and Princeton man, the Democratic nominee's name would become all but synonymous with the United Nations. Then there was the bitter 1960 election loss to the Kennedys, with its nail-biting returns and swirl of rumored cheating in Chicago and Texas.

Nixon harbored a grudging sense that even as he ascended, a tier of the select remained closed off to him. There was a boardroom that he was not allowed to enter, a party to which he had not been invited. Nixon was convinced that for the likes of Voorhis, Hiss, Gahagan Douglas, Stevenson and the Kennedys, life just came easier for the "the dilettantes, the fancy-pants." As the journalist and historian Garry Wills memorably wrote, even as Nixon "worked harder than anyone, . . . he saw others—especially the omnipresent Kennedys—getting an easy ride, laughing at him, undermining the whole point of competitive merit on the human market." With their legacy college admissions and their sinecure appointments, the success of the dilletantes undermined Nixon's belief, instilled by his struggling father, that hard work could set one free, that achievement was a matter of labor. He resolutely maintained that life should be fairer, but then was left vulnerable to suffer depression, what he called "fatalism," when it proved not to be. The repeated blows led him to ramble and rage, his perception of a conspiratorial injustice fueling ire. Then the anger fueled conspiratorial machinations. "The conspiracy of the press," Henry Kissinger recalled, "the hostility of the Establishment, the flatulence of the Georgetown set were permanent features of Nixon's conversation, which one challenged at the cost of exclusion from the inner circle."[9]

Nixon's life story, however, was not the clear-cut path of rejection by elites that he depicted. The stories he told himself, the stories that drove him, the patterns of hurt he experienced were apparent and indeed painful, but not consistently so or foreordained. After all, even though he was rejected by some elite circles—the Kennedy crowd, the Georgetown set—he had still been elected to the highest office in the United States. Upon closer inspection, Nixon's understanding was a "premature entextualization" in the conspiracist mode, a script expunged of contrary evidence in an effort to thicken the plot. For although the elites might have laughed at Nixon, they were not the exquisitely coordinated force he so often purported them to be. They did not consistently win; he lost to Kennedy, but he beat Voorhis, Hiss, Gahagan Douglas and Stevenson. Moreover, Nixon imagined conspiracies among the privileged elite while ignoring his adversaries hailing from modest stock. His foes were not all born lucky and rich. Many came from poor backgrounds like his own, from the bullying Lyndon B. Johnson, the stale Hubert H. Humphrey to the feisty union leader George Meany. He tussled with dogged *New York Times* reporters Neil Sheehan and Max Frankel and Soviet adversaries in the brash Nikita Khrushchev and the hackish Leonid Brezhnev, whom Nixon liked to describe as a working-class, old "Irish labor boss" type.[10]

The apparent string of wealthy opponents was the type of coincidence that an aggrieved and aggravated conspiracist like Nixon filtered, transforming a complex picture into evidence of a foul scheme, a rigged game. His selective storytelling, drawn from incomplete data, focused on the Kennedy fortune while ignoring LBJ's impoverished roots. It was beside the point that much of the ballot stuffing in the 1960 election involved a working-class political machine in the midwestern city of Chicago and poor counties in Texas. Inconvenient was the fact that Nixon had actually climbed the political ranks at record pace funded by donors of his own. Throughout Nixon's career, he found fault lay in various combinations of communists (at home and abroad), big labor, Jews, Blacks, bra burners, draft dodgers, longhairs, secularists, liberals, the Eastern elite and the press. In his mind, the enemies teamed up.

They revealed themselves to be one and the same only then to revert to form as, in Nixon's mind, one hypothesis for their enmity changed to another. His through line was neither racism nor anti-Semitism nor even the bile he stored up for the elite clique of "Harvards." It was paranoia itself. For even as Nixon switched targets, there was ever one more and then another plot needing to be uncovered and soon. Ill fortune was the fault of homosexuals and whores, only then leftists and Jews. Nixon darted from theory to theory to justify his conspiring—because of his enemies' own plotting, the need for expedient information, because of how leaks were undercutting negotiations with the Soviets, Chinese and Vietnamese, the "extremes of violence and discord in the nineteen-sixties," because of the intellectuals and rich kids.[11]

Scholarship has moved away from dismissing such conspiracism as merely misguided pathology. The conspiracy theory is a seductive mode of thought as one scrambles to make the messy neat, to attribute cause to effect. The philosopher Karl Popper argued that the mind sifts through events to deny the random. "We tell ourselves stories in order to live," as Joan Didion wrote. It is what the sociologist Anita M. Waters called an "aversion to the idea of chance in history." At a tipping point, such mental mapping turns to conspiracism with a radical overreading of phenomena. The wrought story, design or alleged proof becomes irrational because the conspiracist believes there to be a higher rationality of cause and effect than actually exists. The philosopher Brian Keeley has called conspiracists "some of the last believers in an ordered universe." Instead of a benevolent God, the conspiracist imagines nefarious man-made design. This alternative, overly rationalized reality has a chiaroscuro quality, a great scission between black and white, yes and no, the revealed and the hidden, good and bad, the working man against the elite. To rationalize one's goodness, to live in the light, there has to be an evil or wrongdoing taking place "behind reality," in the other world, somewhere in the shadows.[12]

As the historian David Brion Davis observed, the "unprecedented danger" of the conspiratorial crisis of the moment remains ever imminent while past alarms fade to a "time of idyllic harmony." Gain in the present remains a fantasy as the plotters remain "too powerful, too far-flung, too invisible, too clever." This narrative of harm and helplessness in the face of hidden power proves maddening as the hoped-for state remains out of reach. In such an echo chamber of pain reverberating, because reality does not match the alternative idealized world of justice and order, the very conspiracy theory, once a balm for rationalization, irritates, aggravates and frustrates. It draws even more attention to injuries received. The paranoid quest impels and impassions hurt, frustration and anger. Rage, rage and belief in conspiracies, as Charles Paul Freund wrote in the *Washington Post*, becomes an "alternative to despair."[13]

Nixon's life stories developed such a repetitive quality, fixing on persistent ideas and dynamics for how his experiences unfolded. He hewed to conspiratorial scripts: he looked not for the approaching army, but for the Trojan Horse; he feared not the invasion, but the infiltration. Indeed, his paranoia went beyond dehumanizing bigotry that slandered his opponents as being less than himself. As Nixon saw it, in quite opposite fashion, those on his ever-growing list of enemies and traitors were well organized, dangerously powerful, a potent and directed force that needed to be immediately confronted. Thus, Nixon formed plots to counter those of the accused. Such "imitation of the enemy," the scholar Richard Hofstadter contended, was central to such conspiracism. Stealth required stealth; indecency by the offending party countenanced indecency by the offended. Ruin necessitated ruin. With grudge and grievance, Nixon unleashed his own plots to trail, uncover and spoil the winnings of the Kennedy ring or the Harvards. He gathered his personal bruisers to match the best and the brightest, his own team of hatchet men—the Haldemans, Charles Colsons and Murray Chotiners—to help concoct and enact his own conspiracies.[14]

At times, Nixon had homosexuals in his sight, for surreptitiously spreading rot in the country. "I won't shake hands with anybody from San Francisco," the president privately vowed. "Decorators. They've got to do something . . . but goddamn it we don't have to glorify it." To Nixon, homosexuals were dirty, contagious. He abhorred the hit comedy *All in the Family*, convinced that Archie Bunker's leftist son-in-law, Mike Stivic, aka "Meathead," was gay. Mike, played by Rob Reiner, was young, opinionated. He was also married to a woman, an outspoken feminist, Gloria. Nonetheless, Nixon railed, "You don't glorify [gays] . . . anymore than you glorify, uh, whores." His homophobia may have stemmed from the boys' club machismo common in his day, but in his mind's eye, even machismo was laced with conspiratorial theory. "When I say they're born that way," Nixon asserted, "the tendency is there. But my point is, that Boy Scout leaders, YMCA leaders, and others, bring them in the [homosexual] direction, and teachers [too]." The rot arose not from some foul gene or festering neurosis, but from cliques of homosexual ingrates and influencers. In conspirative fashion, one eschatological notion led to another and another, never quite enough. To support his point on the homosexual conspiracy, to bolster his nebulous enmity, Nixon reached for another hypothesis. He posited that homosexuals were a sign, and perhaps a cause, of the end of days. "I don't want to see this country go that way," Nixon railed. "You know what happened to the Greeks. Homosexuality destroyed them."[15]

The homosexual enemy was a social set that Nixon clearly misunderstood. He literally misidentified the liberal *All in the Family's* Mike as gay. The president's fuzzy conspiratorial hypotheses merged in the purportedly homosexual "Meathead," the very incarnation of the president's enemies. Mike was the quintessential antiwar, anti-Nixon counterculturist. He had long hair and talked loud. By challenging Archie, his irascible and archconservative father-in-law, he upended family tradition. To call the leftist Mike gay or liken him to a prostitute was to slander progressive and permissive foes like him, all those anti-Nixonites from the "peace at any price" movement to the younger generation preaching sexual liberation. In Nixon's eyes, the contagions from the likes of homosexuals and the likes of the counterculture were polluting the mainstream. One rancorous hypothesis about gays and whores blurred into another conspiratorial claim about hippies, the highly educated and atheists. "[With] the homosexual, the sixteen-year-old that drinks, the public houses of prostitution, you'll have a decadent society," he charged.[16] His was the double vision of the conspiracist and his trials. Homosexuals like Mike needed to be taken off the air, banished from the light, lest their sickness contaminate the American civic body. Yet at the same time, they needed to be outed from the shadows lest they clandestinely infiltrate the country sexually and, thereby, morally.

Nixon's accusations drew on rumors circulating at the height of the Red Scare during the Harry Truman administration of the "international homosexual," the notion that gays were in league with the Soviet Union. The homophobic and anticommunist charge blurred one deviance with another. The morally suspect became the politically suspect with the claim among anti-communists that "sexual perverts" had "infiltrated our government." The historian David K. Johnson calculated that nearly 5,000 homosexuals were accused of communist espionage and ousted from their government jobs, including more than 400 in the State Department alone. Hiss became the poster child for the overly articulate, "effete" and traitorous liberal stalwart who had penetrated the federal ranks. His public image was made suspect by his murky relationship with Whittaker, a man rumored to be a homosexual, in the 1930s. Inconsistent in his theorizing, so great was the threat, Nixon turned the alleged Soviet-homosexual pact upside down. Instead of the allegation of gays as communists, Nixon looked fondly on "Communist societies." So unlike the infected United States, they were, he attested, "Pure in their public ethics . . . And pure in their private lives. They don't stand for anything." In an authoritarian society, such as the Soviets', he professed, threats like homosexuality were tamped down by the strict state. "Dope?" he remarked. "Do you think the Russians allow dope? Hell no."[17]

As for the rise in marijuana use among American youth, the calculated threat by the usual suspects again shifted for Nixon. He grumbled that "homosexuality, dope, uh, immorality in general" represented more than evidence of societal rot; they were weapons wielded furtively by foes against the United States. "Homosexuality, dope, and immorality are the basic enemies of a strong society, and that's why the Russians are pushing it here, in order to destroy us." On another occasion, Nixon turned his attention to find cause in a no less generic collusion, as when he attributed the cannabis craze to another familiar threat. "You know, it's a funny thing," he told Haldeman. "Every one of the bastards that are out for legalizing marijuana is Jewish. What the Christ is the matter with the Jews, Bob?" The chief of staff responded by suggesting yet another of the regime's stock foes, griping, "I suppose it's because most of them are psychiatrists."[18]

Those once struck by Nixon's choler did not soon forget. To his enemies, Nixon was not just an empty suit or an unprincipled climber, a shape-shifter nonpareil and a cheat. They thought him petulant and mean. The longtime and usually even-keeled diplomat W. Averill Harriman swore that he would "not break bread with that man!" Truman called Nixon a "shifty-eyed, goddamn liar" and a "son of a bitch." The writer James Baldwin went with "motherfucker." The left never forgave Nixon for his red-baiting while in the House. They were horrified by his "rocking, socking" Senate campaign against Gahagan Douglas, by how he characterized her as little more than a paramour of Stalin, by how he "savaged" her.[19]

As Nixon's image waxed and waned, as he seemed to slither out of trouble after trouble, his reputation for quick anger grew. The fearsome figure with the five-o-clock shadow had a talent for infuriating his adversaries. During Nixon's second campaign with Eisenhower, Tennessee governor Frank G. Clement, keynote speaker at the 1956 Democratic National Convention, called Nixon the "vice-hatchet man" for his anticommunist tirades against the general's opponents. Nixon appeared to relish in the thick of political "thievery," in his ever-shifting guises, in a willingness to bend to expediency for political advantage. Critics saw him as an opportunist, a shill, a short-fused tyrant. As he harangued against conspiracies, he was thought to be conspiring, selling the public out to big business, to the basest instincts of greed and bigotry. The popular raconteur and newsman Stewart Alsop estimated that Nixon probably had "more enemies than any other American." Alsop's remark was published in the summer of 1958, still a decade before Nixon was elected president.[20]

Already by 1962—long before Watergate and before his execution of the war in Vietnam—Nixon was complaining that he had been accused of "bigamy, forgery, drunkenness, thievery, anti-Semitism, perjury, the whole gamut of misconduct in public office." Six years later, in the summer of 1968 when he discussed his madman theory with Haldeman as they strolled along a foggy beach, Nixon was already confident in his ability to provide the necessary credibility for the strategic ploy, assured that his choleric reputation would lead foes like Ho Chi Minh to "believe any threat of force that Nixon makes because it's Nixon." Indeed, the plan for nuclear blackmail rested on his established standing as a man whose ruthlessness was known to get the best of him.[21]

In the ensuing years, liberals castigated Nixon for his "law and order" postures and his "Southern strategy" to siphon white voters from the Democratic Party by riling up racial resentment among constituents in the former Confederacy. The left rebelled against his escalating the Vietnam War and the carpet bombing of Cambodia and Laos. They called him a war criminal. The gonzo journalist Hunter S. Thompson went further, as was his fashion: "Nixon's very existence is a monument to all the rancid genes and broken chromosomes that corrupt the possibilities of the American dream." This was still years before Nixon's fall, when, the historian Stephen Whitfield noted, "The darkness of [Nixon's] lower face, the thickness of the eyebrows over the piercing, threatening eyes seemed to become heightened with Watergate."[22]

It was not only Nixon's enemies who suffered his malice. Safire judged that Nixon "had a heart too soon made cold, a head too soon made hot." Nixon rarely gave full credit. He critiqued relentlessly. "On and on and on," recalled Richard Helms, then director of the Central Intelligence Agency. This one was "dumb," that one was "stupid." Nixon grumbled incessantly about the military—"The Air Force in their bombings in Vietnam couldn't hit their ass with their hand"—and railed about the State Department and its "bunch of pinstriped cocktail-drinking diplomats." He was so often drawn to bitterly ruminating over paranoia-driven plots and crude countermeasures that it seemed to Helms that Nixon "never trusted anybody." In descriptions of his anger, in attempts to capture his temper, his deputies' words most often grew generic rather than vivid, diffuse rather than specific. Among Nixon's aides, Alexander Butterfield, the Nixon aide who made sure the president's day ran smoothly and keeper of the White House tapes, struggled to convey the extent of his boss's ire. "I don't think people understood how deep these resentments were," Butterfield relayed. "He hated with a passion, and I don't think anyone has quite captured it yet." Such broad and undefined descriptions suggested a sense of his aides' being overwhelmed by his anger. *Lashing* was the word Haldeman used. The chief of staff recounted that in public Nixon had "to control himself," but behind the scenes "on the airplane or in a hotel room . . . [he] lashed out about all the stuff that everybody had done wrong." In the abusive insularity of the regime, cruelty from the boss could be a badge of honor. For the truest believers in Nixonland, the attention that came with a lashing could be a laurel. As his long-time secretary Rose Mary Woods put it to Haldeman, "The greatest compliment that he can pay to you is to lash at you like that, because that is the evidence that he trusts you, respects you."[23]

The search for the source of Nixon's seemingly endless ire became a subject of popular and scholarly inquiry. In the emerging field of psychohistories, the first tomes on Nixon appeared in the early 1970s. The very term *psychohistory* worked its way into common parlance just then along with all its iterative forms—*psychohistorian, psychohistorical* and *psychobiography,* or what one writer called "academeobehaviorilism."" The application of psychoanalysis to examine the temperaments of historical figures dates to Sigmund Freud's investigation of the life and "individual psychopathology" of Leonardo DaVinci (1910), but it was the developmental psychologist Erik Erikson who popularized the term with two case studies, *Young Man Luther* (1958) and *Gandhi's Truth* (1969). Erikson investigated how his subjects' psyches functioned as they developed throughout their lives. By contrast to more traditional biographies, his approach closely tracked not only change, but also the persistence of themes and mental constructs, such as unconscious compulsions fixed in childhood—what Freud referred to as the "intensely tilled soil from which our virtues proudly emerge." To locate the roots of personality, psychohistories focused particularly on the "identity crisis," the time, usually during adolescence or young adulthood, "when each youth must forge himself some central perspective and direction . . . out of the effective remnants of his childhood and the hopes of his anticipated adulthood."[24]

Psychohistory became popular in the United States during a period when increasingly large numbers of Americans were seeking psychiatric care. In 1970, 1 million underwent mental health treatment in hospitals and private clinics, and another million did so as outpatients. By

1975, the number of patients had risen to 6 million as large private insurance providers and Medicaid expanded benefits to include psychotherapy. As the historian David Greenberg has noted, comics from Woody Allen to Bob Newhart joked about their time on the couch as a psychological vocabulary entered the public lexicon as part of the furniture.[25]

Despite psychohistorians seemingly revolutionary intentions, their work proved to be a stabilizing force. Amid the political and cultural turbulence in the wake of the sixties' revolutions, the psychohistory promised to offer something real—an explanation. Psychohistories served as a counterweight to the dizzying talk of the postmodern, of images, representations and the unknowability of a person. They sought Truth behind the facades of analysands. Instead of deconstructing a postmodern subject into constituent elements and competing forms, psychohistory sought to reconstruct the singular personality, to uncover and unite conscious and unconscious drives. Leading political figures from the archconservative Barry Goldwater to the progressive LBJ had been judged by many as unreliable kooks or madmen. Psychohistory promised a tool to bring to light rational complexities—the "complexes"—behind such powerful men, to find reason in the seemingly unreasonable. At the same time, psychohistory allowed erring leaders to be identified as errant, as exceptions. In this way, the confusion and disappointment in American society could be pinned on deviant, pathological individuals.

As psychohistory became institutionalized in conferences and academic organizations, hailed as the "next assignment" for the academy, the ever-slippery Nixon emerged as a prime subject for the Truth-seeking field. The ensuing portraits of Nixon attempted to explain his "warped character." They described his conflicting desire for closeness and escape from his tight-knit family. They traced a line from his "hateful, raging" father to his "identification with the aggressor" to a need to dole out "equivalent humiliations." Fawn Brodie, the most prominent of Nixon's psychohistorians, concluded that Nixon had learned the "art and necessity of denial" from his "outwardly saintly" but cold mother. The British psychoanalyst D. W. Winnicott speculated that Hannah's intensive care for Nixon's brothers and strangers alike left the future president forever in a state of feeling second-rate. Psychohistorians linked Nixon's grief over the loss of his two brothers to a "fascination with death." Some reached even further with Freudian flourishes common at the time, suggesting "orality," "anality" and "castration anxiety" due to his troubled childhood. Brodie looked for proof of latent homosexual feelings between Nixon and his close confidant Charles G. "Bebe" Rebozo. The more rigorous found much fodder as they aimed to unearth a malicious temperament formed in childhood.[26]

In oral histories and retrospective interviews, acquaintances and family reported a restrained anger in Nixon going back to his earliest years. They recounted the future president's isolating, broody, ruminating moods. Rather than his later explosive reputation, his classmates remembered Nixon as "strained and tightly strung," a "very tense person," "something of an oddball," "slightly paranoid." He was remembered as a largely friendless loner in whom one could sense a controlled resentment. "He wouldn't argue much," his brother Donald recounted, but on one occasion as a boy, Nixon got so angry he was unable to restrain himself. He lost control. He "cut loose" and "kept at it for a half to three quarters of an hour," the younger Nixon remembered. "He didn't leave out a thing. I was only eight, and he was ten." In law school, he displayed a sullen temper, earning him the nickname "Gloomy Gus." As one housemate remembered, he was "somewhat limited in humor." He seemed tense by nature, driven, found most often hunched over his books. Another roommate remarked that when angered, they "could feel his rage," but also that they had missed appreciating "his ineffable loneliness."[27]

Still, for all the sweeping analyses—which one reviewer called "world-historical *chutzpah*"—there was also a hesitance of conclusion in psychohistorians' examination of so distanced a personality as Nixon. They stumbled as they wrote of how "it would seem that . . . perhaps . . . may have . . . quite possibly . . . some evidence that . . ." Many historians criticized Erikson's focus on "great men" with little attention on the forces of cultural origins, social movements and socioeconomic context. Some charged that the Nixon psychohistorians were all Democrats out for political revenge against a long-elusive foe. Social critics like Christopher Lasch and Tom Wolfe condemned the field and American culture more generally for discarding the passionate civil and women's movements of the 1960s for a "culture of narcissism" and an embrace of the "Me" decade in the 1970s. Some skeptics pointed out that psychohistory violated one central tenet of psychoanalysis—namely, that psychoanalysis required intensive one-on-one interaction between analyst and analysand. Others pointed out that if Freud was correct in identifying the early years as the most developmentally critical, how did scholars gather that most crucial data when those years were almost inevitably the most bare of contemporary historical accounts, indeed highly dependent on hearsay. As one critic in the *Nation* carped, how to explain all those "hordes of boys [who] grow up sadly in families with violent fathers and castrating mothers. They don't all turn into Richard Nixons."[28]

Psychohistorical speculation waned when the archived Nixon-related materials began to be released, and Nixon's contemporaries started to share their tales of him in the late 1980s and 1990s. Exhaustively researched biographies of Nixon began to fill bookstore and library shelves. Historians and journalists including Stephen Ambrose, Roger Morris, Herbert Parmet, Melvin Small and Tom Wicker turned from the focus on a fixed personality formed in Nixon's childhood to map the story of how Nixon changed through his life. Some still held to the psychodynamic angle, what Ambrose called the "theme of the unloved boy" that "helped make Richard ambitious, eager to show his parents what he could do," but the longform biographies presented heavily descriptive narratives based on meticulous scrutiny of Nixon's records, revelatory oral history projects and Oval Office tapes.[29]

The longform biographies, as per that genre, sought a narrative through line in Nixon's life. With such pithily weighted titles as *Nixon: The Education of a Politician* or *Nixon: The Life* or *Nixon: A Life*, they traced the corruptive path of a scrappy Dick Nixon from hard-scrabble youth to compromised politico. In chronological arcs, they focused on patterns of ever-accumulating struggles in his treacherous climb. Turning from the temperamental to the social, class became a major driving construct for understanding his resentments. Nixon saw intellectuals and elites as an exclusive gang not dissimilar to the rich kids he went to college with, the ones who had no need to work their way through school. In one often-told story, in the early 1930s Nixon helped found his own counter-exclusive group of peers born of lesser means. At Whittier College, the well-to-do had formed the Franklins, a rowdy "literary society." They were, to Nixon, all fashion. They set the pace, but Nixon was determined to determine his own. He and his friends founded the Orthogonians, fashioning their club after the fraternity stylings of the Franklins. Yet in school photographs, the Franklins donned tuxedoes while the Orthogonians wore open-collared shirts to symbolize, so the biographer Aitken judged, their "proletarianism." Contrary to their country club counterparts, the Orthogonians adopted the "Four B's" as their moral code—Beans, Brawn, Brain and Bowls. As the journalist Rick Perlstein argued in his retelling of the story, the future president began a pattern he would follow throughout his career. As an alternative to the exclusive set, Nixon gathered his own, a "nonspectacular—silent—majority."[30]

Several biographers made particular note of the poverty Nixon experienced during his time at Duke University's law school. They turned to detailed description to capture the depth of Nixon's struggles and perseverance. Nixon and four of his classmates shared a hovel that lacked heat and a working toilet. They called it Whippoorwill Manor: one room with two double iron beds for five dollars a month. Having no sink, they showered on campus. For three years, Nixon ate a Milky Way bar for breakfast. Yet after graduating from Duke third in his class, the glossy Wall Street law firms still turned him away. So, too, the FBI. Hat in hand, he had to return to tiny Whittier, California.

Whereas the psychohistories focused on Nixon's early feelings of deprivation, the longform biographies underscored his ambition as being at the heart of both his success and his failure. Indeed, Nixon's drive and downfall read like a morality tale. Rather than attributing his rage to early experiences, the long sweep of the biographies charted how Nixon's ire grew over the course of navigating the adult world of crass and hardball politics. Wicker wrote that the president's life story was a lesson in how the "power to corrupt embodied the dark, struggling, realistic side of the nation." Morris wrote that the "gradual atrophy of ethics that ended so painfully thirty years later" had begun during Nixon's first campaign against Voorhis. Nixon's resentment grew from the controversy surrounding his prosecution of the diplomat Hiss as a Soviet spy, the Checkers episode, the questionable loss to Kennedy followed by the outright loss in his challenge for the California governorship, the swirling scandals all culminating in his resignation over the Watergate scandal. In place of the harsh critique of psychohistorians, his biographers presented Nixon as a character not to hate but to pity. Ambrose wrote of how "surely this author is not alone in thinking that it must have been a terrible thing to be Richard Nixon." Wicker turned to quoting the introductory note to Joseph Conrad's *Lord Jim*: "It was for me, with all the sympathy of which I was capable, to seek fit words for his meaning. He was 'one of us.'"[31]

In *Witness to Power*, John Ehrlichman's first-person account, Nixon's chief domestic advisor emphasized his boss's predilection for political battle. He wrote, "We fail to recognize that he is an animal which has been groomed to run a special race and has forgotten how to do almost everything else." Nixon agreed. He rejected the temperamental explanations of the psychohistories that concentrated on pain dating back to his formative years. He considered such analysis psychobabble and an affront. Monica Crowley, a close foreign policy assistant, noted, "Of the many criticisms leveled at him, the one he found most egregious was that he was insecure." As Nixon told one journalist, "That sort of juvenile self-analysis is something I've never done."[32]

Nixon preferred the portrayals in the longform biographies suggesting that his rough edges stemmed from his Horatio Algeresque efforts during his adulthood in response to the pointy-elbowed bruising he endured for decades in his long political climb. His was a version of the old saw that power corrupts. "My reaction to the Watergate break-in was completely pragmatic," the former president tried to explain. "If it was also cynical, it was a cynicism born of experience." He circled back to elite conspiracies, to the Kennedy's rough play—"rich" and "ruthless." The Kennedys served ever as his foil. In Nixon's mind, the easy winnings by the exclusive set stood in stark contrast to his hard-fought struggles. Their story, not his, was the tale of ill morals, the foul and injustice in the world spawned from them. "[The Kennedy's] may play softball out on the White House lawn, . . . but it's tackle football all the way," he fumed in his retirement. Compelled to drive home the unfairness, Nixon pointed to Robert Kennedy's battle against Humphrey for the Democratic nomination in 1968, still irking him after more than two decades. The Kennedys bombarded Wisconsin with "vicious anti-Catholic literature," he charged. Humphrey was from Minnesota, and the anti-Catholic mailers were postmarked from Minnesota. "Everybody thought Hubert did it," Nixon charged. Only after the campaign was it discovered that the scurrilous literature had been sent by an aide to Robert Kennedy.[33]

As the longform biographies of Nixon's life moved chronologically through the chapters of his presidency, they eventually arrived at the tangled web of Nixon's crimes. No matter the descriptions, no matter the sympathetic qualifier, the books eventually bulged with account after account of skullduggery. As Bob Woodward and Carl Bernstein first reported, a slush fund of hundreds of thousands of dollars was kept in a safe at the White House for "intelligence work" by the Committee for the Re-election of the President, fittingly, some felt, known as CREEP. Nixon had candidates' families secretly photographed and followed for opposition research. He ordered financial audits of his opponents. He had the Black Panthers surveilled along with anti-war groups, including Students for a Democratic Society. He arranged for a wiretap and burglary of the psychiatrist's office of Daniel Ellsberg, leaker of the Pentagon Papers, and of the home Ron Ridenhour, who leaked word of the My Lai massacre. During Ellsberg's trial, alone, Nixon ordered wiretaps on reporters from CBS, the London *Sunday Times*, *New York Times* and *Washington Post*. Not stopping at the opposition, Nixon also bugged his own staff. For more than a year, the president his ne'er-do-well younger brother, Donald, under electronic surveillance.[34]

At the high-water mark in the publication of the popular Nixon biographies, a school of revisionist scholars emerged in the academy who contended that the portraits to date had failed to depict the "real Nixon." The historians Irwin Gellman and Joan Hoff echoed Nixon's claim that the psychohistorians and his biographers were an "elite group of politicians, journalists and scholars" fixated on ruining his legacy. They criticized these writers as "Nixon-haters" and "Nixonphobes" unfairly and without warrant drawing a caricature of Nixon as a wrathful figure. They charged that previous treatments had been overly influenced by former opponents bent on retaliating against Nixon for his hard-hitting campaign style and former allies bent on revenge for some perceived perfidy. If not political and personal, it was recency bias as biographers lingered not on Nixon's long political career, but too much on the still fresh memory of his demise, short-sightedly reading his early rise and long rule as mere precursors to his fall.[35]

The revisionists characterized Nixon as a man of his times ensconced in the thinking of his era. They argued that the anticommunist tactics that had so marred Nixon's record were "as American as apple pie in the 1940s." Hoff wrote that the former president's use of the racist Southern strategy to garner votes paled in comparison to his longer record of support for the civil rights movement. As for Vietnam and aiding a coup against Chilean president Salvador Allende, Nixon's political excesses were consistent with the "consensus" politics of the Cold War. His extralegal quashing of dissent was the continuation the CIA's espionage against domestic targets in Operation CHAOS and the Army's targeting of leftists abroad under its CONUS program. Hoff argued, "The United States has never fought a war without violating the constitutional rights of its citizens. Vietnam was no exception. What was exceptional was the increased sensitivity of people toward violations."[36]

To see Nixon "objectively," Gellman wrote, was to pierce the "visceral hatred" of his long list of enemies, to see beyond Nixon's political chicanery, beyond the excesses typical of the Cold War era, to evaluate his substantive record. The real Nixon, Gellman maintained, was a "dedicated, efficient public servant" who rose through the ranks through political acumen and hard work, not, as with Watergate, through dirty trickery. Hoff saw Nixon as a pragmatic reformer, citing his far-reaching programs to protect the environment and curb abuses against Native Americans' rights, his attempt to reform welfare through large cash infusions and block grants to states, how he extended welfare support to senior citizens and the disabled, how he poured money into food stamps and his war against cancer. For liberal historians distraught over President Ronald Reagan's small government revolution of the 1980s, the revisionism of

Nixon's record was a project of redemption. Through it, Nixon could be reclaimed if not as a liberal lion and an elder statesman, at least as a powerful, progressive pragmatist. Accordingly, Reagan's tenure was characterized as a turn away from the sweep of liberalism through the second half of the twentieth century. Nixon's domestic policies were recast as an extension of Roosevelt's New Deal and Johnson's Great Society. The Republican Nixon was dubbed the "last of the Big Spenders."[37]

How to square the circle between Nixon the progressive reformer and the ruthless cheat? Between the lonely child and the dogged climber? Between the able statesman and the war criminal? More recently, some authors have emphasized the strong contradictions in Nixon's character. The historian Iwan Morgan argues, "Nixon was *both* much better *and* much worse than the norm." The journalist Evan Thomas in his popular account intertwined the positive and negative valuations of Nixon in writing of how "the fears and insecurities that led him into sinfulness also gave him the drive to push past self-doubt, . . . to see, often though sadly not always, the light in the dark." The biographer John Farrell's bestselling *Richard Nixon: The Life* returned to the psychohistorical perspective, treating Nixon's fraught upbringing as a basis for a life of recurrent, raging victimhood. Like the revisionists, Farrell also placed Watergate "in a different context, part of a continuum [in American politics] . . . no sole breach of faith."[38]

A wave of cultural histories in the last two decades have produced far-reaching reevaluations of Nixon, eschewing the task of arriving at a singular understanding of the former president. Daniel Frick wrote of how Nixon came to project the United States' dueling self-images: on the one hand, a gallant Horatio Alger; on the other, a thieving and imperialist crook. He was a bogeyman for his anti-communism just as he was a champion for his silent majority. For Nixon supporters on the right, he fought against the intellectual, effete class. For Nixon detractors, he embodied the corrupt and controlling politician. He became a symbol of the culture wars and the answer to the very question of who is un-American. As Perlstein concluded, "Nixonland . . . is the America where two separate and irreconcilable sets of apocalyptic fears coexist," with the Hisses, Stevensons and George McGoverns, and the hippies pitted against the Goldwaterites, John Birchers and Bible-thumpers.[39]

Rather than focusing primarily on temperament or class or a cynicism grown from politics, the cultural historians looked to a generational frame to understand Nixon's ire. They argued that Nixon was not alone or exceptional in his conspiratorial ideation. The scholar Kathryn S. Olmsted wrote of how his cohort was raised at a time of suspicion, of loyalty tests, an FBI run amok by J. Edgar Hoover and a CIA flexing its newborn, covert muscles. Conspiracy theories began to circulate and amass about Pearl Harbor, the Bay of Pigs, the Kennedy assassination. The creeping power of the New Deal and then the Great Society's welfare state provided ample fodder for accusations of corruption and maleficent design. After all, as Olmsted noted, Nixon's generation came of age under the manic suspicions of communist infiltration of the government, a conspiracy, as Joseph McCarthy preached, "on a scale so immense as to dwarf any previous such venture in the history of man."[40]

This Cold War motif, an obsession with brainwashing and group-think, was not confined to the right but found traction among liberal and radical intellectuals as well. Matching the right's feverish worrying over socialist communism, the American left was gripped by suspicions about the controlling hand of capitalism. Big business was said to have become a mind-numbing force crippling the individual, rendering him a company man, a bureaucrat, an atomized slave. In the popular nightmare vision laid out by William H. Whyte, Jr., in *The Organization Man* (1956), the human capitalist cogs speak in a new patois of "administrator" and "manager." Their new shrines were the "conference table, the workshop, the seminar, the skull session . . . , the project team." The highest value among Organization Men developed into the tenet of "belongingness"—that is, "the deep emotional security that comes from total integration with the group." Whyte's fears echoed the mass social "contentment" in Aldous Huxley's *Brave New World* (1932) and the stifling conformity of George Orwell's *1984* (1949). Rather than pursuing individual achievement, rather than organizing rebellion or collectively disagreeing, Organization Men band together in elevating, even cherishing the soul-stultifying efforts of group work. In the age of Nixon, conservative anti-communism and liberal anti-corporatism became twin and overlapping anxieties over modern society's descent into collectivism. Both the left and the right worried that championing of the masses would overtake the long-valued ideal of individualism. Both were concerned about the casting aside of the hard-labor, thrift and competition of the long-cherished Protestant Ethic. In both nightmare visions, the nation itself, bureaucratization, mass media and the overwhelming force of mind control—whether by elites in big government or big business types—were said to threaten the founding values that Americans once held dear. In the end, as the sociologist C. W. Mills worried in the polemical *White Collar* (1956), the individual would always be "somebody's man, the corporation's, the government's, the army's."[41]

Perlstein and Kevin Mattson—as several of Nixon's biographers had done, including Parmet and Wicker—identified the "real Nixon" as part of a cultural subset of such Cold War frustrations, in the furious silent majority that elevated him to the presidency. This imagined Caucasian community of Organization Men set their sights on the life of comforts promised by the post–Great Depression, postwar boom of Pax Americana only then to be forced to make sense of the difference between the abundance of national wealth and their experiences of unpaid mortgages and halted upward mobility. Like Nixon, few of these "forgotten men" served with distinction in the military. They returned home from war to idle in the perfectly unexceptional pleasures of Ozzie and Harriet, the perfectly content nuclear family. They scrimped and saved for the title to an average house on an above-average block, an Oldsmobile in the garage, a roomy ice box and a cabinet for the television. Like Pat Nixon, their wives wore not mink but Republican cloth coats. They experienced a sense of anomie, of alienation from the good life, of being left out and left behind. Richard Hofstadter and his liberal contemporaries in Nixon's day termed their unrequited angst "status anxiety." Only then war broke out again—this time in Southeast Asia—spilling over into protests, riots and violence on American streets. Rights movements led by a younger generation challenged, fought over and overturned ingrained notions of race, class and gender. Then, for the working and middling classes came the scourges of recession, inflation, oil embargos and de-industrialization.[42]

And the elite on the left did laugh. Instead of celebrating the generation of struggling veterans or sympathizing with suffering middle-aged middle managers, a counterculture of sex, drugs and rock n' roll glamorized itself as freer, as hipper, as living the high life. They pilloried conservatives as boring, as missing out, as pathologically jealous, as "squares." The ascendant liberal elite trumpeted the New Deal order and the Cold War fight as a time for "consensus." They celebrated a government empowered to great feats in the twentieth century, from Roosevelt's Tennessee Valley Authority to Eisenhower's Interstate Highway System, from welfare and increased services to uplift the poor and working classes to expanding civil rights to women and minorities, especially Blacks. As revisionist historians have charged, the scholarly establishment in Nixon's day championed the progressive agenda as not only right but rational. They diagnosed conservative leaders as proselytizing with a uniquely "paranoid style." Social scientists of the New York intellectual set like Hofstadter, Daniel Bell and Seymour Martin Lipset concluded that the raging conservative flank was fueled chiefly by populist grievance and discontent, by a backlash against social and cultural change. Conservatives, not the countercultural left, were the true extremists. As Bell dubbed them, they were the "radical right."[43]

Many historians have more recently come to understand this era of conservatism in its "multiple strands" as a long-standing, vibrant and intellectually rooted political tradition rather than an acerbic backlash to the 1960s as commonly leveled against the right-wing by Nixon's liberal contemporaries. Conservative thought far predated the Nixon generation and the liberal revolutions of the New Deal era, stretching from the eighteenth-century Anglo-Irish theorist Edmund Burke to twentieth-century writers George Santayana and T. S. Eliot. Rather than merely status anxiety and a rejection of the counterculture, modern conservativism broadly preached its own message of libertarianism, traditionalism and anti-communism. This ethos combined Nixon's sentimentalism with his Gospel of Achievement. Like Nixon, the right glorified the tenacity of the underdog Horatio Alger working his way up and Mr. Smith on his way to clean up Washington. They promoted an ethos of hard work, of the laboring man. In their caricature of the right as unhinged, bizarre and archaic, the contemporary social scientists Hofstadter, Bell and Lipset accused their conservative adversaries of conspiracism. In doing so, however, they overlooked many of their opponents' often constructive pushes for local, rather than federal, government, for competition, rather than control and a fear of the brutalizing, communist states.[44]

In the postwar years, migration to the Southwest, to Orange County, California, to Scottsdale, Arizona, to Fort Worth, Texas, provided a base for the sunny Americanism of Ronald Reagan to unite neoconservative hawks with social conservatives. An anti-communist ethos against the power of the state in general brought free marketeers and traditional Christians together. Populist concerns focused on the moral, "the autonomy of communities, the erosion of individualism, the authority of the family and the place of religion in national life." As the historian Lisa McGirr described it, the word spread through church circles and coffee klatches, barbeques and bridge clubs, rallies and study groups that conservatives called Freedom Forums. Far from simply a bottom-up, working-class revolt or a revanchism fomented by outcasts and those left behind by the New Deal order, the philosophies of great, if controversial, thinkers such as the Austrian economist Friedrich Hayek to the German-American philosopher Leo Strauss undergirded the libertarian and traditionalist effort. The University of Chicago economist Milton Friedman promoted the "unshackling" of the American free market from high taxes and regulatory constraints. As the historian Donald T. Critchlow wrote, the right's preoccupations—"fiscal responsibility, returning power to the states, peace through military strength, and the importance of individual responsibility in maintaining civil society"—became mainstream.[45]

While running for the presidency in 1964, Arizona senator Barry Goldwater translated the nineteenth-century laissez-faire ideal into a conservative movement to become the point of the political spear. His assault on FDR's welfare state cut more sharply than the anodyne suburban uplift and "old-fashioned" community building of the broader conservative constituency. Goldwaterism was an embrace of the moniker of the "radical right," as the senator insisted, "Extremism in the defense of liberty is no vice." His mission served as a counterassault against the counterculture's gains, a political awakening for a generation of young right-wingers, emboldening them to compete against the liberal wave of civil rights, women's rights and social reform. "It was learning how to *act*," Perlstein wrote. It was an education in "how letters got written, how doors got knocked on, . . . how to picket, and how, if need be, to infiltrate—how to make the anger boiling inside you ennobling, productive, *powerful*." The senator from Arizona sharpened the conservative mélange of libertarianism, traditionalism and anticommunism to a pique, generating what the scholar Alfred Moore has called a "politics of conspiracy." In *The Conscience of a Conservative*—something of a Little

Red Book for crusading young conservatives—Goldwater warned of nothing less than totalitarianism. Government had become a Leviathan in the "hands of a few men." A small governing elite had bought off the electorate with free programs ranging from housing to hospitalization—all under the "veil" of helping the needy. Welfarism was as "absolute as the oriental despot," Goldwater wrote. Public education inculcated the nation's youth with the mentality of the "mass mind." The United States was not, as Reagan began preaching in the 1970s, a "city upon a hill." America had become a degenerate society led by the traitorous few. Goldwater opined about the trappings of a New Deal conspiracy, "I fear Washington and centralized government more than I do Moscow."[46]

In *The Emerging Republican Majority* (1969), an exegesis that caught conservatives' attention, Nixon Justice Department aide Kevin Phillips advocated wooing the "heartland" to the conservative cause. He called for focusing on mainstream resentment against the liberal wedge issues of "moral permissiveness, experimental residential, welfare and education programing [*sic*] and massive federal spending." Analogous to Goldwater's politics of conspiracy, Phillips argued that the "whole secret of politics [was] knowing who hates who." As civil rights movements pressed the issue of lingering racial inequality in the public square, a backlash of "soft" segregationist tactics spread to the North. Moderate conservatives banded together to preserve racial stratification through redlining, zoning of city blocks and defense of "property rights" in the suburbs. Charismatic evangelical leaders like Jerry Falwell and James Dobson promoted traditionalism through "pro-family" ideologies to combat the insurgent women's and gay rights movements and the emergent secular culture. A group of corporate titans funded a campaign for "Christian libertarianism" to replace the Social Gospel of the New Deal with a Gospel of Free Enterprise. They constructed media empires, think tanks and elaborate political campaigns to counter those relied on by the liberal establishment.[47]

Nixon in his Hiss days brought a moderate face to the anti-communism fight on behalf of the fervent House Un-American Activities Committee. In the 1968 and 1972 presidential elections, Nixon provided a moderate face for the emergent conservative cause. He took up the mantle of wooing white working-class and suburban conservatives, playing on Goldwater's populism and its politics of grievance, its air of conspiracism, but without the overt calls to extremism, racism and Southern revanchism. To conservatives in the South, Nixon promised southern Supreme Court nominees, a slowing of the integration of schools by opposing busing and any programs of "enforced" integration. He preached a strict bill of law and order to those concerned with violence on the streets and across college campuses, those upset by challenges to the social hierarchies of race and the flourishing women's rights movement, to those threatened by an uproarious counterculture. "The first civil right of every American is to be free from domestic violence," he espoused.[48]

In a groundbreaking advertisement campaign for the 1968 presidential election, Nixon's team created a common language for the still evolving revolutionary new medium of television. It featured a vernacular with flashes of images—of underdogs, of farmers and hard hats—to invoke a sense of common and communal fortitude. The sequences of laborers harkened to the hallowed idea of the centrality of hard work rather than a lament over social circumstance or systemic rot. "Have you noticed? The same faces reappear in different spots," one of his admen remarked. "The same pictures are used again and again. They become symbols, recurring like notes in an orchestrated piece. The Alabama sharecropper with the vacant stare, the vigorous young steelworker, the grinning soldier." Nixon's was a populist call-to-arms for those "non-demonstrators and non-shouters" who did not think but labored for their paycheck, who were being left behind, who, as Nixon said, did not just "wail and bellow."[49]

In accepting the 1968 Republican nomination for president, Nixon spoke defiantly of "forgotten men." In conspiracist fashion, he mapped out the by-then familiar chiaroscuro of light and dark, of revelation and lies, of us versus them, drawing a dividing line through the American body politic. He railed vaguely but with a forceful defiance against the dark, the "old voices, the voices of hatred, the voices of dissension, the voices of riot and revolution"—throwing together a conspiracist's admixture of enemies, an alliance of corrupt New Dealers of a previous generation and the rowdy demonstrations of the new hippy set. He rallied those in the light, the Ozzie and Harriets, "those who did not break the law, people who pay their taxes and go to work," those who "love this country [and] are angry about what has happened to America." His focus turned from Vietnam to law and order, from fighting the foreign abroad to confronting the un-American at home, from the new battles afoot to battles long passed. "Did we come all this way for this? Did American boys die in Normandy, and Korea, and in Valley Forge for this?" Nixon beseeched the crowd gathered in the Miami Beach Convention Center.[50]

On stage at the convention, as Nixon's voice lifted, his smile appeared genuine. It was a rare moment for him, looking, in his populist guise, at ease. Yet after the speech, in the glow of one of his greatest oratory triumphs, that very night, Nixon became inconsolable. He grew even more embittered, his sense of grievance stirred, for it was not just a performance. In his grievance, he felt only more alone; in success, he felt alone. "Success," Kissinger noted, "seemed to unsettle Nixon more than failure. He seemed obsessed by the fear that he was not receiving adequate credit." That night, still wound up, Nixon took his bottomless plaint to his speechwriter, Safire, raving against the press again, against those who wrote the "official" accounting. He preemptively struck out against the critics he believed were ever plotting against him. "None of them could write a speech like that," Nixon charged as he ruminated over criticism yet to be leveled. "They call me intelligent and cool and no sincerity and then it kills them when I show 'em I know how people feel." He groused to Safire for an hour-and-a-half, until three in the morning. He insisted that the elite were engaged in battle not only against his middling constituents, but against Richard Nixon himself. The populist story and his own woe he blurred into one. Their fight became his own, as he saw himself as the avatar for the disenchanted conservative. "And they hate me for it . . . They won't like the speech, will they? The *New York Times* and those boys. Fuck 'em," he railed, deflecting, preemptively shielding himself with an unwavering sense of being wronged.[51]

In late 1967, Nixon tested a name for his target constituency of the wronged and aggrieved, his hard hats, calling them the "broad and vital center." He suggested the "great majority of Americans, the forgotten Americans." He tried the "real majority." Only days before a speech on Vietnam delivered as president on November 3, 1969, did he settle on the "great silent majority." It was an odd turn of phrase. "You know," Safire—a renowned etymologist, himself—noted, "to join the silent majority means to die and go on and become part of a cemetery." To prepare the speech, Nixon requested briefing books and news clippings and cleared his afternoons. It was late nights, sometimes until two in the morning, hunched over yellow legal pads or dictating to his lead secretary, Woods, in the White House, in his hideaway in the Executive Office Building, in the Lincoln sitting room, alone for nine days at Camp David. "[It would be] the biggest audience that I'd had up to that time in the presidency, and I think the biggest audience that any president has had up to that time," Nixon later boasted. To generate viewer interest in the speech, the administration chose not to distribute advance copies to the press—no means to "destroy the effect," he explained.[52]

Nixon took his time as he spoke to the millions of Americans gathered that November night around their television sets to watch the innocuously titled "Address to the Nation on the War in Vietnam." He re-viewed at length the history of U.S. involvement in Vietnam to a nation already too well versed in the quagmire. He made a point of highlighting the complicity of Eisenhower, Kennedy and Johnson. He invoked the domino theory, arguing that the fall of Vietnam would lead to the collapse of Southeast Asia. He adopted, as the *Washington Post* described, "the veneer of tough talk." He had a plan for victory and a gradual with-drawal of troops, a "peace with honor." The time frame, however, had to remain secret because, if given a withdrawal date, the North Vietnamese would "simply wait until our forces had withdrawn and then move in."[53]

It was only in the last section, nearly two-thirds into the talk, that Nixon addressed his own constituency directly, only then that the speech became historic. He pivoted to woo the newly christened silent major-ity. "If a vocal minority prevails over reason," over "the will of the ma-jority," he inveighed as Goldwater had, "this Nation has no future as a free society." Nixon raised the stakes once again. It was the script of the populist and the conspiracist, of the notion that power had been high-jacked by a cavorting few. A vocal minority, those marchers and demon-strators, threatened the very character of the nation. They threatened to rule not by ballot, but by shouting, by drowning the majority's voice. Such was the disquieted rumblings of the "silent center," the "emerging majority." Nixon's political strategy rested on "the millions of people in the middle of the American political spectrum . . . who do not picket or protest loudly." In the speech, Nixon had first spoken out against the North Vietnamese, the foreign adversary. Then, in well-established American tradition, he turned to implicitly label his domestic adversar-ies, the vocal minority—those protestors, the government, the rich—as not patriotic, as un-American. He contended that in the rhetorical tit-for-tat, the New Left were the true "radicals." In firing up a populist rage, Nixon channeled Joseph McCarthy's "I'm just a farm boy" populism—the rah, rah, fight, fight-against-the-effete establishment at the heart of the Wisconsin senator's anti-communist campaign. He called his adversaries the "new barbarians," insinuating that so far from his patriotic followers, his foe was an invading horde, as he rejected the "phony youth culture" of the Beatles and the Rolling Stones, as he touted his supporters as the true Americans. For Nixon's battle was not merely a war of ideas, but a clash of cultures.[54]

The morning after the silent majority speech, Nixon boasted that he had received telegrams, in the "high thousands," from a new army of Americans. They were clerks, farmers and struggling veterans, those with their faces flashing in his 1968 ad campaign, those who supported the war, who loved country music and disdained the marijuana and LSD fads. Nixon's goal was to turn back the clock to a wayward nationalism. Haldeman called it a "revival of the 'World War II'" generation. Within two weeks, hundreds of thousands Nixon followers would march on Veterans Day to show support for a military under attack from the "vocal minority." Thousands gathered at State and Madison in Chicago to celebrate their war heroes, to see flyovers in downtown Milwaukee, helicopters equipped with loudspeakers over Gary, with forty-one bands over two days in Birmingham. Those backing the war in Vietnam drove with their headlights burning during the day. "Be seen if not heard," a man adorned in a flag pin and pro-Nixon buttons called out over a loudspeaker as he motored through Manhattan.[55]

The Nixonites saw themselves as counterrevolutionaries, as nationalist revanchists. They were reclaiming the United States as their own. They had sat on their couches silently watching protests on their television; now they had decided to join an army of the silent majority. On that Veterans Day, they posed with Nike missiles in Long Beach, gathered at village houses and state houses, flags flying, generals and admirals and young troops in formation with hats removed, color guards and firing squads volleying gun salutes, with bugles blowing taps and wreathes laid. Resolutions were read in support of the Constitution, of the president. A generation of aggrieved conservatives echoed Nixon's call for law and order, embracing his fiery ire against the left and their protests. His anger, his madness was not only evocative; it was central to their demonstrations. The gatherings on that Veteran's Day by Nixon's followers were, *Newsweek* described, full-throated "counterattack[s] . . . not only over the war itself but over the legitimacy of dissent." It was a turn by the "non-shouters" to shout at the shouters with whom they took issue. The conservative cry matched protest with protest, a demonstration against the despised action of demonstration. It was the "imitation of the enemy," as Hofstadter had predicted.[56]

Fifteen thousand attended the Freedom Rally held at the Washington Monument. They turned counterculture fashion and hip insults upside down, proudly and defiantly declaring themselves "squares." They were mostly white, middle aged, no beards, no mustaches. They wore red, white, and blue armbands to protest the popular attacks against patriotism. A well-shorn country band from rural Virginia performed Merle Haggard's "Okie from Muskogee," a current hit on the country music chart. As they strummed, the lyrics remonstrated against a spiritual, patriotic, and moral decay threatening the nation:

> We don't smoke the marijuana in Muskogee
> We don't take our trips on LSD
> We don't burn our draft cards down on Main Street
> We like living right and being free.

The young coordinator of the massive rally had been an avid Goldwater supporter. Like so many unreconstructed hawks, he did not back Nixon's plan for a gradual withdrawal from Vietnam. He wanted "victory . . . over coexistence" with the communists, even rollback in North Korea.

Speeches from the dais echoed that call, decrying the "Hanoi-crats," dubbing the leftist revolt—not the radical right—as the true "neo-Nazi or neo-Fascist movement."[57]

According to an internal White House poll conducted in the months following Nixon's historic speech, 73 percent of Americans considered themselves part of the silent majority. Fifty-eight percent of respondents considered Nixon's treatment of the North Vietnamese too soft. Another internal poll showed that 76 percent of those who identified as part of the silent majority opposed the anti-war protests, 74 percent saw anti-war activities as hurting the war effort and the nation's future. The White House cheered. One aide's memo read, "Never in history has a speech rather than an event changed opinion so greatly."[58] Nixon's speech was heard by a generation disturbed by the overturning of social and cultural norms. His ability to tap into their aggrievement derived not only from his own temperament, as suggested by the psychohistorians, or from his political battles, as argued by his longform biographers. As cultural historians have written of Nixon, in his resentments he was also a man of his times. There was "something in the air" as he fomented and manipulated a conservative reaction against leftist talk of revolution, against the elite cabals of Georgetown, of the ivory towers and Hollywood. He harnessed a wave of grievance and conspiracism that had flowed from McCarthy to Goldwater, from the Bay of Pigs to the Kennedy assassination, from the forgotten man to the silent majority.

There was still another unresolved facet in Nixon's conspiratorial mentality—a compulsive focus on the rich and privileged that went beyond simple antagonism. Kissinger would later theorize, "Nixon was afraid of Harvard, and he was attracted to it." Nixon seethed against Jews, believing them to be members of a conspiratorial clique, even as he relied heavily on a handful of Jewish men in his chief foreign policy advisor Kissinger, close advisor Leonard Garment, communications director Herb Klein and Council of Economic Advisers chairman Herbert Stein. And just so, Nixon grossly distrusted high-priced lawyers, even when he worked diligently in a white-shoe, New York firm in the early and mid-1960s. A master of congressional wheeling and dealing in the cloakroom, he nonetheless railed throughout his political career against his brethren behind the curtain. Nixon depended on certain press outlets to damn his enemies while scornfully insisting the entire press corps be damned. Indeed, the two-term congressman, the two-term vice president, the twice-elected president himself became the establishment no matter how insistently he claimed to be outside the tent pissing in. Always the anxious social climber, in true ironic fashion, Nixon aspired to what he so despised. He had in him what the psychologist Lawrence Schiff has called the "obedient rebel." That is, even as Nixon harangued against the rotten status of the status quo, he clung to and achieved a standard vision of success.[59]

During the "wilderness years"—after losing to Kennedy in the 1960 election and to Pat Brown in the California gubernatorial race two years later—Nixon did not retreat to his childhood climes and his law firm in Whittier or to the kind of rustic farm he so often spoke of in his populist rants. Instead, he moved to New York to join the ranks of the prestigious. The historian Small notes that it was during this time in the wilderness, seemingly at his political nadir, that Nixon "develop[ed] his interest in fine wine." Later, in retirement, Nixon would buy an apartment on Fifth Avenue and a mansion in Saddle River, New Jersey. In addition to the early memoir *Six Crises*, he wrote nine more books. He became a respected voice in foreign policy and a catch on the speaking circuit. Despite his rage against the Eastern powers that be, he provided his daughters an easier life than the one he had experienced growing up. Off they went to Finch and Smith; Julie ended up marrying an Eisenhower. Nixon treated himself to a Rolodex of memberships at exclusive clubs—the Metropolitan, the Links men's golf clubs, the Bel Air Country Club—more than twenty such.[60]

Nixon did not just want to destroy. Countering and at the same time emulating his adversaries, he wanted to foster what he called a New Establishment to fend off and usurp the existing order. He wanted a focus on television over print, new media rather than old, conservative voices rather than the traditional liberal drumming. "For eight years I was not invited to a White House luncheon or dinner by either Johnson or Kennedy," he grumbled in a memorandum to Ehrlichman not long after entering the Oval Office. He instructed that guests to White House dinners not be from the same "tired old lists," not just congressional leaders and Washington éminences grises. He wanted supporters from across the country, Blacks, Mexicans "and other ethnic groups, particularly Italians." He wanted his own establishment of the once-excluded. As common to the conspiracist's plot, the aim was not merely to defeat but to replace, to wrench free the gifts and treasure of those most hated. In such fashion, Nixon created his own exclusive inner circle, his own cabinet of elites with its own crass patois, secretive plotting and arcane organization, his own cadre of supporters among business leaders and the white middle class.[61]

With additional materials from Nixon's archive having been made available since the 2000s, more recent Nixon scholarship has circled back to its reproving roots, once again trying to find the "real" Nixon and present a true, "objective" view of the former president. Plentifully sourced studies have detailed the Nixon White House's "thievery" and his base execution of the Vietnam War. With access to more extensive and revealing resources, these historians discarded the revisionist' perspective to largely argue that Nixon had little interest in domestic affairs past the next election. Newly released White House tapes revealed nefarious designs. "We're up against an enemy, a conspiracy," the tapes recorded Nixon repeating. "They're using any means. We are going to use any means." As for those "left-wingers" and "bastards," from Hiss to Ellsberg, Nixon's tapes exposed his strategy of leaks and rumors. "Convict the son of bitch in the press," he barked to his deputies. From the Oval Office recordings, Kutler learned that Nixon "knew virtually everything about Watergate and the imposition of a cover-up from the beginning." Post-revisionist scholars like Kutler concluded that the Watergate break-in was not an aberrant slip of character much less an isolated "third-rate burglary"; they returned to an earlier thesis to explain Nixon's activities. As summed up by Kutler, "[A] corrosive hatred . . . decisively shaped Nixon's own behavior, his career, and eventually his historical standing." It was a hatred that dated back to his first term as president, to his political wrangling in the 1960s, to his first congressional campaign to a lifetime of feeling left out.[62] In these reexaminations, Nixon appears once again as turgid, corrupt, lashing out at subordinates with an ire swirling, promising to match alleged conspiracy with conspiring of his own, willing to bend rules for even short-term victory. Past criticism has come full circle. Nixon again comes across as a man bent on retaliation for grievances against a shifting cast of intellectuals, homosexuals, bra burners and Jews. Nixon reemerges as a symbol of American corruption at home with Watergate, and the brutality of American imperialism abroad with the war in Vietnam, invasion of Cambodia and abetting the coup against Allende. In 1973, at the height of Watergate, Woodward wrote a descriptive string to gloss the Nixon administration: "criminality, abuse of power, obsession with real and perceived enemies, rage, self-focus, and small-mindedness." Forty years later, in 2014, in reviewing an anti-Nixon exegesis by former White House lawyer John Dean, Woodward again let loose, as old critiques of the former president return to the mainstream. It was "a White House full of lies, chaos, distrust, speculation, self-protection, maneuver and counter-maneuver," Woodward wrote, adding that Nixon's regime had "a crookedness that makes Netflix's 'House of Cards' look unsophisticated."[63]

Still, in the attempt to depict the gravity of Nixon's politics of retribution, the latest, most serious accounts of Watergate and Vietnam fail to capture a certain playfulness in Nixon's scheming. After all, Nixon took to the game so much that his name became synonymous with "dirty tricks." His victims reported the feeling of having been played, for there was a boyish, immature quality of clowning, hazing, towel-snapping among the perpetrators, as if their fear mongering and other plotting were a ruse. It was as if the Nixon campaign were a political fraternity, not so different from his Orthogonian days, with not just enmity but a desire to construct its own exclusive gang of fellow conspirators. Its bag of dirty tricks contained the "martyrdom theory." In 1972 Nixon suggested that the campaign "not hit [George] McGovern too hard, so as not to martyr him." But, then again, Nixon's team developed the "reverse martyrdom theory." The campaign needed to deliver a decisive blow to a politically weakened McGovern, "hit him again while he's down to keep him down." Nixon loved the lark in which the campaign killed its opponents with exaggerated kindness, hoisting their foes on their own petard. "Our opponents are not bad men," Nixon instructed his deputies to relay to the press. "They are sincere, dedicated radicals. They honestly believe in the radical, liberal left."[64]

Nixon sicced his young crew on the 1972 Democratic contenders for the presidential nomination. At an Edmund Muskie press conference, they released rats with ribbons reading "Muskie is a rat fink." They sent out a press release on Citizens for Muskie stationery, purporting that the Democratic challenger Henry "Scoop" Jackson not only had an illegitimate daughter, but had also been caught in a homosexual dalliance by the police not once but twice. They spread a rumor that Humphrey had been caught driving drunk with a "known call girl." *Washington Post* editor Ben Bradlee, a former JFK confidante and no fan of Nixon, cut to the quick, complaining that Nixon's campaigns were run like a "sleazy hotel in the Caribbean." As a candidate, he played by just three rules, Bradlee explained: "Fill 'em up with booze if they're for us. Buy 'em off if they're neutral. Knee 'em in the groin if they step out of line."[65]

Nixon turned again and again to grievance to justify his conspiring. Psychohistorians looked to his childhood to locate the source of his aggrievement. Biographers pointed to an ever-accumulating sense of being wronged over the course of his political career, and then revisionists upended the debate by arguing that it was Nixon's critics who had invented the notion that bitterness and woe had guided the former president. Cultural historians shifted the debate to note that a conspiratorial mentality had consumed much of Nixon's generational cohort. In his retirement, Nixon offered yet another hypothesis to defend his career of connivance: No longer was he spurred on by intellectuals, commies or Jews. He foreswore political gamesmanship, instead justifying his wily ways by writing starkly of battle. "I would like to believe an enemy is a friend you haven't met," he suggested. "Unfortunately, it is seldom true." Enmity fueled democracy, Nixon argued. His conspiring was part of the electoral fight, a competition of force, but more than just competition. It was the clash of opposing forces, not a clash of ideas, but a rage-filled contest of us versus them. The only alternatives to the battling style of democratic politics, Nixon maintained, was following a path of single-minded authoritarian dictatorship or surrendering to the "consensus government" of the Soviet state where all, at least in theory, agreed to adhere mindlessly to the commune's decree. And just so, to Nixon's telling, by such thinking, dirty tricks represented the ultimate form of anti-authoritarian democracy. It was the freedom to hoodwink. His was the freedom to conspire.[66]

Interlude Three

We've got to play it recklessly. That's the safest course.
—Henry Kissinger, 1972

THE NATIONAL SECURITY COUNCIL briefed President Dwight D. Eisenhower that in a nuclear war, the Soviet Union would obliterate the federal government. With two-thirds of the population dead, dying, or in need of care, hospitals would be overrun, as would banks and grocery stores and hardware stores. The economy would crater. All told, American society would collapse. A preemptive first strike to destroy the Soviets' entire nuclear arsenal was not an option because they had secured a capacity to retaliate with a strike of their own. Only deterrence could prevent annihilation, that is, the only way to stave off a nuclear winter was to maintain the credible threat that nuclear war with the United States was simply too dangerous to consider.[1]

To this end, Eisenhower and his military strategists developed a doctrine of "brinkmanship," of "massive retaliation." They threatened the United States' enemies with counterattacks, outlining a strategic course predictable in its disproportion. The retired general-cum-president warned that if an adversary attacked an American ally, the United States would clobber them. If an opponent hit the United States, they would be destroyed. Eisenhower told his director of policy planning, "We must be ready to throw the book at the Russians should they jump us."[2] According to such strategic calculus, given the outsized might of the U.S. military arsenal, any prospective enemy would consider an attack prohibitive; in strategic parlance, the prospective enemy's advance would be contained, its use of weapons deterred. As neither superpower could act without risking annihilation, the Cold War would settle into an equilibrium of mutual assured destruction, or MAD. The key to threatening massive retaliation, in maintaining MAD, lay not only in the power of U.S. force, but also in the credibility of the threat.

This grand strategy had a critical strategic flaw, however. Would an American president really unleash his nuclear arsenal on Argentina or Algeria or Laos if their leaders stepped out of line? How would the commander in chief contend with the fear of such states falling under the sway of communism like dominos? Was the promise of massive retaliation a credible threat to stymy a possibly communist, possibly nationalist anti-colonial rebellion from spiraling toward civil war? Would an American president really rain down a nuclear holocaust on Korea or Vietnam? And more, would he hazard the possibility of mutual, nuclear annihilation with a Soviet Union that may or may not be aiding that possibly communist, possibly nationalist rebellion? As Eisenhower said worryingly to Secretary of State John Foster Dulles in 1956, "What should we do if Soviet *political* aggression, as in Czechoslovakia, successively chips away exposed positions of the free world?" Dulles had no answer.[3]

In the 1960s as guerrilla forces, nationalists, and communist rebellions spread in the postcolonial gray areas of the Cold War, the liberal critic Arthur M. Schlesinger, Jr., judged the threat of massive retaliation far too blunt an instrument to employ against such "encroachments too small." Henry Kissinger had previously laid out this shortcoming in Eisenhower's strategy in his surprising bestseller *Nuclear Weapons and Foreign Policy* (1957), which Nixon reportedly read with keen interest. Kissinger argued that the overwhelming use of force at the core of MAD was just not credible in the case of nationalist conflicts. For instance, the United States would not wreak massive nuclear havoc on the North Koreans even if armed by the Chinese and Soviets, and indeed, especially if so armed. Kissinger suggested deterring with more "limited," tactical capabilities, such as "smaller, less destructive" nuclear arms to keep the "enemy off balance"—that is, weapons whose use was more conceivable than Eisenhower's potentially vestigial, elephantine nuclear arsenal. Kissinger warned, "The enormity of modern weapons makes the thought of war repugnant, but the refusal to run any risks would amount to giving the Soviet rulers a blank check."[4]

Yet, counter to his stolid image and professed steady doctrine, Eisenhower did at one point attempt to operationalize a nuclear threat in an attempt to make the superbombs strategically useful beyond the defensive policy of deterrence. During the final stages of the Korean War, he issued a back-channel nuclear threat to the Chinese via Indian prime minister Jawaharlal Nehru. The gambit became known as the Dulles ploy. Vice President Nixon took note. During a visit to India in May 1953, Dulles "dropped a hint"—a message meant to be conveyed to China's Mao Zedong—that if the peace talks with Pyongyang collapsed, Eisenhower would escalate the conflict. The Americans were prepared for "stronger, rather than lesser, military exertion." They promised to extend the "area" of the conflict. Via the Indian prime minister, Dulles cryptically passed along a warning to Mao that it would be "difficult to know what [the] end might be."[5]

Dulles never explicitly mentioned nuclear weapons, and Nehru apparently did not relay the veiled threat to the Chinese. In August 2017, the historian William Hitchcock, drawing on previously secret documents, laid bare the enduring Republican myth that the Dulles ploy had ended the Korean War. Key, however, to the conflict's settlement in July 1953 was the death of Soviet leader Joseph Stalin a few months prior, on March 5, 1953. Stalin had ardently supported his comrades in North Korea, but his unstable coterie of successors saw the continuing conflict as a costly quagmire. Moreover, having gained Mao's approval, the North Koreans had decided by April—a month after Stalin's death and still a month before the Dulles ploy—that they would make concessions to conclude the war. Thus, as Hitchcock concluded, "No threat was made, and no threat was delivered."[6]

In the 1950s, however, absent the hindsight of historians like Hitchcock, the Dulles ploy appeared to have been a success; the Koreans agreed to an armistice after Nehru had supposedly passed along the Americans' veiled threat. The gall excited Nixon. He credited the scheme as key to his own thinking, maintaining that he had learned nuclear strategy at Eisenhower's knee. Once in the Oval Office, he and Kissinger would hanker for the opportunity to use it, with Kissinger later goading Nixon to employ the by-then mythic Dulles ploy, to nuclear saber-rattle, to quell the 1971 Jordanian crisis.[7] In Nixon's enthusiasm to later associate his former boss's doctrines with his own foreign policy, however, he ignored one key difference. Steady strength and intimidation had stood at the heart of Eisenhower's strategic vision, not the kind of rash threats that appealed to Nixon and Kissinger. Massive retaliation by Eisenhower was expected as a matter of strategy, and thus a dependable deterrent, not induced and feared as a fit of rage. Indeed, the tricky nature of the Dulles ploy was particularly striking because it was a rare deviation from Eisenhower's usually strict course. Far from a madman theory, Eisenhower's grand strategy lacked the irrational, the out-of-control abandon and the randomness at the center of so many of Nixon's subsequent foreign policy gambits.

Perhaps Nixon drew a lesson from the Dulles ploy, but more likely, his antecedent faith in strategic gambling led him to give undo credit to the coercive gamesmanship of his mentor's one-time act of nuclear chicanery. Nixon had made a career out of formulating the "big play," the "grand gesture." He was known for his love of poker. "As good a poker player as, if not better than, anyone we had ever seen," one of his Navy shipmates recalled. In contrast to Eisenhower's stolid forbearance, Nixon's constitution was that of a risk taker, despite his conservative, controlled demeanor, and his career trajectory proved it—running for a House seat and winning against the impressive Jerry Voorhis; challenging the beloved Helen Gahagan Douglas for a seat in the Senate; contending for the presidency at forty-seven years of age.[8]

Nixon was not alone in being inspired by Eisenhower's nuclear strategy. The limitations of brinkmanship and massive retaliation as doctrines spurred political scientists to find alternative approaches. The strategic uncertainty of the postwar nuclear age stimulated grand, new thinking at universities and in the burgeoning new world of defense think tanks. By the late 1950s, a decade before Nixon proposed his "madman theory" to H. R. Haldeman, in conference rooms and coffee klatches at Harvard in the east and the RAND Corporation in the west, academics the likes of the future Nobel Prize–winning economist Thomas Schelling, future Pentagon whistleblower Daniel Ellsberg and future national security advisor Kissinger batted around new theories of nuclear deterrence. Unconvinced by Eisenhower's reliance on the reliability of predictable massive retaliation, in place of traditional cost-benefit analyses, of the idea of wars as rational trade-offs, of one front lined up against another, the best and the brightest of the nuclear age turned instead to the virtues of bargaining, leverage and vulnerability. If Eisenhower, the ultimate predictable leader, failed to halt the Sino-Soviet advance, what about the unpredictable? The "wizards of Armageddon," as the journalist Fred Kaplan so dubbed them, looked to the utility of the impulsive and the random.[9] Their thinking harkened back to millennial-old questions about the power of the irrational—back to Plato to Shakespeare and Rimbaud—as they, the first wave of nuclear strategists, became the latest generation drawn to the question of the usefulness of madness.

For this first generation of nuclear strategists, the very world seemed to be going mad. The rational appeared outmoded. One scientific revelation after another defied basic reason: the relativity of time, the titanic power of the tiny atom, mind-bending notions like curved space, the overturning of centuries-old dictum like the conservation of mass and energy. As Secretary of War Henry Stimson declared in May 1945, the nuclear bomb was not merely a new weapon but a "revolutionary change in the relations of man to the universe." The entire world, not just armies, could be consumed and in a flash. It was, as the noted French sociologist Raymond Aron warned, "homicidal madness." Indeed, one leading nuclear strategist, Herman Kahn, invented a Doomsday Machine to count the days to Armageddon. Kissinger turned to myth. "In Greek mythology," he wrote, "the gods sometimes punished man by fulfilling his wishes too completely. It has remained for the nuclear age to experience the irony of this penalty."[10]

Fear stoked fear, and the Soviets stoked it more. They launched *Sputnik*, the first man-made satellite, thermonuclear bombs and intercontinental ballistic missiles, frightening Americans with purported (although untrue) bomber and then missile superiority. In turn, new military inventions called for new techniques of war and coercion. The scientific breakthroughs of World War II necessitated the recruitment of scientists to the defense industry. The sheer scope of the "military-political problem" demanded the input of computer scientists, physicists, mathematicians, engineers and economists. New techniques demanded new thinkers, who pondered new strategies. Fear stoked investment, which built a bureaucracy of specialists. Put simply, Schlesinger wrote, World War II "made the scientist a partner . . . in the enterprise of defense; the nuclear age made the association irrevocable."[11]

An atomic brain trust of young scholars emerged, focusing on data-driven policy making as the scales of influence began to tip in favor of intellectual acumen over worldly savvy or veteran experience. The historian Niall Ferguson referred to this generational cohort as the "academic-intellectual complex." They were also called the "whiz kids." With more than a bit of mocking critique, the journalist David Halberstam went with the "best and the brightest." Lyndon Johnson preferred the "Harvards." Bank-rolled by the Air Force and fashioned after the military planning rooms of World War II, the RAND Corporation, for research and development, was founded in May 1948. A new caste of defense intellectuals peopled this "original cold war Think Tank." The central endeavor for the scientific-technological elite became the quantifying and systematizing of decision-making throughout the public sector. Matrixes and massive calculations in hand, RAND scientists convened to patter and ponder, often obsessively, over existential destruction. War was deemed too costly. The atomic bomb was too bluntly powerful a weapon to drop, transforming any use, however heroically conceived, into villainy. So powerful seemed the threat of nuclear attack and retaliation that scholars and policy makers began to dream of world government, of the end of war itself.[12]

And yet, as Bernard Brodie, one of the keenest nuclear thinkers of that period, concluded, "War [had become] unthinkable but not impossible, and therefore we must think about it." Brodie stood out in laying down key suppositions in the post–World War II Atomic Age. Laying the foundation for what would become the prevalent understanding of MAD, he disabused his peers of any first-strike fantasies, of preemptively bombing a nuclear opponent into submission without the high risk of counterattack. "From now on [the nuclear weapon's] chief purpose must be to avert [wars]. It can have almost no other useful purpose," Brodie argued. An attempt to destroy

the enemy's nuclear weapons was too great a risk, he asserted. It was therefore necessary to convince the enemy, likewise, that its nuclear stockpile was
of no use or, more particularly, of too great a risk to use. "Deterrence of war
is the only rational military policy for a country in the nuclear age."[13]

The defense intellectuals endeavor to rationalize the irrational led them
to wrestle with such ideas as the infinite, the uncertain and the paradoxical,
to frame the existential but endemically interdependent standoff between
the nuclear powers, to capture the abstract absurdity of unfathomable
destruction. The wizards of Armageddon transformed the grave into the
incidental, the inconceivable into the feasible, the unthinkable into thought.
They balked at the sanctification of their atomic theory. They preferred the
low, even the base, to the highly abstract. "One does not do research in a
cathedral," the feisty and sometimes furious nuclear theorist Kahn crowed.
Instead, the nuclear fraternity traded in wry metaphors: Russian roulette,
driving "chicken," jockeying in a traffic jam. They conceptualized global
nuclear standoffs as discreet rounds of chance and bluster. They began to call
themselves game theorists.[14]

John von Neumann, once the "chief mathematical wizard" at the
Manhattan Project, which developed the atomic bomb during World War II,
has been credited with devising the basic concepts of game theory. With it, he
transformed the fundamental conceptions of nuclear war and strategic
deterrence. A Hungarian expatriate, von Neumann had mastered calculus by
the age of eight. It was said that he could memorize a column of the telephone book at first sight. He invented an early computer that could process
40,000 words at once for its computations, besting an earlier model of
twenty-seven. Intriguingly, he called this proto-processor a Mathematical
Analyzer, Numerical Integrator and Computer, or MANIAC. Its earliest
tasks in 1953 included thermonuclear calculations. In 1956, the MANIAC I
became the first computer to best a human in a chess-like game. Von Neumann had borrowed the core of his new theory from the basic strategic
structure of poker: No player acted independently. A participant's winnings
turned on the simple but often-overlooked precept that "what I do depends
on what you do, and what you do depends on what I do." This elegant insight

about conflict and cooperation would soon be applied across a range of fields, from nuclear war to the economic marketplace. With this, game theory usurped the previous model for predicting complex interactions, which had assumed that consumers and suppliers independently maximized their profits. By comparison, game theory attempted to calculate the outcome of actors' sequential choices, reactions and, crucially, their expectations of one another's actions.[15]

Von Neumann's innovation provoked a strategic revolution, with RAND and Harvard as Mecca and Medina. The whiz kids were inspired not just by horror but by also hope and swagger. They thought of the nuclear issue as a newly discovered and still indecipherable shore and themselves as pioneers in a new era of discovery. Their commitment was imbued with a blend of fatalism and scientific positivism. Alain Enthoven, the thirty-three-year-old economist and head of the Directorate for Weapons Systems Analysis in the Department of Defense was so confident of the salubrious quality of their work that he avowed their breakthroughs in strategy and organization equivalent to the boom in "medicine during the latter half of the 19th century." He professed that RAND's operational analysis had "reached the point in which [the nuclear] can do more good than harm."[16]

The London *Times* described how the exclusive community of whiz kids of the Atomic Age roamed "freely through the corridors of the Pentagon and the State Department like the Jesuits through the courts of Madrid and Vienna three centuries ago." The *Wall Street Journal* reported glib stories of "fuzzy-cheeked whiz kids with computers telling battle-scarred dogfaces how to fight and win wars." For Kissinger and the lot of the Harvard-RAND brain trust, victory depended more and more on the "genius-statesman"— not just the sane-, rational- or experienced- but the super-minded, that was, the brilliant. Discounting the military experience of an Eisenhower or a Gen. George S. Patton, Kissinger and company believed in the supremacy of creative strategic thinking—not strength or forbearance—as the lynchpin of foreign relations. They came to believe that independent research institutions like RAND could serve as a loyal opposition to the generals, a key to maintaining civilian control over the military. In the nuclear age, as the scientist Kahn argued, "Reality has left experience behind, and central as 'common sense' is, it is not enough." Borrowing the French statesman Georges Clemenceau's dictum, he exhorted, "War is too important to be left to the generals."[17]

With reputation the centerpiece of nuclear bargaining strategies, toughness became a currency. Nixon, for one, relished a good testicular metaphor. To him, John F. Kennedy was a "Stevenson with balls." He wanted a staff with "the balls of a brass monkey," and he regularly ordered "nut-cracking." For the RAND set, toughness was not a test of muscles but a mind-fueled match of masculinity. Their machismo ethic rejected women as thinkers or equals. Bravado and bluffing became a central preoccupation of the young, cocky and often crass nuclear crew. Kissinger foresaw a day in which all battles—atomic missilery aimed one against another—would develop into "stylized contests of the feudal period," peacock affairs of florid intimidation, demonstrations of will more than strength. Such was the new Great Game.[18]

Extending von Neumann's game theory, Schelling extrapolated that nuclear standoffs were not classic military confrontations or any other type of game but, specifically, "*bargaining* situations." Given the mutual nature of deterrence, standoffs between the superpowers needed to center on tradeoffs at the negotiating table rather than fallout on the battlefield. Schelling had begun his career in Denmark and France as an economist helping to implement the Marshall Plan. As Tyler Cowen, one of his students, remarked, "Tom is an unassuming guy who looks as if he sells Hush Puppies at the local mall." Once at RAND, the unassuming Schelling wrote in the tradition of the Fool, his precepts upside-down riddles of power turned on their head. Paradoxically, he described how weakness and vulnerability could become strengths, how seemingly irrational or mad behavior could serve rational ends. He explained, for example, how it could benefit a hostage to break his own hand to avoid relinquishing his life's savings with the simple signing of a check. Schelling also pointed to how the secret ballot created strength from weakness: as Americans "blind" themselves to how other citizens are voting, they as voters become freer to make their own choices.[19]

Schelling puzzled over how to determine risk: How likely would it be that a radar malfunction or a confused pilot triggered the firing of a nuclear payload, and how could one account for such risk in game theory computations? For nuclear strategists, the hypotheticals began to cascade: How does one calculate whether the probability of 35 million civilian casualties is sufficient to deter a foe's attack? What if a 100 million Americans perished in a few minutes? Kahn worried, at what point "would the survivors envy the dead"? Brodie considered how effective it would be to target the enemy's military and leave civilians and cities vulnerable to future blackmail. What would be of greater advantage: to level a city or take it hostage? Is it better to concentrate on civil defense, or is such defensive infrastructure as radar and bunkers and supply depots throwing good money after bad? Indeed, does a better defense fuel the race for superior offense? Each decision needed to be evaluated by secondary measures like marginal utility and opportunity cost. If nuclear war is inevitable, Kissinger wondered, how can it be kept limited?[20]

It was an intellectual festival posing thought against thought. As Kaplan recounted about one wizard of Armageddon, "[He] saw that once he slipped into the deep, dark pit of nuclear strategy, it was easy to become totally absorbed, living, eating, breathing the stuff every hour of every day." Yet when the strategist "departed from that realm for a while and scanned it from a distance, it seemed crazy, unreal." War had become, as the master strategist Albert Wohlstetter deemed, a "delicate balance of terror." The key was the threat of preemption but also the risk that threat spawned. It was like "stretching a trip wire" before the enemies' path, while depending on the notion that they would stop before tripping.[21]

Schelling's most enduring metaphor for this nuclear gamesmanship in an uncertain strategic age was that of a pair of mountain climbers. The premise: "You're standing at the edge of a cliff, chained by the ankle to someone else . . . You'll be released, and one of you will get a large prize," as soon as the other capitulates and concedes the bounty. The dilemma: If your partner in chains yearns to gain the prize, your only recourse, tossing her off the edge, would throw you off the cliff with her. As she inches you both toward the summit, the risk mounts: a loose rock, a turned ankle, an unintended elbow to the side. The journalist Michael Kinsley helped popularize the dilemma in 2005 when he recounted Schelling's strategic conundrum in the *Washington Post*. He had heard the rules of the game from the master himself as a college student in Schelling's Games and Strategy course at Harvard. Schelling's answer to the mountain climber's impasse, Kinsley explained, you play the Fool. "You start dancing, closer and closer to the edge. That way, you don't have to convince him that you would do something totally irrational: plunge him and yourself off the cliff. You just have to convince him that you are prepared to take a higher risk than he is of accidentally falling off." Madness—defined here as an apparent willingness to take on a seemingly counterproductive risk of losing, as typically defined by game theorists—could be the winning option. By extension, Schelling gleaned the core of what would become Nixon's "madman theory"—the utility of a feigned irrationality, a willingness to play with the trappings of overblown toughness, of suicidality. As Kinsley concluded his recollection of Schelling's talk, "If one of those two folks on the cliff can convince the other that he is just a bit nuts, that makes his threat to drag them both off the cliff much more plausible." It was, as Schelling famously wrote, "the threat that leaves something to chance."[22]

Instead of embracing Eisenhower as a nuclear innovator, the game theorists came to reject his predictable strategy of massive retaliation. As Kissinger put it, in a game of "threats and counter-threats . . . a premium will be placed on irresponsibility." From this perspective, the uncertainty in the madman theory stemmed not from Nixon's history of bitter grievance or Eisenhower's steady strategy or even the Dulles ploy. Rather, the predilection for the irrational move sprang from a gang of political scientists and economists of game, deterrence and nuclear theory. In this context, the madman theory became a reasoned strategy of coercion based on the unreasoning concepts of uncertainty and risk. To a tee, in the 1980 monograph *The Real War*, in what Nixon described as his cri de coeur, the former president laid bare his deep faith not only in the irrational strategy but in this gaming trope. "If the adversary feels that you are unpredictable, even rash, he will be deterred from pressing you too far," Nixon exhorted. Evoking the poker metaphor, he predicted that "the odds that he will fold will increase and the unpredictable president will win another hand."[23]

Intriguingly, by several accounts, it was not Schelling—so focused on uncertainty and risk—or Kissinger—pushing the theories of strategic ambiguity and limited war—but Nixon's future foe Ellsberg who explicitly articulated the potential of affective or cognitive madness as a "strategy of conflict." Ellsberg, one of the nuclear whiz kids, had given three lectures on blackmail and coercion to a seminar Kissinger taught at Harvard in 1959, nearly a decade before Nixon's madman beach stroll with Haldeman, a decade before Ellsberg leaked the Pentagon Papers and Nixon's burglars stole his psychiatric records, long before Ellsberg gabbed on the Dick Cavett Show about his release of the secret Department of Defense documents or was interviewed by *Rolling Stone* as an icon for whistleblowing, as the anti-Nixon. In the last of the three Harvard lectures, "Political Uses of Madness," Ellsberg reviewed critiques of Eisenhower's massive retaliation. He emphasized the lack of credibility in a nuclear threat that amounted to "massive suicide-murder." Echoing Schelling, Ellsberg lectured the seminar, "Though no one rationally could choose war, still one might choose a *risk* of war." Hazarding such a risk was a matter of taking the irrational route, a step historically condemned by political scientists. "The first method," he explained, was "simply to be unpredictable; to seem 'a little' erratic, impulsive, unstable." The key to the threat was the centrality of performance, one of the two poles of the madman theory. Not, is it true that I will follow through with my threat?, but "Is it what I want my opponents to think I believe?"[24]

Ellsberg pointed to Adolf Hitler as an exemplar of the irrational madman. Hitler's recklessness froze the great powers into a state of appeasement because his moves did not add up on traditionally strategic grounds. The Führer seemed rash in the invasions of his neighbors. He appeared out of control as he risked world war for minor land gains in Europe, gambling a lot for relatively little. His actions could not be logically anticipated because the potential costs outweighed the benefits, and the German chancellor could not be reasoned with. His risk-taking and unpredictability proved advantageous, at least for a while. He sent only one division across the Rhine—a bluff his neighbors proved unwilling to call—for the threat was that of an irrational strategist, a threat of unpredictability, the advantage of the willing risk-taker over the reasoned actor. In other words, the other pole in the madman theory, as Ellsberg explained, is that "madness helps."[25]

Yet, unlike Nixon, as the historian Jeffrey P. Kimball has emphasized, "None of these civilian strategists [at RAND and Harvard] . . . actually advocated a madman strategy of ambiguity, irrationality, uncertainty, unpredictability, or excessive force and ruthlessness." Among Schelling, Ellsberg and their colleagues, none advocated the policy Nixon (and Kissinger) would adopt. Before joining the Nixon administration, Kissinger consistently protested that high risk and irrationality were the dastardly ploys of the Soviet autocracy and its guerrilla cronies. He argued forcefully for reliance on predictability in "phases which permit an assessment of the risks and possibilities for settlement at each stage before recourse" to action. Just so, Ellsberg vigorously maintained that he considered the Hitler/madman strategy "as being a possibly effective, but extremely dangerous" approach. The Hitler analogy was meant to be a warning against playing the madman. Ellsberg expressed horror at the suggestion that Nixon and Kissinger had employed it.[26]

Still, arguably, the ultimate influence on Nixon was his greatest foreign adversary, Soviet Premier Khrushchev—the then loudest of mad conspirers on the world's stage. In a 1985 interview with *Time*, Nixon praised Khrushchev as the "most brilliant world leader" that he had ever met. He argued that Khrushchev's master stroke during the Cuban Missile Crisis was his ability "to use the universal fear of war to put pressure on Kennedy." The Soviet premier got his first taste of setting unpredictable ultimatums during the October 1956 Suez Crisis, vowing to enter the conflict on the side of Egypt if the British, French, and Israelis refused to halt military operations. He took to the ploy. Over and again he played the nuclear card, threatening Soviet use of nuclear weapons in Lebanon in July 1958, in the Taiwan Straits in August 1958 and in West Berlin in April 1959. Khrushchev played loose and provocatively. Most unlike Eisenhower, he was unpredictable, choking off Berlin, shipping nuclear-tipped missiles to Cuba, pounding his shoe on the lectern at the United Nations, proclaiming *My vas pokhoronim!*—"We will bury you!" Further unnerving his foreign counterparts, Khrushchev developed a habit of speaking of mass annihilation off-the-cuff, "Eight will be enough to destroy Western Germany, six will wipe out France." Of course, he pressed, "We might lose Leningrad . . . But Leningrad is not Russia, whereas Paris is France, and London is England."[27]

Within a week of war-mongering to the United Nations in 1960, the inconsistent Khrushchev reversed himself, announcing to a Polish crowd that "never, never, never [would the USSR] launch any war" against the West. Khrushchev boasted of the destructive greatness of the Soviet military machine only to turn around in unpredictable fashion to advocate for the "friendliness of all nations." He assuaged Henry Cabot Lodge, the U.S. ambassador to the United Nations, "You continue to enjoy roast beef, I borscht, and you have yours and I have mine." It was this inconsistency more than his over-the-top rhetoric alone that led many to fear "Hurricane Nikita." As early as 1959, the journalist Joseph Alsop, adopting the words of *Hamlet's* Polonius, wrote of a "method in Khrushchev's madness." Khrushchev's words were a mix of "lunacy," "a familiar combination of boasts of strength to inspire fear and protestations of peacefulness to promote wishful thinking." Like Ellsberg, Alsop saw Khrushchev's mad malarkey as "the combination that worked so well for Adolf Hitler, until the very last round."[28]

The Soviet leader nurtured his reputation for rashness and bellicosity. He incessantly alluded to madness: the madness of Western imperialists, a mad revanchist militarism growing in West Germany, the madness of the Chinese splitting the communist bloc, the madness of an assault on the Soviet Union, the "sheer madness" of nuclear war itself. In 1970 he even began referring to his predecessor, Stalin, as a madman, although at the same time deny doing so. For Nixon, Khrushchev represented the essence of the feinting madman. Looking back in 1983, Nixon fawned. Khrushchev was "a man that does not lose his temper. He uses his temper . . . He puts on a show, but he is cold when it matters." Three and a half decades later, in the fall of 2017, both the *Jordan Times* and the *Japanese Times* ran a syndicated think piece by Nina L. Khrushcheva, a professor of international affairs at the New School and the granddaughter of the Soviet premier. In an essay addressing President Donald Trump's foreign policy bluster, she, too, dubbed her grandfather the original strategic madman.[29]

In the fall of 1970, just as Ellsberg began copying and compiling what would become known as the Pentagon Papers, he met with Kissinger for lunch. They ate on a little patio at the so-called Western White House, Nixon's estate in sun-drenched San Clemente. Ellsberg caught a glimpse of Nixon riding by in a pink golf cart, "scowling and looking very grim." His best friend, Bebe Rebozo, followed in an identical pink cart. "You know, I've learned more from Dan Ellsberg about bargaining than from any other person," Kissinger, equally well known for his cloying flattery as for his gravelly German purr, said, greeting his one-time fellow whiz kid. Their reunion came amid Nixon and Kissinger's secret bombing campaign of Cambodia, a strategic feint that many thought was motivated by an attempt to scare the Soviets and Chinese with sheer unpredictability. "You have a good memory," Ellsberg replied. To which the seated national security advisor retorted, "They were good lectures," referring to the talks Ellsberg had given to Kissinger's Harvard seminar eleven years earlier. "I was taken aback," Ellsberg would recount. The idea that his strategic analysis influenced a man he came to call a war criminal "made the hair on the back of my neck stand up."[30]

Nixon's fascination with the madman theory was not directly drawn from Ellsberg as the latter feared. He had been taken with the Dulles ploy before Ellsberg spoke to Kissinger's class on the matter. In his memoirs, Nixon wrote that he was impressed when the South Korean strongman Syngman Rhee—that "wise old man," Nixon called him—took the American president aside to lobby for "the importance of being unpredictable in dealing [with] the Communists." Further, Haldeman and Nixon's beach break from speechwriting, when they first bandied about the idea of the madman theory, occurred in the summer of 1968. Kissinger and Nixon had first met at a Christmas party in 1967 but only for five minutes. Kissinger did not meet to talk with Nixon until the morning of Monday, November 25, 1968, at the Pierre Hotel in Manhattan, a few months after the beach talk, before Kissinger would have had the opportunity to convey the strategy suggested in Ellsberg's lectures.[31] It seems, instead, the uncertainty and the potential of madness in the nuclear age was de rigueur. The fear lingered that yet another world war would come, after all, one had already followed another one. The specters of madmen like Hitler or Stalin lingered. Khrushchev blustered with unpredictable threats on the world stage as the stalemate in the Cold War continued to baffle and worry. The loud banter of the reward of risk echoed in the circles of strategic thinkers, through the hallways of Harvard and RAND, of the White House and the Kremlin. By some degree of intellectual osmosis, Nixon adopted Schelling's lesson of dancing on the cliff's edge. Through further discussions with Kissinger, he would make it central to American foreign policy.

In the mad world of strategic thinking, strategists played loose and free with the notion that through irrational means, a player could gain the rational ends he sought. Mistaking Eisenhower's Korean ruse for success, parroting Hitler or Khrushchev, worrying over proxy wars too small to warrant the threat of nuclear annihilation, coaxed on by Kissinger, it seems Nixon's adoption of the madman theory was a matter of a rash man for a rash era. The key for Schelling, and later Nixon, was to "visibly . . . make yourself a little bit out of control," cultivating "a reputation of irrationality," so that your "foe would believe in your self-destructive threats." It was what Andrew Solomon, in his psychological study of madness, would call the "potential power of the disorderly personality." The performance of geostrategic madness, however feigned, was not Eisenhower's predictable massive retaliation. It was not a balance of power held in static check, not a rationalized mutually assured destruction keeping the machinations and threats of the nuclear armed states under control. The madman theory was a matter of risk-taking. Unpredictable threats proved endemic to those first and middle years of the Cold War. For the threat would not be that you would retaliate with nuclear force, but that you *might*.[32]

6 | Madness in Play

The "Madman Theory" in Foreign Policy

THEY SAT IN THE CLUTTER of the national security advisor's office in the basement of the White House as Henry Kissinger dispatched secret instructions to longtime Nixon counsel Leonard Garment. It was the summer of 1969, just months into Richard Nixon's first term as president. As part of a cultural exchange, Garment would soon be headed for Moscow to attend an international film festival. Kissinger explained that the visit provided the administration an interesting opportunity. The U.S. press had depicted Garment as a Nixon confidant, as a man the president trusted with his word. No doubt the Soviets would test Garment's knowledge as he made the round of delegations. They would be eagerly fishing for information on the newly installed American leader, his policy stances and his personality. Garment was to meet with Georgy Arbatov, a senior advisor to General-Secretary Leonid Brezhnev. "If the chance comes your way," Kissinger told Garment, laying out a script, apologize to Arbatov for the president's sometimes erratic behavior, but then tell the Soviets that Nixon had a "dramatically disjointed personality." Understandably, the president was "more than a little paranoid because of years of bashing" by his myriad enemies. Kissinger tasked Garment with relaying that the American president was "when necessary, a cold-hearted butcher," especially toward those who would challenge him to "tests of strength." Garment should convey that Nixon was a "visionary," but, the national security advisor added, he should also suggest that Nixon could get a bit out of control.[1]

Landing in Moscow in mid-July, Garment met first with the U.S. ambassador, Llewellyn Thompson. The high-level diplomat offered a pair of his best notetakers for Garment's meeting with the senior Soviet adviser, yet Garment demurred. He preferred to be more informal, to go alone. That was not possible, the ambassador objected. It was against protocol. The Soviets were tricky. They would have five people in attendance. Would Garment not want to match their numbers? To have a safeguard? "I have my reasons," Nixon's counsel insisted. "I go alone or not at all."[2]

Garment later expressed surprise at the scheme Kissinger had worked out for him, but he offered no misgivings, no questioning of the ruse as too dangerous, too far-fetched or screwball for Nixon's liking. Indeed, he relished the chance to conspire. Garment met Arbatov and his coterie at the Moscow Institute for United States Studies. There were not five to the group but, by Garment's count, "eight or ten chunky, impressive-looking professionals," several of whom he judged to be KGB. Introducing himself, Garment quickly related his life story, touching on "my Russian father, the family's struggle out of poverty, working in the dress factory, my religious awakening[,] . . . early interest in socialism, then music." He sprinkled in some Nixon-like aphorisms: "All circles can be squared," and "There is no such thing as contradiction, only a constrained grasp of complexity." He spoke of his years of legal work with Nixon and their friendship. At the president's request, Garment said, he was heading a council to establish "national goals," something of an American "five-year plan," a venture Garment thought might appeal to his Soviet audience with their predilection for central planning. So it went for half an hour, Garment remembered: "Talk, talk. Scribble, scribble. I was, as jazz musicians say, cooking," when, finally, the moment arrived. Garment told his Soviet hosts that as was Nixon's reputation, the commander in chief was a "complex [of] contradictions." He was "predictably unpredictable." It was a matter, the president's close confidant explained to his Soviet interlocuters, "that Nixon is somewhat 'crazy'—immensely intelligent, well-organized, and experienced, to be sure, but at moments of stress . . . unpredictable and capable of the bloodiest brutality."[3]

During this middle phase of the Cold War—after Joseph Stalin's threatening tenure and Nikita Khrushchev's early blustering, but before the more hopeful years of superpower détente—the unimaginable threat of joint annihilation seemed, at least in theory, to provide stability. The United States and Soviet Union were at a standstill. As the game theorist Thomas Schelling theorized, with the pair of nuclear powers teetering on the cliff's edge, chained together by the risk of mutual annihilation, neither dared make a move against the other. The fear of mutual assured destruction (MAD) in the post–Cuban Missile Crisis era was thought to have created an equilibrium, what the historian John Lewis Gaddis called the "long peace." A strategic balance was said to have developed that made cool heads prevail as neither could survive war with the other. Within this MAD framework, the Cold War continued to sway between what the historian Raymond Garthoff called "détente and confrontation," an ebb and flow of arms buildups, hostility and negotiation. After Stalin's death in March 1953, hopes had run high for a rapprochement with the Soviets until they violently quelled a rebellion in East Berlin the following July. Subsequently, optimism for a peaceful coexistence re-emerged at high-level meetings in Geneva in 1955 only to be dashed again, by the Soviets' crackdown in Hungary in 1956. Three "high-level reciprocal visits" took place in 1959, leading to a planned presidential visit by Eisenhower to Moscow and a summit in Paris, only to be abruptly canceled after an American U-2 reconnaissance airplane was spotted near Moscow on May Day 1960.[4]

Nixon's primary achievement in foreign policy is considered by many to be his cooling of the Cold War, building a détente that tran-scended the precarious MAD standoff, lessening tensions between the United States, China and the Soviet Union through trust-building sum-mitry, arms control, cultural and professional exchange and increased trade. He entered office promising a shift in U.S. nuclear policy from a "superiority" of arms that fed competition with the Soviets to a "sufficiency" of weapons to maintain a credible deterrent. He committed to delicate back-channel diplomacy to develop personal relations with the aim of overcoming ideological difference and cultural misunderstandings. Nixon believed, the historian Robert D. Schulzinger asserted, "The fact of having reached an agreement was more important than the details of it." Nixon's grand strategy, however, also depended on swift confrontation. Rejecting Harry Truman's steady containment of the Soviet empire and the predictability of massive retaliation that Eisenhower promised, Nixon maintained that in an unstable world, an equilibrium between the superpowers could only be sustained by rattling his saber. As Schelling described his pair of precariously enchained mountain climbers, a threat was considered credible only when thought to be imminent and unpredictable. To be believed, one had to appear to be willing to do the unbelievable. To convince the Soviets that the United States remained resolute in its course, Nixon insisted, "[The] real possibility of irrational American action is essential."[5]

Applying the "madman theory" to Vietnam and Jordan, and later in wars between India and Pakistan and in the greater Middle East, Nixon and Kissinger repeatedly threatened the Soviets and their client states with imminent nuclear retaliation. Their strategic posturing amounted to what the scholars William Burr and Jeffrey P. Kimball termed a "nuclear specter." Time and again Nixon and Kissinger acted the madmen, latter-day ogres, bullies, in his words, "obsessed," "angry," not able to be restrained. They were convinced that the play of nuclear alerts, feinted carrier maneuvers, stand-downs and airlifts provided successful tests of détente. Without such coercive moves, Kissinger insisted, "We would have had a Soviet paratroop division in [Vietnam] this morning."[6]

For Nixon, these standoffs were not merely dispassionate tactical maneuvers but tests of will, the latest in his lifelong crises. The predicaments terrified him but also invigorated him by their potential for coercion. "The major problem . . . is that the Russians retain their respect for you," Kissinger goaded Nixon during the Middle East crisis, in Jordan, in the winter of 1971. The national security advisor knew how to play on the president's insecurities and his dogged striving. He pressed, "If we do nothing, there's a certainty of disaster. This way there is a high possibility of one, but at least we're coming off like men." Planning a counterassault against the North Vietnamese, in the spring of 1972, the two convened to reexamine the possibilities of the madman ruse. "We'll escalate it . . . [W]e've got to pour things in there . . . The wilder we look the better," Kissinger instructed. The strategy was not simply a one-off plan. "We've done it in Jordan. We did it in India-Pakistan. And we've got to play it recklessly," Kissinger stressed. "That's the safest course." Kissinger did not catch the irony, and neither apparently did the assenting Nixon, but irony was the very point. From recklessness came safety. From madness came calm.[7]

Nixon won his first presidential election on the promise of a "swift peace" in Vietnam. Yet as the war offered no easy resolution, the issue of potential furor back home in the United States nagged. Almost a decade and a half later, in 1983, Nixon could still recall the very number of protestors and casualties. "From the time I came into office in 1969 until April of 1970, . . . there had been a total of eighteen hundred demonstrations on college campuses. But worse, there'd been two hundred and fifty cases of arson," he said, reciting the extent of the upheaval. "There had been over six hundred injured, two-thirds of them being police, and, in addition to that, there had been at least eight killed." Nixon remembered clearly one incident in particular: the firebombing of fellows' offices at the Center for Advanced Studies in Behavioral Sciences at Stanford University. Of the incident in May 1970, he remarked, "[A] visiting Asian scholar, a noted anthropologist, had a twenty-five-year research project that he'd been working on there burned, destroyed, a whole lifetime's work." The scholar, Mysore Srinivas, had pioneered field work to study the caste system in his native India. The destruction of his research was, to Nixon, "senseless," "mindless" ruin.[8]

"Even the term 'authority' has acquired for many a sinister cast," remarked Daniel Patrick Moynihan, Nixon's advisor for urban affairs, about the turmoil besetting the United States in the late 1960s. Nixon called the dissenting generation "bums," self-important free-riders, dirty, lazy. He believed that the country's youth had been "given too much, too easily." He was convinced that the younger generation had not worked hard enough to earn a place on the political stage, whereas he had devoted his days and nights to gain what he had missed out on in his poor upbringing. "And this weakened them," Nixon concluded. A "virus of dissent," *Time* called the demonstrations spreading across the nation in 1968—all to the unrelenting beat of the daily body count of fallen soldiers in Vietnam. "Every day in the paper . . . young men from Kansas," returned in body bags, Senator Robert Dole of Kansas recalled. He simply remembered, "You meet the parents."[9]

In May 1969, after only a few months in office, Nixon and Kissinger presented the North Vietnamese with an ultimatum. If they failed to agree to the Americans' peace terms by November 1, the one-year anniversary of Johnson's halting bombings of North Vietnam, the United States would "resort to any means necessary." It was a classic threat of force, following Eisenhower's escalatory strategy of "brinkmanship." Nixon and his team named it Operation Duck Hook, considered by some to be a forerunner of the United States' "shock and awe" bombardment of Iraq in 2003 under President George W. Bush. If the North Vietnamese ignored the November deadline, Nixon would forgo restraint and launch a four-day blitz and harbor-mining offensive. American airpower would target twenty-nine Vietnamese installations—military and economic. Nixon's team began to bandy about a rash of escalatory tactics. One contingency called for an invasion of North Vietnam; another ordered a nuclear detonation to cripple the Chinese railroad pass into Vietnam. Nixon settled on a fixed schedule for the incursion. After four days of bombing, Nixon would give Hanoi four more days to sue for peace, or the assault would be repeated.[10]

As the deadline for Duck Hook neared, however, Hanoi served Nixon a "cold rebuff." Brinkmanship had failed, or perhaps Nixon had failed at Eisenhower's brinkmanship. The North Vietnamese dismissed the November 1 ultimatum threatening massive retaliation. They demanded a complete U.S. withdrawal and elections in South Vietnam without condition. The communist leadership was "determined to fight to the end." Secretary of Defense Melvin Laird and Secretary of State William P. Rogers lost their nerve, arguing to Nixon that a barrage had little chance of working against the resolute communists, and Nixon flinched.[11] He recognized that he could not afford to unleash such a massive conventional force without risking chaos abroad and a torrent of discontent at home. The decision to shelve Operation Duck Hook proved a key turn. Nixon recognized that to maintain credibility at the peace table, he had to remain popular domestically: he had to adhere to his campaign promise of de-escalation while only in secret amping up coercion of the North Vietnamese and the Soviet leadership. The anti-war movement not only irked the president personally, the demonstrators had undercut him on policy. His acting chops would be tested as he would have to play two parts at once: credible action abroad, deniable facade at home.

The backup plan, Nixon resolved, was to employ the madman theory. If a predictable threat of outright force as planned for Operation Duck Hook failed to intimidate, he would turn to an unpredictable nuclear feint. He would threaten a preemptive nuclear strike even though he had no intention of following through with it. He chose coercion through deception, performance over action, that is, he would play a trick. He and Kissinger set about orchestrating a worldwide alert that pantomimed an imminent nuclear attack if the North Vietnamese continued to refuse to adhere to the November deadline. He amassed attack aircraft, strategic bombers, Polaris submarines, aircraft carriers and destroyers. The operation deployed U.S. military assets from the Atlantic and the Pacific, from the United States, Western Europe, the Middle East and Southeast Asia. The gambit was referred to euphemistically as a Joint Chiefs of Staff Readiness Test or an Increased Readiness Posture. One of the largest clandestine operations in U.S. military history, it would last from October 13 to October 30. A nuclear alert would surely "jar" the North Vietnamese at the Paris peace table. It was, at last, the strategy of conflict and risk that the game theorists had conceived, a cocking of the rouletted revolver, pressing the accelerator in a game of chicken. Nixon called on his poker skills to bluff. Echoing Schelling, they aimed, as Kissinger later attested, to send a "signal that things *might* get out of hand."[12]

Scholars of history, politics and foreign policy did not readily accept that Nixon had indeed dabbled in the mad arts. At the time and for several decades thereafter, there was little public awareness that he had implemented his madman theory. His foreign policy could be brutal, certainly bullying. Secretive, without a doubt. There were suggestions of some irrationality, especially after Watergate. Was it an act though? An account of such mad play as Kissinger's instructions to Garment was not revealed to the public until Garment published his memoirs in 2001. For decades, Nixon chief of staff H. R. Haldeman's recollection of his walk on the foggy beach with Nixon in 1968, recounted in a single paragraph of his 1978 memoir, remained the only firsthand account of Nixon's risky strategy. Haldeman's disclosure of the madman theory had been shocking enough to merit a syndicated Associated Press article. Mentions of the madman idea appeared in the *New York Times* and *Washington Post*. Notably, five years after Haldeman's account, Seymour Hersh, the dauntless reporter of war crimes, laid out Nixon's use of the madman theory more fully in *The Price of Power*. In this sprawling study of the massive (and messy) web of misdeeds committed by Kissinger during his White House tenure, Hersh detailed the canceled plan to carpet bomb North Vietnam in the oddly named Operation Duck Hook. By best accounts, the name derives from a botched golf swing that curves far off course, usually into a trap or hazard. Its selection remains inexplicable, like naming a space shuttle *Icarus*.[13]

Beyond the tabled plans for Duck Hook, Hersh documented Nixon's madman ploy against the North Vietnamese, including the full-scale nuclear feint by the Strategic Air Command (SAC) in October 1969. It was an altogether disproportionate attempt at strong-arming, Hersh contended. If taken seriously by Moscow, the operation might have escalated had the Soviets chosen to defend their communist client, ending in joint mass casualties and a cloud of radioactivity stretching over Southeast Asia. Hersh also reported a "signaling" operation aimed at the Cambodians in April 1970 as further employment of mad coercion. The "signal": Nixon ordered not only the secret campaign to carpet-bomb military targets in Cambodia, but also deployed four carriers and twenty additional warships to blanket the coast. It was, Hersh wrote, "the most enormous armada since the invasion of Normandy in World War II." Nixon called the mass forward deployment of U.S. forces on the sea "irresistible military pressure" meant to threaten not only the further pummeling of Cambodia but to convince the North Vietnamese that if they continued the fight, their forces would be next in line for obliteration.[14]

Hersh in *The Price of Power* repeated a steady beat of "madman theory, . . . madman theory, . . . madman theory," calling out Nixon's strategy nineteen times to drive home the centrality of the irrational gameplay in Nixon's foreign policy. Still, his understanding of the theory in his exhaustive study was inchoate. He focused on the bullying aspect. The primary feature for Hersh was the excessiveness of overwhelming force; his emphasis was far more on a description of Eisenhower's notion of brinkmanship and massive retaliation than Nixon's risk-laden strategy of feinted operations. Hersh missed or discounted the centrality of the theatrical performance of power and unpredictability as the key to the mad ploy. He overlooked the sense of trickery. Moreover, the significance of the nuclear strategy was somewhat lost amid Hersh's consuming focus on Kissinger's transgressions. As the historian Walter LaFeber wrote in the *Washington Post*, Hersh's far-ranging, 600-page indictment strained under the weight of Kissinger's myriad "double-crosses, character assassinations, labyrinthine conspiracies, and just plain criminality."[15] In the post-Watergate era, scholars and journalists scattered their sights in the course of unravelling the seemingly endless machinations of the Nixon administration, trying to make sense of the sheer depth and scope of malfeasance, the counter-cutting charges, the reams of declassified documents yet incomplete and later the tapes. Less than a decade after Nixon's resignation, few had yet to focus on his foreign policy as history.

The flourishing generation of revisionist historians in the late 1980s and 1990s rejected Haldeman's precocious assertion that Nixon had actually implemented his madman theory in foreign relations. Just as they looked to rescue Nixon's progressive reforms from the quagmire of Watergate, they also sought to shine light on his achievement of détente in the shadow of Vietnam. They wrote of how Nixon's realpolitik aimed to liberate the Cold War from what the historian Joan Hoff called the "procrustean ideological" frame. This generation of scholars dismissed the beach stroll with Haldeman as a single-sourced fancy, a "weakly grounded" claim, a settling of scores by the former chief of staff after a stint in prison. After all, in the same memoir in which he first mentions the madman theory, the square-jawed Haldeman, known for his own "cruel" and "humiliating" tactics, pins the entire organization of the Watergate break-in on his former boss. In the same book, he relates his disgust quite dramatically. In one passage that particularly caught the attention of newspapers, Haldeman floridly reminisces, "I saw both greatness and meanness in Nixon in such bewildering combination that years later, peering out of a hotel window at the White House . . . , I muttered out loud: 'Nixon was the weirdest man ever to live [there].'" The madman theory that Haldeman described sounded, by definition, crazy. Even as recently as the fall of 2019, Kissinger's special assistant Winston Lord flatly dismissed the madman theory as fantasy—not worthy of consideration—in a discussion at the Harvard Kennedy School.[16]

The historian Kimball's crucial work uncovering Nixon's mad strategy unfolded over the course of two and a half decades, beginning with a conference paper in 1990 for the Society for Historians of American Foreign Relations at the University of Maryland. Two years later, in 1992, SAC officially corroborated the existence of a nuclear readiness test during October 1969 but disclosed no motive. Those who took note of this seemingly tangential military exercise in the Pacific assumed that the feint of force must have been aimed at deterring the Soviets from attacking their newly turned adversaries, the Chinese. The idea that a full-scale nuclear alert had been aimed at influencing the North Vietnamese at the negotiating table seemed severely "strained logic," "convoluted at best." It was not until the late 1990s, as a post-revisionist school gained ascendency, with further revelations from the archives, that scholars came to believe that unpredictability, rather than overwhelming force, had been at the heart of Nixon's Vietnam War strategy. Only in August 2002, a decade after the first public admission of the 1969 nuclear alert, did Kimball and William Burr firmly establish that the massive maneuvering of U.S. forces had been intended to intimidate North Vietnam into caving to the November 1 ultimatum and not meant as a deterrent to halt Soviet aggression. The documentary evidence came in response to a Freedom of Information Act request filed eight years prior. The Associated Press, Agence France-Presse and the National Security Archive's website picked up the finding as the madman theory hit the mainstream. Awareness peaked when Kimball and Burr's findings drew the attention of *NBC Nightly News* and its anchor Brian Williams. In 2015, in *Nixon's Nuclear Specter*, the post-revisionist scholars Burr and Kimball finally laid out the definitive account of Nixon's use of the madman theory in Vietnam. Of particular note, Laird, Nixon's secretary of defense, personally wrote to the authors confirming that Vietnam, not Sino-Soviet relations, had been "Nixon's real reason" for the 1969 SAC nuclear alert. Laird explained the rationale—that the terror stoked by the nuclear exercise might end the war. Specifically, he recalled Nixon emphasizing, "I just want to keep them off balance. Keep them questioning what I will do."[17]

On October 15, 1969, two weeks before the deadline of the November ultimatum, just as the nuclear feinting exercises in the Pacific secretly began, Nixon's hand was undercut. In 10,000 high schools across the United States, students skipped classes to demand a halt to the Vietnam War. The mass demonstration, dubbed The Moratorium, was promoted as "a march against death." Organizers collected endorsements from the United Auto Workers, the National Council of Churches, the Pittsburgh City Council even Midas Mufflers. A hundred thousand gathered in Boston Common to hear South Dakota senator George McGovern speak as a skywriter sketched the peace sign above them. Another 100,000 converged on Bryant Park in New York City. Celebrities, including Woody Allen, Lauren Bacall and Shirley McLean, showed up to root on the crowd. As Nixon directed his secret nuclear maneuvers in the Pacific, the protestors wore black armbands to mourn the war's dead. Rallies and prayer vigils filled the streets. Church bells tolled. Black crepe draped municipal buildings. And just as "We Shall Overcome" had been the hymn of the civil rights movement, the gathered adopted John Lennon's new hit, "Give Peace a Chance," as the day's anthem.[18]

Nixon tried to transmit rumors to the press through John Ehrlichman, his domestic affairs advisor, that the demonstration was fueled and funded by communists. Haldeman believed that Nixon genuinely "suspected that [the protestors] were being aided and abetted, if not actually inspired by Communist countries." Yet far from a grand conspiracy, the broad protest could not be pinned on a small group of unkempt, intellectual basement dwellers. In East Meadow, Long Island, the longtime ambassador and statesman W. Averell Harriman, who had headed President Johnson's 1968 peace talks with the North Vietnamese, spoke to a crowd of 15,000. Both Vice President Spiro T. Agnew's daughter and Secretary of Defense Laird's son joined the demonstrations, and across the pond, just steps from the U.S. embassy in London, William Jefferson Clinton, then a Rhodes Scholar, gathered with hundreds to dissent in Grosvenor Park. By best estimate, some 2 million Americans demonstrated that day. "It was a display without parallel," judged *Life* magazine, the "largest expression of public dissent ever seen in this country."[19]

As six inches of snow did not deter 3,000 Americans from marching in Denver, as the tally of anti-war demonstrators reached 11,000 in rural Iowa, unknown to the protesting Americans, an undeterred Nixon proceeded with his nuclear readiness test. As millions marched at home, in the most visible maneuver of Nixon's feint, the president unleashed an aerial parade of eighteen B-52s in Operation Giant Lance. The massive bombers—bearing eight turbo engines, with 185-foot wingspans, capable of speeds of up to 500 miles per hour—were known as Stratofortresses. Each held four thermonuclear bombs. They flew eighteen- to twenty-four-hour ovular "vigils" over frozen Artic cliffs. U.S. aircraft, operating in radio silence, performed stand-down maneuvers to make it appear like regular missions were being called off. As one CIA report explained, "[A] stand-down in military air activity is one of the classic indicators of preparations to initiate hostilities." The maneuver signaled that the airplanes were ready, if needed, to "respond to a[ny] possible confrontation."[20]

In addition to the nuclear feint, Nixon came to believe that if he wanted to do something "drastic," Haiphong Harbor, the major port in North Vietnam, was the "only target worth doing it to." Just as he had stepped back from the overt force of Duck Hook, he dared not actually mine North Vietnamese waters. Instead, through a coordinated series of naval measures, Nixon attempted to trick the communists into believing that the United States imminently intended to plant bombs in their main commercial artery. Variously known as the mining readiness test or the mining feint, the key to the bluff was balancing public ignorance with convincing "indicator actions," at once credible, threatening and deniable. The feint escalated gradually from an inventorying of available mines to airlifting 150 mines based in the Philippines to releasing "empty mine drogue parachutes" off the port of Haiphong to pantomiming a threat to blockade. The exercise rested on the assumption that Chinese and/or Soviet spy rings were closely monitoring American activities in the South Pacific. The U.S. Navy concurrently proceeded with a smaller maneuver at the Yokosuka Naval Base, in Japan. The Japanese port was known to employ local workers and longshoremen from socialist unions who harbored anti-American sentiment and ties to the Soviet Union. They would surely leak word of the mining exercise. To an inquiring *Washington Post* reporter and the concerned Senate Foreign Relations Committee chairman, J. William Fulbright, administration officials passed the mining ruse off as an "annual inspection on a surprise basis," a "normal configuration 'Charlie,'" just some "training exercises."[21]

For the next part of the script, Nixon met with the Soviet ambassador, Anatoly Dobrynin, to deliver clearly the message. They convened in the Oval Office in the early afternoon on October 20, seven days into the nuclear ruse and eleven days before the November ultimatum deadline.

Nixon planned to play the madman. The dean of superpower diplomacy, Dobrynin would serve as Soviet ambassador to the United States for twenty-four years, from presidents Kennedy to Ronald Reagan, from general secretaries Khrushchev to Mikhail Gorbachev. He was a calming influence, friendly but wary, an artist of the back channel who began his entreaties reassuringly with "Henry, mind you, you should realize . . ." or "Let's take some first simple steps, like a child, in trusting one another." He had an affability thought to be, at the time, quite "un-Russian." Steeped in American culture, he liked fishing in Florida, betting at the Kentucky Derby. He played chess with national security advisors Robert McNamara and Zbigniew Brzezinski. Still, one career diplomat remarked, "You shouldn't treat him as a friend at court." Dobrynin was not a reformer but an assiduous messenger, and, as the *New York Times* noted, "no more duplicitous than he had to be."[22]

The level-headed Dobrynin quickly passed Moscow his notes on the unusual Oval Office meeting with Nixon, the impending November ultimate deadline looming. The Soviet diplomat expressed concern about the president's state of mind, for if the American president was acting mad, Dobrynin certainly bought the performance. Nixon had begun with an overview, skipping from topic to topic, speaking of summitry in Helsinki and Vienna—which Nixon noted had had a "good past"—then dissecting the muddle of the Middle East. Nixon goaded his Soviet interlocutor, pointing to his interest in a détente with Beijing, implying a U.S. tilt in tenuous Sino-Soviet relations. Then the topic turned and swiftly. Dobrynin recorded that on speaking of Vietnam, Nixon seemed not tough as the president intended, but "visibly nervous." He accused the Soviets of wanting the war to continue in order to take advantage of the Americans' domestic unrest. The Soviets had sat on their hands and done nothing to advance peace since the United States stopped bombing North Vietnam the previous year—that is, the president smirked, unless one counted their suggesting an oblong table for the negotiations in Paris. Throughout a half-hour monologue, Nixon circled back to the crisis in Vietnam. He "rambled, repeating himself and losing his train of thought." The effect was alarming to the Soviet diplomat. Nixon pointed out that he had another three years and three months in office and announced that, in that time, he would not allow the Soviets "to break" him. And he would *never*—Dobrynin emphasized to his bosses in the Kremlin, noting that the president had repeated the word twice—accept a humiliating defeat. After his "long-winded monologue," Dobrynin noted, Nixon finally paused to catch his breath.[23]

As they continued to converse, the ranting Nixon—"having cooled off a bit"—emphasized that not all he said should be taken literally. He valued mutual understanding and even-keeled leadership, so everyone need stay calm, "without high emotions." But, Dobrynin tried to convey, the president again, in speaking, "got excited." Nixon could just not understand the Soviets' unconditional support of the North Vietnamese. He reverted to rambling. Then, his mood shifting, the president became "again amicable." In finishing the notes to his leadership team, Dobrynin concluded that "apparently, this is taking on such an emotional coloration that Nixon is unable to control himself."[24]

After escorting the Soviet ambassador to his car, Kissinger returned, elated, to the Oval Office. He thought Nixon had performed his mad act perfectly. "I wager that no one has ever talked to him that way in his entire career! It was extraordinary," cheered the national security advisor. Later that evening in a telephone call, the two set the plan for the following day. It was, indeed, the same basic script that Kissinger had conveyed to Garment for his film festival visit to Moscow. Kissinger would raise the issue of Vietnam in his next meeting with Dobrynin, shake his head in frustration, and tell him, "I am sorry, Mr. Ambassador, but he is out of control." Kissinger would insist that Dobrynin did not know the real Nixon. "I am very close to the President," Kissinger would explain, and from enemy to enemy, standoff to standoff, Nixon had "been through more than any of the rest of us put together. He's made up his mind and unless there's some movement . . ." Kissinger would again shake his head and walk out.[25]

For all the nuclear exercises against the Vietnamese that October 1969, for the myriad military maneuvering and for all of Nixon's mad bluster and risk, his ploy "ended with a whimper." The scholars Scott Sagan and Jeremi Suri determined that the feinted nuclear venture fell far short of its goals. The action was what the military considered a "cheap signal"—more bravado than resolve, more riverboat gamble than keen strategic exercise. In part due to the extreme secrecy within and between the White House, the Pentagon and the military commands, Nixon and Kissinger's nuclear alert mixed ambiguous intent with poorly executed coordination. They also failed to game China's reactions. In response to Nixon's feint, the Chinese mobilized close to a million soldiers, 4,000 airplanes and 600 ships for the war they expected to come. They also put forces on alert to use their (relatively small) cache of nuclear weapons.[26]

A SAC historical study deemed Nixon's exercise "discernible but not threatening to the Soviets." Accidents in execution, for instance, bombers flying too closely together, had posed the most serious risk. Suri and Sagan concluded that Nixon and Kissinger's ploy brought together the "worst of all worlds," being "both ineffective and dangerous." In one sense, however, their escapade worked quite effectively, though not in bullying the North Vietnamese to settle for peace. The war would grind on for three more years. Yet, by 1969 Moscow appeared to truly believe that Nixon was off kilter. Dobrynin had sensed a "growing emotionalism" and "lack of balance" in the American commander in chief, worrying to Politburo members about the potentially stark repercussions of a president who could not "control himself even in a conversation with a foreign ambassador."[27]

Was Nixon simply acting crazy to menace his communist counterparts or had he lost control? Was his anger an act or did his frustration with Ho Chi Minh and the North Vietnamese fuel his actions? Even if the ploy were an actual strategic exercise, was Nixon's choice of a nuclear gamble inherently a mad idea premised on undue risk? Was his dance on the cliff's edge a rational choice to best an irrational foe or the illogic of an unreasoning player caught in an unreasonable situation? Nixon had rehearsed the readiness test against the Vietnamese in advance. He carefully prepared the entire nuclear ploy through the month of October. With meticulous calculation, he implemented his plan with only five others completely in the loop. Nixon saw his role as a performance, coolly playing the devil's advocate only then advocating against the devil as he sloughed off one role to take on another. Yet he also did tend to lose control of his emotions. Nixon was prone to imagine conspiracies against him and to fashion conspiracies in response. He personalized conflicts like those in Southeast Asia as affronts to him and his authority, seeing an unreasoning foe unwilling to concede to what he imagined were his rational demands. The standoff in Vietnam and the Soviets' refusal to rein in their client state frustrated him terribly. The demonstrations at home only exacerbated his anger as a direct attack on his character. After Hanoi's refusal to accept the November 1 ultimatum, Haldeman noted in his diary that Nixon was "as bitter and disappointed as I ever saw him."[28]

Throughout Nixon's life, his frustrations had fueled feverish ruminations and schemes of retaliatory trickery. In such trying circumstances, Nixon could be both mad with frustration and putting on a performance of madness—employing his anger—to coerce. The heightened stakes of such crises invigorated the president; the chance for the "big play" titillated his mood. From Kissinger's perspective, the president had played the knave in a grand performance; from Dobrynin's vantage, Nixon had lost his grip. The madman theory worked in that even to the historian, the difference between acting mad and true madness, or some combination of the two, remained and remains hazy. Nixon's motives elude as the line between temper and control remained unclear—and purposely so!

Nixon carried on rattling the saber, toying with his adversaries with gestures not only disproportionate but unpredictable. He teetered on the mountain's cliff in an aim to intimidate, acting the madman as he adopted measures that appeared—in an era of mutual assured destruction—to take on undue, catastrophic risk. A year after his feint in Southeast Asia, he unsheathed his terrible sword once more, not in the Pacific but in the Middle East. On September 1, 1970, for the second time in three months, Palestinian fedayeen attempted to assassinate Jordan's King Hussein, an American ally. Buoyed by Hussein's apparent weakness, the Popular Front for the Liberation of Palestine hijacked three international airliners. Hussein feared an uprising. He ordered tanks to surround and shell dissenting strongholds in Palestinian refugee camps. Tanks from Syria, a Palestinian and Soviet ally, invaded Jordan as Israel threatened to engage. Nixon worried that a "Soviet-inspired insurrection" might topple Hussein's Hashemite regime. He considered the Arab-Israeli conflict not chiefly a regional struggle but a "superpower psychodrama," another proxy war directly linked to the battles for control of and credibility in the developing world. He worried about a "ghastly game of dominoes, with a nuclear war waiting at the end." When Nixon met with the Israeli prime minister, Golda Meir, in the Oval Office on the morning of September 18, he found her in a "very stern mood." She, too, argued that the Arabs were only as capable as the Soviets allowed them to be. They could not operate their surface-to-air missiles without their sponsor state's assistance, she told Nixon. Further goading Nixon's worry, she told him that the Israelis had spotted Soviet pilots over the Suez Canal.[29]

Once again, to de-escalate, Nixon turned to the threat of escalation—what he would call a "very hard but very quiet line." Bogged down in the Vietnam quagmire, the Americans, should the need arise, lacked the spare military forces necessary for a successful counterassault against the uprising that threatened Hussein. The public had made clear, "No More Vietnams." So, less than a year after the SAC nuclear feint against Hanoi, Nixon again considered evoking the nuclear specter to bully his adversaries into submission or, in the least, gesture to his adversaries that he was willing to play chicken, to cock the revolver, to load his most dangerous arsenal. Nixon insisted to Kissinger that they needed to play the game with clandestine and "cool" detachment to make credible the threat; ironically, a more overt signal to the Soviets, he was convinced, would look like "bluffing." He ordered "maximum readiness," placing 20,000 American troops on alert. The Sixth Fleet assembled in the eastern Mediterranean. The Pentagon deployed a "cruiser, fourteen destroyers, and supporting ships . . . [and] an embarked marine battalion" with an extra carrier, the *John F. Kennedy*, to boot. Nixon threatened Hussein's foes with the might of conventional force, and if the Soviets intervened, he was determined to flash the nuclear option. "There's nothing better than a little confrontation now and then, a little excitement," he told Kissinger with renewed vigor.[30]

The situation threatened to devolve into another Cuban Missile Crisis, but in the Middle East and not due to antic intimidation by Khrushchev, but by Nixon. "We never create the impression with the Russians that the US will always act rationally," he told the *Chicago Sun-Times* in an off-the-record comment as the standoff unfolded. Kissinger judged Nixon's wayward remark to the *Sun-Times* as evidence that his usual "self-discipline" had been "breached by emotion," that he was overheated, amped up by the excitement of the crisis. The national security advisor found the president far from the "cool and detached" demeanor he had intended to deploy against the Soviets, but instead "charged up" by the action, "carried away by the spirit of the occasion." Ultimately, Brezhnev calmed his allies, convincing the Syrians to retreat to their border, and Hussein quelled the uprising, expelling the Palestine Liberation Organization to Lebanon, though not before the *Sun-Times* editors published Nixon's candid statement in their next edition, on September 17. The president had disclosed his core strategy, boasting, "The real possibility of irrational American action is essential to the US/Soviet relationship."[31]

During the 1971 war between Pakistan and India the following winter, Nixon again employed the grand bluff strategy with esprit, again deploying U.S. naval forces. He aimed to bolster the United States' West Pakistani allies against their Indian adversaries. After a destructive cyclone ripped through East Pakistan, the government in Islamabad, located in West Pakistan, had failed to provide necessary aid. With a larger population than West Pakistan, East Pakistan won a parliamentary majority in the following elections. In an attempt to hold on to power, the West Pakistanis unleashed a "reign of terror," openly slaughtering (mostly Hindu) Bengalis in East Pakistan. The number of dead remains highly disputed. By a CIA estimate, 200,000 Bengalis had been murdered by the halfway mark of the genocide, some 10 million Bengali refugees flooding into India. The international community looked on. Nixon hedged for time. "I wouldn't put out a statement praising it, but we're not going to condemn it either," he told Kissinger.[32]

Pakistan's president, Yahya Khan, launched an airstrike against India to preempt Prime Minister Indira Gandhi from strongly intervening. Gandhi, nonetheless, sent a massive Indian force into East Pakistan in support of Bengali nationalists. Nixon and Kissinger were dependent on Yahya as a back channel for their burgeoning rapprochement with the

Chinese, whereas they saw Gandhi as a "Soviet stooge." Identifying yet another "superpower psychodrama," worried that East Pakistan would become a "cesspool" for communist infiltration, that the unrest might spread to the Middle East to threaten Iran, Israel and even the Suez Canal, Nixon became convinced that he had to act. He grew alarmed at the prospect of a third world war, as the Chinese would side with their allies in West Pakistan and the Soviets with the Bengalis in East Pakistan. Kissinger encouraged Nixon to intervene in yet another test of will. "Your card [is only as strong as] your willingness to jeopardize it," he pressured the president. Nixon dispatched ten ships, including the nuclear-powered aircraft carrier U.S.S. *Enterprise*, a force capable of overwhelming the Soviet fleet stationed in the Bay of Bengal. On the direct hotline to Moscow, he warned Brezhnev, "in the strongest possible terms to restrain India with which . . . you have great influence and for whose actions you must share responsibility."[33]

Failing to mention his own encouragements of the president, Kissinger later remarked that Gandhi had put his boss in an irrational mood. Of all the players in the regional mire, Nixon particularly disdained the Indian prime minister. Gandhi hailed from a longline of Brahmin leaders who comprised the Nehru-Gandhi dynasty. "Nixon and Mrs. Indira Gandhi were not intended by fate to be personally congenial," Kissinger wrote. "Her assumption of almost hereditary moral superiority . . . brought out all of Nixon's latent insecurities." Nixon referred to her as "that bitch" and "that witch" while judging the brutal Yahya a "thoroughly decent and reasonable man." As Kissinger purported to worry over the president's judgment, the national security advisors' erratic mood scared his colleagues. One Department of State official reported to Haldeman about Kissinger "rant[ing] and rav[ing]" over the cascading war between India and Pakistan and the potential for global conflict. On hearing about the extent of Kissinger's rages, Nixon grew concerned, "Henry's gotten past the point of basic stability."[34]

As the nuclear stakes heightened with the U.S. and Soviet fleets circling in the Bay of Bengal, Moscow pressed Gandhi to back down and accept a cease-fire with the assurance that East Pakistan would be granted independence as Bangladesh. Gandhi maintained that she never had any intention of going any further than aiding the East Pakistanis; she had no desire to invade West Pakistan and certainly none to start a hot war with the Chinese. Just as in the Jordanian crisis, Nixon and Kissinger gave themselves and their naval feint primary credit for the cease-fire, for providing the necessary pressure on the Indians and the Soviets to maintain the balance of powers. "A heroic thing," Kissinger declared. Encouraged by the final settlement between the South Asian powers, in the year to come, he and Nixon continued to kibitz about possible opportunities gleaned from more feints against North Vietnam. For the madman theory was not a one-off tactic but a strategic ploy whose potentialities they, like moths, returned to again and again. "Mr. President, our major thing now is to get across to the Russians, to the Chinese, and to Hanoi that we are on the verge of going crazy," Kissinger concluded. "This is how we broke the India-Pakistan situation last year." It was a pure bluff, Nixon assented. "With nothing," he said. "With nothing," Kissinger agreed.[35]

The following spring, in April 1972, Nixon and Kissinger returned to consider their pattern of risk-laden schemes, this time in response to a North Vietnamese incursion into South Vietnam, and this time, pressing beyond strategic feint to the use of overwhelming military force. Known as the Easter Offensive, Hanoi's assault had marked a shift from guerrilla tactics to traditional war. Unleashing the most intensive fighting in four years, the incursion was considered at the time a "new chapter" in the conflict. The Soviets had heavily armed their communist allies with antiaircraft, long-range artillery and armored tanks. The North Vietnamese sent twelve divisions across the border, scrambling South

Vietnam's haphazard defenses, slaughtering civilians. There were accounts of public executions of South Vietnamese partisans, mass murder, some buried alive. "Thousands of panicking South Vietnamese soldiers fled in confusion . . . , streaming south down Route 1 like a rabble out of control," the *New York Times* reported.[36]

The assault by the Vietnamese was "more than just an offensive. It was a full-scale invasion," a "crisis of the first magnitude," a "barbaric strain of North Vietnamese brutality," a rattled Nixon assessed. Most of all, he was shocked by the strategic ramifications. "Vietnamization," his plan to hand over the fighting to the South Vietnamese, appeared to have been an unrealistic overassessment of his allies' ability to defend themselves. He feared that the Kremlin, encouraged by its client state's successful Easter Offensive, might step away from the negotiating table and arm its client state in the north with greater impunity. The Soviets might be spurred on to reinvest in the proxy battles of the Cold War, even reconsider the steps the superpowers had been taking toward détente and arms control. Nixon envisioned his "structure of peace" collapsing in the wake of Hanoi's brazen campaign. Chaos in Southeast Asia could trigger renewed civil strife, reinvigorating communist fervor and nationalist insurrection in the still unresolved conflicts in the postcolonial Middle East and even Latin America. "Allies . . . would question our judgment and our mastery of events," Kissinger worried. Then, Nixon imagined his greatest achievement slipping away, as if swallowed by quicksand, as he feared that China might reconsider their burgeoning rapprochement.[37]

Nixon and Kissinger warned Dobrynin that they would cancel the culminative, forthcoming arms control summit in Moscow if the Soviets failed to curb Hanoi's aggression. Brezhnev insisted that he "knew nothing of [the planned North Vietnamese] offensive," but Nixon found that hard to believe. The president was also "disgusted" by the Pentagon's indecision and paltry plans for a response. His mood grew dark, distempered and fatalistic. He contemplated whether his lifelong fight against the communists might be doomed, as the current crisis set off misgivings that dogged and rattled him, eliciting ambivalences over the Cold War battle he rarely shared, suggestions of a frailty bound up in his cause. "If we fail it will be because the American way simply isn't as effective as the Communist way in supporting countries abroad," he wrote in his diary. He judged the situation a moral hazard. For, ironically, he feared that U.S. support, far from strengthening allies, weakened them, preventing the South Vietnamese from striving and toughening, from pursuing the kind of lonely Romantic venture that he conceived as his own path, as the "American way." As he wrote in a note to himself, "We give them the most modern arms, we emphasize the material to the exclusion of the spiritual and the Spartan life, and it may be that we soften them. On the other hand, the enemy emphasizes the Spartan life, not the material, emphasizes sacrifice." He concluded that the North Vietnamese had the "will to win," while his allies in the south remained content not to lose. Whether pitched at the military brass in Washington or leaders in Saigon, Nixon's harsh admonishes bore a note of loneliness, a worry that he was surrounded not by the toughness he so valued, but by a vulnerability he could not control.[38]

Throughout the month of April, in the lead-up to the thunder and fury of what would be known as Operation Linebacker, Nixon let loose his worry with the ramblings of a warmonger. His mood unsettled and erratic, he resolved to undertake a drastic and risky approach that would exceed the SAC readiness test of 1969, the Jordanian crisis and the India-Pakistan war. "I want everything that can fly, flying," he told Kissinger and Adm. Thomas Moorer, chairman of the Joint Chiefs of Staff. "Good God! In the Battle of the Bulge they were able to fly even in a snow storm. The Air Force has got to take some goddamn risks, just like the Air Force took some risks in World War II." Nixon suggested "tak[ing out] the dikes" in Haiphong. A wary Kissinger demurred, pointing to the potential cost of 200,000 lives. Nixon clarified, "Well, no, no, no, no, no, no, I'd rather use a nuclear bomb. Have you got that ready?" Again, Kissinger pressed back, stammering, "Now that, I think, would just be, uh, too much, uh . . ." Nixon cut him off. "A nuclear bomb, does that bother you? . . . I just want you to think big, Henry, for Christ's sake."[39]

At night, in search of peers, Nixon turned to studying the risk-laden maneuverings of World War II leaders. He mulled over Winston Churchill's writings as he contemplated the ramifications of total war versus the consequences of inaction. "Hué is like Verdue," he insisted. "You can't lose Hué." John Connally, secretary of the treasury, former Texas governor and a fierce, close confidant of Nixon, encouraged the president: "Don't worry about killing civilians. Go ahead and kill 'em. People think you are now. So go ahead and give 'em some." Haldeman agreed, adding, "There's pictures on the news of dead bodies every night. A dead body is a dead body. Nobody knows whose bodies they are or who killed them." Put the summit with the Soviets at risk; "forget the domestic reaction." Nixon assented as he judged both a recalcitrant Moscow and an overly dovish Washington hindrances to ending the war.[40]

"Henry, we must not miss this chance," the president instructed as April passed into May. "I'm going to destroy the goddamn country [North Vietnam], believe me, I mean destroy it, if necessary. And let me say, even [use] the nuclear weapon if necessary. It isn't necessary." Nixon hastened to add, "But, you know, what I mean is, that shows . . . the extent to which I'm willing to go." Clarifying the scheme again, the president addended his comment. "By a nuclear weapon," he explained, "I mean that we will bomb the living bejeezus out of North Vietnam and then if anybody interferes we will threaten [with] the nuclear weapon." Speaking to Moorer, Connally and Kissinger, Nixon suggested disregarding casualties in weighing his plan's advantages. "You are not to be too concerned about whether it slops over," he stressed. "The most important thing is to get those military targets. If it slops over, that's too bad." As his mood boiled, Nixon professed the underlying goal of Operation Linebacker. "If it costs the election, I don't give a shit . . . we are going to win the war," he said, his taping system silently recording the session. "We are going to cream North Vietnam," that "shit-ass little country."[41]

In the mode of the discarded Operation Duck Hook, Operation Linebacker unleashed the power of the U.S. Air Force and naval aircraft against North Vietnam, beginning on May 9. Based in Guam and Thailand, almost 140 B-52s—"America's brutes in the air"—bore a capacity not discharged for nearly a decade. As Nixon vowed to Kissinger, "They have not given us any way to avoid being humiliated and since they have not, we must draw the sword." Adding another note of Teddy Roosevelt–like gusto, he declared, "What distinguishes me from Johnson is that I have the *will* in spades." The Americans bombed railroads, bridges, road arteries, warehouses, power plants, oil depots and enemy troop concentrations fifty miles north of Hanoi and south to the Demilitarized Zone. Navy ships including six aircraft carriers assembled in Tonkin Bay in an area known as Yankee Station. They mined Haiphong Harbor, cutting the North Vietnamese off from Soviet arms and fuel shipments. Bombers ruined rail lines designed for Chinese resupply efforts.[42]

On news of the mining and air assault, anti-war groups called for "emergency mass march[es]" in U.S. cities and on college campuses across the nation. The *Washington Post* reported "clashes between police tear gas and nightsticks and demonstrators' rocks and fists" from Berkeley, California, to Carbondale, Iowa, to Gainesville, Florida. High school students stormed the Capitol in Washington, DC. They milled around the Cannon House Office Building and shut down the galleries of the House of Representatives. An estimated 2,500 demonstrators blocked traffic on Park Avenue in New York City with another 2,500 clogging 106th Street on the Upper West Side. Students staged a "mock war" in front of International Telephone and Telegraph Corporation headquarters. From surrounding buildings, they dropped pictures of bombs connected to tiny parachutes that splattered red paint on impact. On the ground, some protestors played dead; others in military uniform steered "survivors" into "concentration camps."[43]

Returning to his understanding of grand strategy as a game of poker, Nixon wrote in his diary, "We have very few cards to play at this point." He had maintained a semblance of control over his frustration, holding back his fiercest ire, as he ordered a massive assault on North Vietnam's military infrastructure rather than a reign of terror targeting its civilian populations. In lieu of a full-scale conventional assault abroad that would have threatened to transform the generally nonviolent domestic demonstrations into chaos, Nixon emphasized the need to turn again to the nuclear specter of feigned force. Feinting was still necessary for his game however more harshly he played. Nixon had clarified to his National Security Council, "We are not going to use nuclear weapons" but the option must ever be "hanging over" the adversary. He had again circled back to his central thesis, stressing the method in the madness, vowing that the "more reckless we appear" the better.[44]

Nixon noted the subsequent exchange between Kissinger and Dobrynin in his memoir. The two met in the White House Map Room on May 11. A day earlier, during the aerial assault, the Americans had mistakenly sunk a Soviet ship, killing one sailor. Surprisingly, Dobrynin had spoken neither of the lost ship or of canceling the impending summit between the superpowers. Kissinger finally broached the subject. "*Should* we have asked any question about the summit," Kissinger pressed. "No, you have handled a difficult situation [the Easter Offensive] uncommonly well," Dobrynin responded. For in the ironic fashion of the MAD era, out of instability, with the flurry of American retribution, a steadiness continued to prevail. The détente between the superpowers held as the two agreed to move forward with their upcoming arms limitation conference. The following day, as the two diplomats made plans for the summit, they discussed possible gifts to exchange. The Soviets would give Nixon a hydrofoil; Brezhnev passed word that he would not mind another American automobile to add to his well-admired collection.[45]

In October 1973, conflict in the "gray areas" of the Cold War again threatened to erupt into war between the superpowers as yet another test of the madman theory enfolded. Syria and Egypt surprised the Israelis on their high holiday of Yom Kippur with an assault on the Golan Heights and across the Suez Canal. The Israelis were overrun, their casualties horrific—1,000 deaths within the first day—and damage to their weaponry extensive including 500 tanks, a third of its force, within the first week. Frightened by their losses and stunned by the Arabs' gall, the Israelis ordered that nuclear warheads be attached to Jericho missiles.[46] The cascade of events rattled both the Soviets and the Americans. They saw the defeat of their respective clients—Egypt and Syria for the Soviets, Israel for the Americans—as portending the collapse of their influence in the Middle East. Both superpowers sent resupplies of arms, tanks, aircraft and antiaircraft missiles. Moreover, just as the conflict escalated in the Middle East, Nixon was being bruised and distracted by the ongoing Watergate scandal. Amid the October war, in what became known as the Saturday Night Massacre, the attorney general and deputy attorney general of the United States both resigned rather than carry out Nixon's order to fire Watergate special prosecutor Archibald Cox. With the White House further preoccupied by corruption scandals that led to the forced resignation of Vice President Spiro T. Agnew, Kissinger, now secretary of state, picked up the mad torch.

On the one hand, Kissinger feared that the Israelis would again humiliate the Arabs. In 1967, the Israelis' defeat of the combined forces of the Arabs in six days of fighting, had spurred on a crippling Arab oil embargo against the United States. On the other hand, Kissinger feared that a "desperate Israel might activate its nuclear option." He further worried that if the Soviets dispatched forces to Egypt, establishing a bridgehead in the Middle East, they would never leave. An introduction of Soviet ground troops could spin the conflict out of control, countermeasures leading to countermeasures. The attack by Egypt and Syria had itself surprised the Americans, and now they detected a Soviet ship headed to the Mediterranean, believed to be armed with nuclear weaponry. Moscow placed seven airborne divisions on alert, suddenly stood down a key airlift—to send planes with reinforcements to Cairo instead?—and another heavy sealift—with weapons bound for Egypt? Kissinger in his memoir simply described "ominous reports in especially sensitive areas." Alexander Haig, Nixon's then chief of staff, judged that it was the Soviets, this time, who were playing a risky game of chicken. Kissinger swore he was willing to "go to the mat."[47]

By the first week's end, with the Israelis overrun, the "US Sixth Fleet and the Soviet Mediterranean Squadron circled each other a few hundred miles out to sea, their commanders' fingers on the button," Abraham Rabinovich, a chronicler of the October War, recounted. Fifty-some Soviet ships aggressively flanked fifty-some U.S. vessels. Below the surface, submarines patrolled. Overhead, U.S. planes circled, their missiles aimed to fire. The Israelis and Egyptians engaged in the first naval battle to employ radar-targeted missiles. Ashore they let loose the largest recorded tank melee since World War II. By the end of the second week of the crisis, the Israelis had swiftly driven back the Arab offensive. They penetrated the Syrian border within firing range of Damascus. The forces of the bellicose Gen. Ariel Sharon seized bridgeheads on the Suez Canal. The Israelis cut off supply lines and encircled Egypt's Third Army in the Sinai desert.[48]

In the face of Egypt's impending defeat, Brezhnev threatened action. It was left, again, to Ambassador Dobrynin to pass the word on the night of October 24: "I will say it straight," said the Soviet diplomat, reading the missive from Brezhnev to Kissinger over the telephone. The

Israelis had "brazenly challenged" the UN Security Council resolution calling for a cease-fire. The only choice was to send a joint Soviet-American military force of peacekeepers to end the war immediately. "If you find it impossible to act jointly with us in this matter," Brezhnev warned, and Dobrynin relayed, "we should be faced with the necessity urgently to consider the question of *taking appropriate steps unilaterally.*"[49]

By the time Kissinger received Brezhnev's curt warning, at 9:50 p.m., Nixon had gone to bed upstairs in the White House residential quarters. He wished not to be disturbed. "I don't think we should get him," Kissinger said to Haig. Nixon was "too distraught" over the brewing Watergate scandal. The president had spoken to Kissinger earlier that evening about his enemies' plots not only to take his office but his life. Reportedly, he been seen drinking heavily. In Haig's retelling, after hearing of Brezhnev's ultimatum, Nixon warned, "This is the most serious thing since the Cuban Missile Crisis." Later that night, Haig poked his head into the president's room, and according to his retelling, "With a wave of his hand, [Nixon] said, 'You know what I want, Al; you handle the meeting.'"[50]

At 10:40 p.m., downstairs from where the president slept, a small group of the National Security Council members convened in the White House Situation Room for what one attendee called a "curious little rump NSC meeting." Kissinger chaired. Far from the staid, calculatingly rational actor, he seemed "quite upset" to attendees. He denounced Brezhnev's bullying, "Why . . . without any warning all day then 'bang' we receive the Brezhnev threat?" The Soviets were "seizing on any opportunity offered by the Israelis in violation of the ceasefire." In the throes of Watergate, at a "moment of maximum US weakness," the Soviets were "throwing détente on the table since we have no functional President," Kissinger fretted to the council. "If the Soviets put in 10,000 troops into Egypt what do we do?" Those in attendance noted the "funny things going on" with Soviet naval deployments. Haig worried about the real possibilities of a third world war. "If we . . . put Marines or troops into the Middle East it will amount to scrapping Détente," Kissinger warned. What should be the next move? A "rational plan" or a "move of desperation"?[51]

Periodically throughout the meeting in the basement of the White House, as the gathering stretched on, eventually lasting from 10:30 p.m. to 3:30 a.m., Kissinger or Haig would exit to go visit the residence, purportedly, to brief Nixon and return with his judgment. Helmut Sonnenfeldt, a high-level advisor on the NSC, thought the routine actually quite typical. "Nixon did not particularly care to participate in meetings where he was under pressure to make a decision," Sonnenfeldt recalled. "He wanted to keep his distance, make up his mind . . . There were too many people in the room, and he didn't like large meetings." Deputy Secretary of State Kenneth Rush in his recounting of events, however, asserted, "We never did know whether Nixon approved; all we knew was that Kissinger said so." Haig would call it "B-A-L-O-N-E-Y" that the president had not been kept abreast of the debate.[52]

Kissinger laid out three options at the meeting. To counter the Soviet threat, they chose the most capricious route. They would not wait to meet force with force; instead, they would again engage unpredictably, once again dancing on the cliff's edge. At 11:30 p.m., in Nixon's name, the rump NSC raised the country's nuclear alert to DEFCON (Defense Condition) III—the highest state of peacetime readiness since the Cuban Missile Crisis. The 82nd Airborne Division from Munich went on alert. Seventy-five B-52 nuclear bombers in Guam were ordered to stand down. Two thousand troops headed for an area south of Crete as the aircraft carrier *Franklin D. Roosevelt* joined the *Independence* to threaten Soviet resupply routes. A third carrier was also dispatched to the Mediterranean. A message was sent to Egyptian president Anwar Sadat asking him to "consider the consequences for your country if the two great nuclear countries were thus to confront each other on your soil." After the NSC meeting, Kissinger sent a quick demand to Do-brynin: "Desist from all actions until we have a reply." He would not abide further threats from Brezhnev. In his memoirs, as Kissinger related years later, "Two could play chicken."[53]

Five hours later, at 11:30 a.m. Moscow time, an extraordinary meeting of the Politburo convened. "The Americans say we threatened them, but how did they get that into their heads? What has that to do with the letter which I sent to Nixon?," an astonished Brezhnev protested. The Soviet general secretary insisted his message through Dobrynin had been misunderstood. His ultimatum to the Americans, however harsh, had been canned bluster, a push to speak further, not a challenge to a crippled president. Some in the room grumbled, "We should have responded to mobilization with mobilization." There was a suggestion to send 50,000 to 70,000 soldiers from the Ukraine and the northern Caucasus. They needed to rescue the Egyptians in the Sinai and occupy the Golan Heights. "Who could have imagined the Americans would be so easily frightened?," asked one minister. "It is not reasonable to become engaged in a war with the United States because of Egypt and Syria," another argued. The KGB chief, Yuri Andropov, called for calm. Far from a rational actor, Nixon was "not playing by the rule," he affirmed, but "we shall not unleash the Third World War." "Where is the brink, the line between peace, and a nuclear war?," asked Foreign Minister Andrei Gromyko. "What about not giving any response to the American nuclear alert?," another minister suggested. "Nixon became too nervous; let us cool him down."[54]

Victor Israelian, head of the Foreign Ministry and a member of the Kremlin's Middle East task force, attended the historic meeting of the Soviets' response to the American's DEFCON III escalation. "Nobody liked or supported the idea [of capitulation]," Israelian recounted. The Politburo, however, could not risk calling the NSC's aggressive bluff; the actions in the name of the American president had proven too unpredictable to counter with strong measures of their own. The madman strategy appeared to have worked; the erratic feint brought calm. The Soviets decided to send seventy "observers" in a "business-like operation" to Egypt to meet with American representatives immediately. Within two days, by 4:00 a.m. on October 26, the Israelis and Egyptians agreed again to a cease-fire. Prime Minister Meir expressed great appreciation to the Americans, giving credit to Nixon's nuclear gambit. "We are convinced that thanks to the [DEFCON] alert declared by the President of the United States . . . undesirable developments were averted," she stated.[55]

For all the Soviet ministers' serious discussions at the late-night Kremlin meeting, Israelian related that there had been little they could do in terms of choices. Before the raised nuclear alert, the Soviets had already placed airborne and amphibious divisions on alert, doubling their ships in the Mediterranean to total near 100, with 23 submarines in tow (to the Americans' 60). The Soviet's minimal action, their agreeing to observers and negotiations, "the Kremlin's calm response," Israelian recounted, was the only option due to Soviet "unpreparedness." The general staff had not planned a countermeasure for over-the-top American nuclear posturing in the Middle East. Brezhnev's threat had, indeed, been bluster of his own. They had no other options than to continue by diplomatic means. Further, Brezhnev had another international matter to attend: The day following their emergency Politburo meeting he was to host the World Congress of Peace-Loving Forces in the Soviet capital. More than 3,000 attendees from seventy countries were set to descend upon Moscow. It was to be a grand "propaganda show," Israelian recalled. If the Soviets proceeded to fire missiles at the Americans and Israelis, how could Brezhnev pass himself off as the "greatest of peace lovers" to his global guests? He would look a fool.[56]

A decade later, Nixon recounted his performance during the 1973 Arab-Israeli War. "It isn't important what I might have done," he said. He turned to the game theorists' familiar analogy. "[M]y answer goes back to my poker-playing days. When you got a hole card, you never show it unless they call you."[57] That is, the best strategy is not to show an unplayed asset unless necessary. It was an odd comment, for far from not revealing the ace up his sleeve, time and again, Nixon, and later Kissinger, took the ace out to wave it for their enemies to see, maneuvering the U.S. nuclear arsenal to the front lines to threaten adversaries. Nixon played not the steady containment of Truman's grand strategy or the predictable, massive retribution promised by Eisenhower. His was a strategy for a new age, akin to the unpredictable craft of game theory that Schelling, Herman Kahn and Daniel Ellsberg studied in their offices at Harvard and RAND. Although Nixon's nuclear ruse failed to end the Vietnam War and his madman theory proved only arguably decisive in Jordan's civil war or the Indo-Pakistani standoff, the world did not explode in a conflagration. Nixon's nuclear specter appeared to contain crises as regional conflicts by threatening that a large-scale superpower response would devolve into global annihilation. The equilibrium of MAD held. Nixon and Kissinger maintained that not employing their rash strategy would have been even riskier. They held fast to the notion that the only sound course for fending off escalation was the credible threat of further escalation, and that the only credible threat of further escalation was a show of irrationality.

This conclusion nonetheless rested on an assumption out of Nixon's control: If the Soviets had reacted to Kissinger's gambit with a nuclear threat in kind, the world could have exploded. While there remains conflicting evidence about whether the madman strategy proved the difference between victory and defeat for their client states—Soviet weakness appeared as much if not a greater factor as the Americans' maneuvering in the outcomes of the Cold War battles—to take such a chance as the White House's nuclear games in the Pacific and the Middle East was to risk, as Schelling put it, that matters "*might* get out of hand."

Seemingly at a loss, the granite-faced Gromyko became forlorn over the Americans' furious bluster. For the Americans had, just as game theorists conceived, proved unpredictable. "[They] put forces on alert so often," Gromyko complained, "that it is hard to know what it meant."[58]

Furthermore, despite Nixon's insistence on the reasonableness of his strategy, he did not simply act mad. He made decisions under intense pressure, piqued by the possibilities, elated by the power of the irrational, concerned over the lack of toughness and frailty of his deputies and allies. So "charged up," so "carried away by the spirit of the occasion," during the Jordanian civil war, he baldly revealed his secret strategy of acting irrationally to the editors of the *Chicago Sun-Times*. Disgusted by Indira Gandhi, he hurled furious epithets and threats at the Indian prime minister while expressing little concern over the genocide of Bengalis in East Pakistan. In his fury in response to the Easter Offensive, he vowed retribution on the "shit-ass little country." He unleashed an aerial assault on North Vietnam, mining Haiphong Harbor, threatening to his advisors to employ nuclear weapons. He was drawn to acting out of control, to intimidating his foes with the force of apparent irresponsibility. He advocated cool and calm detachment, yet he acted far from what he preached. He was titillated by employing the madman theory, to demonstrate his singular resolve amidst crises akin to the Romantic tales of his rough and heroic idol Teddy Roosevelt.[59]

In a televised news conference two days after the 1973 nuclear scare in the Middle East, Nixon informed the nation of the root of his administration's actions. Drawing on the heroic Cold War mythos of mad strategic gambling, he declared the Middle East standoff the "most difficult crisis we have had since the Cuban confrontation in 1962." His remarks were another grand television performance; there was no talk of his having missed the key strategic meeting of the rump NSC. "Even in this week, when many thought the president was shell-shocked, unable to act, the president acted decisively," he proclaimed. He attributed his credibility to his willingness to continue the bombing of North Vietnam despite public outcry. He credited Brezhnev's capitulation to his own reputation for resolve. "I have a quality which is—I guess I must have inherited it from my Midwestern mother and father—which is that the tougher it gets, the cooler I get," he remarked. Nixon returned to the notion of international affairs as a test of his will, to his toughness. "I suppose because I have been through so much, that may be one of the reasons that when I have to face an international crisis, I have what it takes." Toward the end of the press conference, when asked about his rumored disturbed temperament, the president finally lost his nerve, a simmering ire under his reserved performance. "Don't get the impression that you arouse my anger," he declared to the inquiring journalist. "You see, one can only be angry with those he respects."[60]

7 | Madness Controlled

To China and the "Indefinite Shore"

IN FEBRUARY 1972 Nixon dined with the then septuagenarian French philosopher André Malraux. It was just days before Nixon's historic trip to the People's Republic of China (PRC). He would be the first president of the United States to visit the PRC and the first to travel to a nation with which the United States had no diplomatic relations. The eight-day trip would also be the longest foreign visit by an American commander in chief. With the trip to China, Nixon hoped his lifelong battles might finally land him the role and moniker that, in his first inaugural, he deemed the "greatest honor history can bestow." For even through his shifting incarnations, through his moods, both high and low, his pushes for détente and mad confrontation, Nixon had remained stalwart in yearning for the esteemed title of "peacemaker."[1]

That February night, Nixon shared with Malraux a story about Abraham Lincoln. "People who knew Lincoln said that they always felt he was looking beyond the horizon—as if there were a space between the earth and the sky where his gaze was focused," Nixon told his French guest. He had read the anecdote in Carl Sandburg's biography of the great and tragic president. It was a sentimental tale Nixon was drawn to, one which he repeated in interviews, in his memoirs, to visitors like Malraux. The veracity of the story was not the president's chief concern. According to the tale, according to Nixon's telling, on the very day of Lincoln's assassination, he had told his cabinet of a dream he had had the night before. The soon-to-be-martyred president dreamt of being "in some 'singular indescribable vessel' moving with great rapidity toward an indefinite shore." It was a dream, Nixon relayed to Malraux, that Lincoln had had before each of the great battles of the Civil War—a vision, Nixon was convinced, conjured by great men like Charles de Gaulle, like Mao Zedong and, he implied, like himself in his imminent voyage to the far-off East.[2]

The tale Nixon told Malraux of Lincoln resembled high adventure stories akin to his memories of childhood, of reading about foreign lands in *National Geographic* in front of his aunt's fireplace, of the train on the Santa Fe line pulling out of his town of Yorba Linda to some place glorious out on the horizon. There was a note of anticipation, but also of an anxiousness and loneliness in Nixon on the verge of his visit to Beijing. He described a striving in Lincoln, a purpose to an end that could never be defined, that he would never reach. The fabled story of Lincoln's last cabinet meeting was reminiscent of the Moses tale, a prophet who led his people to freedom but never to reach it himself. It resembled Nixon's own experience of constantly striving only to be undercut, to remain Nixon Agonistes, alone, in his "singular indescribable vessel." Nixon returned to one particular point the French philosopher made during their meeting. Although Malraux had "raised hell about Vietnam," Nixon recalled that his guest stressed that however embattled the president may be, although "everybody is ready to say the United States should get the hell out . . . you've got to always try to stand very firmly." Malraux insisted that the United States "play a role . . . in the world," not shirk off its duties to safeguard Europe and Japan, not become an "island." Nixon added, "He only says let it be an intelligent role."[3]

Nixon called himself a "pragmatist" in international affairs. After becoming president, however, the man now so often considered the realist *sine pari* chose to hang the presidential portrait of Woodrow Wilson alongside that of Dwight Eisenhower in the Cabinet Room. In addition, the desk he chose to sit behind in the Oval Office had, he thought, belonged to Wilson, a man who abhorred the pragmatic realists and passionately promoted the notion of universal principles and collective security in the twentieth century. Although Nixon's intention was clear, the desk turned out not to be Woodrow's but that of Henry Wilson, a shoemaker who became Ulysses S. Grant's vice president. Nonetheless, Nixon described Wilson as he might have described Lincoln or himself. As the historian Garry Wills suggested, both thought themselves a "lonely misunderstood leader, . . . an introspective intellectual . . . out of place in the glad-handing world of politics."[4]

In contrast to Nixon's portrayal of himself as a great and commanding peacemaker, scholars have come to write of the rapprochement between Washington and Beijing as a response to diminishing American strength throughout the 1960s. The forces of international trade, economic interdependence and financial globalization had challenged the United States' preponderance of power both abroad and at home, undermining the sovereignty of the nation. In 1971 the United States ran a trade deficit, its first time since 1893. With the country bogged down with half a million troops deployed on the Indochinese Peninsula, Henry Kissinger compared the United States to a "weary tyrant." Nixon worried it had become a "helpless, dispirited giant." Kissinger would recall how non-communist Asian governments were anxious that "the United States might shed *all* its responsibilities and turn its back on *all* its interests in the region." Both Nixon and Kissinger feared that a loss of what the game theorist Thomas Schelling was calling "face" threatened not just American commitments in Asia but also the United States' closest allies in Europe. NATO had begun to fracture as France pulled out of its integrated military structure. West German chancellor Willy Brandt initiated a rapprochement with the Eastern bloc. Chinese premier Zhou Enlai warned his American counterparts, "Powder kegs have been set up everywhere." The administration feared the emergence of "future Nasser-types" in Latin America and Africa just as, in the Far East, a Japanese economic "miracle" undercut the Americans' economic might.[5]

As president, Nixon upended decades of his own anti-communist cant, or what Kissinger called an "abstract crusade," what Eisenhower had designated the United States' "mission to fight communism all around the world." In Nixon's 1968 acceptance speech for the Republican's nomination, he announced that Americans did "not seek domination over any other country." He advocated a course to sustain the bipolar hegemony that had grown out of the post–World War II accords, a peaceful coexistence in which the United States would be "as firm in defending our system as [the communists] are in expanding theirs." In a major address to Congress in February 1970, Nixon maintained, "[The] more that policy is based on a realistic assessment of our and others' interests, the more effective our role in the world can be." It was not the internal ideological fervor of the PRC or the Soviet Union, or their social and economic structures, that undercut the world's order, it was the communists' external steps to enlarge their empires that radically challenged global accord. He sounded like Kissinger, like a latter-day Prince Klemens von Metternich, both men enamored with the eighteenth-century, Austrian diplomat and his strategy of realpolitik. Far from the Wilsonian trappings of universal self-determination, Metternich, like his Anglo-Irish counterpart Lord Castlereagh, stressed that rulers shared not ideals but strategic interests, and interests conflicted. Only the ability of powerful and stable states to balance their objectives with others'—interests traded for interests—could provide a stable international framework.[6]

In Nixon's view, a negotiated détente with the communists became a matter of "linkage," constructing a web of such interlocking strategic objectives. The Americans' recognition of the PRC would depend on China's cooperation in bringing peace to Vietnam. Strategic arms limitations and increased trade with the Soviets would depend on Leonid Brezhnev's reducing crackdowns on political dissent in the Eastern bloc and his support of communist movements throughout Europe. Because the United States could no longer dominate the world, Nixon argued, international stability depended on a balance among China, Japan, the Soviet Union, the United States and Western Europe. He pressed for a status quo among the great powers to shore up alliances and defend against the revolutionary movements upturning the postcolonial world. Whether right- or left-wing regimes, whether the likes of the Philippines' anticommunist Ferdinand Marcos or China's Communist Party chairman Mao, Nixon consistently favored authoritarians over dedicated democrats for their reliability in suppressing radical and reform movements. He could deal with "strongmen," Nixon maintained. "This is the time men have to be strong. I don't have contempt for strong men that disagree with me—like Communists. I respect them." It was the idealists, he said, the "intellectuals who put themselves on a high moral plane and are just weak," whom he could not abide. "Clowns, dilettante intellectuals . . . [They] bite us like sand flies."[7]

The historian Jeremi Suri further observed how Nixon's easing of tensions with the Chinese was not only a hard-nosed strategy for dealing with opponents abroad, but also at home. Détente with the communists could undercut protestors vehemently, and sometimes violently, rebelling against their states' leaders. Nixon hoped that a rapprochement with the Chinese would lead his one-time adversaries to press their client state, North Vietnam, to stand down. The Vietnam War would be settled not between soldiers fighting in the jungle or with masses demonstrating in the streets but in back-channel negotiations, between representatives of the people, furtively, between elites. By quelling tensions between Washington and Beijing, by quieting the fighting between Hanoi and Saigon, Nixon and Kissinger and Mao and Zhou could spend their political capital on stabilizing the unrest extending from Berkeley to Wuhan, where demonstrating partisans revolted against the upheaval of Mao's Cultural Revolution. By mitigating international friction, by thawing Cold War state-to-state relations, the leaders, thereby, hoped to curtail domestic turmoil.[8]

In this game of realpolitik, Nixon imagined a chessboard not of competing beliefs and consuming affectations, thinking instead about which strategic pieces to play; to this end, there was more to gain. With the cold precision of a geostrategic engineer, the president envisioned reorienting the world map to position the United States triangularly between the two skirmishing communist states of China and the Soviet Union. He could initiate a new phase of the Cold War in which the United States would have the leverage to tilt the balance of events to favor one or the other empire. Kissinger quipped, "With conscientious attention to both capitals, we should be able to have our mao tai and drink our vodka, too."[9]

As Nixon's moods vacillated and his allegiances altered, however, his notion of his role was not quite so realistic, never as entirely unsentimental as his national security advisor's. In the most private of moments, the two kibbitzed over their shared aims, but while Nixon was taken with Kissinger and the realpolitik vision, he was not so singularly minded. Kissinger's biographer Walter Isaacson described a profound cynicism in the national security advisor's wily attempts to accumulate power and sway. "In dealing with other people, [Kissinger] would forge alliances and conspiratorial bonds by manipulating their antagonisms," Isaacson wrote. The master diplomat did not rely simply on rational calculations of personal, partisan and national interests, but often sought to gain his adversaries' "approval through flattery, cajolery, and playing them off against each other." Nixon lacked Kissinger's fine-tuned affective control. He set out on a cynical path, but then waffled or faltered. He sought compromise only to be tempted by a greater vision. He attained a goal only then to question its import or worry over the credit he would receive. Despite Nixon's efforts to tamp down his anxieties and reservations, he often found that he could not. With one confidant and then another, throughout the day and into the night, for hours, Nixon ruminated over which move to play. Haldeman reached for a metaphor to characterize his boss's irresolution: "He's [like] a dog who is getting ready to lie down . . . He's trying to decide how he's going to settle . . . and he makes these circles and circles."[10]

Nixon vacillated on how to position the United States in the world as elusive and determinedly so. As he insisted to Kissinger, "We cannot, either in the past, or in the present, or in the future . . . be too forthcoming in terms of what America will do." Nixon believed that the United States should not "beat our breasts" with determined bravado, but then again, neither should it shirk away and "wear a hair shirt" with endless guilt. He and Kissinger would extract the United States from Vietnam, he acknowledged, but then he hesitated; he would not apologize for his nation's strength and swagger. "Who does America threaten? Who would you rather have playing th[e] role [of the superpower]?" Then, again, Nixon retreated. As he ruminated with Kissinger, he returned to his much-used poker metaphor rather than to the United States' dominant role. "I mean there's a lot of people that could look at their hole cards here," he remarked, considering various players and their hidden advantages.[11]

From crisis to crisis, for a lifetime, even after acquiring a crew of close confidants and drawing millions of supporters, Nixon remained a loner. To attain the popularity necessary for his relentless self-advancement, he traded alliances. He ingratiated himself among overlapping Republican fiefdoms of old guard and new, East Coast and West Coast, economic royalists and libertarian chauvinists. He courted Confederate revanchists with his Southern strategy only then tried to secure domestic support through broad progressive programs. So, too, behind closed doors, in calculatingly realist fashion, he alleged an interchangeability of foreign comrades. He argued that unions of trusted

"friendship" between nations—in which belief matched belief, sentiment united with sentiment—would prove hollow, wholly insufficient
to secure rational and enduring strategic alliances. "Speaking here,"
Nixon privately told Zhou in Beijing, "the Prime Minister knows and I
know that friendship—which I feel we do have on a personal basis—
cannot be the basis on which an established relationship must rest." He
recounted a lesson from a professor in his first year at Duke law school:
"A contract was only as good as the will of the parties concerned to keep
it. As friends, we could agree to some fine language, but unless our national interests would be served by carrying out agreements set forward
in that language, it would mean very little."[12]

Mystique and "face" remained at the forefront of Nixon's thinking.
By the time he was elected president, a hardened Nixon spoke of the Vietnam War as a cause that needed not a "victorious peace" but merely an
"honorable end." He was convinced that if he were seen as abandoning
Saigon to the communists, if he could not guarantee the South's (apparent) sovereignty, he would lose his own legitimacy as a leader abroad and
at home. By the time Kissinger first secretly met with the Chinese in
July 1971, Nixon had been discussing with him the need for at least a patina of credibility in their withdrawal from Vietnam. They would insist on
guaranteeing a "decent interval" between the time the Americans evacuated and Saigon fell. As Nixon would judge, "If a year or two from now
North Vietnam gobbles up South Vietnam, we can have a viable foreign
policy if it looks as if it's the result of South Vietnamese incompetence."[13]

Yet, however determined, far from an assured man, Nixon ever
weighed his options. In portrayals of himself and in other's portrayals
of him as a keen strategist of foreign affairs, there was an element of flexibility. In private talks with Zhou, after Nixon laid out his realpolitik
vision of how great powers achieved a state of balance, after setting forth
that nations had not "friends" but "alliances," he slipped back into a Wilsonian script of universal self-determination. "It is the right of every

nation . . . to survive and develop," he told the Chinese premier as the two shared their philosophic outlooks. In particular, Nixon insisted on free, fair and open elections in South Vietnam as the keystone for a negotiated resolution and peaceful coexistence. Through the rest of his term and after leaving office, Nixon defended the veracity of his avowed commitment to democracy in Southeast Asia that he had made to Zhou. He tried to hide the degree to which self-interest, expedience and cynicism dominated his Vietnam strategy, the degree to which his military retreat from Saigon became guided by a desire to extricate the United States without losing face, regardless of South Vietnamese casualties. Unlike Kissinger, who spent a career proselytizing the virtues of realpolitik, Nixon wanted the historical record to read that he had been a man not of exigencies but of principles. However facetious or revisionist or self-deluding, he argued that he never sold out the South Vietnamese, that the real Nixon had endeavored to secure their independence, that the real Nixon was guided not by a decent interval but by decency. "When I see the terrible holocaust that has been visited upon the people of South Vietnam, Cambodia, and Laos [after the U.S. withdrawal], I say that any government with any moral sense whatever was justified in trying to prevent that from happening," he insisted in a far-ranging interview with his former aide Frank Gannon in April 1983. "And I think history will record, when we get further away from the trauma of defeat, that . . . as President Reagan has said, it was a just war, if any war at all is just."[14]

There was a plasticity to Nixon's strategic vision, but there was also a constant. In discussing his imminent breakthrough to China, whether détente arose from strategic weakness or strength, whether he sought international order between the great powers or to buoy self-determination for the rest, Nixon was keenly aware of his role. He wished not to be remembered primarily as the red-baiter of his congressional days or the average Joe of the silent majority. He dissociated from strong-arm foreign affairs, carpet-bombings of cities (Hanoi) and the mining of harbors (Haiphong). As befitted a boy who had been president of his school classes and his law school's bar association, and a congressman turned senator then vice president and president, striving proved to be the singular constant in Nixon's foreign policy. He liked the coining of phrases that gave off an air of a masterly mind at work, like "linkage," "Nixon Doctrine," and "Vietnamization." He yearned to lead the nation through an epochal event that would be considered side-by-side with John Kennedy's moonshot. For even if his foreign policy at times came off the cuff, even when his grand strategy was not an unprecedented stroke of genius, even if it proved inconsistent, even when his policies sprung not from strength of character and country but from a position of vulnerability, Nixon hungered to be seen as the genius-statesman, the foresighted leader, the heroic Lincoln, singular and lonesome.[15]

Nixon hung Theodore Roosevelt's portrait in the Cabinet Room alongside those of Eisenhower and Wilson. "The credit belongs to the man who is actually in the arena, whose face is marred by dust and sweat and blood," Roosevelt had said, and Nixon repeatedly quoted. Nixon titled his third and final memoir *In the Arena* (1990) as he turned his focus to another version of his staged performances, the figure of the gladiator. Far from the grime of politicking, he aimed for a sublime presentation. And as with his hero Roosevelt, Nixon, too, focused not merely on victory but on grievance. Roosevelt derided those who failed to strive. The bystander, the observer, the waylaid, all should be mocked if not scorned. "It is not the critic who counts; not the man who points out how the strong man stumbles," said Roosevelt, and Nixon railed, "I have contempt for men who won't take chances. I call them gutless wonders." He maligned the press, the protestors, the naysayers, those on the sidelines. They were not doers; they were feeble critics, sickly. As for the man in the arena, a disdainful Roosevelt spat out and Nixon quoted, "If he fails, at least he fails while daring greatly, so that his place shall never be

with those cold and timid souls who know neither victory nor defeat."
Action was to be cherished. Roosevelt urged the celebration of "the
man . . . who errs, who comes short again and again; because there is
not effort without error and shortcoming."[16]

As Nixon met with Malraux before his departure to Beijing, he had
thought that speaking looked painful for his White House guest. The
philosopher had recently suffered a stroke. "[The] whole left side of his
face was drooping, and the words could hardly come out," Nixon described. "I admire a guy who goes over physical disability." As was so
often the case, he felt for the maligned underdog, the "poor guy," "fighting it all the time." And to Nixon's delight, the feisty Frenchman responded to his story of Lincoln in kind. "When [Malraux] talked about
China, . . . a torrent of words came [out]," Nixon recalled. The Frenchman cheered his American host on his imminent voyage to Beijing with
the promise of adventure and significance. "You are about to attempt one
of the most important things of our century," he said to Nixon. Malraux
had been a lifelong adventurer of the old imperialist kind. He described
foreign policy as an attempt to leave a "scar on history." At twenty-two,
in 1923, a swashbuckling Malraux had been imprisoned in Cambodia
for art theft. He traveled to China in the 1930s and briefly got to know
Mao and Zhou. He became a hero of the French Resistance in World
War II and then de Gaulle's long-serving minister of culture. Later in
life, he traveled through East Pakistan, to Saudi Arabia and then to Yemen on a quest to unearth the long-lost capital of the Queen of Sheba.
He was known for his storytelling, elaboration and grandiosity. As one
press advisor complained about Malraux, "I felt I was listening to the
views of a romantic, vain, old man who was weaving obsolete views into
a special framework for the world as he wished it to be." Nixon, however,
was taken with his much-disparaged guest.[17]

So to Nixon, Malraux had spoken of the historic trip to Red China
just as Nixon had spoken of Lincoln's indeterminate voyage. "I think of

the sixteenth-century explorers," Malraux said, and Nixon would repeat, "[those] who set out for a specific objective but often arrived at an entirely different discovery." It was as if the trip to China took him not only to a far-off shore, but also back in time to the fabled oceanic adventurers of exploration. Both Nixon and Malraux traced the roots of the president's historic journey to a legendary lineage. With Nixon's trip to China, as they framed it, far from the grit and grind of realpolitik and the compromised exigencies that became synonymous with his name, a "new Nixon" was entering the land of epics, the dangerous and the divine. Nixon would dub it the "week that changed the world."[18]

To understand Nixon's strong desire to become the peacemaker, some scholars have pointed to Hannah Milhous, Nixon's mother, and her Quaker pacifism, indeed a propensity toward peacemaking "inherited from his mother" as he wanted so much to please her "saintly" ways. As the historian Margaret MacMillan put it, "He longed to be good." Yet, for Nixon, peacemaking proved at once an emulation and a rebellion. Nixon had discerned by his college days that achieving peace was not as his mother had preached. It was not her pacificism that could end war, he came to believe, but the letting loose of unadulterated war—or at least the threat of it. "Illogical? Insane? Yes, but the fact we must acknowledge is that man can be inspired to fight for the cause of peace," he wrote in a college essay. Nixon dreamt of joining not the ranks of his mother's Quaker purity but the warring peacemaker: "Wilson led his country into war," the young Nixon proselytized. "He fired his soldiers with patriotic zeal; he revitalized the Allied troops; all because he had an ideal, the ideal of World Peace." Nixon shed the Quaker pacifism of his childhood for pacifism through pacification. "My beliefs are shattered, but in their place a new philosophy has been built," he expounded with the alacrity of conversion. And still through his young adult life, after returning from war in the South Pacific as a naval officer, having seen bombs dropped and men dead, he appeared "to be dreaming about some new order which would make wars impossible," one friend recalled. "He impressed us in those days as an idealistic dreamer." In the afterglow of Wilson and then Franklin Roosevelt's wars, Nixon saw the world as mutable, one that could fall into great conflict but, just as well, he believed, could through conflict progress.[19]

Nixon made himself a student of foreign affairs. As he had throughout his life, he cherished the chance to do what he called his "homework." Upon entering the House of Representatives, he toured Europe in a congressional group assessing the prospects for the Marshall Plan. Nixon would for most of his career tout himself as a hardline cold warrior. He presented himself not as a realist, but an ideologue. He rejected China's inclusion in the United Nations. He ran as vice president on Eisenhower's ticket, decrying that Harry Truman had "lost China" to the communist world. His anti-Chinese resumé ran long, duly warning of the Red empire's authoritarian crimes against its people and its imperial designs to bully its neighbors. When it came to anti-communism, he quipped, "I didn't need to be lobbied. It would be like carrying coals to Newcastle." In Nixon's second debate with Kennedy in 1960, he compared China's threatening the islands of Quemoy and Matsu to Hitler's aggression in Danzig. He saw the war on the Indochinese Peninsula as a fight against further communist expansion. As he formulated in a 1965 address, "[The] confrontation is not fundamentally between Vietnam and the Viet Cong . . . but between the United States and communist China." He maintained that without communist meddling in Pacific affairs, there would not have been enough support among fledgling revolutionaries to fight a Cold War in Southeast Asia. In effect, Nixon suggested, if not for Chinese intervention in North Korea or North Vietnam, liberal democracy or at least an authoritarian capitalism would have taken root.[20]

China duly played its part as a U.S. adversary. Mao rallied his people around the idea of the United States as China's chief foe, the symbol of capitalism in all its corruption. In Mao's telling, with Europe past its prime, the United States now stood as the last vestige of the old world, the last imperial power in Asia. As for Nixon, the chairman taunted him as the "jittery chieftain of US imperialism" and the "God of Plague and War." The Chinese *People's Daily* sprayed metaphors that could have been penned by one of Nixon's fiercest domestic adversaries, a Hunter S. Thompson or a Gore Vidal. The paper declared Nixon a "hypocrite priest and a 'gangster' who, while talking peace, 'holds a blood-dripping butcher's knife.'"[21]

As Nixon's career progressed, he dallied with different strategic modes. He worked hard to burnish his foreign policy credentials. Under Eisenhower, he hopped from state to state on official visits. He attempted to distance himself of his image as a crusading red-baiter, to refashion himself as a serious man, a man of the world. Still, at times, he regressed. In his years in the wilderness, after his 1960 political defeat to Kennedy, he continued to give well-worn stem-winders. "It happens that we are on the right side," he starkly insisted to the conservative Bohemian Club of San Francisco in the summer of 1967. He boasted with ideological zeal that Americans were on "the side of freedom and peace and progress against the forces of totalitarianism and reaction and war."[22]

On July 25, 1969, only months into his presidency, Nixon announced what became known as the Nixon Doctrine. During a diplomatic junket to Guam after observing the Apollo 11 splashdown and recovery in the Pacific after the first moon landing, Nixon held a press conference. In the afterglow of the great American adventure to space, Nixon promised a venture of his own. He declared that he would not back down from the threatening communists in China, North Korea and North Vietnam. He would not retreat from obligations in the Pacific as had the British, the French and the Dutch. He would uphold the U.S. promise to continue aiding Japan, Malaysia, Singapore, South Korea and Thailand. The United States would remain a great Pacific power. More ominously, Nixon spoke of assuring security agreements by helping its Asian allies with "internal security."[23]

Key to the policy, Nixon announced, was that the United States would no longer simply rely on force and military occupation but would instead focus on economic and military aid to friendly regimes. Nixon promised to withdraw American troops from South Vietnam—flood it with arms and training for its soldiers—and allow the Vietnamese to wage their own battle. For this policy shift, he adopted a term coined by his Secretary of Defense William Laird: "Vietnamization." Being brought to heel in the jungles of Vietnam, the United State would nonetheless maintain its standing as the defender of democratic rights, albeit from a distance. It was an imperial sleight of hand. In retreat, Nixon insisted, the United States would still retain its place as leader among nations, a role reminiscent of FDR's proclamation of it as the "arsenal of democracy." Nixon trumpeted, "Asia for Asians," a renewed U.S. commitment to self-determination. "That is what we want, and that is the role we should play. We should assist but we should not dictate." As was his want, Nixon offered a maxim in the form of a recollection. He recalled advice he had passed along to the Pakistani president, Gen. Ayub Khan. "The role of the United States in . . . any of those countries which have internal subversion is to help them fight the war but not fight the war for them."[24]

Far from a well-laid plan, however, Nixon's delivered his expansive remarks at a 6:30 p.m. press conference at the Top O' the Mar, an officers' club in Guam. The White House held back on releasing a transcript and said the president's remarks were meant "for attribution but not direct quotation." Nixon had consulted neither Kissinger nor his national security staff.[25] Back home, liberals welcomed the notion of disentangling the United States from quagmires abroad, and conservatives cheered on the plan to reinvest in allies. Those on the far right, however, feared the old hand was growing soft.

Winston Lord, Kissinger's Asia specialist, would characterize the Nixon Doctrine as neither a grand strategy nor a master plan, one "not at all different from the rhetoric of past policy." The historian Jeffrey P. Kimball has called the Nixon Doctrine "ambiguous," "inconsistent" and "imprecise." The doctrine retained U.S. commitments to allies assumed at the end of World War II. Kimball observed that the turn to Vietnamization was not a revolution but a return to Eisenhower-era policy. Between 1955 and 1961, Nixon's mentor had supported counterinsurgency and nation-building in Southeast Asia with a minimal U.S. footprint. Eisenhower had already pledged to invest in solidifying South Vietnam's capability to combat subversives both domestic and foreign. Nixon's concurrent, covert military plans only added confusion to the purported grand strategy of his purportedly new doctrine of disentanglement. Far from overseeing an offensive retreat, the president was well underway in planning the fabled and ultimately aborted Operation Duck Hook, aimed at leveling North Vietnam with American air and naval power. Within months, Nixon would employ the "madman theory" by threatening North Vietnam with a full-scale nuclear alert.[26]

As the Nixon Doctrine proved irresolute—after two more protracted years of fighting communists in Southeast Asia, after both troop withdrawals and escalatory bombing, after promises of peace but no apparent end to the war—in mid-July 1971, seemingly in a flash, Nixon announced from NBC studios in Burbank, California, that he would be traveling to China to meet with his communist adversaries. Like his impromptu remarks in Guam, Nixon put on a show, a coup de théâtre in fewer than 400 words. The broadcast, presented live on all three major television networks, shocked the millions watching at home. To hear about the planned pursuit of peace with the Chinese from a man who had built his career battling the Red peril was a "shattering jolt," the *Washington Post* reported. The newspaper marked the announcement as no less surprising as Hitler and Stalin's rapprochement in August 1939 and their agreement to divvy up Poland. With the Nixon Doctrine, the president had pledged to maintain the status of the United States as an arsenal for democracy for its allies. Now, he had seemingly shifted from being an ideologue championing the anti-communist crusade to a realist in the pursuit of international stability. It marked such an alarming reversal that the phrase "Nixon going to China" entered Americans' lexicon, denoting just such an alarming reversal. Indeed, the cliche developed further, to *"only* Nixon could go to China"—only a leader like Nixon, with his furious, anti-communist past, would have the political capital and the credibility to make such a risk-laden overture. As the historian John Lewis Gaddis observed, ironically only for a red-baiter like Nixon could such a diplomatic maneuver "take on the aura of statesmanship rather than softness."[27]

In Mao, Nixon had found a willing partner with an even more ruthless reputation. Loudspeakers strung through the streets of Beijing announced the news of Nixon's visit, but Chinese authorities eschewed any mention of realpolitik. Like Nixon, Mao transmitted a message in the language of the visionary, cloaking the strategic breakthrough in terms of class struggle. He maintained to his people that the new dynamic between the powers stemmed from the weakening of the Americans' position throughout the 1960s. The rapprochement grew out of a U.S. "awakening" of students, clergymen, Blacks, the working class and even some businesspeople and military personnel fed up with U.S. meddling in the South Pacific. "[The] masses of the American people . . . are very good," the loudspeakers blared, "only a handful [of the] monopoly capitalist class" stood in the way of a peaceful coexistence or even a socialist revolution.[28]

Crucially, relations between the People's Republic and the Soviet Union had cratered. Animosity between the Chinese and the Russians dated back at least to the thirteenth and fourteenth centuries, to the Yuan (Mongol) dynasty, at times to all-out invasion, at times to familiar, if not familial-like, spats between competing and neighboring powers, between the younger brother and the "erstwhile Elder Brother," though which of the two was which remained an open question. Russians historically considered the Chinese as having an Eastern, barbaric *dysha* (soul) rather than one grounded in Orthodox or Western Christendom. Buried in the folklore of animosity, with no small amount of Orientalist condescension, the Russians slighted Mao as the next Genghis Khan or the latest radical in the tradition of the Boxer Rebellion (1899–1901). Stalin, in his own game of realpolitik, had even made a pact with Mao's archrival, the Nationalist Chiang Kai-shek, toward the end of World War II. After Stalin's death, Nikita Khrushchev refused to share the plans for the atomic bomb with an upstart communist China that he considered too radical. Deepening the discord, Khrushchev's very public denunciation of Stalin's cult of personality threatened in 1956 to undercut Mao's own.[29]

Peripheral skirmishes aside, between 1956 and 1969, the Soviets armed their divisions along the Chinese border with short- and medium-range nuclear-tipped missiles capable of reaching cities in northern China. The Brezhnev Doctrine, put forth by Khrushchev's successor in 1968, further spooked Mao with its insistence on meddling in the affairs of the socialist world. Mao criticized the Soviets' invasion of Czechoslovakia that summer, calling the incursion the "most barefaced and typical specimen of fascist power politics played by the Soviet revisionist clique." With China's population booming at three times that of the Soviet Union, Mao was not to be ignored. By 1964 China had developed an atomic bomb and by 1967 a hydrogen bomb. Mao positioned a bulwark of forces in the Soviets' backyard, in Mongolia. Rumors circulated about first strikes by the Soviets against the Chinese nuclear arsenal.[30]

By the early 1970s, as Mao's health deteriorated, his control also began to slip. Like Nixon, he was acting from a position of dwindling strategic strength. Surrounded by adversaries in India, the Soviet Union,

South Korea, Japan, Taiwan, the Philippines, Singapore and South Vietnam, China confronted what the historian Wen-Qing Ngoei has called an "arc of containment" on nearly all fronts. Mao's worst fear was of China being carved up: the north to Moscow, the south to Washington, the east to Tokyo, and Tibet to New Delhi. So impressed, Mao ordered the *People's Daily* to publish Nixon's first inaugural address, in which the American president pledged to undertake the course of the "peacemaker." The *Reference News*, the leading internal newsletter circulated to Communist Party and military leaders, tipped off readers to a quickening pace of the rapprochement. It was an unprecedented move. By improving relations with the Americans, a weakened Mao saw an opportunity to paint the Soviet Union as the "social-imperialist country" and the true "bastion of reactionary forces in the world." By pledging peace with the United States, Mao saw himself as the one triangulating. He believed he could "borrow the strength of the barbarians to check the barbarians." Indeed, Kissinger—as ever, stressing strategic considerations over ideological suasion—would write that realpolitik was the traditional style of Chinese geostrategy. Surrounded by twelve unsettled neighbors, and following the teachings of the general and philosopher Sun Tzu, the Chinese could not hope for the decisive battle or unconditional surrender so central to Western warfighting that demanded a final surrender of its foes. Instead, Kissinger wrote, "[The] Chinese ideal stressed subtlety, indirection and the patient accumulation of relative advantage."[31]

The evening following Nixon's announcement of his upcoming trip to see Mao, the press spotted Nixon outside one of his favorite Los Angeles haunts, Perino's Restaurant. After a dinner of hot crab legs with mustard sauce and handshaking, Nixon declared it a "beautiful night." As the *Chicago Tribune* observed, "Even . . . Haldeman and John D. Ehrlichman, known for their dour expressions, wore broad smiles." Nixon biographer Garry Wills called it the "happiest time in Nixon's life." Still, as well-wishers greeted the famous diners in the restaurant's foyer, Kissinger remembered noticing a reserve in the president's celebration. "There was a mutual shyness; Nixon was always ill at ease with strangers, and the other guests were not comfortable in approaching," Kissinger judged. "In his hour of achievement Richard Nixon was oddly vulnerable, waiting expectantly for recognition without quite being able to bridge the gulf by which he isolated himself from his fellow man."[32]

Both U.S. adversaries and allies were disturbed by Nixon's sudden announcement, which, Kissinger recounted, "rattled [Ambassador Dobrynin's] teeth." It was reported that the leaders of Taiwan displayed "a blend of dignified reserve and controlled rage." William Rusher, publisher of the *National Review* and a stalwart supporter of Taiwanese independence, called the move one of "the greatest historical double-crosses of all time." Indeed, after Nixon's announcement, a new word entered the Japanese lexicon: *shokku* (great shock).[33] At least, such was the shokku in the summer of 1971, such was Nixon's masterly show.

It was during Nixon's years in the political wilderness, as the turmoil of the 1960s stretched on, that his thoughts began to shift from a vision of ultimate victory over totalitarianism to a goal of international order balanced by great if disagreeing powers. He had publicly broached his desire for a normalization of relationships with China in a 1967 journal article he penned with the assistance of William Safire for *Foreign Affairs*. Nixon contented that the "free world" must not let fester "a billion of its potentially most able people to live in angry isolation," left "to nurture its fantasies, cherish its hates and threaten its neighbors." The "irritants" of Taiwan and Vietnam should no longer drive the great powers into war. He called for a "new world," "new leaders," "new people," "new ideas." By banding together, the Americans and Chinese could not only check the Soviets, they could, as Kissinger would write, "reduce Indochina to its proper scale—a small peninsula on a major continent" whose conflict could no longer act as a proxy battle between the communist and capitalist worlds.[34]

Far from Nixon's "bolt-from-the-blue" staging, negotiations between the United States and the People's Republic had secretly been underway since the beginning of Nixon's first term. As was so often the case with Nixon, the sudden announcement of his trip to China had been timed for dramatic effect. This "new Nixon" was a performance of his power to reshape the world with a seemingly snap decision. It was a show that masked a long rehearsal process. Before his televised declaration for a détente with China, Nixon had already reduced patrols by the Seventh Fleet along the Chinese coast of the Taiwan Straits. Trade, travel and tariff restrictions had been loosened as delegations of professionals traveled from one country to the other. Coyly, Nixon dropped a hint to *Time* in the fall of 1970. "If there is anything I want to do before I die, it is to go to China," he told the magazine. So, too, Mao's estimation for the Americans had been growing. The United States was "changing from monkey to man," Mao quipped to his diplomats, "not quite man yet, the tail is still there . . . but it is no longer a monkey, it's a chimpanzee, and its tail is not very long."[35]

The rapprochement with China had been at Nixon's initiative. Although he would omit it in his memoirs, Kissinger at first pooh-poohed the effort for accord. "Our Leader has taken leave of reality. He has just ordered me to make this flight of fantasy come true," Kissinger complained to his deputy, Alexander Haig, in February 1969. On an airplane ride soon thereafter, Haldeman returned to the main cabin after speaking with the president to sit with the national security advisor. "You know, he actually seriously intends to visit China before the end of the second term," the chief of staff said. "Fat chance," Kissinger shot back. In China, Mao's leading advisor, a wary Zhou Enlai, compared the American president to a woman of loose morals, "tartering [*sic*] herself up and offering herself at the door." Yet Nixon insisted, "Nations must have great ideas or they cease to be great." Far from the madman or the cynical realist, Nixon's visionary aplomb sounded much like a Malraux, a de Gaulle or a Churchill. Talks with China developed from "feelers" first tested in December 1969, behind the scenes of a Yugoslav fashion show in Warsaw, and continued at the U.S. consulate in Hong Kong and at CIA stations in Romania and Pakistan. The White House left the congressional leadership out of the loop as Nixon, step-by-step, explored his options for improving relations with Mao. He referred to the People's Republic rather than to Red China or Communist China at a dinner in October 1970 with the Romanian dictator Nicolae Ceausescu. The Chinese invited an American table tennis team to visit in the spring the following year, the first such invitation since 1949. They were told not to shake hands or converse, but Mao allowed his country's team to forgo the standard brandishing of their *Little Red Books*. Zhou even instructed his squad to humor the Americans, to let them win a few games.[36]

For Kissinger's first visit to China, in July 1971, he slipped away from Pakistan to China, disappearing for forty-eight hours, complaining officially of dysentery or what the diplomats called a "Delhi belly." With Kissinger secretly in China, Nixon spoke at length to a group of media executives at a Holiday Inn in Kansas City. He planned his remarks to further tip off the Chinese to his grand strategic pivot. Forgoing the type of ideological exhortations against the Red menace that had made him famous, Nixon called for an "era of negotiation rather than confrontation." He outlined a structure of peace balancing the power of the five "superpowers": China, Japan, the Soviet Union, the United States and Western Europe. As with the communists' intramural sparring, he pointed to Western Europe and Japan as the United States' "real potential rivals," suggesting that an internecine capitalist battle could help level the diplomatic and economic playing field. This notion of all nations as "rivals" rather than some as allied as "friends," amounted to a

Metternich-like calculation, replacing the pursuit of ideologically based alliances with the pursuance of national interests. Nixon's talk attracted "relatively little attention" in Kansas City, he would note in his memoirs. Yet in Beijing the following morning at breakfast, Kissinger "found a copy of [the] speech, with Chou's underlinings and marginalia."[37]

The subtle Sino-U.S. dance spanned three years. Along the way, Kissinger changed his tune, letting go of his initial misgivings. "So delicately arranged," he would wax about his operations, "so stylized [were the negotiations] that neither side needed to bear the onus of an initiative, so elliptical that existing relationships [with other allies] on both sides were not jeopardized." The wording on the origin of the summit proved tricky, however. Rather than Nixon hankering to go to China or the Chinese beseeching the United States, the two sides agreed that Zhou, "'knowing of' the President's desire, had extended the invitation." As Kissinger presented Nixon with the carefully worded invitation, he described it as "the most important communication that has come to an American president since the end of World War II.[38]

Kissinger had wanted the focus of the summit to remain on the delicate diplomacy behind closed doors, between a handful of world leaders, without the distraction of a media spectacle. Nixon, however, wanted a dramatic diplomatic performance, a historic public demonstration, a proper setting for his grand venture. The pomp was not merely to feed his ego. As the historian Tizoc Chavez has observed, the actorly Nixon believed in the power of spectacle. He had gathered the importance of veneer from his election loss to Kennedy, the value of mystique, the importance of the medium as much as the message. His press team numbered sixty, and another sixty-seven technicians worked with their Chinese counterparts for three weeks ahead of the visit. Along with Nixon's retinue of 150—including staff, military personnel and Secret Service officers—ninety members of the U.S. press corps were invited on the trip. Heavyweight anchors and correspondents, four from each television network, accompanied the president to the People's Republic, including Walter Cronkite, Dan Rather, Eric Sevareid and Barbara Walters. The affair was to be captured in full color by television, with the latest technology transmitting the images and sound across the Pacific live via satellite. With Beijing thirteen hours ahead of the United States, tours of the great Chinese landmarks would be held in the mornings for live broadcasts during prime time on the East Coast. Each spectacular moment would to be staged and directed for an American audience agape at the first handshake, at the Great Wall, at the Forbidden City, as a Chinese band fiddled "America the Beautiful."[39]

From the White House lawn on February 17, 1972, before entering his helicopter on the first leg of his voyage to China, Nixon was swept away by his own vision. His trip to China was not merely like the "indescribable" voyages of the Atlantic explorers of yesteryear, his would be the most modern-day of trips. To a crowd of 3,000, including a thousand children, gathered on the South Lawn, Nixon announced, "If there is a postscript that I hope might be written . . . , it would be the words on the plaque which was left on the moon by our first astronauts when they landed there: 'We came in peace for all mankind.'" Nixon reveled in the adventure, elated as he neared his dream of having his own moon shot, of what he truly longed for, of being Kennedyesque. "What would [Mao] think if he could see Kennedy," he asked Kissinger. "He would have thought Kennedy was a lightweight," the national security advisor answered. "You think so?," the president pressed. Kissinger assured him: "Mao would have had total disdain for Kennedy. He would have felt about him the way De Gaulle did. De Gaulle had absolutely no use for Kennedy."[40]

Haldeman delighted in the momentous, even metaphysical nature of the circus. The chief of staff had been aboard the *Spirit of '76*, the president's plane, when it set out for Beijing. "It was kind of an odd feeling because they covered the actual takeoff," he recounted and marveled, "we were on the plane watching the TV covering the takeoff." On the long journey, Nixon excitedly buried himself in his briefing books and practiced using chopsticks. "Because of a lack of communications," he remarked, drawing again on the fancies of exotic adventure, "we are as much a mystery to them as they are a mystery to us." The *New York Times* borrowed Nixon's by then common refrain to headline its coverage: the flight of 11,510 miles to Hawaii then Guam and then Beijing was "Like a Trip to the Moon."[41]

The *Spirit of '76* landed northeast of the Chinese capital, at the time still commonly called Peking in the United States. As the Nixons descended the ramp, Zhou clapped, and the first couple clapped in turn. Nixon had imparted to Haldeman that the first handshake was "the key picture of the whole trip." At the 1954 Geneva convention, Secretary of State John Foster Dulles had refused to shake Zhou's hand. The Chinese premier would recount that Walter Bedell Smith, Dulles' deputy, wanting to give a friendly salutation but not daring to break with his boss's protocol, "held on to a cup of coffee with his right hand while shaking Zhou's arm with his left." To signal a new era, Nixon resolved to change course and in style. He stage-managed the greeting himself. He had lines painted on the runway indicating the optimal angle for the plane to land to showcase himself and Pat descending the stairway. The dozen-plus staff on the *Spirit of '76* were barred from exiting until after the ritual greeting. As Kissinger recalled, Haldeman even had a "burly aide" block the aisle. The cameras caught the figures of Nixon and Zhou's nearing, both wore long overcoats, the president's a slim charcoal number, the premier's bulky and black. Both leaders had gray-fringed hair, combed straight back and receding. They both leaned in, and as Nixon would write with a flourish, "When our hands met, one era ended and another began."[42]

As the pair departed the airport in a gray, silk-curtained limousine, Nixon recalled Zhou returning the flowery pronouncement The Chinese premier declared, "Your handshake came over the vastest ocean in the world—twenty-five years of no communication." Gaunt but fluid in his movements, Zhou's charisma stemmed from his noticeable intensity, as if attuned to every moment, concentrating on each moment. Like Nixon's idol de Gaulle, Zhou was a man of both self-assurance and distance. Kissinger noted, "[Zhou] fill[ed] a room by his air of controlled tension, steely discipline, . . . as if he were a coiled spring." He was said to be ever the master of a room's chatter even when not saying a word. Kissinger wrote, "In some sixty years of public life, I have encountered no more compelling figure." Nixon simply told Haldeman, "Zhou enchanted me." For Nixon was apparently not the only grand performer racing through the streets of Beijing that late February day. Just as Nixon chose from his many-sided roles, so, too, did Zhou. The two men were a match, an ensemble. As one high-ranking diplomat described the savvy Chinese premier, "There was not a grain of truth in him. It's all acting. He is the greatest actor I have ever seen." He described how Zhou would "laugh one moment and cry the next and make his audience laugh and cry with him."[43]

Nixon saw in Zhou an inversion of the madman theory. Zhou, ever the master of his emotions, seemed not at all inclined toward irrational risk. Nixon and Kissinger judged their Chinese counterparts as "fanatic[s]" in their aims, but "hard realists" in their means. They had no doubt that there was a madness. Was it not Mao who said that he had no fear of nuclear war? "We may lose more than 300 million people. So what?" Mao once boasted. "War is war. The years will pass, and we'll get to work producing more babies than ever before." To Nixon's eye, the madness of the Chinese leadership remained hidden. The chairman and premier displayed to their American guests the affective control of effusive emotion that Nixon had so mightily attempted to tamp his entire life. In Zhou, Nixon saw a formidable force and yet a performer bereft of the distraction of feeling. His affect was smooth in temperament, seemingly stripped of emotional investment. The threat so brandished in Nixon's madman theory was all but hidden from the American president. Nixon considered the display "Chinese courtesy."[44]

"Games of *guanxi*" or "relationship games" is how the Sinologist Richard Solomon described the courtesy displayed by the Chinese. Far from Khrushchev, Brezhnev or Nixon's bombastic threats, far from Kissinger's unsentimental realpolitik, the Chinese leaders lavished their guests with hospitality, with banquets and innumerable multicourse banquets. In place of irrational threats let loose or rationalized plays of policy transaction, they cajoled through subtle flattery. What did the president prefer for his breakfast? At what temperature did he want his room to be kept? Did he desire more tea? How hot? The Chinese gave their guests grand tours of their ancient civilization, then they demonstrated modern-day displays of mass martial and gymnastic regiments. Solomon wrote that Chinese leaders made their diplomatic moves "through the cultivation of good will, obligation, [and] guilt." Nixon had misread his host when he spoke to Zhou about the need for a carefully constructed "alliance" rather than trusting "friendship." "Their whole idea is to inculcate in outsiders coming to the Middle Kingdom a sense of obligation for their hospitality," reflected Lord, Kissinger's deputy and the future ambassador to China. "They want us to feel that friends do favors for other friends."[45]

Indeed, Marshall Green, assistant secretary of state for East Asian and Pacific affairs, recalled a strict reprimand on the eve of their departure. Trading in his usual lectures, Kissinger warned his deputy to eschew Metternich, realpolitik and talk of interchanging objectives. "Never . . . use the language of the marketplace in dealing with top Chinese officials. Don't talk about deals or quid-pro-quos," Kissinger instructed his team as they finalized preparations for their bilateral meetings. Instead, the national security advisor directed Green to focus on personal diplomacy, believing the Chinese would respond only to appeals to their guanxi, to their courtesy and ideals. As Kissinger dictated, "Always talk about principles." The Chinese are the "real puritans," he poked Green, "not like you New Englanders."[46]

In a broad Orientalist stroke, both Nixon and Kissinger essentialized Chinese courtesy not as specific to Mao or Zhou, but as a cultural trait held by their people as a whole. It was, Nixon wrote, the "subtlety of the Chinese which is most impressive." It was, Kissinger proffered, the "Chinese way." The national security advisor saw a culminative greatness in how Zhou "possess[ed] the sense of cultural superiority of an ancient civilization" that "softened the edges of ideological hostility by an insinuating ease of manner." Kissinger also saw great shame. He instructed his deputies to allow their Chinese counterparts to vent their frustrations after "decades of humiliations at the hands of the imperialist West." Although he did not say as much, Kissinger appeared to be speaking from his personal experience. About Foreign Minister Ji Pengfei, he cautioned, "[He] may well spend two full days sounding off . . . before he is willing to get into substance. Don't interrupt him. Let him get it out of his system. If you interrupt to rebut him, he'll start all over again—and you'll get nowhere." For even as he spoke in awe of the Chinese control of their feelings, contradictorily even paradoxically, Kissinger also saw the Americans' diplomatic overture as a venture to help tame the overly emotional Chinese, to bring them into the international community, "to join [them] in rational and constructive relationships with the outside world."[47]

Given the degree of Zhou's guanxi, Nixon's advance team had expected nearly half a million Chinese gathered at the airport for the president's landing. Yet, despite Nixon's later fulminations over the first handshake, the Chinese did not roll out the red carpet for the president on his arrival that morning in late February 1972. Contrary to Nixon's later rosy recounting of the landing of the *Spirit of '76*, the Chinese welcome was strictly delimited, appearing almost perfunctory. There were forty-two officials, a 350-man honor guard, no crowd. The muted salutations registered in stark contrast to other recent diplomatic receptions. For the president of Somalia, the Chinese reportedly ushered "two thousand dancers and three hundred thousand people in the street." During a visit to Francisco Franco in Madrid, the Americans had been met by "miles and miles of people packed solid." In Beijing, instead of a warm, uproarious welcome to the American commander in chief, he was greeted with wordy placards that read "Long Live the People's Republic of China" and "The Basic Theory That Guides Our Thought Is Marxism-Leninism." The Americans' retinue of 800 numbered more than double that of the Chinese on the tarmac. No children passed out flowers, no one twirled batons. One sign at the airport terminal ominously read, "Make trouble fail, make trouble fail again, until their doom / This is the nature of all imperialists and capitalists and they cannot go against it."[48]

During the half-hour drive through the northern Chinese countryside, the Americans saw flashes of barren farmland and shabby peasants, drawn cattle. Beijing itself smelled of burning coal. As the historian MacMillan described, in accord with a socialist aesthetic, cobbled streets and intricate arches from the centuries' old city had been bulldozed to make way for sprawling avenues and acres of squares, emblems of China's march to modernity. Medieval walls were leveled to construct ring roads. Still, no throngs gathered on the motorcade's route. No flags nor welcoming banners flew save, as Kissinger noted, "the huge portraits of Marx, Engels, Lenin and Stalin" alongside Mao's ever-present face. One State Department official who caught glances of Beijing between the curtains of his car's windows recounted, "It appeared to be almost a ghost city. The few pedestrians moved slowly, their faces impassive, as if they were suffering some form of combat fatigue." He thought it the result of the tumult of the Cultural Revolution. Kissinger recalled their cars sweeping through Tiananmen Square only to encounter a "vast . . . emptiness."[49]

Haldeman caught a different view. Driving through the main arteries of the Chinese capital to the Diaoyutai State Guest House, the chief of staff reported seeing crowds. "As you looked down the side streets," he swore he saw "quite a large gathering of people one block away, being held off by a barrier." He assumed the Americans were quite the curiosity. The stray bystanders on foot and on bicycle, shabbily dressed in worn blue clothing, "studiously paid no attention to us," Haldeman recounted. "It almost appeared that [the Chinese on the street] had been put there for the purpose of ignoring us." Indeed, British diplomats would later learn that bicyclists had been ordered to ignore the caravan, for the Chinese were intent on not making a hullabaloo for the launch of the historic visit that Nixon and Malraux had compared to the great explorations of the New World, to the world-altering ally summits of World War II, to the landing on the moon.[50]

By way of justification, the Chinese later explained that since the United States and China did not have formal relations, they could not treat Nixon's arrival as a formal state visit but merely as "bilateral communications." Kissinger suggested that the Chinese thought a "celebration . . . premature and perhaps [might] weaken [their] negotiating position of studied equanimity." Or, perhaps, he wrote, it was to assuage the North Vietnamese, who were furious at the Chinese for agreeing to the meeting in the first place. In any case, it was clear that the Chinese were directing the summit. Their courtesy was carefully titrated; the Americans would have to play along. In the next act, Zhou surprised Nixon with an announcement. At 2:30 p.m., on the first day of the visit, after an "opulent lunch" as Kissinger recalled, the Chinese premier said simply, "Chairman Mao would like to see the President." The Americans had fifteen to twenty minutes to ready themselves. Nixon had no time to shower.[51]

Kissinger took the invitation as a good omen. "Appointments were never scheduled [with Mao]; they came about as if events of nature," he would later write. In Nixon's retelling, the sixty-five-minute meeting with Mao, not even an hour-and-half after they had landed in Beijing, came as a delightful surprise. Worried about State Department leaks to right-wing hawks or left-wing doves back stateside, Nixon broke with protocol and went with only one Secret Service agent, no staff, no interpreter, relying instead on the Chinese translator. As a frazzled Haldeman remembered, when he told Ronald Ziegler, the press secretary, of the president's immediate departure, he took a bite of the tangerine he was holding, "getting about half the tangerine . . . peeling and all."[52]

Nixon's visit with Mao marked the first meeting between the Chinese leader and American officials in a quarter century, since the Truman administration. Zhou, Kissinger and Lord joined them, but added little to the conversation. By the time of Nixon's trip to China, Mao had already become a fabled figure in his own time. Like Nixon, he had climbed with an upward mobility nearly unimaginable. The chairman's story was "an extraordinary saga of a peasant's son from southern China who conceived the goal of taking over the Kingdom of Heaven," Kissinger would write. In his own sentimental spin on the chairman's life, Kissinger downplayed Mao's "occasionally murderous revolutionary" ways, treating the "appalling bloodletting" of the Cultural Revolution as aberrant. The former national security advisor simply described how Mao "attracted followers, led them on the Long March of six thousand miles, which less than a third survived, and from a totally unfamiliar territory fought first the Japanese and then the Nationalist [Chinese] government, until finally he was ensconced in the Imperial City." Kissinger attributed the extraordinary feats not to an ideological commitment to communism but to Chinese culture, to Mao's ability to "exude the self-assurance of knowing that he was heir to a tradition of uninterrupted self-rule which had spanned three millennium."[53]

Mao lived in a sparse house that had been inhabited by court mandarins during China's imperial age. Brown slipcovers draped the furniture.

Books filled its shelves and were heaped in mounds on tables. Next to the chairman was a cup of jasmine tea and his spittoon. He rose in greeting although he needed help. "I can't talk very well," he simply said, his speech interrupted by a persistent cough and a swollen throat. The Americans were unaware of the degree to which the seventy-eight-year-old was ailing. There had been rumors of strokes, congestive heart failure, an addiction to sleeping pills. He had a lung infection and a doctor on call down the hall in case of emergency. A loose-fitting wardrobe had been sown for him to accommodate his swollen limbs. The meeting with the Americans took place in Mao's book-lined bedroom, outfitted as a makeshift hospital ward. His medical equipment was "hidden in a giant lacquer chest and behind potted plants"; his bed had been removed from the room. Instead of considering the obvious disarray as a possible sign of a mind slipping, cluttered in thought, disorganized, however, Kissinger defended the style of the chairman's haunt as if one of Mao's rationalizing supplicants. Justifying the disordered room before him, he opined, "[The] all-powerful ruler of the world's most populous nation wished to be perceived as a philosopher-king who had no need to buttress his authority with traditional symbols of majesty." Kissinger described with enthusiasm how the chairman's halting words were "ejected from his vocal cords in gusts," each with a "new rallying of physical force until enough strength had been assembled to tear forth another round of pungent declaration."[54]

In preparation for the meeting, Nixon had gathered a few acting notes of his own. He was to match courtesy with courtesy, shorn of confrontation or bluster. Eschewing the dry negotiations of diplomatic policy or strategic consideration, of linking one objective for another, the president undertook to engage in a game of guanxi with Mao. He tried to draw closer to the founding father of the People's Republic by pointing to their similarities, how they both had come from common stock, how both struggled with managing intellectuals, how both were taken with great power. Nixon performed his part well. The two men fondly shared their domestic grievances—Nixon trying to fend off the China lobby on his right flank, Mao purportedly having uncovered a coup by his chosen successor, Lin Bao. They spoke of the need for secrecy between great leaders. They spoke of Mao's predilection for "rightists." The right was consistent; the left swung too much in favor of the Soviets, he remarked.[55]

Even more than philosophizing, the two leaders gossiped. They bounced from one topic to another, from Mao and Chiang slandering each other as "bandits" to the virtues of a first female American president to ribbing Kissinger about his reputation for cavorting with young women. Mao played on Nixon's gripes, taking a swipe at Lyndon Johnson, calling him a "gangster," and Nixon knew how to play to Mao's most pressing concerns. As he remarked, "We must ask ourselves—again in the confines of this room—why the Soviets have more forces on the border facing you than on the border facing Western Europe." The president then pivoted from shared sentiment, trying to reassure his host that he had no designs on the Chinese empire by expounding on his own version of cold realpolitik. Although Kissinger had warned his deputies to speak only of principles and not quid pro quos, Nixon, nonetheless, turned to realistic exigencies. "What is important is not a nation's internal political philosophy. What is important is its policy toward the rest of the world and toward us," he told Mao. What was important was "to build a world structure in which both can be safe to develop in our own ways on our own roads." For neither wanted to dominate the other, he reassured. "We don't threaten each others' territories."[56]

Nixon found his new diplomatic partners astonishingly self-deprecating. Their feelings and tempers, he imagined, were always held in check. In one particular exchange, Kissinger remarked that he had assigned selections of Mao's omnipresent *Little Red Book* in a course he had taught while a professor at Harvard. Mao demurred, "These writings of mine aren't anything. There is nothing instructive in what I wrote." Nixon chimed in, "The Chairman's writings moved a nation and have changed the world." At that, Mao retorted, "I haven't been able to change it." With an affable gentility, the chairman—the one-time revolutionary leader who brought 750 million Chinese to heel—simply added, "I've only been able to change a few places in the vicinity of Peking."[57]

Nixon appreciated the subtle and friendly manner of his Chinese hosts, how different from the brash grandiosity of the Soviets and their obsession with bigness. He recalled being moved when Mao held his hand for more than a minute while making a particularly poignant point. "What impressed me and others in our party was that . . . rather than being the hands of a peasant, . . . [they] were the hands of a literary man," Nixon recalled. It was as if his very hands had been erased from his years of hardship. Mao's was no calloused paw. His fingers were "very delicate, very fine and very expressive," as if they themselves exuded Chinese courtesy.[58]

Moreover, Nixon was impressed not only by Mao's soft façade, but also by a striving he sensed in the chairman that matched his own, an "almost tangible . . . overwhelming drive to prevail." In the Chinese leader's presence, the American president felt "vibrations of strength" beneath the ritualized gentility. Nixon sensed an "animal magnetism" similar to LBJ or Khrushchev. Mao parried Nixon's flattery, "People like me sound a lot of big cannons." Zhou laughed. Nixon noted that in Mao's company, even the self-assured Zhou became "very deferential and reserved." The chairman was the kind of leader Nixon idealized, men with vision and mystique, strength and poise, men who seemed to titrate their feelings. Chinese subtlety was a force distilled.

Mao's informal banter might have indicated that he did not deem Nixon worthy of detailed, face-to-face negotiations. When Nixon alluded to the Indo-Pakistani conflict or relations with the Japanese, Mao de-

Chinese Communist Party chairman Mao Zedong meeting with Nixon and national security advisor Henry Kissinger in his bedroom-turned-study in Beijing, February 1972. *Courtesy of the Richard Nixon Presidential Library and Museum.*

clined to discuss geostrategy. "All those troublesome problems I don't want to get into very much. I think your topic is better—philosophic questions," the chairman insisted. He played down the Taiwan issue as inconsequential when compared to the world's balance of power and demurred from speaking of the Soviets. He wove queries for his guests throughout their conversations, knitting in maxims and comments sometimes tinged with sarcasm. He called Nixon's memoir *Six Crises* "not a bad book." As for Kissinger, Mao proffered that as a "doctor of philosophy," should he not have the answers? Kissinger later characterized Mao's smile as "penetrating and slightly mocking." Nixon seemed to miss any hostility in the repartee if, indeed, the chairman's rough humor had been a slight. Instead, he wrote of how much he appreciated conversing about "philosophical questions," what a relief it was not to crawl around in the political dirt. The two did seem to get along quite well: at sixty-five minutes, the meeting lasted fifteen minutes longer than scheduled. An inspired Nixon left the chairman with a riddling phrase on power and restraint all his own. "You will find I never say something I cannot do. And I always do more than I can say."[59]

In the late afternoon, Nixon and Kissinger returned to their worried American retinue, unharmed. The president's admiration for his hosts deepened through his visit to China. After the chilly initial greeting on the tarmac, the disinterested crowds and the surprise and impressive meeting with Mao, the Chinese buttered up their American guests with eight-course banquets. As Kissinger and his aides stowed away with their counterparts to grind out the details of a communiqué, their hosts, no longer holding back, put on a show for Nixon, Pat and their retinue. The network morning shows in the United States broadcast four-hour dinners live from the Great Hall of the People, a two-story Stalinist-style behemoth, stretching along one side of Tiananmen Square. The cavernous dining room held more than sixty tables, 900 guests and a "battalion of white-jacketed waiters." A Chinese Army orchestra struck up "Home on the Range" and "Turkey in the Straw." The *Washington Post* reported, "President and Mrs. Nixon awkwardly chopsticked their way through . . . shark's fin, steamed chicken in coconut milk and sweet melon," and for the Americans' particular pleasure, the Chinese served bread and butter, all presented on lazy Susans.[60]

After several courses, Nixon rose to toast the Great Hall, quoting Mao, emulating the brutal leader with trite pronouncements on striving and destiny. His words pointed to another trait the two men shared. Mao, too, was a great sentimentalist, papering over atrocity with emotions at once too much, yet too little. "So many deeds cry out to be done, and always urgently the world rolls on," Nixon toasted, repeating one of the chairman's phrases. "Time presses. Ten thousand years are too long, Seize the day, seize the hour!" Nixon spoke of peaceful coexistence, but not one based on Wilsonian democratic principles. Retreating to the spirit of realpolitik, instead of fighting an ideological war, Nixon stressed concomitant spheres of influence for the great powers. He toasted to a "long march together, not in lockstep, but on different roads leading to the same goal."[61]

"The atmosphere in the Great Hall was electric," an aide to Kissinger cheered. "Surely everyone there, and every TV watcher, must have sensed that something new and great was being created in the US-China relationship." Lord, so taken by the scene, judged there to be 10,000 in the Great Hall, erring in the room's capacity by a multiple of more than ten. Periodically, attendees raised their glasses and shouted, "Gan-bei" (Bottoms up). The Chinese and Americans downed their sharp mao-tais. Nixon compared the cocktail to wood alcohol. Dan Rather, the CBS correspondent, called it "liquid razor blades." Haldeman was proud of his boss. Nixon made the rounds of the massive and solemn Great Hall. Going table to table, the president, so often shy and awkward on such public occasions, looked each toastee "squarely in the eye," Haldeman jotted in his daily diary. Nixon "raised his glass and clinked the other person's, took a quick sip, then he raised his glass again and gave a little staccato bow to the individual, marched to the next individual, and repeated the performance." Nixon called his daughters after the meal. They had seen the banquet on television, starting at six o'clock in the morning East Coast time. Their father's use of chopsticks and his toasting had impressed them. Nixon was elated as "more people than . . . [at] any time in the history of the world" had heard a speech live, and it was his.[62]

In the next act, in yet another display of power, performance and guanxi, the Chinese turned to dramatic spectacle to woo their guests. Some 20,000 spectators gathered in a packed stadium for a gymnastics exhibition. The athletes walked in step, swinging their arms, and then standing ramrod to salute the premier and the visiting Americans. The crowd's behavior was choreographed. As Haldeman described it, "Overhead lights [hung] for the television cameras, and as each section was lighted from time to time, the people in it would all automatically start cheering for the camera." He noted the "regimentation is enormous." Haldeman described the gymnasts in the way that Kissinger and Nixon spoke of Mao and Zhou. They exhibited a "level of control" that was "almost total." Indeed, Lord described how the Chinese were "geniuses at protocol." He had studied the intricate games of guanxi, taking for example a tour of the Summer Palace, a lavish expanse of imperial gardens and compounds, lakes and bridges, dating to the twelfth-century Jin dynasty. "If they have two hours to cover the Summer Palace," he explained, the focus was never to allow their guests to feel anxious about possibly having missed other important sites. The Chinese hosts broke the tours into twenty-minute segments. "If you stop for longer than they expected to look at the Empress's Jade Boat . . . instead of pushing you and saying that we're not going to get through everything," Lord noted, the hosts quietly conferred among themselves to determine which later twenty-minute segment to jettison. "So you end up getting through on time in terms of what the schedule says but you never feel rushed."[63]

Nixon was particularly taken by the subtle yet immense power at the heart of Zhou's guanxi. A snowstorm the night and morning of the president's scheduled visit to the Great Wall appeared to all but cancel the Nixons' chance to see the Chinese wonder. Zhou, however, had other plans. With a snap of his fingers, at least as it appeared to Nixon, the premier arranged for thousands of laborers, through the night, to clear the streets for the president's visit to the wall. In another seeming aside, at one of the state dinners, the Nixons expressed their fondness for the country's giant pandas. Pat had earlier in the day toured a zoo and was delighted. Zhou immediately offered to give two pandas to the American people as a symbol of their two nations' détente. Nixon was jealous of how the Chinese premier's swift deliveries stood in stark contrast to the Americans' planned surprise gift of a pair of thick-furred musk oxen.

To the president's consternation, even news of the gift had leaked to the media in advance of his trip.[64]

During fifteen subsequent hours of meetings, Nixon only became more taken with Zhou. He found the Chinese premier's stamina "unbelievable." He marveled, "We'd go on for two or three hours in the morning and three or four hours in an afternoon, and then [Zhou] would spend half the night working with Kissinger on the details of memoranda . . . that we had discussed earlier in the day." Nixon gathered that the premier went to bed well past midnight. His meetings with Zhou, attended by their accompanying deputies, proved to be extraordinarily unusual ones between chief negotiators. Nixon and Zhou moved back and forth between theoretical critiques and wide-ranging geostrategic aims, punctuated with good-natured bantering. Nixon, laying on the flattery, said, "Having read the transcripts of conversations [Zhou] had with Dr. Kissinger, I think the Prime Minister can handle himself with anyone in the world." Zhou demurred. "No, I don't feel I am in a position to take such an exaggerated position. The knowledge of any one person is limited," he replied. Nixon promised that he was a "new Nixon," different from his anti-communist days serving Eisenhower. "The world has changed since then," Nixon said, adding that he had too. He noted that both he and Zhou had been actors in their youth, and that that was how he had met his wife. Zhou mentioned that he liked the name of the president's plane. The *Spirit of '76*, he appreciated, alluded to a "pioneer spirit," in the case of the United States dating back 200 years. In turn, Nixon described their meeting as a great voyage: "As we begin these meetings we have no illusions that we will solve everything. But we can set in motion a process which will enable us to solve many of these problems in the future."[65]

The pair spoke of a "conceptual roadmap" looking forward. The Americans were not asking the Chinese to "compromise principles,"

Nixon assured, and "there will be no disclosures to the press unless we agree." Zhou appreciated the desire and need for secrecy. The differences between the men became most marked when Nixon asserted the importance of the U.S. presence in the Pacific to maintain stability. Zhou insisted that Taiwan was just as important as the U.S. handling of matters with the Soviets. "The place is no great use for you, but a great wound for us," Zhou lectured. He called Taiwan a "sacred territory" and, perhaps even more important, said an American presence there was a sign of imperialists meddling in China's internal affairs. Yet, looming in the background, drawing the two sides together, was the Soviet threat—what Zhou referred to as the "international context." By definition, a détente between the Americans and the Chinese represented a challenge to Soviet expansion, or what Zhou at times referred to as the Soviets' desire for "hegemony." They agreed that the United States and China needed closer relations to counter any short-term stunts the Soviets might have in mind.[66]

In the final joint statement that became known as the Shanghai Communiqué, the two sides exhibited not a grand meeting of the minds and ideals, but their aspirations for a "peaceful coexistence" to take root. It was a step toward the "normalization of relations," an expression of the desire of both powers neither to endanger the international community nor to seek sole dominion in the Asia Pacific. Together the Americans and Chinese could affirm progress in easing tensions. They established "separate commitment[s]" to "oppose" any nation's attempt to dominate world affairs. In an "unprecedented feature," Kissinger noted, more than half of the joint declaration concerned not agreement of shared ideas but a recognition of the two powers' conflicting positions. Each reaffirmed its obligation to its respective Korean ally and agreed to disagree over the war in Vietnam. In a masterful turn of linkage between interlocking interests, the Americans consented to "progressively reduce" the U.S. troop presence in Taiwan "as the tension in the area diminishes," meaning in Vietnam. In concurring that these local tensions were not the most pressing issues in need of immediate, concrete resolutions, the United States and China implicitly affirmed that easing tensions between the two great powers took precedence.[67]

Still, the Shanghai Communiqué maintained the trappings of moral mission as each side was given space to give vent its fundamental principles and aspirations. In a nod to a Wilsonian desire for universal self-determination and faith in reaching an ultimate peace among nations, the United States maintained its duty to promote "individual freedom and social progress for all the peoples of the world, free of outside pressure or intervention." In their commitment to the communist class struggle, the Chinese avowed, "Wherever there is oppression, there is resistance. Countries want independence, nations want liberation and the people want revolution—this has become the irresistible trend of history." The cleverness of the document's construction was that depending on the reader's predilection, either its realist or ideological components could be read as the most important aim. On the one hand, in the opening section, the chief concern appeared to be the need for a stable peace over the settling of local scores. On the other hand, the communiqué concluded by acknowledging the fundamental differences between the powers, with each side spelling out its ultimate goal for the ordering of a just world.[68]

The visit to Beijing and the Shanghai Communiqué were demonstrations of international courtesy and restraint by China and the United Stated, far from the antics of madmen. The proclamation signaled a desired rapprochement between two great powers with the ability to incinerate each other with their nuclear arsenals, providing an opening for negotiation, trade and a transition from menacing rivals to cordial adversaries. Mao and Zhou refused to aid the United States directly in ending the war against the North Vietnamese. China actually competed with the Soviets in increasing military assistance during

1971/72, each trying to assert proof of their revolutionary goals. Ultimately, however, Beijing pressed Hanoi to reach a final settlement with the United States. Most importantly, the historian Evelyn Goh argued, in the long run the "decision for rapprochement . . . nullified Washington's rationale for the Vietnam War, which had been to contain the revolutionary expansion of Communist China."[69]

The editorial board at the *Washington Post* feted the occasion by reiterating Nixon's pronouncement that his week in China had "changed the world," that the summit had ushered forth a "historic new era." The liberal Republican senator Jacob Javits, often a thorn in Nixon's side, called the burgeoning détente "the most portentous foreign policy development for the United States since the end of World War II." The reviews of Nixon's diplomatic venture were largely effusive although some critics suspected that the seemingly swift reversal of course might be another of the president's schemes. The visit would be "best remembered as a television image," a jaded *New York Times'* Max Frankel contended. "It was not anything [Nixon] did there that was particularly important. It was to be seen there that made him." Frankel dismissed the display as more postmodern trickery, more medium over message, feeding once "forbidden fruit to a hungry television audience at home." Years later, piling on, Kissinger would call Nixon's China gambit a "monomaniacal obsession . . . with public relations."[70]

Yet Kissinger also lavishly praised the accord in his tome on foreign policy, *Diplomacy* (1994). He considered the negotiated peace a "veritable diplomatic revolution." Minimizing Nixon's central role, he credited the precarious Sino-Soviet split as key to the Sino-U.S. alignment against their mutual, unmanageable foes in Moscow. "Necessity dictated that rapprochement occur, and the attempt would have had to be made no matter who governed in either country," Kissinger ultimately judged. He attributed the smoothness, speed and scope of the rapprochement to realpolitik, waving aside the importance of diplomatic fellowship and guanxi games. He argued that Nixon's success was due not to "personal relations" or to "Mao's motives" but to the "unprecedented emphasis on the analysis of the national interest," by the Americans in particular, on a single-minded realism that focused on "balancing incentives."[71]

William F. Buckley, Jr., one of the most articulate anti-communist American hawks and a skeptic of the diplomatic efforts with China, had drawn one of the prized seats on the *Spirit of '76* for journalists covering the Beijing visit. He thought that Nixon's arrogance had gotten the best of him, that the communists had played Nixon, that the president had been blinded by the dream of being a peacemaker. As Nixon gave his opening toast in the Great Hall of the People, Buckley was transfixed by Zhou's face, remarking, "one could not help but reflect that the smile must have been similar on the face of his hero, Stalin, when the boys got together to toast peace and dignity, and self-determination of all peoples, at Yalta." Anti-communist conservatives in the China lobby who, likewise, held fast to securing Taiwan's independence, were irate. In retrospect, the historian Nancy Bernkopf Tucker has come to similar conclusion, that the Americans sold out their Taiwanese allies. She wrote that Nixon rolled over and then "relied on secrecy and 'China fever' to mask the collateral damage." In China, Nixon had made it crystal clear that Taipei was expendable. "Principle one," he had told Zhou, "There is one China, and Taiwan is a part of China. There will be no more statements made—if I can control our bureaucracy—to the effect that the status of Taiwan is undetermined." Nixon promised progress on the matter in his second term and, without Watergate, he might very well have made good on it.[72]

Perhaps fueled by the great esteem in which Nixon held Zhou and Mao, or perhaps to garner the greater credit for détente, Nixon in his own personal act of guanxi, began to proselytize that "under Mao the lives of the Chinese masses have been greatly improved." In actuality, the greater opening of China to the world that Mao promised Nixon provided minimal benefit to the Chinese people, at least in the near term. Even as Mao welcomed powerful leader after powerful leader on his red carpet, during the chairman's lifetime, conditions for the overwhelming majority of his people remained poor. The elite could travel a bit more, tour the world, visit expatriate relatives, yet, as the historians Jung Chang and John Halliday observed, the mainland remained a "tightly sealed prison" for the mass of its citizens. A mere half-dozen more books were translated from English to Chinese—one of them being the "not so bad" *Six Crises*. An opening to major trade to China began in 1972 with the importation of $4.3 billion of equipment from the United States and Japan, yet the opening of greater trade relations between the United States and the People's Republic would have to wait until the late 1970s after Deng Xiaoping finally consolidated his hold on power.[73]

As for Nixon's greater geostrategic designs, there is little evidence that the triangulation strategy of tilting toward the Chinese had effect on U.S. relations with the Soviets. The strategic arms limitations agreement, to be signed at a summit in Moscow the following summer, had already been agreed upon two months before Nixon's visit to Beijing. Moreover, the era of détente between the superpowers and Americans' threat of tilting favor toward the Chinese did not halt the Soviet Union from continuing to sponsor revolutions around the globe. Indeed, the historian Gaddis argued that a "reverse linkage" ensued. As the Americans' tied their hands in the competition over the world order, the Soviets stretched and flexed their military muscle. Between 1970 and 1977, the Americans brought home 207,000 troops, while the Soviets ballooned their military investment, deploying an additional 262,000 internationally. They sent aid to communist revolutionaries in Portugal, dispatched Cuban soldiers to Angola and smuggled arms and advisors to Marxist uprisings in Somalia, Ethiopia and Yemen.[74] In the long run, the military expansion of the Soviets led to imperial overstretch, in particular to the invasion and quagmire in Afghanistan that would contribute significantly to the eventual downfall of the Soviet Union. Moreover, most disappointing to Nixon and Kissinger in terms of their vision of linked interests, neither the Chinese nor the Soviets lifted a finger to stop the North Vietnamese from overrunning South Vietnam in 1975.

Ultimately, the "structure of peace" Nixon envisioned with the balancing of power into a protracted détente depended on stability and the legitimacy of state authority, but there could be little stability given the imbalance in the developing world. The superpowers' desire to maintain their spheres of influence compelled them to intervene in the revolts and civil wars accompanying the collapse of colonial rule. Détente could not abide a vacuum. Kissinger complained, "We are now living in a never-never land in which tiny, poor, and weak nations can hold up for ransom some of the industrialized world." Despite congressional attempts to limit the country's international investments, for all the talk of an "era of negotiation" and for all the withdrawals of troops from foreign soil, the Nixon Doctrine was premised on continuing to fund the counter-insurgency and counterterrorism efforts of U.S. allies. Markedly, Nixon propped up right-wing dictators far more often than leftist movements. In the Philippines, he invested in Marcos' police state that cracked down on political opponents, eventually declaring martial law, dissolving Congress, banning strikes and rallies and arresting 30,000 journalists, activists, union leaders and senators from opposing factions. After a coup in 1965 brought Suharto to power in Indonesia, American aid underwrote his purge of the military, ban on rival political parties, suppression of student groups and killing of nearly half a million. Nixon also sent support to authoritarians in Chile, Greece, Iran, and South Korea in addition to anti-Marxist forces in Angola and Portugal.[75]

The historian Mattias Fibiger dubbed Nixon's strategy "authoritarianization." In the name of international stability and domestic security, the United States supported anti-democratic strongmen, enabling them to consolidate their rule. As the historian Daniel Sargent wrote, Nixon "invoked the specter of social destabilization, even revolution, to rationalize the seizure of power." Nixon's moves reflected the realpolitik influence of Metternich and Lord Castlereagh. The realist diplomat-philosophers had championed state security not as a foundation for liberal development, but as a goal to preserve a status quo structure of peace. They were essentially rightists, favoring a steady, the heavy-fisted conservative rather than the overturning leftist reformer. They promoted the strongman's craft as what Kissinger called the "art of restraining the exercise of power," a devotion to control both internationally and internally. Metternich and Lord Castlereagh warned that crusaders for a peace of shared higher ideal were not just wrong but dangerous, that a universalism based on ideology would lead to radicalism and revolutionaries that threatened to level civil society for utopian aims. Such extremity ultimately brought the Terror after the French Revolution and later the Bolsheviks, Kissinger, himself, argued in his doctoral dissertation. "Righteousness is the parent of fanaticism and intolerance," he warned.[76]

Still, even as Nixon's strategy suggested realistic and oftentimes frustrated compromise, at times, a wavering Nixon slipped back into another well-rehearsed script of ideals and the necessity for "moral war." He returned to his anti-communist cant, his days determined to fight the Red peril in those areas—outside of the Soviet and Chinese spheres of influence—where the Americans could hold sway. He countenanced his support for dictators on the right with the need to quash radicals on the left. To expand freedom and advance toward liberal democratic rule, he maintained, a strong leader first needed to establish control, rule of law and law and order, upholding the need for state security not merely for the sake of international stability, but as a requisite precursor for economic and political development. He would point to Lincoln as the "supreme idealist" who "broke laws," "usurped arbitrary power" and "trampled individual rights" in order to save the Union. When he toasted the Shanghai Municipal Revolutionary Committee on his first visit to Beijing, Nixon turned again not to the hard edges of realpolitik but to the sentimental to commune with his hosts. "We have seen the progress of modern times, . . . a bridge across 16,000 miles and 22 years of hostility which have divided us in the past," he said, reveling in the spotlight of his grand journey. With words in the grandiloquent tradition of Wilson, reminiscent of Nixon's heady collegiate essays, the president promised his communist hosts the utopian machination so feared by realists like Metternich, Castlereagh and Kissinger. He put forth the Americans' ideological goal written into the Shanghai Communiqué: to "build a new world, a world of peace, a world of justice, a world of independence for all nations."[77]

This philosophy provided an alternative rationale for Nixon not only for détente but for prolonging the Vietnam War. To coerce Hanoi to the negotiating table, he repeatedly bombed North Vietnam then spread the stalemated war into Laos and Cambodia. Yet rather than bullying realism, it was a "question of moral war," Nixon lectured Kissinger and Haldeman on a retreat to Camp David in June 1971. At the same time that Nixon was secretly negotiating to meet with his Chinese adversaries, as he bandied about the notion of the "decent interval," Nixon slipped back into youthful drawl, pontificating about the bloodiest of means for unambiguous ends. "You hear that the US is imperialistic and aggressive. But we build up our enemies after wars, and we ask not one acre," he attested. He insisted to his national security advisor and chief of staff that self-interest did not define the American cause: "What will we get ourselves out of Vietnam? Nothing . . . If we retreat from the world scene, who's left? With all our stupidity, with all our impetuousness, what other nation in the world is more idealistic than the United States?"[78]

To his audience of Kissinger and Haldeman, Nixon compared his campaign in Southeast Asia to the defenders of democracy during World

War II. He looked back to his service in the Navy. He recalled as a congressman traveling through Germany researching the Marshall Plan, standing on a hill, surveying the carnage leveled by the Americans. "And you could certainly say that was immoral, to have killed all those people, to have bombed the areas and so forth," Nixon proffered, but "would Hitler conquering that area be more moral?" In justifying his foreign policy, Nixon cast himself, as he had through so much of his career, as the buttress against a bloody totalitarianism. He compared himself to his idols de Gaulle and Churchill—charismatic leaders who adopted autocratic styles in the name of expansive liberal aims. "[T]he North Vietnamese bombing is a tragedy," he said, but also deemed it "even more immoral" to quit and run, to appease, to allow one domino after another to fall into totalitarian rule. Haldeman recalled that Nixon got quite worked up ruminating over the bloody quagmire in Vietnam, insisting that he was following FDR and Truman's butchering model of warfare, that he refused to "go out of Vietnam whimpering."[79]

In 1983, in an extended interview with his former aide Frank Gannon, Nixon remained both resolute and stymied in justifying the course of his foreign policy during his presidential tenure. As he attempted to convey his abiding philosophy, he repeated what had once been the pacifist mantra his mother passed down. "As a matter of fact, war compromises principles. War is evil. All war is wrong. All killing is wrong," Nixon asserted. Yet turning the subject over in his mind as he so often did, Nixon turned from one mentor to another, from Hannah Milhous Nixon to Eisenhower. The conundrum of a just war arose, he noted, "when Eisenhower ordered the bombing of Dresden, which was a civilian target, and forty million [sic] Germans burned to death in one night." To him, the air assault "certainly was immoral," but, he implored, "it would have been more immoral to allow Hitler to rule Europe. That's what it gets down to." Still not content, he revisited the question. Trying to convince his interviewer, or perhaps himself, Nixon repeated his previous words almost verbatim pointing to the example of Dresden: "Now, that was immoral, but it would have been more immoral to allow Hitler to rule Europe." His conclusion, almost identical to his first response—quite simply, the crux of Wilson's aim for the necessity to grant war for the highest ends—was not to allow the ideology of fascism to grip Europe. Nixon's parable told not only of the costly human casualties, but also of how such questions tested a leader's decisiveness, fortitude, goodness. As was so common to Nixon's thinking, the action on the battlefield was a projection of the will of the singular leader. It was exhilarating, mind-bending, exciting for Nixon, but also lonely. "Those are decisions that leaders have to make, and sometimes they are terribly difficult," he insisted. "That was a difficult one for Eisenhower, as he often told me thereafter."[80]

In *Diplomacy*, Kissinger attempted to reconcile the contradictions in the thirty-seventh president's mismatched visions. Nixon's former national security advisor wrote, "In Nixon's mind Wilsonianism and *Realpolitik* would merge." Kissinger tried to bring the two Nixons together: one a man of commitment and one of compromise, a devoted ideologue who spoke of a transcendent peace and a combative realist convinced of the centrality of power. Ultimately, Kissinger calculated that Nixon turned away from the hope of a utopian outcome. Amid the unfolding and intransigent international turmoil of the 1970s, further beleaguered by the war at home, Kissinger wrote, control, the rule of law and order, had broken down. The American people could no longer maintain the "wholesome diplomacy" of Wilson in which "the international order is essentially benign, and its diplomacy . . . an expression of goodwill." Kissinger granted, "Traditional American values remained as important as ever." Foremost, however, Nixon's commitment to liberal democracy "provided the inner strength for America to move through the ambiguity of the world."[81] Kissinger's understanding of Nixon was a vision of the hardened but faithful, persisting through a lapsed world. It was a tricky formulation.

According to Kissinger, Nixon matched means to ends, contrary to pragmatic tradition. He argued that in quite the opposite fashion of pragmatism, in which morally ambiguous means can bring virtuous ends, that his former boss envisioned Americans' virtue as the means to gird stable but morally ambiguous ends. By sustaining its greatest ideals, the United States could contain the Soviet Union; not contain the Russians in order to spread great ideals. It came down to strength through peace: A free United States, so buoyed by its own democratic values and institutions, could provide not liberty but stability to Europe, the Middle East and Southeast Asia. It was, according to Kissinger, using Wilson to reach Metternich, idealism for realpolitik. Safire crafted a simpler formulation to express the idea, describing his former boss as an "idealistic conniver."[82]

And here one sees the standard difficulty of trying to identify a coherent philosophy behind Nixon's wavering foreign policy, his shifty and shrouded strategies, or what the historian Jussi M. Hanhimäki called his "elusive grand design."[83] With nearly two decades to mull over, in *Diplomacy*, Kissinger painted a portrait that was all too neat. He projected his own proclivity for realpolitik onto his former boss. He imagined that Nixon's commitment lay ultimately in the compromising realm of strategic tradeoffs while writing off his boss's moralizing as flummery. Kissinger did not let stand the man riven with contradiction, one who hailed his mother's pacifist aims yet condemned her pacifistic means, who could praise both the realist and the idealist, who could build his career on battling the communist threat and then rest his legacy on making peace with the leading communist powers. In an attempt to synthesize Nixon the man, Kissinger fashioned the image of the president solely as a strategic figure—cunning and calculating. He failed, could not see, or chose not to take into account the man of many moods who schemed furtively in the cloakroom only to dream of bursting forth gallantly in the arena. He did not take fully into account how his boss's mind was rent, divided between peacemaker, pragmatist and madman, how he struggled. Kissinger's theory fell flat as he tried to draw a singular portrait of a Nixon on the world's stage, as he stressed a "merging" in Nixon's mind rather than a cognitive dissonance.

The motives of the "real Nixon" continue to elude. Nixon wavered and flip-flopped, switching priorities, insisting on one route of action with one set of advisors only to about-face and choose another. He could be *the* prince or *a* prince. He could trade strategic interest with his adversaries through cold calculation, or he could coax interlocutors with rehearsed flattery. He foreswore goodwill in the world, only then venerated the decency of the common man. His support of rightist dictators might have been influenced by the hard-hearted calculation of Metternich or inspired by the remorseless crusading of Wilson. His strategies were ever in flux as he tried to balance between the pressures exerted by Congress, the Departments of State and Defense, the anti-war movement, allies' uncertain commitments and economic downturns. Ultimately, he was a "man of many masks" with all the contradictions that undergirded the madman theory. At times, Nixon grasped for control, and at others let loose his temper; he performed, and he raged. He vilified communists at home, but summited and banqueted with the Chinese. He withdrew troops from Southeast Asia only to bomb the "bejeezus" out of North Vietnam, and then within a month, he signed a historic nuclear arms limitation agreement with the Soviet Union.[84]

There were 5,000 inside the hangar at Andrews Air Force Base and another 10,000 outside to meet the *Spirit of '76* after a seven-and-a-half-hour flight from Anchorage. "It's sort of like seeing the astronauts coming back from the moon," one bystander commented. Hugh Sidey of *Life* wrote, "My God, it's like the arrival of the king." Nixon's daughters Julie and Tricia were in attendance. So, too, were Vice President Agnew and even the Russian ambassador, Anatoly Dobrynin. Taiwan's ambassador was notably absent. The onlookers clustered together to see the president, once the red-baiter, return from his trip to visit Mao and Zhou, until recently "crusaders for world revolution." Nixon announced to those gathered that his trip provided the "basis for [a] structure of peace" but "no magical formula." Soon enough, sentiment overtook him. Nixon described the American redwood sapling that he had gifted the Chinese. "Just as we hope that those saplings that we left in China will grow one day into mighty redwoods, so we hope, too, that the seeds planted on this journey for peace will grow." Haldeman called it "great television." Gallup reported a 98 percent approval rating for the visit, the highest recorded for any event to date.[85]

After Beijing, Nixon persistently pressed his staff to promote him as a "man of peace," or, as he ordered Haldeman, "Mr. Peace." He wanted "to keep the China story alive" and worried that Kissinger was getting too much credit for the burgeoning detente. Nixon sent a seventeen-paragraph memorandum to his chief of staff listing talking points to circulate to administration allies in the media. "RN goes into such meetings better prepared than anyone who has ever held this office," Nixon wrote. He wanted any hint of expediency or cynicism expunged from the record and insisted that his aims, unlike Kissinger's, were steadied by ideals, not diplomatic calculus. As he added in his bulleted memorandum for the press, Nixon "never gives an inch on principle. As a matter of fact, he is perhaps more rigid on principle than his advisers would want him to be." He also possessed the "qualities of subtlety, humor[,] . . . speaking more quietly when he is making the strongest points." Nixon described himself not only as stalwart in his thinking, but ascetic in his conduct. It was simply a matter of self-control, perhaps courtesy. He "never takes a drink during the course of the meetings." Further, Nixon "carries it to the extent of resisting the temptation which [are] so obviously presented to him, particularly with the Chinese, of eating nuts and other goodies put before him." Kissinger had a reputation for snacking loudly and constantly during high-level meetings. Nixon ordered Haldeman not to disclose the memo but to pose the bulleted items to Kissinger as "simply your observations with regards to points you think he might well make."[86]

If there was a through line, a "merging" in Nixon's mind as Kissinger aimed to identify, an ultimate drive in his grand designs, it was his admiration for Theodore Roosevelt, his desire to emulate the rough-riding president. Nixon strove to be the great man in the arena, fated to suffer loneliness at the top. Nixon scribbled a note, a grand and singular vision, almost a short tone poem, in an attempt to formulate an identity for himself: "Foreign Policy = Strength . . . Must emphasize—Courage. Stands alone . . . Knows more than anyone else. Towers above advisers. World leader." For all the chatter of strategic play, of a hard-nosed realism, in going to China, Nixon yearned for the trappings of an epochal event that would be compared to Kennedy's moonshot. He hungered for the performance, to be thought of as the genius-statesman, the peacemaker nonpareil, a man like Lincoln leading his people to the "indefinite shore."[87]

Conclusion

IT WAS NOT THE CRIME of breaking into the Democratic National Committee headquarters at the Watergate complex in 1972 that proved to be Richard Nixon's downfall. There was no direct evidence he had advance knowledge of the act. Instead, the president's misdeed was to instruct the CIA to halt the FBI's investigation into the break-in. He spoke of hush money to quiet his ne'er-do-well henchmen from testifying to Congress. He was caught on tape speaking of "thievery," a tape that he had tried to hide from the prying press, the courts, from the court of public opinion. It was the cover-up that became the scandal. "It was the cover-up not the crime" that became the cliché. Central to the story was not Nixon as a third-rate burglar, but as an obstructionist, crook, conspirator; central was how the president cheated, lied and tried to hide in plain sight for all to see. As the Watergate scandal simmered then subsumed, questions nagged for answers. Why had Nixon sent such bungling goons to carry out his dirty tricks? Why had he tried to sabotage an election he was already set to win in a landslide? Why break into the offices of an organization for which, as H. R. Haldeman would say, he had "total disregard"? Why would Nixon then so desperately try to cover up an offense in which he had no obvious part? Why not destroy the tapes? Most vexing, why tape himself at all?[1]

The swirl of questions drew in the public with a centripetal force. With each leak and admission, the Watergate scandal came to be viewed as not simply a bungled batch of crimes but a case study into Nixon's psyche. If one could answer the maddening questions underlying

Watergate, then one might understand that missing element that defined the seemingly pathologically flawed president, his penchant for secretiveness, vindictiveness, the source of his rage. According to this logic, Nixon-watchers rejected dismissing the obstructionist crimes as political machination or expediency or simply an error in judgment. They refused to settle on an instrumental objective for the "White House horrors," as Ehrlichman called the mess of foul play. Instead, in the still-definitive account of the scandal, the constitutional historian Stanley I. Kutler argued, "The wars of Watergate are rooted in the lifelong political personality of Richard Nixon." The Watergate scandal was seen not as distorting Nixon's character but revealing it. "It was a reflection of the Nixon paranoia," the *Washington Post's* Bob Woodward judged. The crimes fell in line, "another in a pattern, . . . a mentality," said John Dean, Nixon's former counsel turned government witness.[2]

Nixon was a man who wanted to be "in the arena," go for the "big play," be the visionary "peacemaker," but with Watergate, with the whole nation spellbound, he became the man of the cover-up. He hid instrumentally, and he hid affectively. He hid to get things done—the cloakrooms, the shuttle diplomacy, the grand nuclear bluff, the hush money. And he hid because he felt he had so terribly much to hide—his awkwardness, his clumsiness, the sense that he had an anger too great, a rage that could overwhelm him. The Watergate incarnation of Nixon resonated not as a "new Nixon," but as an old role that dogged him since his debate with John Kennedy, since publicly prosecuting the vaunted Alger Hiss, since he savaged the impressive Jerry Voorhis, even since his lonely, reclusive days as a child. The Nixon of Watergate was coated in a seedy veener. One woman from his hometown of Whittier sensed, "There's something about the guy I just don't like." It was a judgment both resolute in its conclusion and selective in its focus, casting aside the winning appeal of the young up-and-comer of Nixon's first political campaigns. Gone was the "Honest Dick" of his Checkers speech. Gone was the world-traipsing Nixon of the diplomatic junket and grand over-tures of peace. "To say that he was in disgrace was an understatement," Jonathan Aitken, his most sympathetic and semiofficial biographer, wrote. "The bombardment of vilification from his political and media opponents . . . made him the most despised man in America."[3]

A "firestorm" is how Haig recalled the year leading up to Nixon's res-ignation on August 9, 1974. Of the Watergate break-in, the president insisted in public, "No one in the White House staff, no one in the administration, presently employed, was involved in this very bizarre in-cident." In private, he barked to his subordinates, "I don't give a [exple-tive deleted] what happens. I want you all to stonewall." After weeks of televised hearings, after both dogged and sprawling newspaper cover-age, Nixon by the summer of 1973 appeared to be losing his grip on his carefully crafted image. His counsel, Dean, admitted to a cover-up. His assistant, Alexander Butterfield, disclosed the existence of the White House tapes. Nixon rambled at press conferences; he shoved Ronald Ziegler, his young press secretary, in front of cameras. On October 20, 1973, in the so-called Saturday Night Massacre, he attempted to halt the investigation by having the Watergate special prosecutor, Archibald Cox, fired. Nixon's attorney general, Elliot Richardson, resigned rather than carry out Nixon's order to dismiss Cox, as did his deputy, William Ruckelshaus, but the acting attorney general, Robert Bork, followed through with the president's demand. Haldeman and Ehrlichman re-signed in disrepute and ultimately served time for perjury, conspiracy and obstruction of justice. The popular liberal critic Stewart Alsop wrote in *Newsweek* that the president was on the "naked edge of a nervous breakdown," as rumors swirled among aides and reporters that Nixon was drinking too much, perhaps even on the verge of a stroke. It was said that Haig, chief of staff, pressed Nixon's doctors to stop providing him so many sleeping pills. Nixon's son-in-law Ed Cox, married to daughter Tricia, was reported to be worried that he might commit suicide.[4]

The scandal brought to life one of Nixon's chief nightmares: his reputation, carefully crafted through highs and lows, across decades, was out of his control. After sixteen months, fifteen statements, eight press conferences and four television appearances, "There was too much piled up," Haldeman remembered. Adding to the firestorm was news that the president had unpaid taxes. A corruption scandal had forced Vice President Spiro Agnew to resign. Nixon continued to battle until the following summer, when, on August 5, 1974, the public heard Nixon plotting to pay off the Watergate burglars on the "smoking gun" tape, recorded in the Oval Office. Editorials in nearly every newspaper in the United States called for the president's resignation. Nixon's approval rating dropped to 23 percent; the president's closest Republican colleagues urged him to step down. On August 8, Nixon finally announced his decision to resign, effective the following day at noon.[5]

Nixon soon thereafter fell into a depression. His daughter Julie Nixon Eisenhower described Christmas 1974 as the "lowest point in my father's life." He described his mood as a bout of "fatalism," that dogged, dark humor he suffered after major defeats in his life. He cloistered himself, agreeing to see only a few visitors. In his palatial home in San Clemente, California, surrounded by the ocean, a three-hole golf course and an office with an extraordinary view, he found himself despondent. On one visit, Bob Finch, a former aide and confidant, found a man inconsolable. Ziegler, another lasting confidant and aide he kept on staff after the White House would retreat alone with the former president for six and even eight hours, reminiscing, ruminating, Nixon alternating between long monologues and long silences, drinking scotch. Ziegler described a man faced with "humiliation after the shame of humiliation."[6]

Nixon was hospitalized in September 1974 for a severe bout of phlebitis, a substantial clot, his left leg "swollen to nearly three times its normal size." The operation to remove the clot lasted seven hours, followed by three more hours to resolve an abdominal hemorrhage. He thought the experience near-death. His doctor reported him in "deep despair, anguish and mental torment." Cox worried. Between the pardon and the phlebitis, "It's not that he's not sharp. He grasps things as quickly as ever. But the mental letdown plays on the physical," his son-in-law reported. "Each plays on the other and that cycle makes both worse." Nixon's legal fees amounted to a reported $750,000 and he owed $200,000 in unpaid back taxes. He resigned from the California Bar Association and carried large mortgages. Living on an $80,000 a year pension, at one point his bank account reportedly fell to $500. To pay bills, Nixon cut staff, his Secret Service detail, even let Ziegler go. He sold his two beach homes in Key Biscayne to generous donors. Adding to Nixon's torment, in the spring of 1975, Saigon fell to the North Vietnamese. To match public disgrace, his private life nearly collapsed when Pat suffered a stroke the following summer.[7]

Yet, remarkably, even the shameful depths of the post-Watergate tumult, the torment of major illness and massive debt did not defeat Nixon. After an eighty-minute, exclusive interview with James Kilpatrick in 1974 just before Nixon left the White House, *Time* had headlined his apologia as a "Stout If Rambling Defense." The president was leaving behind a trail of discarded reputations through his political career, one shed for the next—red-baiter, average Joe, big spender, old-guard conservative, warmonger, peacemaker, an overrated blowhard. After resigning from office, Nixon was determined to reinvent himself once again. He sought to cement his credit as the president who ended the war in Vietnam and initiated détente with the Chinese and the Soviets. What was more, Nixon hoped to become a roving diplomat without portfolio. For the rest of his life, even in his lowest days in retirement, he turned again to hard work as a panacea. He relied on routine, beginning each day of work promptly at 7:00 a.m., dressed in jacket and tie, as if still in office. He read the *New York Times*, *New York Daily News* and *Wall Street Journal*. For lunch he adhered to a strict diet: a tin of salmon with a little mayonnaise on rye crackers. For all his cynicism and paranoia, and so seemingly incongruous to his bouts of "fatalism," Nixon had the ability to maintain a faith that he could rebound. Framing his downfall as another crisis, another "test of will" in the fashion of his hero Theodore Roosevelt, he felt reinvigorated. He turned to a mentor's words, quoting Charles de Gaulle with an admixture of a phrase that combined hard work and an element of daring, of playing chicken and Russian roulette: "[A] leader must endure strict self-discipline, constant risk taking and perpetual struggle."[8]

In the years following his resignation, journalists, critics and historians struggled to characterize his legacy, never quite sure of the moving target of a man so determined to resurrect his reputation. News outlets from *Newsweek* to *New York Magazine* to *U.S. News & World Report* would publish profiles and interviews tentatively announcing the return of the "old China hand" and his new role as the "sage of Saddle River" after he and Pat left California and then New York for New Jersey. Correspondents would go on to write of the former president with a hesitancy as contradictory notions of Nixon seesawed, uncertain which incarnation was the "real Nixon"—the addled, Watergate crook or the able, elder statesman, the madman or the sage.[9]

Over the course of three years, the former president drafted *RN: The Memoirs of Richard Nixon* (1978), his second and longest autobiography. He toyed with his readers, promising to divulge, while, as his biographer Stephen Ambrose described, "leaving everything opaque." For all the autobiography's circumlocution, for all its elision of feeling, its lack of clarity on the most pressing of issues, the public remained titillated by Nixon's ongoing defenses. Sales brought in $2.5 million. In due course, far from retreating to an easy life of rest and contemplation, Nixon made a show of his redemption. He earned $1 million for an exclusive, 1977 televised interview with the British journalist David Frost, during which he reprised his attack on the media. The press had "too much power and it's power that the Founding Fathers would have been concerned about," he told Frost. "There is no check on the [television] networks . . . [or] the newspapers." As for Carl Bernstein and Bob Woodward's *The Final Days* (1976), their follow-up to *All the President's Men* (1974), Nixon was scathing. "All I say is Mrs. Nixon read it and her stroke came three days later." He circled back, reworking his anger into a pithy life lesson by grounding himself in the sentimental. "I made so many bad judgments," he admitted. "The worst ones, mistakes of the heart rather than the head." By the end of the interview, Frost wrong-footed Nixon on the details of the Watergate scandal as the former president slumped in his chair through his defense, concluding, "I let the American people down. And I have to carry that burden with me for the rest of my life." Of the nearly 55 million American viewers, 44 percent found him more sympathetic than before the interview, but 72 percent still thought him guilty of obstruction of justice, and 69 percent thought he had lied even to Frost. The longtime CBS and NBC journalist Marvin Kalb thought the questions "soft," the answers "rambling and murky." Yet "all that was irrelevant," Kalb wrote, because "Nixon was back on the tube."[10]

Most significantly for Nixon, he returned to China for nine days in March 1976. Mao Zedong himself had sent the disgraced president an invitation. Nixon was still a "virtual hermit," still the "country's No. 1 controversial figure," *Newsweek* wrote. The conservative standard-bearer William F. Buckley called Nixon a "pariah." The *Washington Post's* Joseph Kraft judged the trip a "sleazy act" that prioritized Nixon's rehabilitation efforts over the United States' foreign policy interests. Nixon contended that his visit served to legitimize Hua Guofeng, successor of the recently deceased premier, Zhou Enlai, and once in Beijing, he revisited his greatest days, that "week that changed the world." He stayed at the same guest house as when the president. He feasted again in the Great Hall, toasting mao-tais, listening again, to the Chinese play "America, the Beautiful" and "Turkey in the Straw." He met with Madame Teng

Ying-Chao, Zhou's widow, and once more with Mao despite the eight-two-year-old chairman's ailing health. At the beginning of his trip, the Chinese in Tiananmen Square appeared wary, backing off from the visiting American. Yet, *Newsweek* reported that, by the end of Nixon's travels, in Canton "tens of thousands of people poured into the streets to give the fallen President a tumultuous welcome that rivaled anything he had received in better days."[11]

In 1980 for the next stage of the disgraced former president's rehabilitation, Nixon moved with Pat into a four-story brownstone on the Upper East Side of Manhattan and then to a twelve-room, million-dollar home in Saddle River, New Jersey, with six fireplaces, a nursery for his grandchildren, a well-manicured garden and a well-fortified wall. The staff called it "The Residence." Ever the "obedient rebel," both suppliant and defiant, Nixon maintained a rancor for the exclusive crowd—insisting that he avoided the "beautiful people," "trendies," "art crowd," "Henry's crowd"—even as he and Pat treated themselves to dinners out at the swanky French restaurants Lutèce and Le Cirque. Nixon gave top-billed televised interviews with national news anchors Tom Brokaw, Peter Jennings and Ted Koppel and CNN late-night talk show host Larry King. He wrote opinion pieces outlining his thoughts on American grand strategy for the loftiest presses—the *New York Times*, *Wall Street Journal*, *Los Angeles Times* and *Time*.[12]

At the Residence, Nixon hosted "stag dinners" with media magnates and foreign policy establishment types, serving his growing wine collection, capped off with vintage port and cognac. He welcomed conservative intellectuals like Norman Podhoretz and Irving Kristol, liberal writers such as Norman Mailer and John Steinbeck, even old political rivals, among them Hubert Humphrey and George Wallace. For a man who spoke so often of never looking back, of shielding himself from the past, Nixon's mood shifted when he held court, spinning the story of his life as triumph rather than ruin. He spoke of his accomplishments, his adventures, regaling his guests about the time "de Gaulle told me . . ." and "So Ike lets out a yelp and . . . ," and "That was the time Khrushchev took me aside to say . . ." At one such gathering, the former president spoke for four hours to three longtime *Newsweek* correspondents over turtle soup, fillet of beef and Chateau Lafite Rothschild '61. He let loose, commenting on how he had become an object of fascination, gleefully recounting how crowds gaped, wondering, "What makes this guy tick?" Nixon dazzled his audiences, mapping out the world's issues, offering his impressions and advice about one country and the next, all while cracking jokes about the usual suspects—liberals, the media, intellectuals. When the inevitable question arose about what lesson he had learned from the Watergate scandal, Nixon quipped with a simple, rehearsed response: "Destroy the tapes."[13]

In the spring of 1986, Katherine Graham, publisher of the *Washington Post* and Nixon's one-time arch enemy, ordered "The Rehabilitation of Richard Nixon," a six-page lead story with a three-page interview, a twelve-photograph spread, and Nixon's smiling visage on the front page. And it was not just the press, literati and foreign policy movers and shakers that Nixon allured. He turned the charm on for two of his most prominent biographers: the former British MP Jonathan Aitken and the historian Joan Hoff. After long interviews with the former president, both left convinced that the image of the shifty, hunched political animal was a fabrication. He wore his years well—sharp, fit for his age, cynical but delightfully adroit with humor, even charismatic. Aitken and Hoff became two of his greatest rehabilitators. They were confounded by how a "tiny minority of Nixon haters" had so hijacked and tarnished his image, particularly, his generous domestic record, by how this charming old man and his "riveting dark eyes" had been transformed into the demon of his age.[14]

Nixon had returned to the scene as a "new Nixon," a man content, regaling interested journalists about how he settled his mind playing golf, taking long walks and watching baseball with his grandson Christopher. One visiting reporter observed, "No Watergate books but six elephants on the shelves." She described Nixon's home as having an "Oriental feeling," with "rice-paper walls and Chinese decorations," as if an ode to the nation that, for Nixon, exuded courtesy, that he hoped would define his legacy, as if capturing that moment in time that the American press had compared with landing on the moon. Another reporter, however, relayed an uncertainty in his host's presence that recalled how journalists, critics and onlookers had for years puzzled over Nixon's incongruous movements. Nixon's "eyes fluttered and his face tightened at the slightest interruption," the *Newsweek* correspondent remarked. "There was something so obviously rehearsed, calculated, unspontaneous."[15]

Indeed, it is hard to imagine that defeat had finally transformed the former president into a man of relaxation and leisure. The image of a deck-reclining and duck-hooking Nixon was another exaggeration, if not a fabrication. Pat would later reveal her husband's restless moods. "Nobody could sleep with Dick," she would recount. "He wakes up during the night, switches on the light, speaks into his tape recorder or takes notes, it's impossible." Despite insisting that he had finally found contentment, Nixon continued to work at a frantic pace. His then chief of staff, John Taylor, described his boss as a man competing against an ever-ticking clock. Nixon's age became a worry. "He never undertook any activity lightly . . . It pains him. He feels guilty," Taylor relayed. "So a lot of our morning meetings were taken up with the question of whether such and such a project would be worth the effort. Above all, would it make an impact on the course of events?" A sense of defiance in the face of unfairness continued to drive Nixon, Taylor observed. Nixon in his diary returned to the portrait he once shared with the adventurer André Malraux, just before his first trip to China, and to the notion that his journey had been a lonely one—"aching," "yearning," with "almost physical pain." Far from a new course, he saw himself again as the aggrieved, up against an elephantine if ill-defined force. "We're out now, so they try to stomp us . . . kick us when we're done. They never let up, *never*," Nixon complained to his then communications director, Kenneth Clawson.[16]

Marking his official return to public life in 1981, Nixon joined the former presidents Gerald Ford and Jimmy Carter at the funeral of the slain Egyptian president Anwar Sadat. He set off to lecture on foreign policy without notes, giving sweeping tours d'horizon at fundraisers attended by the Republic Party elite, even to rousing success at the Oxford Union in London. "While I had retired from politics," a defiant Nixon told the British crowd, "I had not retired from life . . . So long as I have a breath in my body, I am going to talk about the great issues that affect the world." He traveled five times to the Soviet Union and toured every other country in Eastern Europe except Poland and East Germany. He visited the exiled shah of Iran in Cuernavaca, King Khalid in Jidda, King Hussein in Amman and President Habib Bourguiba in Tunis. The former president reached yet again for the sentimental to capture his elation, reclaiming the story of his adult life as he had his rough childhood, both of them "hard but happy." He quoted de Gaulle quoting Sophocles, "One must wait until the evening to see how splendid the day has been." He returned to his worn script, not to a "new Nixon" but to an old one, a more comfortable fit, to the tale of Horatio Alger. "Through work, willpower, luck, brass, and political skill," he had recovered.[17]

Journalists began writing of Nixon as a "gray eminence," a "king-maker" even "something of a statesman." His readmittance to the exclusive community of foreign policy thought leaders galvanized him. He publicly criticized Carter's advocacy of international human rights and spoke in support of peaceful relations with authoritarians like Gen. Anastasio Somoza of Nicaragua. "One principle that I have followed is that whether it's in Vietnam or it's in Iran, you don't grease the skids for your friends," the so recently exiled Nixon championed the need for abiding loyalties. "If the United States does not stand by its own friends we are going to end up with no friends." He then flew to China to meet with Chairman Deng Xiaoping, then to 10 Downing Street to meet with Prime Minister Margaret Thatcher.[18]

The once-fallen president even began to acquire something of a rock star patina. *Rolling Stone* included him on its 1986 list of "Who's Hot: The New Stars in Your Future." He helped mediate a union dispute among Major League Baseball players, umpires and management. He was photographed engulfed by autograph seekers at a Burger King in New Jersey. He expressed a mixture of delight and trepidation at his restored popularity of a sort as he could not help but question the motives of those who watched, who waved and stared. When asked about unexpected feting, he mentioned the "bashing" he received on every anniversary of the Watergate break-in. "So you relive it then, but as far as I'm concerned I never look back," he insisted. He deflected with a line he often used: "Remember Lot's wife. Never look back." It was a subtle but distinct disclosure, suggesting that he indeed continued to relive the painful Watergate scandal, but then catching himself, insisted that he never looked back. It was a familiar formulation as Nixon claimed to be in control of his emotions even as he teetered on the edge of a sentiment that threatened to overwhelm him.[19]

With a former aide who remained a confidant, Nixon discussed the subject of Watergate with contrition. "I brought it on myself," he said before waving the affair off as a "series of blundering mistakes, not a grand scheme driven by malicious intent." He circled back not to his own culpability but to grievance, to yet another conspiracy against Richard Nixon. "I knew that I was a target," he continued. "I had been a target ever since Alger Hiss, because during that case I did the worst thing that you can do to the press: prove that they were wrong." The issue was one of different "standards," he added, one for Republicans, one for Democrats. "And then there were standards for me." It was not the substance of the Watergate cover-up, he argued just moments after taking full responsibly. He was a marked man. The left detested him for continuing the war in Vietnam, while the right sought to crucify him for détente, he charged. "I should have known that I was somebody who couldn't even sneeze in the goddamned White House without having somebody order an investigation."[20]

"Are you saying that if it weren't Watergate it would have been something else," the former aide asked her one-time boss. "That's my theory," Nixon answered. Watergate was the "sword," but without Watergate, there would have been another knife in the back, he thought. Another former aide asked Nixon how he thought posterity would view him. Nixon returned to the theme of his exclusion. "Again," he said, "having in mind that most [historians] are liberal, most of them are Democrat in terms of party persuasion, and most of them are obsessed by style, I'm going to strike out on all three scores." Then Nixon pivoted to another conspiracy by his anti-war critics. Agitated, he charged that the spectacle over Watergate and his forced resignation were a great show trial brought on *not for his continuing* the Vietnam War, but because he *ended* it. He recalled how Henry Kissinger had passed on word from his "friends at Harvard." They could not "bear the thought that you did it," the national security advisor had goaded the president. The "virulence" of the peaceniks, the counterculture and the intellectual elite, Nixon claimed, was "due to the fact that . . . we had succeeded when they said we couldn't."[21]

As the Cold War threatened to turn hot in 1980, Nixon strongly advocated a show of military force to combat Soviet adventurism in the Third World. In contrast to the message of détente that had defined Nixon's presidency, he returned to the earlier days of his staunch anti-communism, pushing to prove to the Soviets that the Americans were not afraid to act. His book *The Real War* (1980) presaged Ronald Reagan's amping up the rivalry against a revanchist "evil empire." He wrote of a "choice between surrender and suicide, against red or dead." The polemic proved to be a best seller not only at home but also in France and England, selling out its first run within a week. Nixon continued to publish best sellers at a marked pace, circling around his foremost ambition, around the notion of how to make peace and how to become a peacemaker, with titles including *Leaders* (1982), *Real Peace* (1984), *No More Vietnams* (1987), *1999: Victory without War* (1988) and *Beyond Peace* (1994). The biographer Ambrose described Nixon's prose as lecturing, like he was a "speechmaker rather than a book writer," stringing together proclamations rather than analysis, favoring rhetoric over argument. He found the part a comfortable fit, the writerly role, that of the didact, not to relay or relate but to convince or command.[22]

However static the titles and tone, over time, the former president's foreign policy advice oscillated with a typically Nixonian balance of exigencies. After his renewed ideological hardline of the early 1980s, by the middle of the decade he had turned to a strategy he dubbed hardheaded détente—a "combination of détente and deterrence." During the so-called Reagan Revolution, which looked to restart the Cold War and the arms race against the Soviets, Nixon became a, perhaps the, American figure who embodied the strategy of détente, the need for a peaceful coexistence with the communists, a symbol beyond his Watergate and Vietnam-era villainy. As the decade wore on, as the Eastern Bloc disintegrated and the Soviet Union threatened to collapse, Nixon distanced himself from his "red or dead" rhetoric. He insisted that between the superpowers, "there can be no real peace in the world unless a new relationship is established." In his round of speeches, he delivered a clear message: "The United States wants to reduce tension and the Soviet Union needs to reduce tension." As he wrote in 1990, "The time is ripe for a deal."[23]

In 1992, in a secretly distributed memo that Nixon himself soon leaked to fifty foreign policy opinion leaders, including Kissinger, Zbigniew Brzezinski, Brent Scowcroft and Hugh Sidey of *Time*, Nixon harshly criticized George H. W. Bush. He condemned Bush for not offering more substantial economic aid to post-Soviet Russia, for a "pathetically inadequate response." The leaking was vintage Nixon, a bold pronouncement masked in mystery, a shrouded missive the contents of which, through his own connivance, soon appeared in a front-page *New York Times* news analysis by Thomas Friedman. In the memo, a little more than four pages long, Nixon argued that economic stability needed to come before political reform and foreign policy concerns. The ever-flexible Nixon traded realpolitik for neoliberal nation building, declaring that building the Russian economy was "the most important issue since the end of World War II." He reached again for the Wilsonian rhetoric that had once infused his anti-communist campaigns. "Today the ideas of freedom are on trial," he wrote. "If they fail to produce a better life in Russia and the other former Soviet republics, a new and more dangerous despotism will take power, with the people trading freedom for security and entrusting their future to old hands with new faces." With keen foresight, he predicted not a return to communism but an "extremist Russian nationalism." Even as he shifted in his strategic advice, however, he returned to a trope that had spanned his career. Like the game theorists, he wrote of the most weighty issues with mundane metaphor, making the inconceivable understandable by transforming the existential into the tangible. "To play in this game," Nixon wrote, "we must have a seat at the table. To get a seat at the table, we must be ready to put some chips in the pot. The stakes are high." Adding one more dig at Bush, he chided the administration for "playing as if it were a penny ante game."[24]

Among foreign policy establishment members trying to make sense of Nixon's sprawling legacy, there remained considerable disagreement on the rejuvenated Nixon. The liberal critic Arthur Schlesinger, Jr., described Nixon's "imperial presidency" as a great power grab abroad and at home. Similarly, William Bundy, advisor to Kennedy and Johnson, argued that the "thievery" in the Nixon White House had infected the administration's foreign policy from the secret bombing of Cambodia to aiding the coup against Chile's Salvador Allende. Still, other foreign policy hands claimed that Nixon's malfeasance and resignation had not strengthened but "weaken[ed] the institution of the presidency." Some including the political scientist James David Barber questioned Nixon's centrality in reaching a détente with the Chinese and Soviets. Others like the hawkish Richard Pipes stated that détente with the Soviet Union, once again confrontational and adventurous by the time of the Reagan era, had proven to have no staying power at all.[25]

In flurries of reappraisal and reproach, as the former president seemed never to sate the public's curiosities, a psychological lens was applied not to understand Nixon personally as had a generation of psychohistorians, but to assess Americans' ongoing obsession as a culture with the ever-reinventive former president. Monica Crowley, Nixon's amanuensis in his last years, trumpeted the notion that Nixon had specifically been chosen for derision by the likes of Schlesinger on the left and Pipes on the right. She suggested that "Nixon-hating"—what the revisionist historian Irwin Gellman called "Nixonphobia"—had become a "national psychological exercise aimed at convincing ourselves that our recent history is not as damaged as it seems. We claimed his political scalp as a prize to show that those wrenching years produced at least one ostensibly righteous result." That is, in Nixon's "wrongdoing, we found shelter from our own." The Nixon critic William Boot also pathologized the relationship between Nixon and the American public. On the fifteenth anniversary of Watergate, in his essay "Nixon Resurrectus," Boot described a "love-hate relationship with elements of sadomasochism and mutual bondage." Nixon and the American public could not live without each other, Boot charged. For they enjoyed too much despising each other's company. "Those were the days," one *New Yorker* correspondent opined in the summer of 1986, recalling the dizzying cascade of events during the Watergate scandal. "Nixon was 'crazy,' unpredictable, enigmatic. One day, out of the blue, he would impound congressionally authorized funds, the next, he would declare Charles Manson guilty when the man was still on trial." Nixon made Reagan's Iran-contra scandal look "dull," the reporter wrote.[26]

Cultural historians also took up the issue of the seemingly insatiable fascination with the former president. Far from Nixon's static recriminations against his enemies, from the sour image so often conjured by his critics, from the acrid caricature Nixon so thoroughly feared would define his legacy, these cultural historians reimagined the lifelong politician as a one-man cast of shifting characters to match the public's mood. From David Greenberg to Daniel Frick to Mark Feeney, scholars embraced the former president as prismatic. Greenberg wrote, Nixon's "images overlapped, mingled, coexisted"; they were "constantly changing, always contested." Whereas Nixon thought himself a diplomat, others thought him tricky. He was a "cardboard saint," or "his heart [wa]s pure," or he was "something of an intellectual." Nixon was either a two-dimensional wise guy or the most complicated of men. Indeed, the historian Hoff argued, compared to the TV-ready, poll-tested politicians of the 1990s like George H. W. Bush and Bill Clinton, Nixon with all his passions and his panics had become a psychological tonic for a disillusioned, baby-boomer generation. In this way, most surprisingly, the secretive and rehearsed Nixon had been reinvented as a nostalgic symbol of a more "authentic" time.[27]

As none quite sufficed to describe the "real Nixon," Hunter S. Thompson, fumbling to put his finger on the matter, scrambled a mix of metaphors. Nixon had "the integrity of a hyena and the style of a poison toad," the gonzo journalist cracked. Thompson had traveled on Nixon's campaign trail in 1972, gaining rare access. He insisted that the ever shifting candidate—the "real Richard Nixon," the "new Nixon" and the new "new Nixon"—was little more than a windup doll, a brand-new, yet old-fashioned model, a "plastic man in a plastic bag." Like so many of Nixon's foes, he wanted to diminish the enraging president as weak, even as Thompson tried to illustrate his great power. Nixon was both a regular politician and a rare chimera, a feeble lowlife and a creature to be terribly feared. Thompson, whose pen would capture a generation, returned to the familiar theme that had bedeviled so many of Nixon's portraitists. The quest to root out the "real Richard Nixon," the phrase-ripping Thompson wrote, was to unmask the "man behind the masks or maybe to find that there was no mask at all."[28]

The longtime *New York Times* reporter Tom Wicker thought he witnessed a rare, intimate Nixon beyond the guise. At some late hour in 1957, Wicker caught a glimpse of the then vice president. The forty-four-year-old's footsteps "clack[ed across] the tiled floor" of the abandoned Senate lobby that they both knew well. The young politician, creeping into middle age, was alone save for his Secret Service agent, and to Wicker's eye, he betrayed "no sign that he realized anyone was nearby." Wicker felt at that moment that he might be witnessing the private Nixon, just for a few moments—a scenelet of the "real Richard Nixon," peeled of public affectation. No Haldeman, yet. No Kissinger. No Colson.[29]

Wicker would not have been hard to espy in the Capitol lobby. Tom—not Thomas, as he insisted for his byline—was by no means an embedded reporter, no slinking sleuth for the Gray Lady. Pudgy, yet hulking, with a meaty handshake, Wicker carried himself like a Southern boy with a languid, North Carolina drawl. He favored a paisley silk tie, monk-strap shoes and, on occasion, an olive green three-button suit with fire engine red suspenders. In the years to come, the barrel-chested Wicker would cover what was supposed to be a routine presidential parade through Dallas on November 22, 1963, and mediate between New York police and rioting inmates at Attica. Yet as his and Nixon's paths neared in the Capitol in 1957 at that late hour, Nixon had no "politician's ready greeting" to offer the (at times overly) genial reporter—no handshake or backslap, no joke at hand, not even a nod of recognition of the "rather ruffled" giant of a reporter. Wicker recalled that apparently without noticing his presence, the vice president simply continued to amble "along rather slowly, shoulders slumped, hands jammed in his trouser pockets, head down . . . eyes apparently fixed . . . on the ornate Capitol floor."[30]

In this private, unrehearsed moment, out of public view, the vice president emanated an air of the inscrutable, a man "hard to fathom," a "man bound up in his inner being, unaware that he was meeting another person, unaware of the impression he was making, unaware even that he was making an impression." Wicker had never seen Nixon that up close. In Nixon's most private of moments, he had no pride of power. There was no lilt in his step. Wicker had thought Nixon taller, perhaps with "better posture." He was hunched, Wicker noted, and his "face seemed darker than could be accounted for by the trademark five o'clock shadow." To the *New York Times* veteran, the still young politico seemed "profoundly unhappy," his presence "unappealing." He simply seemed alone. And then, just like that, Wicker watched the vice president retreat to his "inner-sanctum hideaway somewhere in the bowels" of the Capitol. A rare moment for conclusion passed.[31]

Notes

ABBREVIATIONS

FA-OHP   Foreign Affairs Oral History Project, Association for Diplomatic Studies and Training, https://adst.org/oral-history/oral-history-interviews/

JVP   Jerry Voorhis Papers Claremont College, California

Moynihan Papers   Daniel P. Moynihan Papers, Manuscript Division, Library of Congress, Washington, DC

Nixon-Gannon   Richard Nixon, interview by Frank Gannon, Walter J. Brown Media Archives & Peabody Awards Collection, University of Georgia Special Collections Libraries, Athens, Georgia

NSA   National Security Archive, George Washington University, https://nsarchive2.gwu.edu/

OHP-CSUF   Oral History Program, Richard M. Nixon Project, California State University, Fullerton

OHP-RNL   Oral History Project, Richard Nixon Presidential Library and Museum, Yorba Linda, California

RNL   Richard Nixon Presidential Library and Museum, Yorba Linda, California

WHSF   White House Special Files, Richard Nixon Library and Museum, Yorba Linda, California

WHSF-CMC   White House Special Files, Contested Materials Collection

WHSF-SMOF   White House Special Files, Staff Member and Office Files

INTRODUCTION

1   H. R. Haldeman, with Joseph DiMona, *The Ends of Power* (New York: Dell Publishing, 1978), 82–83. For Nixon's routine of taking calming walks on the beach, see Theodore H. White, *The Making of the President 1968* (New York: Harper Perennial, 2010), 296; H. R. Haldeman, interview by Raymond H. Geselbracht, OHP-RNL, Apr 11, 1988, 15.

2   Haldeman, with DiMona, *Ends of Power*, 82–83, emphasis in the original.

3 Marvin Kalb, *The Nixon Memo* (Chicago: Univ of Chicago Press, 1994), 193;
   Jeffrey P. Kimball, email interview by author, Sep 29, 2017. For examples of
   Haldeman as a man of "mystique" and turn to postmodernism, see H. R. Halde-
   man, *Haldeman Diaries: Inside the Nixon White House* (New York: G. P. Putnam's
   Sons, 1994), Thursday, January 8, 1970, 117, and Wednesday, July 1, 1970, 179;
   Henry Kissinger, "Watergate: Nixon's Germans," *Time*, Mar 8, 1982; Bruce
   Tucker, "'Tell Tchaikovsky the News': Postmodernism, Popular Culture and the
   Emergence of Rock 'N' Roll," *Black Music Research Journal* 22 (2002): 23–30.
4 John Ehrlichman, "Ehrlichman Reviews Haldeman," *Time*, Mar 6, 1978; Ethel
   Payne, "The Real Nixon: The Inside and Lowdown on the Man with Eyes on
   the White House," *Chicago Defender*, Jul 15, 1957, 1; Garry Wills, *Nixon Agonistes:
   The Crisis of the Self-Made Man* (New York: First Mariner Books, 2002), xv;
   William Safire to Richard Nixon, memorandum, "Approaches to 1972," Nov 11,
   1970, box 45, folder 29, WHSF-CMC, 10; Alexander Butterfield, interview by
   Timothy Naftali, OHP-RNL, Jun 12, 2008, 10.
5 Richard Hofstadter, *The Paranoid Style in American Politics* (New York: Knopf,
   2012), 3–40.
6 Lucien Febvre, *A New Kind of History: Writings of Lucien Febvre* (New York:
   Routledge, 1973), 12.
7 Doc. 22, "Kissinger," memorandum, Aug 10, 1972, William Burr and Jeffrey P.
   Kimball, "Nixon, Kissinger and the Madman Strategy during the Vietnam War,"
   National Security Archive Electronic Briefing Book no. 517, May 29, 2015, NSA.
8 For examples of denials of the theory's existence, see Fred Greenstein, "A
   Journalist's Vendetta," *New Republic*, Aug 1, 1983; Joan Hoff, "Richard M.
   Nixon," in Fred Greenstein, ed., *Leadership in the Modern Presidency* (Cambridge,
   MA: Harvard Univ Press, 1995), 185–89. Joan Hoff, *Nixon Reconsidered* (New
   York: Basic Books, 1995), 177–78. For debate on its denial, see Jeffrey P. Kimball
   and William Burr, *Nixon's Nuclear Specter: The Secret Alert of 1969, Madman
   Diplomacy, and the Vietnam War* (Lawrence: Univ Press of Kansas, 2015), 77;
   Jeffrey P. Kimball, email interview by author, Sep 29, 2017.
9 Jeffrey P. Kimball, "Trump's Madman Gambit," *U.S. News and World Report*,
   Dec 30, 2016. See also Burr and Kimball, *Nuclear Specter*.
10 Henry Kissinger, *Nuclear Weapons and Foreign Policy* (New York: HarperCollins,
   1957); Herman Kahn, *Thinking about the Unthinkable* (New York: Avon Library,
   1962); Thomas Schelling, *Arms and Influence* (New Haven, CT: Yale Univ

Press, 1966); John Lewis Gaddis, *Strategies of Containment* (Oxford: Oxford Univ Press, 1982); Thomas Schelling, *Strategy of Conflict* (Cambridge, MA: Harvard Univ Press, 1981); Fred Kaplan, *The Wizards of Armageddon* (Stanford: Stanford Univ Press, 1991); Jonathan Schell, *The Fate of the Earth* (Stanford: Stanford Univ Press, 2000), emphasis in the original.

11　Kimball, "Trump's Madman Gambit"; Timothy Naftali, "The Problem with Trump's Madman Theory, *Atlantic*, Oct 4, 2017; Nina Khrushcheva, "The Return of the Madman Theory," *Japan Times*, Oct 5, 2017; Phil Levy, "Trump and the Half-Madman Theory of International Negotiations," *Forbes*, Apr 25, 2018; James Hohmann, "Trump Suggests His Embrace of the 'Madman Theory' Brought North Korea to the Table," *Washington Post*, Feb 26, 2019; Keith Johnson, "Trump's 'Madman Theory' of Trade with China," *Foreign Policy*, May 10, 2019; Stephen Collinson and Caitlin Hu, "Trump's Threat to Iranian Culture Rekindles the 'Madman Theory' of International Relations," CNN, Jan 7, 2020; Rick Wilson, "This Isn't the Madman Theory. This Is a Madman President," *Daily Beast*, Jan 28, 2020.

12　For a range of positive and negative outcomes of the madman theory, see M. Sinaceuer, "The Advantages of Being Unpredictable," *Journal of Experimental Social Psychology* 49 (2013): 498–508; Stephen Walt, "Things Don't End Well for Madmen," *Foreign Policy*, Aug 16, 2017; Seanon Wong, "Stoics and Hotheads: Leaders' Temperament, Anger and the Expression of Resolve in Face-to-Face Diplomacy," *Journal of Global Security Studies* 4, no. 2 (Apr 2019): 190–208. For evolutionary theory, see Andrew Little and Thomas Zeitzoff, "A Bargaining Theory of Conflict with Evolutionary Preferences," *International Organization* 71, no. 3 (Summer 2017): 523–57

13　Lionel Trilling, *Sincerity and Authenticity* (Cambridge, MA: Harvard Univ Press, 1973), esp. 2, 139–41.

14　For historiographical reviews on the history of emotions, see Rob Boddice, *The History of Emotions* (Manchester: Manchester Univ Press, 2018); Nicole Eustace et al., "'AHR' Conversation: The Historical Study of Emotions," *American Historical Review* 117, no. 5 (Dec 2012): 1486–531; Barbara H. Rosenwein, "Worrying about Emotions in History," *American Historical Review* 107, no. 3 (June 2002): 821–45; Peter N. Stearns, "History of Emotions," in *Handbook of Emotions*, 2nd ed., ed. Michael Lewis and Jeannette M. Haviland-Jones (New York: Guilford Press, 2000).

15 Trilling, *Sincerity*; Rosenwein, "Worrying about Emotions," 834–37; Nixon-Gannon, Jun 10, 1983, part 1. For Nixon's revulsion to emotional display, see also Nixon-Gannon, Apr 8, 1983, part 2.

16 Garry Wills, "The Enigma of President Nixon," *Saturday Evening Post*, Jan 25, 1969, 25; James Chace, "The Five-Power World of Richard Nixon," *New York Times*, Feb 20, 1972, SM14; Stanley I. Kutler, *The Wars of Watergate* (New York: W. W. Norton, 1992), 33.

17 For psychohistories and the temperamental theories, see James David Barber, *The Presidential Character: Predicting Performance in the White House* (Englewood Cliffs, NJ: Prentice Hall, 1972); Earl Mazo and Stephen Hess, *Nixon: A Political Portrait* (New York: Harper and Row, 1968); Bruce Mazlish, *In Search of Nixon: A Psychohistorical Inquiry* (New York: Basic Books, 1972); David Abrahamsen, *Nixon vs. Nixon* (New York: New American Library, 1977); Fawn Brodie, *Richard Nixon: The Shaping of His Character* (New York: W. W. Norton, 1981). For long-form biographies and developmental theories, see Jonathan Aitken, *Nixon: A Life* (New York: Regnery, 1994); Stephen Ambrose, *Nixon*, vol. 1, *The Education of a Politician, 1913–1963* (New York: Simon & Schuster, 1988); Stephen Ambrose, vol. 2, *Nixon: The Triumph of a Politician* (New York: Simon & Schuster, 1989); Stephen Ambrose, vol. 3, *Nixon: Ruin and Recovery, 1973–1990* (New York: Simon & Schuster, 1991); Roger Morris, *Richard Milhous Nixon: The Rise of an American Politician* (New York: Henry Holt & Co., 1989); Anthony Summer, *The Arrogance of Power: The Secret World of Richard Nixon* (New York: Viking, 2000); Tom Wicker, *One Of Us* (New York: Random House, 1991).

18 For revisionism, see Irwin F. Gellman, *The Contender: Richard Nixon: The Congress Years, 1946–1952* (New York: Free Press, 1999); Herbert S. Parmet, *Richard Nixon and His America* (New York: Little, Brown & Co., 1989); Hoff, *Reconsidered*, 1995; Melvin Small, *The Presidency of Richard Nixon* (Lawrence: Univ Press of Kansas, 1999); Iwan W. Morgan, *Nixon* (London: Oxford Univ Press, 2002). For cultural histories of Nixon, see David Greenberg, *Nixon's Shadow* (New York: W. W. Norton, 2003); Daniel Frick, *Reinventing Richard Nixon: A Cultural History of an American Obsession* (Lawrence: Univ Press of Kansas, 2008); Mark Feeney, *Nixon at the Movies* (Chicago: Univ of Chicago Press, 2004); Rick Perlstein, *Nixonland: The Rise of a President and the Fracturing of America* (New York: Scribner, 2009), 46. Greenberg, *Shadow*, xxvi.

19 Aitken, *A Life*, 5; Nixon-Gannon, Apr 8, 1983, part 1; Wicker, *One of Us*, xii–xiii.

20 Alexander Butterfield, interview by Timothy Naftali, Jun 12, 2008, OHP-RNL, 28.

21 Febvre, *New Kind of History*, 16; Nixon-Gannon, Apr 8, 1983, Part 2; William Safire, *Before the Fall* (New York: Routledge, 2017), 689.

22 Haldeman, with DiMona, *Ends of Power*, 82–83.

1. THE ACTING LIFE OF RICHARD NIXON

1 Nixon-Gannon, Jun 13, 1983, part 1; Nixon-Gannon, Feb 9, 1983, part 5; Andrew Hacker, "Is There a New Republican Majority?," *Commentary*, Nov 1969, 65.

2 Jules Witcover, "Nixon for President in '68?," *Saturday Evening Post*, Feb 25, 1967, 96; Stephen Ambrose, *Nixon*, vol. 1, *The Education of a Politician, 1913–1963* (New York: Simon & Schuster, 1988), 122; Roger Morris, *Richard Milhous Nixon: The Rise of an American Politician* (New York: Henry Holt & Co., 1989), 357; Nixon-Gannon, Feb 9, 1983, part 2, 5; Richard Nixon, *RN* (New York: Simon & Schuster, 1990), 42–43; Stewart Alsop, "The Mystery of Richard Nixon," *Saturday Evening Post*, Jul 12, 1958; Stewart Alsop, "Nixon on Nixon," *Saturday Evening Post*, Jul 12, 1958, 26–27. For Kennedy and Nixon's friendship, see Jonathan Aitken, "The Nixon Character," *Presidential Studies Quarterly* 26 (Winter 1996); Morris, *Richard Milhous Nixon*, 357; Evan Thomas, *Being Nixon* (New York: Random House, 2016), 107–8; Witcover, "Nixon for President," 96.

3 For striking internal examinations of his need for frivolity, see Frank Leonard, memorandum, "There's Something about the Guy I Just Don't Like," Mar 29, 1971, WHSF-CMC, box 1, folder 2; William Safire, *Before the Fall* (New York: Routledge, 2017), 602.

4 Safire, *Before the Fall*, 6; Nixon-Gannon, May 13, 1983, part 2; Stewart Alsop, "Campaigning with Nixon," *Saturday Evening Post*, Nov 5, 1960; Garry Wills, "The Enigma of President Nixon," *Saturday Evening Post*, Jan 25, 1969, 25–27, 54–58; William F. Gavin, "'Source Material': His Heart's Abundance. Notes of a Nixon Speechwriter," *Presidential Studies Quarterly* 31, no. 2 (Jun 2001): 362; Edwin Diamond, "Tape Shock: The Nixon Transcripts," *Columbia Journalism Review*, Jul 1, 1974, 5–9; Stephen Hess and David S. Broder, "Durability in Drive for Power Is Demonstrated: Alive, Nevertheless," *Washington Post*, Dec 1, 1967, A18, emphasis in the original.

5 Dwight Chapin, interview by Timothy Naftali, OHP-RNL, Apr 2, 2007, 10, 7; Alexander Butterfield, interview by Timothy Naftali, OHP-RNL, Jun 12, 2008,

10; Lamar Alexander, interview by Timothy Naftali, OHP-RNL, Jun 27, 2007, 31, 39; Christopher Matthews, *Kennedy and Nixon: The Rivalry That Shaped Postwar America* (New York: Simon & Schuster, 1998); Rick Perlstein, *Nixonland: The Rise of a President and the Fracturing of America* (New York: Scribner, 2009), 22.

6   Lou Cannon, *President Reagan: The Role of A Lifetime* (New York: PublicAffairs, 2000), 32; Richard E. Neustadt, *Presidential Power and the Modern Presidents* (New York: Free Press, 1991), esp. 68; Timothy Raphael, *The President Electric: Ronald Reagan and the Politics of Performance* (Ann Arbor: Univ of Michigan Press, 2009), esp. 92–94.

7   Fred I. Greenstein, *The Hidden-Hand Presidency: Eisenhower as Leader* (New York: Basic Books, 1982); Steven Watts, *JFK and the Masculine Mystique* (New York: St. Martin's Press, 2016); Raphael, *President Electric*.

8   Safire, *Before the Fall*, 602.

9   Tom Wicker, *One of Us* (New York: Random House, 1991), 3; David Greenberg, *Nixon's Shadow* (New York: W. W. Norton, 2003), xxix; Douglas Hallett, "Real Nixon Is Better Than the Mask," *Wall Street Journal*, Aug 24, 1970, 6; Safire, *Before the Fall*, 600, 605.

10 Greenberg, *Nixon's Shadow*; Bela Kornitzer and Richard Nixon, *Real Nixon: An Intimate Biography* (Charleston: Literary Licensing, LLC, 2011); Gary Allen, *The Man Behind the Mask*, (Belmont, MA: Western Islands, 1971); Harold Spalding, *The Nixon Nobody Knows* (New York: Jonathan David Publishers, 1972); Frank Leonard, memorandum, "MR. PRESIDENT . . . the Man," n.d., WHSF-SMOF, box 1, folder 1: Desmond Barker, Jr.: Media; Alan Lotten, "Politics and People," *Wall Street Journal*, Apr 19, 1973, 20; Bill Millinship, "Will the Real Nixon Now Stand Up," *Observer*, Nov 12, 1972, 12; Colman McCarthy, "Golf as a Clue to the Real Nixon," *Washington Post*, Aug 25, 1969, A24; Leonard, "There's Something"; Don Oberdorfer, "The 'Real Nixon' an Enigma," *Washington Post*, October 13, 1968.

11 Theodore White, *The Making of the President 1968* (New York: Harper Perennial, 2010), 169.

12 Marshall McLuhan, *Understanding Media: The Extensions of Man* (Cambridge, MA: MIT Press, 1994), 7–21; Marvin Kalb, *The Nixon Memo* (Chicago: Univ of Chicago Press, 1994), 12; Neustadt, *Presidential Power*, esp. 68; Lawrence Stone, "Revival of Narrative," *Past and Present* 85, no. 1 (Nov 1979): 3–24; George G.

Iggers, *The Historiography of the Twentieth Century* (Hanover, NH: Wesleyan Univ Press, 1997), 97–133.

13 Joe McGinnis, *The Selling of the Presidency* (New York: Penguin, 1968), 181, 195; Hallett, "Better Than the Mask," 6.

14 Greenberg, *Nixon's Shadow*, 68.

15 Greenberg, *Nixon's Shadow*, xv–xvi; Oberdorfer, "'Real Nixon' an Enigma," A1; Stephen I. Kutler, *The Wars of Watergate* (New York: W. W. Norton, 1992), 45; Nixon, *RN*, 178.

16 Nixon-Gannon, Feb 9, 1983, part 1; Morris, *Richard Milhous Nixon*, 108, 125, 130, 145.

17 Jonathan Aitken, *Nixon: A Life* (New York: Regnery, 1994), 63; Morris, *Richard Milhous Nixon*, 110, 108, 125, 130, 204–25; Thomas, *Being Nixon*, 10–11; Mark Feeney, *Nixon at the Movies* (Chicago: Univ of Chicago Press, 2004), 20; Eleanor Harris, "The Richard Nixons: National Spotlight," *Washington Post*, Mar 11, 1956, AW18; "Fighting Quaker," *Time*, Aug 25, 1952, n.p.; Kay Marten, "They're Proud of Nixon," *Chicago Tribune*, Oct 28, 1956; Nixon, *RN*, 18, 23; John Farrell, *Richard Nixon: The Life* (New York: Doubleday, 2017), 71–72; Nixon-Gannon, Feb 9, 1983, part 3.

18 "Fighting Quaker"; Alsop, "Mystery," 53–72; William Lee Miller, "The Debating Career of Richard M. Nixon," *Reporter*, Aug 19, 1956, 11, JVP, box 58, folder 21: Repercussions in Later Years; Richard Nixon, Pre-Presidential Papers: 1946, RNL, box 1, folder 1: Campaign, Speech File; Ambrose, *The Education*, 68; Greg Mitchell, *Tricky Dick and the Pink Lady: Richard Nixon vs. Helen Gahagan Douglas* (New York: Random House, 1998), 41; Morris, *Richard Milhous Nixon*, 131, 192.

19 Richard Nixon, *Six Crises* (New York: Doubleday, 1962), 1–72; Farrell, *Richard Nixon*, 97; Nixon-Gannon, Feb 9, 1983, part 5; Fiora Rheta Schreiber, "Pat Nixon Reveals for the First Time. 'I Didn't Want Dick to Run Again," *Good Housekeeping*, Jul 1968, 188.

20 Walter Goodman, *The Committee: The Extraordinary Career of the House on Un-American Activities Committee* (New York: Farrar, Straus & Giroux, 1968), 261; Kathryn S. Olmsted, *Real Enemies: Conspiracy Theories and American Democracy, World War I to 9/11* (Oxford: Oxford Univ Press, 2009), 96; Nixon-Gannon, Feb 9, 1983, part 6; "Hiss Pictured as Red Spy, Stooge, Liar," *Washington Post*, Nov 22, 1949, 1. For "slovenly" examples, Irving Howe, "Alger Hiss

Retried," *New York Times*, Apr 9, 1978; Sam Tanenhaus, *Whittaker Chambers: A Biography* (New York: Modern Library, 1998), 505–6.

21 Nixon-Gannon, Feb 9, 1983, part 6; Nixon, *Six Crises*, 1–72.

22 Farrell, *Richard Nixon*, 108; Mary Spargo, "Never Saw Him, House Probers Told," *Washington Post*, Aug 6, 1948, 1; "Alger Hiss Denies All Red Accusations Made by Chambers," *Washington Post*, Aug 6, 1948, 1; Alexander Feinberg, "Alger Hiss Denies Ever Turning Over Any State Papers," *New York Times*, Dec 13, 1948, 1; Edward Ryan, "Hiss Confronts Chambers," *Washington Post*, Aug 26, 1948; Murrey Marder, "Hiss Denies All Charges by Chambers," *Washington Post*, Jun 1949, 1; *Hearings before the Committee on Un-American Activities, House of Representatives* (Washington, D.C.: US Government Printing Office, 1948), 993.

23 Nixon-Gannon, Feb 9, 1983, part 6; C. P. Trussell, "President Is Blunt," *New York Times*, Aug 6, 1948, 1; Morris, *Richard Milhous*, 401; Marder, "Hiss Counsel Calls Accuser Mental Case," *Washington Post*, Jul 1949, 1; Nixon, *Six Crises*, 9; Nixon-Gannon, Feb 9, 1983, part 6.

24 Nixon-Gannon, Feb 9, 1983, part 6.

25 Nixon-Gannon, Feb 9, 1983, part 6; William Fitzgibbon, "The Hiss-Chambers Case: A Chronology since 1934," *New York Times*, Jun 12, 1949; Janny Scott, "Alger Hiss, 92, Central Figure in Long-Running Cold War Controversy," *New York Times*, Nov 6, 1996.

26 Nixon-Gannon, Feb 9, 1983, part 6; "Alger Hiss Admits He Knew Chambers after Confronting Him," *Washington Post*, Aug 8, 1948, 1; C. P. Trussell, "Hiss and Chambers Meet Face to Face; Clash in Testimony," *New York Times*, Aug 26, 1948, 1; Howe, "Alger Hiss Retried"; Conrad Black, *Richard M. Nixon: A Life in Full* (New York: PublicAffairs, 2007), 130.

27 James Keogh, *This Is Nixon: The Man and His Work* (White Fish, MT: Literary Licensing, 2012), 41; Fredrik Logevall, *Embers of War* (New York: Random House, 2012), 222–23.

28 Nixon, *RN*, 70–71; Nixon, *Six Crises*, 70.

29 "Funds Flow in for Nixon," *New York Times*, Sep 26, 1952, 14; Eleanor Harris, "The Darkest Hours of the Richard Nixons," *Washington Post*, Mar 4, 1956; Ward Just, "GOP Nominee Richard Nixon," *New York Times*, Aug 9, 1968, A14; Robert S. Cathcart and Edward A. Schwarz, "The New Nixon or Poor Richard," *North American Review*, Sep–Oct 1968, 8–12; Nixon, *Six Crises*, 73–130.

30 Nixon-Gannon, Apr 8, 1983, part 2; Nixon, *Six Crises*, 93; Nixon, *RN*, 97; Safire, "On Political Loyalty," *New York Times*, Jul 18, 1974, 35; Irwin Gellman, *The President and the Apprentice* (New Haven, CT: Yale Univ Press, 2015), 39.

31 Felix Morley, "On Senators," *Barron's*, Sept 29, 1952, 3; W. C. Bryant, "'Nixon Affair' Deflates Happy Mood aboard Ike's Special Train," *Wall Street Journal*, Sep 20, 1952, 1; "Nixon Should Withdraw," *Washington Post*, Sep 20, 1952, 1; Morris, *Richard Milhous Nixon*, 761–63, 776; Nixon, *Six Crises*, 83–86; Gellman, *The Apprentice*, 33; Arthur M. Schlesinger, Jr., *Journals, 1952–2000* (New York: Penguin, 2008), 155.

32 Morris Landberg, "Nixon's Expense Fund Totals $18,235," *Star News* (AP), Sep 21, 1952, JVP, box, 58, folder 21: Repercussions in Later Years of Nixon 1946 Campaign; Nixon, *Six Crises*, 100; Nixon, *RN*, 98–101.

33 David S. Broder, "Controversial Aide Reenters National Politics," *Washington Post*, Feb 23, 1969, A3; JVP, box 58, folder 24: Murray Chotiner; Alsop, "Mystery," 62; H. R. Haldeman, interview by Raymond H. Geselbracht, OHP-RNL, Apr 11, 1988, 24; Nixon, *Six Crises*, 83–85, 107–13.

34 Gellman, *The Apprentice*, 43; Richard Nixon, transcript, Sep 23, 1952, American Rhetoric: Top 100 Speeches, https://www.americanrhetoric.com/speeches /richardnixoncheckers.html (hereafter Nixon, "Secret Fund Speech").

35 Nixon, "Secret Fund Speech."

36 David Halberstam, *Powers That Be* (Champaign: Univ of Illinois Press, 2000), 465; Morris, *Richard Milhous*, 835, 839.

37 Clayton Knowles, "GOP Officially Closes Book on Nixon Expense Fund Case," *New York Times*, Sep 26, 1952, 1; Robert W. O'Brien and Elizabeth J. Jones, *The Night Nixon Spoke: A Study of Political Effectiveness* (Los Alamitos, CA: Hwong Press, 1976), 9; Morris, *Richard Milhous Nixon*, 852–53; Knowles, "Closes Book on Nixon," 1; Greenberg, *Nixon's Shadow*, 52–53; Kenneth Ungerman, "Nixon Clean as Hound's Tooth; Will Stay—Ike," *Atlanta Daily World*, Sep 25, 1952, 1; Alsop, "Mystery"; Earl Mazo, *Richard Nixon: A Political and Personal Portrait* (New York: Harper and Brothers, 1959), 136.

38 Nixon, *Six Crises*, 123; Gellman, *The Apprentice*, 29.

39 Black, "Privacy in Public," 16; Nixon-Gannon, Apr 8, 1983, part 2; "Truman Is Silent on the Two Funds," *New York Times*, Sep 26, 1952, 14; "Stevenson's Funds," *Chicago Tribune*, Sep 30, 1952, 14; Nixon, *RN*, 100.

40 Gellman, *The Apprentice*, 30; "Nixon's Technique of Youthful Sincerity and Blasting Truman Draws Big Crowds," *Wall Street Journal*, Oct 10 1952, 6; William G. Wearts, "Democrats Called Spineless by Nixon," *New York Times*, Oct 10, 1952, 19; Morris, *Richard Milhous Nixon*, 857–58; Elie Abel, "Truman, Acheson Assailed by Nixon," *New York Times*, Oct 8, 1952, 14; "Administration Is Spineless, Nixon Charges," *Chicago Tribune*, Oct 10, 1952, 3; "Nixon Speech Clothes Adlai in 'State Department Pinks,'" *Washington Post*, Oct 10, 1952, 12.

41 Farrell, *Richard Nixon*, 217; Nixon, *Six Crises*, 183–234; Tad Szulc, "US Flies Troops to Caribbean as Mobs Attack Nixon in Caracas," *New York Times*, May 14, 1958, 1.

42 Nixon-Gannon, Sep 7, 1983, part 3; Nixon, *Six Crises*, 183–234; Tad Szulc, "Nixon Cuts Tour Short," *New York Times*, May 15, 1958, 1; Lester Tanzer, "Nixon Unhurt as Red-Led Mob Attacks Car in Caracas," *Wall Street Journal*, May 14, 1958, 2; Lester Tanzer, "Reds in Caracas," *Wall Street Journal*, May 16, 1958, 8; "Report Nixon Death Plot," *Chicago Tribune*, May 13, 1958, 1.

43 Nixon, *Six Crises*, 183–234; Szulc, "Troops to Caribbean," 1; Nixon-Gannon, Sep 7, 1983, part 3; Tanzer, "Nixon Unhurt."

44 Don Nixon to Richard Nixon, WHSF, box 2, folder 23, Jan 9, 1971; Szulc, "Troops to Caribbean," 1; Alsop, "Nixon on Nixon," 26–27.

45 Safire, *Before the Fall*, 21; Nixon-Gannon, Sep 7, 1983, part 1; Farrell, *Richard Nixon*, 298.

46 Farrell, *Richard Nixon*, 283; Kutler, *Wars of Watergate*, 51; Gerald S. Strober and Deborah H. Strober, eds., *Nixon: An Oral History of His Presidency* (New York: HarperCollins, 1994), 31; Herb Klein, interview by Timothy Naftali, OHP-RNL, Feb 20, 2007, 32.

47 Nixon, *Six Crises*, 422–23; Chapin, OHP-RNL, 46; Farrell, *Richard Nixon*, 372; Nixon, *RN*, 354–55; Edward Nixon, interview by Timothy Naftali, OHP-RNL, Jan 9, 2007, 12.

48 David Wise, "Are You Worried about Your Image, Mr. President?," *Esquire*, May 1973, 24; Witcover, "Nixon for President," 93–97; Stephen J. Whitfield, "Richard Nixon as a Comic Figure," *American Quarterly* 1, no. 1 (Spring 1985): 118. For some similar quipping over Nixon's staid appearance, see "Is 'Benign Neglect' the Real Nixon Approach?," *New York Times*, Mar 8, 1970, E1; Leonard, "There's Something," 7; Oberdorfer, "'Real Nixon' an Enigma," A1; McCarthy, "Golf as a Clue," A24.

49 H. R. Haldeman, *Haldeman Diaries: Inside the Nixon White House* (New York: G. P. Putnam's Sons, 1994), "Friday, January 22, 1971," 27, "Friday, March 28, 1969," 45, "Wednesday, May 21, 1969," 60, "Monday, Feb 3, 1969," 238; Richard Nixon to John Ehrlichman, memorandum, Jan 11, 1969, WHSF, box 1, folder 40; Butterfield, OHP-RNL, 4; Stephen Ambrose, vol. 3, *Nixon: Ruin and Recovery, 1973–1990* (New York: Simon & Schuster, 1991), 585.

50 Butterfield, OHP-RNL, 14–15; White, *Making of the President 1968*, 10; David Greenberg, "Nixon as Statesman: The Failed Campaign," in *Nixon in the World: American Foreign Relations, 1969–1977*, ed. Fredrik Logevall and Andrew Preston (Oxford: Oxford Univ Press, 2008), 47; Roger Ailes to H. R. Haldeman and Dwight Chapin, "White House Television," WHSF-CMC, n.d., box 7, folder 18: H. R. Haldeman: Charles Colson; Morris, *Richard Milhous Nixon*, 100; Hunter S. Thompson, *The Great Shark Hunt: Strange Tales from a Strange Time* (New York: Simon & Schuster, 2011), 175, 191; Chapin, OHP-RNL, 24.

51 On mining punchlines, see Richard Nixon to John Ehrlichman, memorandum, WHSF, n.d., box 1, folder 35: RN Tape; Witcover, "Nixon for President," 95.

52 H. R. Haldeman, interview by Raymond H. Geselbracht and Fred J. Grabske, OHP-RNL, Aug 13, 1987, 34; Henry Kissinger, *The White House Years* (Boston: Little, Brown and Company, 1979), 1175.

53 Raymond Price Jr., interview by Timothy Naftali, OHP-RNL, Apr 4, 2007, 10; Charles Colson, interview by Timothy Naftali, OHP-RNL, Aug 7, 2007; Tom Charles Huston, interview by Timothy Naftali, OHP-RNL, Mar 10, 2008, 35; Leonard Garment, interview by Timothy Naftali, OHP-RNL, Oct 5, 2007, 27; John Farrell, *Richard Nixon: The Life* (New York: Vintage, 2017), Kindle; Kissinger, *White House Years*, 1175.

54 Ronald Steel quoted in Kutler, *Wars of Watergate*, 34; Joan Hoff, *Reconsidered* (New York: Basic Books, 1995), 341; Ambrose, *Ruin and Recovery*, 531.

55 James MacGregor Burns, "Nixon's Final Appeal to History," *Chicago Tribune*, Jun 6, 1978; Nixon-Gannon, May 27, 1983, part 3; Nixon-Gannon, Apr 8, 1983, part 4; Aitken, "Nixon Character," 241.

56 Ron Ziegler to H. R. Haldeman, memorandum, Nov 16, 1970, WHSF-CMC, box 45, folder 29, 4; Pat Buchanan to Richard Nixon, memorandum, Sep 17, 1971, WHSF, box 1, folder 13: Pat Buchanan: Haldeman 1971. For similar examples of the cult de mystique in the Nixon administration, see Stewart

Alsop, "Nixon and the Square Majority: Is the Fox a Lion?," *Atlantic Monthly*, Feb 1972; Haldeman, OHP-RNL, Apr 11, 1988, 130; H. R. Haldeman, interview by Raymond H. Geselbracht, OHP-RNL, April 12, 1988, 76–77; H. R. Haldeman, interview by Raymond H. Geselbracht, OHP-RNL, Apr 11, 1988, 46, 75; Richard Nixon, *Leaders* (New York: Warner Brother, 1982), 40–80; Ziegler to Haldeman, Nov 16, 1970, 4; Haldeman, OHP-RNL, Apr 12, 1988, 76–77, emphasis in the original.

57 Sarah Booth Conroy, "A Self-Portrait: The Richard Nixons as the First Family," *Washington Post*, Mar 14, 1971, K1; David Oberdorfer, "Nixon Picks His Ground," *Washington Post*, Mar 18, 1971.

58 William Anderson, "Herb Klein Heads an Empire," *Chicago Tribune*, Apr 5, 1971, 1; Wise, "Are You Worried," 121; Anderson, "Herb Klein," 1.

59 Glenn Plaskin, "Barbara Talks about Talking," *Toronto Star*, Feb 28, 1988, H6; Chery Purdey, "Here's Barbara—and Her Ego," *Edmonton Journal*, Jun 30, 1990, G2; Rhys Blakely, "End of an Era As TV's Big Interview Queen Quits," *Times* (London), May 17, 2014, 43; Oberdorfer, "Nixon Picks His Ground," A21; James Conaway, "How to Talk with Barbara Walters about Practically Anything," *New York Times*, Sep 10, 1972, SM40.

60 Oberdorfer, "Nixon Picks His Ground," A21; Conaway, "Barbara Walters"; Tom Shales, "Live From New York! It's Walters vs. Nixon," *Washington Post*, May 8, 1980, C1; Purdey, "Here's Barbara," G2.

61 Conaway, "Barbara Walters"; Wise, "Are You Worried," 120; Kutler, *Wars of Watergate*, 92; Richard Nixon to H. R. Haldeman, memorandum, Jan 4, 1969, WHSF, box 1, folder 35: Television Man; Stuart Schulberg, Letter to the Editor, *New York Times*, Oct 1, 1972, SM77; Haldeman, OHP-RNL, Apr 12, 1988, 77. For a similar denial that Nixon never had a "public relations man," see Alsop, "Nixon on Nixon," 26–27.

62 Aitken, "Nixon Character," 219; Nixon, *Six Crises*, 34–35.

63 Nixon, *Leaders*, 327; Safire, *Before the Fall*, 689, 692.

2. THE SENTIMENTAL LIFE OF RICHARD NIXON

1 Carroll Kilpatrick, "Nixon Honors Soviet War Dead: President Visits Leningrad," *Washington Post*, May 28, 1972, A1; "Calls for Peace," *New York Times*, May 28, 1972, 1; UPI, "Nixon Lays Wreath on Russian Memorial," May 27, 1972, https://digitalcommons.chapman.edu/upi_nixon/170/.

2   Translation from Yvonne Pörzgen, "Siege Memory-Besieged Memory?
    Heroism and Suffering in St Petersburg Museums Dedicated to the Siege of
    Leningrad," *Museum and Society* 14, no. 3 (2016): 418–19; Theodore Shabad,
    "Nixon Talks on TV to Soviet People and Hails Accord," *New York Times*,
    May 29, 1972.

3   Sarah Knott, *Sensibility and the American Revolution* (Chapel Hill: Univ of North
    Carolina Press, 2009), 250–54; Rebecca Bedell, *Moved to Tears: Rethinking the
    Art of the Sentimental in the United States* (Princeton, NJ: Princeton Univ Press,
    2018), 14–15, 28, 37–39.

4   James Yuenger, "Nixon to Address Russ Today," *Chicago Tribune*, May 28, 1972;
    Robert B. Semple, "President Honors Leningrad Dead," *New York Times*,
    May 28, 1972, 1; "Transcript of Nixon's Acceptance Address," *New York Times*,
    Aug 24, 1972, and for video, "The Presidency: Richard Nixon 1972 Accep-
    tance Speech," CSPAN, Aug 23, 1972, https://www.c-span.org/video/?3911-1
    /richard-nixon-1972-acceptance-speech (hereinafter Nixon, "1972 Acceptance
    Speech").

5   Nixon, "1972 Acceptance Speech."

6   William F. Gavin, "'Source Material': His Heart's Abundance, Notes of a Nixon
    Speechwriter," *Presidential Studies Quarterly* 31, no. 2 (Jun 2001): 358, 362–67;
    Karen Hult and Charles Walcott, "Policymakers and Wordsmiths: Writing for
    the President under Johnson and Nixon," *Polity* 30, no. 3 (Spring 1998): 482–83;
    H. R. Haldeman, *Haldeman Diaries: Inside the Nixon White House* (New York:
    G. P. Putnam's Sons, 1994). For notable examples of Nixon's favoring of the
    sentimental, see "Richard Nixon: Checkers Speech," *The History Place*, Sep 23,
    1952, http://www.historyplace.com/speeches/nixon-checkers.htm; "Richard
    Nixon: Address Accepting the Presidential Nomination at the Republican
    National Convention in Miami Beach Florida," Aug 8, 1968, American
    Presidency Project, https://www.presidency.ucsb.edu/documents/address
    -accepting-the-presidential-nomination-the-republican-national-convention
    -miami (hereinafter, Nixon, "1968 Acceptance Speech"; "Girl Gave Nixon
    Theme," *Washington Post*, Nov 7, 1968; Nixon, "1972 Acceptance Speech;
    "April 7, 1971: Address to the Nation on the Situation in Southeast Asia,"
    https://millercenter.org/the-presidency/presidential-speeches/April-7-1971
    -address-nation-situation-southeast-asia; "January 22, 1971: State of the Union
    Address," https://millercenter.org/the-presidency/presidential-speeches

/january-22-1971-state-union-address; "April 30, 1973: Address to the Nation about the Watergate Investigations," https://millercenter.org/the-presidency /presidential-speeches/april-30-1973-address-nation-about-watergate -investigations; "Richard M. Nixon Farewell Address," *The History Place*, Aug 9, 1974 (hereinafter, Nixon, "Farewell Address"; William Safire, "The Way Forward," *New York Times*, Sep 2, 2007; Joe McGinnis, *The Selling of the President* (New York: Penguin, 1968), 115. In Nixon's first campaign for the House and later the Senate, he went beyond the public, employing his family in advertisements, presenting sentimental family portraits with his two toddler daughters: Edwin Black, "Richard Nixon and the Privacy of Public Discourse," *Rhetoric and Public Affairs* 2, no. 1 (Spring 1999): 4–7, 10. On political ads, see Paul Christiansen, *Orchestrating Public Opinion* (Amsterdam: Amsterdam Univ Press, 2018), 74–80; Nixon-Gannon, May 27, 1983, part 1; McGinnis, *Selling*, 115.

7   Rudolf Neuhâuser, *Towards the Romantic Age: Essays on the Sentimental and Preromantic Literature* (The Hague: Springer, 1974), 8; Joanne Dobson, "Reclaiming Sentimental Literature," *American Literature* 69, no. 2 (Jun 1997): 263–88; G. J. Barker-Benfield, *The Culture of Sensibility: Sex and Society in Eighteenth-Century Britain* (Chicago: Univ. of Chicago Press, 1996), 215. For discussions of moral sentimentalism, see Annette C. Baier, *A Progress of Sentiments: Reflections on Hume's* Treatise (Cambridge, MA: Harvard Univ Press, 1991), 1–27; Barker-Benfield, *Culture of Sensibility*, 104–53; Michael Bell, *Sentimentalism, Ethics and the Culture of Feeling* (New York: Springer, 2000), 1–2, 39–43; Dobson, "Reclaiming Sentimental Literature." See etymologies in Marcia Muelder Eaton, "Laughing at the Death of Little Nell: Sentimental Art and Sentimental People," *American Philosophical Quarterly* 26, no. 4 (Oct 1989): 270–71.

8   Harrison Salisbury, *The 900 Days: The Siege of Leningrad* (Boston: De Capo, 2003), 507; Anna Reid, *Leningrad: Tragedy of a City under Siege, 1941–1944* (London: Bloomsbury, 2011), 182; Constantine Krypton, "The Siege of Leningrad," *Russian Review* 13, no. 4 (Oct 1954): 256, 258; Alexis Peri, *The War Within: Diaries from the Siege of Leningrad* (Cambridge, MA: Harvard Univ Press, 2017), 38; Reid, *Leningrad*, 263.

9   Shabad, "Nixon Talks"; Reid, *Leningrad*, 363–64; Julia Popova, "Siege Lines: 75 Years Ago Tanya Savicheva Made the Last Entry in Her Diary," RT, May 13, 2017; Salisbury, *900 Days*, 484; Evan Andrews, "The Siege of Leningrad,"

History.com, Aug 29, 2018, https://www.history.com/news/the-siege-of
-leningrad; Patricia Heberer, *Children during the Holocaust* (Lanham, MD:
Rowman Altimara, 2011), 52–53.

10   Joseph Kupfer, "The Sentimental Self," *Canadian Journal of Philosophy* 26, no. 4
(Dec 1996): 543; David Denby, *Sentimentalism Narrative and the Social Order in
France* (Cambridge: Cambridge Univ Press, 1994), 2–3, 13; Andrew Burstein,
Sentimental Democracy: The Evolution of America's Romantic Self-Image (New York:
Hill and Wang, 1999), 4–6; Robert C. Solomon, "On Kitsch and Sentimental-
ity," *Journal of Aesthetics and Art Criticism* 49 (1991): 1–14; Knott, *Sensibility and the
American Revolution*, 250–54; James Chandler, "The Politics of Sentiment:
Notes Toward a New Account," *Studies in Romanticism* 49, no. 4 (Winter 2010):
561; "Rightful Indignation": Robert C. Solomon, "In Defense of Sentimental-
ity," *Philosophy and Literature* 14 (1990): 14; Bruno Bettelheim, *Informed Heart*
(New York: Penguin, 1991); Baier, *Progress of Sentiments*, 3; on the origin of the
term *philanthropist*, B. Sprague Allen, "The Dates of Sentimental and Its
Derivatives," *PMLA*. 48, no. 1 (Mar 1933): 304.

11   Stewart Alsop, "The Mystery of Richard Nixon," *Saturday Evening Post*, Jul 12,
1958, 62; David Greenberg, *Nixon's Shadow* (New York: W. W. Norton, 2003),
54–55; John Farrell, *Richard Nixon: The Life* (New York: Doubleday, 2017), 94;
Robert S. Cathcart and Edward A. Schwarz, "The New Nixon or Poor Richard," *North American Review* 253, no. 5 (Sep–Oct 1968): 8–12; Gavin, "Source
Material," 358–68.

12   Garry Wills, *Nixon Agonistes: The Crisis of the Self-Made Man* (New York: First
Mariner Books, 2002); Richard Nixon, *RN* (New York: Simon & Schuster,
1990), 26; Jonathan Aitken, *Nixon: A Life* (New York: Regnery, 1994), 26.

13   Farrell, *Richard Nixon*, 3; Nixon to Ginger Rogers, telegram, Dec 12, 1968,
WHSF, box 6, folder 9; Aitken, *A Life*, 4; Stephen Ambrose, *Nixon*, vol. 3, *Ruin
and Recovery, 1973–1990* (New York: Simon & Schuster, 1991), 586; Jonathan
Aitken, "The Nixon Character," *Presidential Studies Quarterly* 26, no. (Winter
1996).

14   Wills, *Agonistes*, 586; Aitken, *A Life*, 26; Margaret MacMillan, *Nixon and Mao:
The Week That Changed the World* (New York: Random House, 2007); 13; H. R.
Haldeman, interview by Raymond Geselbracht and Fred Graboske, OHP-
RNL, Aug 13, 1987, 61; Richard Nixon, *Six Crises* (New York: Doubleday, 1962),
398, 405.

15   Michael Anthony Savile, *The Test of Time: An Essay in Philosophical Aesthetics* (Oxford: Clarendon Press, 1982), 339; Ira Newman, "The Alleged Unwholesome of Sentimentality," *Arguing about Art*, ed. Alex Neill and Aaron Ridley (New York: McGraw-Hill, 1995), 238.

16   Tom Wicker, *One of Us* (New York: Random House, 1991), 9; Wills, *Nixon Agonistes*, 156; Nixon-Gannon, Sep 7, 1983, part 2; Ken Clawson, "5 Years Later: A Loyalist Relives the Nixon Resignation," *Washington Post*, Aug 9, 1979, D1.

17   Robert Dallek, *Nixon and Kissinger: Partners in Power* (New York: Harper Perennial, 2007), 5; Nixon, *RN*, 1; Nixon-Gannon, Feb 9, 1983, part 1; Richard Nixon, *In the Arena: A Memoir of Victory, Defeat and Renewal* (New York: Pocket Books, 1991), 85–86.

18   Virginia Shaw Critchfield, interview by Jeff Jones, OHP-CSUF, May 2 and 9, 1970, "Richard Nixon's Early Years," 16, 42; Mary G. Skidmore, interview, by Greg Brolin, OHP-CSUF, 1977, "Richard Nixon's School Days," 1; Merle West, interview by Robert Davis, OHP-CSUF, 1977, "Richard Nixon as a Relative," 12; Farrell, *Richard Nixon*, 51; Mr. and Mrs. Richard Gauldin, interview by Milan Pavlovich, OHP-CSUF, May 8, 1970, "Early Yorba Linda," 10; Paul Ryan, interview by Milan Pavlovich, OHP-CSUF, May 15, 1970, "Richard Nixon as a Neighbor," 7–8, 12; Gerald Shaw, interview by Jeff Jones, OHP-CSUF, Jun 3 1970, "Life in Early Yorba Linda and Fullerton, California," 7; Jean Lippiatt, "Pat Nixon Was My Typing Teacher," *Saturday Evening Post*, Jun 1, 1971, 29.

19   Nixon-Gannon, Feb 9, 1983, part 2; Nixon-Gannon, Feb 9, 1983, part 1; Dallek, *Nixon and Kissinger*, 5; Nixon, *RN*, 5; Nixon, *Arena*, 85.

20   Roger Morris, *Richard Milhous Nixon: The Rise of an American Politician* (New York: Henry Holt & Co., 1989), 62; West, OHP-CSUF, n.p.; Conrad Black, *Richard M. Nixon: A Life in Full* (New York: PublicAffairs, 2007), 3; Hoyt Corbit, interview by Tom Peters, OHP-CSUF, May 6, 17, 20, 1968, "Richard Nixon: Early Years in Yorba Linda," 9; Critchfield, OHP-CSUF, 21; Mary Elizabeth Rez, interview by Tom Peters, OHP-CSUF, Apr 21, 1970, "Richard Nixon," 14; Aitken, *A Life*, 16; Stephen Ambrose, *Nixon*, vol. 1, *The Education of a Politician, 1913–1963* (New York: Simon & Schuster, 1988), 26.

21   I. A. Richards. *Practical Criticism* (New York: Harcourt, Brace and World, 1929), 252; Pat Buchanan, *Nixon's White House Wars: The Battles that Made and Broke a President and Divided America Forever* (New York: Crown Forum, 2017), 52; Tom Wicker, "Richard M. Nixon, 1969–1974," *Presidential Studies Quarterly* 26, no. 1

(Winter 1996): 254; Witcover, "Nixon for President in '68?," *Saturday Evening Post*, Feb 25, 1967, 93; Nixon, *RN*, 452.

22   Harold Spalding, *The Nixon Nobody Knows* (New York: Jonathan David Publishers, 1972), 40; Rez, OHP-CSUF, 21; Morris, *Richard Milhous*, 42, 49–50, 58, 60, 101–3, 108, 122, 141; Mauricio Mazón, "Young Richard Nixon: A Study In Political Precocity," *Historian* 41, no. 1 (Nov 1978): 42; Cecil E. Pickering, interview by Steven Guttman, OHP-CSUF, Jun 30, 1970, "Nixon: Yorba Linda Childhood," 23; Yoneko Iwatsuru, interview by Milan Pavlovich, OHP-CSUF, Apr 30, 1970, "Early School Days in Yorba Linda, California," 3, 6; Shaw, OHP-CSUF, 39; Skidmore, OHP-CSUF, 1, 3; Critchfield, OHP-CSUF, 4, 12, 21, 24; Alsop, "Mystery," 53–72; Mark Feeney, *Nixon at the Movies* (Chicago: Univ of Chicago Press, 2004), 25; Ambrose, *Education of a Politician*, 27.

23   Aitken, *A Life*, 16–19; Earl Mazo and Stephen Hess, *Nixon: A Political Portrait* (New York: Harper and Row, 1968), 10; Morris, *Richard Milhous Nixon*, 49; James Whitcomb Riley, *The Complete Poetical Works of James Whitcomb Riley* (Bloomington: Indiana Univ Press, 1993), 262, 350, 463.

24   Morris, *Richard Milhous Nixon*, 101–3, 108, 122, 141; Shaw, OHP-CSUF, 46; Richard Perlstein, ed., introduction, *Richard Nixon: Speeches, Writings, Documents* (Princeton, NJ: Princeton Univ Press, 2008), xx; Ambrose, *Education of a Politician*, 67; Iwatsuru, OHP-CSUF, 3, 6; Shaw, OHP-CSUF, 39; Skidmore, OHP-CSUF, 1; Alsop, "Mystery," 53–72; Critchfield, OHP-CSUF, 21, 24; Pickering OHP-CSUF, 23.

25   Nixon, *RN*, 4; Nixon-Gannon, Feb 9, 1983, part 1; Monica Crowley, *Nixon in Winter* (New York: Random House, 1998), 405.

26   Nixon, *RN*, 3–13; Aitken, *A Life*, 12; Solomon, "In Defense," 321; Richards, *Practical Criticism*, 252; Richard Nixon, *Leaders* (New York: Warner Books, 1982), 4–9; Aitken, *A Life*, 12–13, 26; David Greenberg, "Nixon as Statesman: The Failed Campaign," in *Nixon in the World: American Foreign Relations, 1969–1977*, ed. Fredrik Logevall and Andrew Preston (Oxford: Oxford Univ Press, 2008), 54.

27   Nixon, *Arena*, 4–13.

28   Nixon, *Arena*, 573; Nixon, *Leaders*, 6–7, 19; Eleanor Harris, "The Richard Nixons: National Spotlight," *Washington Post*, Mar 11, 1956, AW18; Marie Smith, "Dick and Pat Visit Old Home at Yorba Linda," *Washington Post*, Jun 14, 1959; Alsop, "Mystery," 59; Kay Marten, "They're Proud of Nixon," *Chicago*

Tribune, Oct 28, 1956, 35; Morris, *Richard Milhous*, 33–35, 79; Davis, OHP-CSUF, n.p.; Rez, OHP-CSUF, 5; Farrell, *Richard Nixon*, 46; Corbit, OHP-CSUF, 22; Pickering, OHP-CSUF, 12; Critchfield, OHP-CSUF, 8, 24; Nixon-Gannon, Feb 9, 1983, part 1; Ralph Navarro, interview by Milan Pavlovich, OHP-CSUF, Jun 4, 1980, "Early History of Yorba Linda, California," 17; Shaw, OHP-CSUF, 55; Edward Nixon, interview by Timothy Naftali, OHP-RNL, Jan 9, 2007, 1.

29 West, OHP-CSUF, n.p.; Stewart Alsop, "Nixon and the Square Majority: Is the Fox a Lion?," *Atlantic Monthly*, Feb 1972; Morris, *Richard Milhous Nixon*, 194; Earl Mazo, *Richard Nixon: A Political and Personal Portrait* (New York: Harper & Brothers, 1959), 35; Bela Kornitzer and Richard Nixon, *The Real Nixon: An Intimate Biography* (Whitefish, MT, 2017), 79; Nixon-Gannon, Feb 9, 1983; Shaw, OHP-CSUF, 1; Critchfield, OHP-CSUF, n.p.; Corbit, OHP-CSUF, 1; Davis, OHP-CSUF, n.p.; Perlstein, *Speeches*, xvii; Nixon, *Arena*, 85–94.

30 Aitken, *A Life*, 7, 13–15.

31 Nixon, *Arena*, 8; Davis, OHP-CSUF, n.p.; Aitken, *A Life*, 21; Arthur Burdg, interview by Richard Curtiss, OHP-CSUF, Feb 16, 1970; Corbit, OHP-CSUF, 29; Mr. and Mrs. Gauldin, OHP-CSUF, n.p.; Pickering, OHP-CSUF, 15; Rez, OHP-CSUF, n.p.; Ralph C. Shook, Sr., interview by Richard Curtiss, Feb 10, 1970, OHP-CSUF, "Richard: As Sunday School Student and Neighbor," n.p.; Skidmore, OHP-CSUF, 4; Nixon, *RN*, 4–5; Edward Nixon, OH-RNL, 3; Nixon-Gannon, Feb 9, 1983, part 1. For similar sentimental descriptions of Hannah Nixon, see Nixon, *RN*, 1–13; Richard Nixon, "August 9, 1974: Remarks on Departure from White House," *Presidential Speeches*, Miller Center, https://millercenter.org/the-presidency/presidential-speeches/august-9-1974 -remarks-departure-white-house; Nixon-Gannon, Feb 9, 1983, part 1.

32 Farrell, *Richard Nixon*, 49; Nixon-Gannon, Feb 9, 1983, part 2; Edward Nixon, OHP-RNL, 11.

33 Harris, "Richard Nixons," AW18; Pickering, OHP-CSUF, 7; Davis, OHP-CSUF, n.p.; Stewart Alsop, "Nixon on Nixon," *Saturday Evening Post*, Jul 12, 1958, 26; Nixon-Gannon, Sep 7, 1983, part 2.

34 Nixon-Gannon, Feb 9, 1983, part 2; Morris, *Richard Milhous Nixon*, 95; Francis J. Gavin, *Nuclear Statecraft: History and Strategy in America's Atomic Age* (Ithaca, NY: Cornell Univ Press, 2012), 68.

35 Aitken, *A Life*, 14, 16; Skidmore, OHP-CSUF, 1; Nixon-Gannon, Feb 9, 1983, part 1; Iwatsuru, OHP-CSUF, 3; Nixon, *RN*, 8.

36 Nixon-Gannon, Feb 9, 1983, part 1, 2; Morris, *Richard Milhous Nixon*, 61, 143; Ambrose, *Education of a Politician*, 24; Farrell, *Richard Nixon*, 48.

37 Evan Thomas, *Being Nixon* (New York: Random House, 2016), 10; Ambrose, *Education of a Politician*, 24; Wicker, *One of Us*, 651; Alsop, "Nixon on Nixon," 26; Nixon, *Arena*, 86–87; Nixon-Gannon, Feb 9, 1983, part 1.

38 Sentimentalism survived not so much as a social movement as an artistic trope. It was the dramatizing of the at once fortitude of feelings and fragility of affective bonds. Plots continued to hinge on connections of knowledge most heartfelt, on the said and the secret. We can trace the sentimental's popularity through the antebellum United States in the abolitionists and the feminist likes of Harriet Beecher Stowe, Louisa May Alcott and later Emily Dickenson.

Further, the sentimental also threaded through the Orientalism of E. M. Forester's *A Passage to India*, Flaubert's *L'Éducation sentimentale* and G. W. Goldsmith's dear Oriental, "nature's unspoiled child . . . who cannot comprehend the vices of the Christian world." Well past the Age of Feeling, the sentimental wove through Nathaniel Hawthorne and Herman Melville and, most especially, drenched Charles Dickens in the likes of Tiny Tim, Ebenezer Scrooge and Pip. Dickens's "Dear, gentle, patient, noble . . . mute" (and dead) Little Nell in *The Old Curiosity Shop* is perhaps the standard-bearer of syrupy creations. For an apt analysis of Orientalist sentimentalism, see W. F. Gallaway, Jr., *The Sentimentalism of Goldsmith*, PLMA 48, no. 4 (Dec 1933): 1168–71, and Lisa Lowe, "Orient as Woman, Orientalism as Sentimentalism: Flaubert," *Critical Terrains: French and British Orientalisms* (Ithaca: Cornell Univ Press, 1991), 75–101. For unsparing impatience with Little Nell, see Eaton, "Laughing," 269–82; Anthony Savile, *The Test of Time: An Essay in Philosophical Aesthetics* (Oxford: Clarendon Press, 1982), 331; Michael Tanner, "'Sentimentality,'" *Proceedings of the Aristotelian Society* 77 (1976–77): 130; Mary Midgley, "Brutality and Sentimentality," *Philosophy* 54 (1979): 385.

For what the "standard view" or modernist critique of Sentimentalism, see Deborah Knight, "Why We Enjoy Condemning Sentimentality: A Meta-Aesthetic Perspective," *Journal of Aesthetics and Art Criticism* 57, no. 4 (Autumn 1999): 411–20; Eaton, "Laughing," 269–82; Richards, *Practical Criticism*, 241–54; Savile, *Test of Time*, 236–50; Tanner, "'Sentimentality,'". For literary reviews, especially feminist, see Sean Epstein-Corbin, "Pragmatism, Feminism and the Sentimental Subject," *Transactions of the Charles S. Peirce Society* 50, no. 2

(Spring 2014): 220–45; Joanne Dobson, "Reclaiming Sentimental Literature," *American Literature* 69, no. 2 (Jun 1997): 263–88; Cindy Weinstein, *Family, Kinship, and Sympathy in Nineteenth-Century American Literature* (Cambridge: Cambridge Univ Press, 2004).

39 Richards, *Practical Criticism*, 241–42; Eaton, "Laughing," 269–82; Baier, *Progress of Sentiments*, 152; Kupfer, "Sentimental Self" 551, 554; Midgley, "Brutality and Sentimentality," 385.

40 Nixon, "1968 Acceptance Speech"; Nixon, "Bring Us Together"; "Girl Gave Nixon Theme," *Washington Post*, Nov 7, 1968; Nixon, "1972 Acceptance Speech"; Nixon, "April 7, 1971: Address to the Nation on the Situation in Southeast Asia"; Nixon, "January 22, 1971: State of the Union Address"; Nixon, "April 30, 1973: Address to the Nation about Watergate Investigations," Apr 30, 1973; Nixon, "Farewell Address"; Safire, "Way Forward," *New York Times*, Sep 2, 2007.

41 Nixon, "1968 Acceptance Speech"; Nixon, *RN*, 625–28; Nixon-Gannon, Jun 13, 1983, part 3.

42 James Gannon, "Labor and Nixon," *Wall Street Journal*, Feb 27, 1969, 14; Eaton, "Laughing," 269–82. See for examples of his opponents' derision, Fawn Brodie, *Richard Nixon: The Shaping of His Character* (New York: W. W. Norton, 1981), 284; Gavin, "Source Material," 362, 367; "How Nation's Editors React to Nixon Speech," *Chicago Tribune*, Sept 25, 1952, 4; Robert Mason, *Richard Nixon and the Quest for a New Majority* (Chapel Hill: Univ of North Carolina Press, 2005), 71; Don Oberdorfer, "The 'Real Nixon' an Enigma," *Washington Post*, Oct 13, 1968, A1; Garry Wills, "The Enigma of President Nixon," *Saturday Evening Post*, Jan 25, 1969, 25–27, 54–58; William V. Shannon, "The Happy Traveler," *New York Times*, Aug 8, 1975, 21; Hunter S. Thompson, *The Great Shark Hunt: Strange Tales from a Strange Time* (New York: Simon & Schuster, 2011), 185.

43 Jeremi Suri, *Henry Kissinger and the American Century* (Cambridge, MA: Belknap Press, 2007), 206. For similar accounts by Nixon's deputies about his "light" and "dark" sides, see Alexander Butterfield, interview by Timothy Naftali, OHP-RNL, Jun 12, 2008, 2; Dwight Chapin, interview by Timothy Naftali, OHP-RNL, Apr 2, 2007, 78; Henry Kissinger, *White House Years* (New York: Little, Brown, 1979), 1175; Jeb Magruder, *An American Life* (New York: Atheneum), 77; Nixon, *RN*, 843; G. Gordon Libby and Charles Colson quoted in Gerald S. and Deborah H. Strober, *Nixon: An Oral History of His Presidency* (New York: HarperCollins, 1994), 301.

For ambiguity in "admiration and disdain," see especially Ambrose, *Ruin and Recovery*; Farrell, *Richard Nixon*; Betty Glad and Michael W. Link, "President Nixon's Inner Circle of Advisers," *Presidential Studies Quarterly* 26, no. 1, (Winter 1996): 22. For Nixon as part of the silent majority, see Wicker, *One of Us*; Rick Perlstein, *Nixonland: The Rise of a President and the Fracturing of America* (New York: Scribner, 2009). For sympathy/admiration, see Ralph De Toledano, *Nixon* (New York: Henry Holt, 1956); Mazo and Hess, *Nixon*; Conrad Black, *Richard Milhous Nixon: The Invisible Quest* (London: Quercus, 2007); Aitken, *A Life*. For sharp accounts of a failed presidency, see James David Barber, *The Presidential Character: Predicting Performance in the White House* (Englewood Cliffs, NJ: Prentice Hall, 1972); John Ehrlichman, *Witness to Power: The Nixon Years* (New York: Simon & Schuster, 1982); Jeffrey Kimball, *Nixon's Vietnam War* (Lawrence: Univ Press of Kansas, 1998). For examples of the sentimental/brutal in the siege of Leningrad, see Midgley, "Brutality and Sentimentality," 385–89, Reid, *Leningrad*, 7, 22; Alexis Peri, *The War Within: Diaries from the Siege of Leningrad* (Cambridge, MA: Harvard Univ Press, 2017), 106–7; Popova, "Siege"; Andrews, "The Siege"; Wicker, *One of Us*, 9.

44 Wills, *Agonistes*, 17–18; Monica Crowley, *Nixon off the Record* (New York: Random House, 1996), 5; Greenberg, "Nixon as Statesman," 54.

45 Nixon, *Six Crises*, xvi, 426.

46 Wicker, *One of Us*, 9, or Wills, *Agonistes*, 17–18; Chapin, OHP-RNL, 78; Jeb Magruder, *An American Life* (New York: Atheneum), 77; Raymond Price, Jr., quoted in Frank, "Dark Sides"; Butterfield, OHP-RNL, 2; Strober and Strober, *Oral History*, 301; Clawson, "5 Years Later," D1.

47 Henry Kissinger, *Years of Renewal* (New York: Simon & Schuster, 1999), 54.

48 Paul Valentine, "Protests Are Peaceful as Republicans Meet," *Washington Post*, Aug 22, 1972, A8; Kyra Gurney, "Drugs, Protests and Mass Arrests: What Happened Last Time Miami Hosted a Convention," *Miami Herald*, Mar 11, 2019; Andrew Glass, "Demonstrators Disrupt Republican Convention," Aug 22, 1972," *Politico*, Aug 21, 2016.

49 David Broder, "Nixon Sounds Peace Theme in Unity Bid," *Washington Post*, Aug 24, 1972, A1; Robert Semple, "Miami Beach Tent City a Carnival of Protest," *New York Time*, Aug 21, 1972, 1; Valentine, "Protests Are Peaceful," A8; Glass, "Demonstrators"; Gurney, "Drugs, Protests and Mass Arrests."

50 Haynes Johnson, "Nixon at Brightest Point of 20-Year Spotlight," *Washington Post*, Aug 24, 1972, A1; Nixon, "1968 Acceptance Speech."

INTERLUDE ONE

1   Phyllis Lee Levin, "The Private Pat Nixon," *Vogue*, Oct 15, 1972, 85; Roger
    Morris, *Richard Milhous Nixon: The Rise of an American Politician* (New York:
    Henry Holt & Co., 1989), 324; "Those Other Campaigners: Pat and Eleanor,"
    Time, Oct 9, 1972; "The Silent Partner," *Time*, Feb 29, 1960.

2   Judith Viorst, "Pat Nixon Is the Ultimate Good Sport," *New York Times
    Magazine*, Sep 13, 1970.

3   Levin, "Private Pat," 85; Gloria Steinem, "In Your Heart You Know He's
    Nixon," *New York Magazine*, Oct 28, 1968; Jessamyn West, "The Real Pat Nixon,"
    Good Housekeeping, Feb 1971; "Other Campaigners," *Time*; Lenore Hershey
    et al., "The 'New' Pat Nixon: Mrs. Nixon in the New Spring Classics," *Ladies'
    Home Journal*, Feb 1972, 124; "Pat Nixon: Steel and Sorrow," *Time*, Aug 19, 1974;
    Jean Liebman Block, "The Pat Nixon I Know," *Good Housekeeping*, July 1973.

4   Gil Troy, "Pat Nixon," in *A Companion to Richard M. Nixon*, ed. Melvin Small
    (Hoboken, NJ: Wiley and Blackwell, 2011), 49; Lisa Burns, *First Ladies and the
    Fourth Estate* (Evanston, IL: Northwestern University Press, 2008), 112; Mary
    Brennan, *Pat Nixon: Embattled First Lady* (Lawrence: Univ Press of Kansas,
    2011), 66; "Pat into the Fray," *Time*, Dec 6, 1971, 15; *Newsweek* cited in Anthony
    Summers, *The Arrogance of Power: The Secret World of Richard Nixon* (New York:
    Penguin Books, 2011), 286.

5   Ann Beattie, *Mrs. Nixon: A Novelist Imagines a Life* (New York: Scribner, 2011), 77.

6   "The Relentless Ordeal of Political Wives," *Time*, Oct 7, 1974; Julie Nixon
    Eisenhower, *Pat Nixon: The Untold Story* (New York: Simon & Schuster, 1986);
    Lester David, *The Lonely Lady of San Clemente: The Story of Pat Nixon* (Los
    Angeles: Crowell, 1998); Brennan, *Embattled First Lady*; Troy, "Pat Nixon," 65.

7   Kandy Stroud, "Pat Nixon Today," *Ladies Home Journal*, Mar 1975, 132; Eisen-
    hower, *Untold Story*, 21, 58, 85, 88, 143; Viorst "Good Sport"; Brennan, *Embattled
    First Lady*, 35–36; Hershey et al., "'New' Pat," 125; Winzola McLendon, "Pat Nixon
    Today," *Good Housekeeping*, Feb 1980, 129; Flora Rheta Schreiber, "Pat Nixon
    Reveals for the First Time: 'I Didn't Want Dick to Run Again," *Good Housekeeping*,
    Jul 1968, 129.

8   Donald T. Critchlow, *Phyllis Schlafly and Grassroots Conservatism* (Princeton, NJ:
    Princeton Univ Press, 2005), 17.

9   Eisenhower, *Untold Story*, 143; William Safire, "Political Spouse," *New York
    Times*, Jun 24, 1993; Brennan, *Embattled First Lady*, 69.

10   Troy, "Pat Nixon," 54; Richard Nixon, *In the Arena: A Memoir of Victory, Defeat and Renewal* (New York: Pocket Books, 1991, 28. For examples of their daughters' affection, see Julie Nixon Eisenhower to Richard Nixon, letter, Jun 13, 1972, WHSF, RNL, box 3, file 6; Julie Nixon Eisenhower to Richard Nixon, letter, Sep 7, 1972, WHSF, RNL, box 3, file 9; Julie Nixon Eisenhower to Richard Nixon, letter, Mar 1973, WHSF, RNL, box 3, file 14; Julie Nixon Eisenhower to Nixon, letter, n.d., WHSF, RNL, box 3, file 17; Julie and David Eisenhower to Pat and Richard Nixon, letter, n.d., WHSF, RNL box 4, file 12; Schreiber, "Pat Nixon Reveals," 188.

11   Richard Nixon, *RN* (New York: Simon & Schuster, 1990), 23; "Steel and Sorrow"; "Silent Partner"; Eisenhower, *Untold Story*, 17–18, 21.

12   Eisenhower, *Untold Story*, 27; Brennan, *Embattled First Lady*, 1–7, emphasis in original; Levin, "Private Pat," 129; Morris, *Richard Milhous Nixon*, 209; "Steel and Sorrow."

13   McLendon, "Pat Nixon Today"; Eisenhower, *Untold Story*, 35; "Silent Partner"; Levin, "Private Pat."

14   John Farrell, *Richard Nixon: The Life* (New York: Doubleday, 2017), 72; "Silent Partner"; Jean Lippiatt, "Pat Nixon Was My Typing Teacher," *Saturday Evening Post*, Jun 1, 1971, 29, 127.

15   Lippiatt, "Typing Teacher," emphasis in the original.

16   Eisenhower, *Untold Story*, 88; Brennan, *Embattled First Lady*, 20–21; Troy, "Pat Nixon," 54.

17   Garry Wills, "The Enigma of President Nixon," *Saturday Evening Post*, Jan 25, 1969, 54–58; Farrell, *Richard Nixon*, 59, 71; Morris, *Richard Milhous Nixon*, 193.

18   Nixon-Gannon, Sep 7, 1983, part 3; Nixon-Gannon, May 27, 1983, part 1.

19   Eisenhower, *Untold Story*, 92; Will Swift, *Pat and Dick* (New York: Threshold Editions, 2014), 255–56.

20   Diana Klebanow, "Married to Nixon," *USA Today Magazine*, Jan 1, 2015; Hershey et al., "'New' Pat"; Brennan, *Embattled First Lady*, 98; Steinem, "In Your Heart."

21   Schreiber, "Pat Nixon Reveals," 188; Viorst, "Good Sport"; Stroud, "Today"; Levin, "Private Pat"; Brennan, *Embattled First Lady*, 115–17; Helen Thomas, "Pat Nixon, Her First Year as First Lady," *US News and World Report*, Dec 22, 1969, 13; "A Visit with the First Lady-Pat Nixon Interview," ABC News, Sep 12, 1971, https://www.youtube.com/watch?v=ABfQjJGNQ78.

22 Sarah Knott, *Sensibility and the American Revolution* (Chapel Hill: Univ of North Carolina Press, 2009), 1–6; Levin, "Private Pat"; Hershey et al., "'New' Pat"; "Traveling with Pat Nixon—A Different Type of Tour," *US News and World Report*, Jun 20, 1969, 9; Susanna McBee, "Pat Nixon and the First-Lady Watchers," *McCalls*, Sep 1970; Thomas, "First Year." For similar analysis of the sentimental tradition and the sensible woman, see G. J. Barker-Benfield, *The Culture of Sensibility: Sex and Society in Eighteenth-Century Britain* (Chicago: Univ. of Chicago Press, 1996), 104–53; Joanne Dobson, "Reclaiming Sentimental Literature," *American Literature* 69, no. 2 (Jun 1997): 263–88; Michael Bell, *Sentimentalism, Ethics and the Culture of Feeling* (New York: Springer, 2000), 1–2, 39–44.

23 Troy, "Pat Nixon," 55, emphasis in original; Eisenhower, *Untold Story*, 119, 126; Melvin Small, *The Presidency of Richard Nixon* (Lawrence: Univ Press of Kansas, 1999), 16.

24 Betty Glad and Michael W. Link, "President Nixon's Inner Circle of Advisers," *Presidential Studies Quarterly* 26, no. 1 (Winter 1996): 16; "Steel and Sorrow"; Farrell, *Richard Nixon*, 353; Klebanow, "Married to Nixon"; Hershey et al., "'New' Pat"; H. R. Haldeman to Charles Colson, memorandum, "The President's Posture in the 1972 Campaign," Nov 4, 1971, WHSF-SMOF, box 7, file 18.

25 West "Real Pat", 68; John Ehrlichman, *Witness to Power: The Nixon Years* (New York: Simon & Schuster, 1982), 55; Margaret MacMillan, *Nixon and Mao* (New York: Random House, 2007), 277.

26 Hershey et al. "'New' Pat"; Brennan *Embattled First Lady*, 60–61, 130; Brennan; "BookTV: Mary Brennan, 'Pat Nixon: Embattled First Lady,'" BookTV, Nov 12, 2012, https://www.youtube.com/watch?v=-vLyqHSWzsE.

27 Klebanow, "Married to Nixon"; "African Queen for a Week," *Time*, Jan 17, 1972, 12–14.

28 Brennan, *Embattled First Lady*, 31, 56, 66, 75–76; Thomas, "First Year"; Swift, *Pat and Dick*, 244; Schreiber, "Pat Nixon Reveals."

29 Schreiber, "Pat Nixon Reveals"; "Silent Partner."

30 Hershey et al., "'New' Pat"; Block, "Pat Nixon I Know"; John C. Whitaker, "Nixon's Domestic Policy: Both Liberal and Bold in Retrospect," *Presidential Studies Quarterly* 26, no. 1 (Winter 1996): 148–49; Farrell, *Richard Nixon*, 161.

31 Joe McGinnis, *The Selling of the President* (New York: Penguin, 1968), 111; Ehrlichman, *Witness to Power*, 56, 65–66; Morris, *Richard Milhous Nixon*, 594;

Gwendolyn B. King, interview by Fredrick J. Graboske and Paul A. Schmidt, OHP-RNL, May 23, 1988, 15; Farrell, *Richard Nixon*, 400; Glad and Link, "Inner Circle," 16; Swift, *Pat and Dick*, 253.

32   Swift, *Pat and Dick*, 251, 254; Monica Crowley, *Nixon in Winter* (New York: Random House, 1998), 36.

33   Steinem, "In Your Heart."

34   Steinem, "In Your Heart."

35   Steinem, "In Your Heart."

36   Jessie Van Sant, *Eighteenth-Century Sensibility and the Novel: The Senses in Social Context* (Cambridge: Cambridge Univ Press, 1993); Claudia Johnson, "A 'Sweet Face as White as Death': Jane Austen and the Politics of Female Sensibility," *NOVEL: A Forum on Fiction* 22, no. 2 (Winter 1989): 161.

37   Janet Todd, *Sensibility: An Introduction* (London: Methuen, 1986), 20, 110; Elaine Tyler May quoted in Troy, "Pat Nixon," 56. For the feminist turn in the study of sentimentalism, see Dobson, "Reclaiming Sentimental Literature," 263–88; Sean Epstein-Corbin, "Pragmatism, Feminism and the Sentimental Subject," *Transactions of the Charles S. Peirce Society* 50, no. 2 (Spring 2014): 220–45; Carol Kay, "Canon, Ideology and Gender," *New Political Science* 15 (Summer 1986), esp. 70–72; Van Sant, *Eighteenth-Century Sensibility*.

38   "The Nixon Convention," *Chicago Defender*, Aug 24, 1972, 19.

39   Steinem, "In Your Heart."

3. THE WORKING LIFE OF RICHARD NIXON

1   Theodore H. White, *The Making of the President 1968* (New York: Harper Perennial, 2010), 248f; Henry Kissinger, *White House Years* (New York: Little, Brown, 1979), 11–12; Jussi M. Hanhimäki, "An Elusive Grand Design," in *Nixon in the World: American Foreign Relations, 1969–1977*, ed. Fredrik Logevall and Andrew Preston (Oxford: Oxford Univ Press, 2008), 27; Alexander Haig, interview by Timothy Naftali, OHP-RNL, Nov 30, 2007, 7; Jeremi Suri, "Henry Kissinger and American Grand Strategy," in Logevall and Prescott, *Nixon in the World*, 69; Richard Nixon to Henry Kissinger and H. R. Haldeman, memorandum, Jan 15, 1969, WHSF, box 1, folder 43; Kissinger, *White House Years*, 11–12; Walter Isaacson, *Kissinger: A Biography* (New York: Simon & Schuster, 2005), 136; Dwight Chapin, interview by Timothy Naftali, OHP-RNL, Apr 2, 2007, 17.

2   Garry Wills, *Nixon Agonistes: The Crisis of the Self-Made Man* (New York: First Mariner Books, 2002), 24–25; 54–58; Edwin Black, "The Invention of Nixon," in *Beyond the Rhetorical Presidency*, ed. Martin J. Medhurst (College Station: Texas A&M Press, 1996), 105.

3   Nixon-Gannon, Jun 10, 1983, part 4; Stewart Alsop, "Nixon and the Square Majority: Is the Fox a Lion?," *Atlantic Monthly*, Feb 1972, 41. For accounts of Nixon's inability to relax, see John Farrell, *Richard Nixon: The Life* (New York: Doubleday, 2017), 18–19, 59, 358; H. R. Haldeman, interview by Raymond H. Geselbracht and Fred J. Grabske, OHP-RNL, Aug 13, 1987, 93; Frank Leonard, memorandum, "There's Something about the Guy I Just Don't Like," Mar 29, 1971, 7, WHSF-CMC, box 1, folder 2; Roger Morris, *Richard Milhous Nixon: The Rise of an American Politician* (New York: Henry Holt & Co., 1989), 93; Garry Wills, "The Enigma of President Nixon," *Saturday Evening Post*, Jan 25, 1969, 54–58; Jules Witcover, "Nixon for President?," *Saturday Evening Post*, Feb 25, 1967, 93, 95. On Nixon's shyness, see Stewart Alsop, "Nixon on Nixon," *Saturday Evening Post*, Jul 12, 1958, 58–59; Lou Cannon, interview by Timothy Naftali, OHP-RNL, Feb 21, 2007, 21; John Ehrlichman, *Witness to Power: The Nixon Years* (New York: Simon & Schuster, 1982), 12, 65; Eleanor Harris, "The Richard Nixons: National Spotlight," *Washington Post*, Mar 11, 1956, AW18; David Halberstam, "Press and Prejudice," *Esquire*, Apr 1974, 114; H. R. Haldeman, *Haldeman Diaries: Inside the Nixon White House* (New York: G. P. Putnam's Sons, 1994), Thursday, January 30, 1969, 24; Murray Kempton, *Rebellions, Perversities and Main Events* (New York: Times Books, 1994), 418; Evan Thomas, *Being Nixon* (New York: Random House, 2016), 225; Jeb Magruder, interview by Timothy Naftali, OHP-RNL, Mar 23, 2007, 12; Richard Nixon, *In the Arena: A Memoir of Victory, Defeat and Renewal* (New York: Pocket Books, 1991), 3–4; Nixon-Gannon, Feb 9, 1983, part 1; Thomas, *Being Nixon*, 6, 263; Evan Thomas, "The Complexity of Being Richard Nixon," *Atlantic*, Jun 15, 2015; Tom Wicker, "Richard M. Nixon, 1969–1974," *Presidential Studies Quarterly* 26, no. 1 (Winter 1996): 253–54; David Wise, "The Nixon Era Begins," *Chicago Tribune*, Jan 19, 1969, 24.

4   Morris, *Richard Milhous Nixon*, 740; Richard Nixon, *Six Crises* (New York: Doubleday, 1962), 295; Robert Coughlan, "Success Story of A Vice President," *Life*, n.d., JVP, box 58, file 21: Repercussions in Later Years; Nixon, *Arena*, 351–53.

5   K. A. Cuordileone, "Politics in the Age of Anxiety," *Journal of American History* 87, no. 2 (Sept 2000): 515–45; Brian Robertson, "The Forgotten Man: Richard Nixon, Masculinity, and the Path to Power in Southern California," *California History* 94, no. 2 (Summer 2017): 22–40.

6   Cuordileone, "Age of Anxiety," 522–23.

7   Wills, *Agonistes*, 159–60; John Kennedy, *Profiles in Courage* (New York: Harper-Collins Perennial Modern Classics, 2006), 1, 51; Monica Crowley, *Nixon off the Record* (New York: Random House, 1996), 13–14; Kevin Mattson, *Just Plain Dick* (New York: Bloomsbury, USA, 2012), 8. For examples of crisis as key, see Haldeman, *Diaries*, Sunday, January 3, 1971, 230; Richard Nixon, *RN* (New York: Simon & Schuster, 1990), 35, 42, 73; Nixon, *Six Crises*; Richard Nixon, *Leaders* (New York: Warner Brothers, 1982); Tom Wicker, *One of Us* (New York: Random House, 1991), 14.

8   Nixon, *Arena*, 351–52; Wills, *Agonistes*, 156, emphasis in original.

9   Nixon et al., memorandum of conversation, Beijing, Feb 24, 1972, *Foreign Relations of the United States, 1969–1976*, vol. 17, *China, 1969–1972*, ed. Steven E. Phillips (Washington, DC: Government Printing Office, 2006), https://history .state.gov/historicaldocuments/frus1969-76v17/d199; Arthur Schlesinger, Jr., *The Vital Center* (New York: Routledge, 2017).

10 Nixon-Gannon, Feb 9, 1983, part 2; Farrell, *Richard Nixon*, 54; Jonathan Aitken, *Nixon: A Life* (New York: Regnery, 1994), 21; Edward Nixon, interview by Timothy Naftali, OHP-RNL, Jan 9, 2007, 2; Nixon, *RN*, 4–5; Morris, *Richard Milhous Nixon*, 102.

11 Morris, *Richard Milhous Nixon*, 122, 60–63, 92, 133; Nixon, *RN*, 19; Gerald Shaw, interview by Jeff Jones, OHP-CSUF, Jun 3 1970, "Life in Early Yorba Linda and Fullerton, California," 42; Stephen Ambrose, vol. 3, *Nixon: Ruin and Recovery, 1973–1990* (New York: Simon & Schuster, 1991), 467; Stewart Alsop, "The Mystery of Richard Nixon," *Saturday Evening Post*, Jul 12, 1958, 53–72.

12 James David Barber, *The Presidential Character: Predicting Performance in the White House*, 4th ed. (New York: Routledge, 2017), Kindle; Esther R. Cramer, "La Habra and the President," memorandum, Jan 29, 1971, WHSF, box 3, folder 22; "Application for Registration of Historical Landmark," n.d., WHSF, box 3, folder 21; Conrad Black, *Richard M. Nixon: A Life in Full* (New York: Public-Affairs, 2008), 16; H. R. Haldeman, with DiMona, *Ends of Power* (New York: Dell Publishing, 1978), 311. See also, Haldeman, OHP-RNL, Aug 13, 1987, 61;

Florence quoted in Farrell, *Richard Nixon*, 66, William Safire, *Before the Fall* (New York: Routledge, 2017), 21.

13   Nixon, *Arena*, 211–12, 221; Mattson, *Just Plain Dick*, 69; Alsop, "Nixon on Nixon."

14   H. R. Haldeman, interview by Raymond H. Geselbracht, OHP-RNL, Apr 11, 1988, 31; Richard Nixon, "First Inaugural Address of Richard Milhous Nixon," Jan 20, 1969, Avalon Project, https://avalon.law.yale.edu/20th_century/nixon1 .asp.

15   Thomas, "Complexity"; Thomas, *Being Nixon*; 225; Aitken, *Life*, 2; Jeb Magruder, *An American Life* (New York: Atheneum, 1974), 61. For trouble over the Oval Office tape recorder, see Stephen Bull, interview by Timothy Naftali, OHP-RNL, Jun 25, 2007, 9–11; Alexander Butterfield, interview by Timothy Naftali, OHP-RNL, Jun 12, 2008, 10, 41–42; Richard Nixon and Alexander Butterfield, conversation, Feb 16, 1971, 10:28 a.m., in Douglas Brinkley and Luke Nichter, eds., *The Nixon Tapes, 1971–1972* (Boston: Houghton Mifflin, 2014), 3; Ken Hughes, *Chasing Shadows* (Charlottesville: Univ of Virginia Press, 2014), 79.

16   Steve Martin, *Born Standing Up* (New York: Simon & Schuster, 2007), 119; Joe McGinnis, *The Selling of the Presidency* (New York: Penguin, 1968), viii, 32; Thompson, *Great Shark Hunt*, 185.

17   Thomas, *Being Nixon*, 63; David Greenberg, *Nixon's Shadow* (New York: W. W. Norton, 2003), 45.

18   Fiora Rheta Schreiber, "Pat Nixon Reveals for the First Time. 'I Didn't Want Dick to Run Again,'" *Good Housekeeping*, Jul 1968, 188; Alsop, "Square Majority," 46; Safire, *Before the Fall*, 113; Alsop, "Nixon on Nixon," 26–27; Haldeman, *Diaries*, Thursday, February 23, 1970, 130. On Nixon's time spent at the EOB, see Dwight Chapin, interview by Timothy Naftali, OHP-RNL, Apr 2, 2007, 23; Betty Glad and Michael W. Link, "President Nixon's Inner Circle of Advisers," *Presidential Studies Quarterly* 26, no. 1, (Winter 1996): 15; Raymond Price, Jr., interview by Timothy Naftali, OHP-RNL, Apr 4, 2007, 16. For Nixon's shirking confrontation, see Charles Colson, interview by Fredrick J. Graboske and Paul A. Schmidt, OHP-RNL, Sep 21, 1988, 2; Haig, OHP-RNL, 11; Walter Hickel, interview by Timothy Naftali, OHP-RNL, Apr 25, 2008, 23.

19   Aitken, *A Life*, 372–73; Thomas, *Being Nixon*, 198; "How Nixon's White House Works," *Time*, June 8, 1970, 19–27. On Nixon's efficiency and reticence, see

"Counterattack and Counterpoint," *Time*, Aug 13, 1973; "Nation: Ehrlichman Reviews Haldeman," *Time*, Mar 6, 1978; Glad and Link, "Inner Circle," 13–40; Haldeman, with DiMona, *Ends of Power*, 58; Henry Kissinger, "Watergate: Nixon's Germans," *Time*, Mar 8, 1982; "Learning to Live with Scandal," *Time*, Jul 16, 1973, n.p.; Gerald S. Strober and Deborah H. Strober, *Nixon: An Oral History of His Presidency* (New York: HarperCollins, 1994), 339; Haldeman, OHP-RNL, Apr 11, 1988, 52–53; Wicker, *One of Us*, 400.

20   Haldeman, with DiMona, *Ends of Power*, 46–47, 54; Butterfield, OHP-RNL, 18; John Huntsman, Sr., interview by Timothy Naftali, OHP-RNL, Mar 10, 2008, 4, 9. For confusion over Haldeman's name, see Henry Kissinger quoted in Ken Hughes, *Fatal Politics: The Nixon Tapes, The Vietnam War, and the Casualties of Reflection* (Charlottesville: Univ of Virginia Press, 2015), n.p.; "Counterattack and Counterpoint," *Time*, Aug 13, 1973, n.p. For the "cruel" and "humiliating" Haldeman, see Butterfield, OHP-RNL, 14; Christopher Demuth, interview by Timothy Naftali, OHP-RNL, Jan 14, 2008, 29, 32; H. R. Haldeman, interview by Raymond H. Geselbracht, OHP-RNL, Apr 12, 1988, 61; Frederic Malek, interview by Timothy Naftali, OHP-RNL, Sep 17, 2007, 7; Safire, *Before the Fall*, 2.

21   Haldeman, OHP-RNL, Apr 11, 1988, 54, 95; Price, OHP-RNL, 16; Stanley I. Kutler, *The Wars of Watergate* (New York: W. W. Norton, 1992), 86–87; Glad and Link, "Inner Circle," 21; Ehrlichman, *Witness*, 78; Safire, *Before the Fall*, 2.

22   Wicker, *One of Us*, 392, 400; Haldeman, OHP-RNL, Apr 11, 1988, 36. On Ehrlichman as a "teddy bear" and Haldeman as antagonistic to White House staff, see particularly Huntsman, OHP-RNL, 26; Bobbie Kilberg, interview by Timothy Naftali, OHP-RNL, Nov 19, 2007, 6; Gwendolyn B. King, interview by Frederick Graboske and Paul Schmidt, OHP-RNL, May 23, 1988, 12.

23   James P. Pfiffner, *The Modern Presidency* (Boston: Cengage Learning, 2010) 68; Larry Berman, *The Office of Management and Budget* (Princeton, NJ: Princeton Univ Press, 1979), 105–25; Karen M. Hult, "The Administrative Presidency," in *A Companion to Richard M. Nixon*, ed. Melvin Small (Hoboken, NJ: Wiley and Blackwell, 2011), 185–201; Safire, *Before the Fall*, 261. For further on Nixon's "corporate" style, see Farrell, *Richard Nixon*, 352; Joan Hoff, *Nixon Reconsidered* (New York: Basic Books, 1995), 50–60;

24   Hult, "Administrative Presidency," 186–89; Safire, *Before the Fall*, 261.

25   Henry Kissinger, *Diplomacy* (New York: Simon & Schuster, 1994), 142; Haldeman, *Diaries*, Wednesday, September 8, 1971, 351; Nixon and Haldeman,

conversation, in Brinkley and Nichter, *Oval Office Tapes, 1971–1972*, 526; *Chicago Sun-Times* quoted in Isaacson, *Kissinger*, 437.

26 "Kissinger: An Interview with Oriana Fallaci," *New Republic*, Dec 1972, 17–22; Mario Del Pero, *The Eccentric Realist: Henry Kissinger and the Shaping of American Foreign Policy* (Ithaca, NY: Cornell Univ Press, 2010), 44, emphasis in the original; Haldeman, OHP-RNL, Apr 11, 1988, 113, 117; Kissinger, *White House Years*, 140.

27 For discussion of the Three Germans and the "Berlin Wall," see Chapin, OHP-RNL, 10, 41; Pat Buchanan to H. R. Haldeman, memorandum, n.d., WHSF-SMOF, box 1, folder 20, 1; Haig, OHP-RNL, 7; "How Nixon's White House Works" n.p.; "The Need to Protect a President," *New York Times*, Feb 17, 1978, A17; Harrison Salisbury, *Without Fear or Favor: The New York Times and Its Times* (New York: Times Books, 1980), 232; Wicker, *One of Us*, 400, emphasis in the original

28 For Nixon's regimented routine, see Butterfield, OHP-RNL, 4, 15, 35; Haldeman, *Diaries*, Sunday, January 26, 1969, 22; Haldeman, with DiMona, *Ends of Power*, 73; Haldeman, OHP-RNL, Aug 13, 1987; Haig, OHP-RNL, 23, 29; Richard Nixon to John Ehrlichman, memorandum, Jan 4, 1969, WHSF, box 1, folder 34; Schreiber, "Pat Nixon Reveals," 188; Price, OHP-RNL, 16.

29 Aitken, *A Life*, 373–83; Hoff, *Reconsidered*, 55–56.

30 Christopher F. Karpowitz, "What Can a President Learn from the News Media? The Instructive Case of Richard Nixon," *British Journal of Political Science* 39, no. 4 (Oct 2009): 755–80; Haldeman, OHP-RNL, Apr 11, 1988, 81–82.

31 Karpowitz, "News Media," 755–80; Butterfield, OHP-RNL, 16; Don Oberdorfer, "Nixon's Digest," *Washington Post*, May 9, 1971, A1, A3.

32 Milton Viorst, "Nixon of the O.P.A.," *New York Times*, Oct 3, 1971, SM70; Hoff, *Reconsidered*, 52; Nixon, *RN*, 35, 42, 73; Ward Just, "GOP Nominee Richard Nixon," *New York Times*, Aug 9, 1968, A14.

33 Stein quoted in John C. Whitaker, "Nixon's Domestic Policy: Both Liberal and Bold in Retrospect," *Presidential Studies Quarterly* 26, no. 1 (Winter 1996): 134. For the puzzle over Nixon's progressive turn once president, see Atiken, *A Life*, 353; Richard P. Nathan, "A Retrospective on Richard M. Nixon's Domestic Policies," *Presidential Quarterly* 26, no. 1 (Winter 1996): 155–56; Hoff, *Reconsidered*, 136; Alex Wadden, "A Liberal in Wolf's Clothing," *Journal of American Studies* 32, no. 2 (Aug 1998): 203–18. For revisionist analysis of this progressive

turn, see further Herbert S. Parmet, *Richard Nixon and His America* (Boston: Little, Brown and Co., 1989), and Melvin Small, *The Presidency of Richard Nixon* (Lawrence: Univ Press of Kansas, 1999). For the orthodox view of Nixon as political opportunist, see Elizabeth Drew, *Richard M. Nixon* (New York: Simon & Schuster, 2007); Rowland Evans, Jr., and Robert D. Novak, *Nixon in the White House: The Frustration of Power* (New York: Random House, 1971); Jonathan Schell, *The Time of Illusion* (New York: Alfred A. Knopf, 1975).

34 Moynihan quoted in Aitken, *A Life*, 375; Dominic Sandbrook, "Salesmanship and Substance: The Influence of Domestic Policy and Watergate," in Logevall and Preston, *Nixon in the World*, 85–103; Whitaker, "Domestic Policy," 138.

35 Farrell, *Richard Nixon*, 378, 382, 372; Whitaker, "Nixon's Domestic Policy," 131–33.

36 Hugh Davis Graham, "Richard Nixon and Civil Rights: Explaining an Enigma," *Presidential Studies Quarterly* 26, no. 1 (Winter 1996): 99; Whitaker, "Nixon's Domestic Policy," 134; White, *1968*, 147; Sandbrook, "Salesmanship and Substance," 89; Pat Buchanan to H. R. Haldeman, "Neither Fish nor Fowl," memorandum, Jan 14, 1971, WHSF-SMOF, box 1, folder 4: Pat Buchanan: April 1971; Whitaker, "Nixon's Domestic Policy," 134.

37 Parmet, *Richard Nixon and His America*; Hoff, *Reconsidered*, 52–69; Safire, *Before the Fall*, 261; Hult, "Administrative Presidency," 185–201; Nixon, *RN*, 267, 426.

38 James T. Patterson, *Freedom Is Not Enough* (New York: Basic Books, 2010), 113; Jill Quadagno, *The Color of Welfare* (New York: Oxford Univ Press, 1994), 123–24; Nixon, *RN*, 352–53.

39 Daniel Geary, "The Moynihan Report: An Annotated Edition," *Atlantic*, Sep 14, 2015; Patterson, *Freedom Is Not Enough*, 124; Susan D. Greenbaum, *Blaming the Poor* (New Brunswick, NJ: Rutgers Univ Press, 2015), 3–7.

40 Whitaker, "Nixon's Domestic Policy," 133, 158–60; Scott Spitzer, "Nixon's New Deal: Welfare Reform For The Silent Majority," *Presidential Studies Quarterly* 42, no. 3 (Sep 2012): 455–81; Alex Wadden, "A Liberal in Wolf's Clothing," *Journal of American Studies* 32, no. 2 (Aug 1998): 203–18; Edmund Burke, "The Nixon Poor Law Reform," *Family Law Quarterly* 4, no. 4 (Dec 1970), 355–62; Hirschel Kasper and L. J. Hausman, "Nixon's Family Assistance Plan," *New Republic*, Mar 1970, 8–10; Leonard J. Hausman, "The Politics of Guaranteed Income: The Nixon Administration and the Family Assistance Plan," *Journal of Human Resources* 8, no. 4 (Fall 1973): 411–21; "Family-Assistance Plan: A Chronology," *Social Services Review* 46, no. 4 (Dec 1972): 603–8; "Welfare Reform Plan Bigger Than Nixon's

Is Urged by Johnson-Appointed Commission," *Wall Street Journal*, Nov 13, 1969, 7; Jonathan Spivak, "Lack of a Consensus among Nixon Aides Threatens Passage of Welfare Reform," *Wall Street Journal*, Jun 9, 1970, 6; Romain Huret, "Richard Nixon, The Great Society, and Social Reforms: A Lost Opportunity?," in Small, *Companion*, 205; Jack Rosenthal, "Income Aid Plan Based on Need Proposed by Presidential Panel," *New York Times*, Nov 13, 1969, 1.

41 Greenbaum, *Blaming*, 9–13; Jill Quadagno, "Race, Class, and Gender in the US Welfare State," *American Sociological Review* 55, no. 1 (Feb 1990): 11–30.

42 Spitzer, "Nixon's New Deal," 472–73; George Shultz to John Ehrlichman, memorandum, 1970, Moynihan Papers, series I, box 255, folder 10: Blue Collar; Hausman, "Guaranteed Income," 411. For a gendered and racial analysis, see Spitzer, "Nixon's New Deal," 455–81; Quadagno, *Color of Welfare*; Quadagno, "Race, Class," 11–30.

43 Farrell, *Richard Nixon*, 29; Irwin Gellman, *The President and the Apprentice* (New Haven, CT: Yale Univ Press, 2015), 142, 144, 150, 167, 568.

44 Quadagno, *Color of Welfare*, 122; Farrell, *Richard Nixon*, 251–52.

45 Graham, "Civil Rights," 94; Hoff, *Reconsidered*, 78; Kutler, *Wars of Watergate*, 64; Patterson, *Freedom Is Not Enough*, 109–28.

46 Graham, "Civil Rights," 94; Kotlowski, "Civil Rights Policy," 221–22; Dean J. Kotlowski, *Nixon's Civil Rights* (Cambridge, MA: Harvard Univ Press, 2002), 218–19, 226; Daniel Frick, *Reinventing Richard Nixon: A Cultural History of an American Obsession* (Lawrence: Univ Press of Kansas, 2008), 151–60; John David Skrentny, *The Ironies of Affirmative Action* (Chicago: Univ of Chicago Press, 1996), 189.

47 Patterson, *Freedom Is Not Enough*, 117–20; Quadagno, *Color of Welfare*, 124; Shultz to Ehrlichman, memorandum, Moynihan Papers, "Blue Collar, 1970"; Spitzer, "Nixon's New Deal," 465, 472–73; Hausman, "Guaranteed Income," 411.

48 Graham, "Civil Rights," 93–106; Hoff, *Reconsidered*, 109–10; J. Larry Hood, "The Nixon Administration and the Revised Philadelphia Plan for Affirmative Action," *Presidential Studies Quarterly* 23, no. 1. (Winter 1993): 145–67; David Rosenbaum, "Shultz Appeals to House on Jobs," *New York Times*, Dec 21, 1969, 39; Donald Janson, "Minority Hiring Upheld by Court," *New York Times*, Apr 24, 1971, 36; Kotlowksi, "Civil Rights Policy," 225; Huret, "Social Reforms," 207; Hult, "Administrative Presidency," 207.

49 "Philadelphia Plan Draws Meany's Fire," *Chicago Tribune*, Jan 13, 1970, 6;
    Graham, "Civil Rights," 95.

50 "Richard M. Nixon Farewell Address," *History Place*, Aug 9, 1974; Nixon, *RN*,
    1088.

51 Farrell, *Richard Nixon*; Nixon, *Six Crises*, 296.

52 Nixon, *RN*, 267; Wicker, *One of Us*, 397.

53 Mary McGrory, "The Real Nixon Won Out over the Fictional One," *Los Angeles
    Times*, E5; Strober and Strober, *Oral History*, 338; Farrell, *Richard Nixon*, 352;
    Wicker, *One of Us*, 250.

54 Ehrlichman, *Witness*, 77; Reeves, *Richard Nixon*, 601.

4. MADNESS IN THE ACT

1   Roger Morris, *Richard Milhous Nixon: The Rise of an American Politician* (New
    York: Henry Holt & Co., 1989), 258, 261; South Pasadena–San Marino Citizens
    Committee for Voorhis, "Political Forum," JVP, box 58, folder 2: Campaign
    Material. Richard Pearson, "Ex-Rep. Jerry Voorhis Dies; Lost Race To Nixon,"
    Washington Post, Sep 12, 1984; John Farrell, *Richard Nixon: The Life* (New York:
    Doubleday, 2017), 2; Jerry Voorhis to editor of the *Observer Review*, Nov 21, 1968,
    JVP, box 58, folder 21: Repercussions in Later Years; "What Others Think about
    Him," Voorhis campaign advertisement, *Monrovia Journal*, Oct 31, 1946, JVP,
    box 89, folder 24: Campaign 1946 Ads; William Costello, "1946—The First
    Campaign," *New Republic*, Oct 12, 1959, JVP, box 58, folder 13; Jonathan Aitken,
    Nixon: A Life (New York: Regnery, 1994), 115. For Voorhis obituaries, see Glenn
    Fowler, "Jerry Voorhis, '46 Nixon Foe," *New York Times*, Sep 12, 1984; "Former
    Nixon Foe H. Jerry Voorhis Dead At 83," *Associated Press*, Sep 11, 1984; "Ex-Rep";
    Pearson, "Ex-Rep. Jerry Voorhis Dies."

2   Aitken, *A Life*, 126; David Greenberg, *Nixon's Shadow* (New York: W. W.
    Norton, 2003), 24; "Voorhis-Nixon Debate," program, Oct 28, 1946, RNL,
    Campaign 1946, box 1, folder 5: Correspondence Jul–Nov; Paul Bullock to
    Jerry Voorhis, letter, Aug 26, 1946, JVP, box 58, folder 5: Notes for Debates
    w/Nixon; "Jerry Voorhis Returns," *South Pasadena Review*, Aug 23, 1946, 3, JVP,
    box 58, folder 10: Newspaper Articles Pro and Con; "New Faces in the House,"
    Time, Nov. 18, 1946; Costello, "First Campaign," 14. On the handsome Nixon,
    see Ernest Brashear, "Who Is Richard Nixon," *Trainman News*, Oct 6, 1952.

3   "Nixon Says," pamphlet, n.d., RNL, Campaign 1946, box 1, folder 7: Ephemera; Greenberg, *Nixon's Shadow*, x–10; Lisa McGirr, *Suburban Warriors: The Origins of the New American Right* (Princeton, NJ: Princeton Univ Press, 2001), 23–25; Pamela Hallan-Gibson, *The Golden Promise: An Illustrated History of Orange County* (Albany, NY: Windsor Publications, 1986), 47–62; Kevin Starr, *Endangered Dreams: The Great Depression in California* (New York: Oxford Press, 1996), 121–50, 181–230; Kevin Starr, *Embattled Dreams: California in War and Peace, 1940–1950* (New York: Oxford Univ Press, 2002), 3–27, 61–122, 156–89, 309–39; M. J. Heale, "Red Scare Politics: California's Campaign against Un-American Activities, 1940–1970," *Journal of American Studies* 20, no. 1 (Apr 1986): 10–13.

4   Bullock to Voorhis, Aug 26, 1946; "Nixon Accepts Challenge of PAC Forces," *Monrovia News Post*, Sep 2, 1946, JVP, box 58, folder 13; "Don't Be Fooled Again!," *Glendora Press-Gleaner*, Oct 25, 1946, 5, RNL, Pre-Presidential Papers: 1946 Campaign, box 1; "Voorhis Endorsed by PAC?," *Whittier News*, Sep 11, 1946, JVP, box 58, folder 6: PAC-Communist Issue in Campaign; "Voorhis Denies Endorsement or Support of CIO-PAC," *Alhambra Post Advocate*, Sep 11, 1946, JVP, box 58, folder 6: PAC-Communist Issue in Campaign; "Nixonites Offer Proof PAC Backing Voorhis; Congressman Denies," *Whittier News*, 8, JVP, box 58, folder 6: PAC-Communist Issue in Campaign.

5   Richard Nixon, *RN* (New York: Simon & Schuster, 1990), 37; Costello, "First Campaign," 14; Morris, *Richard Milhous Nixon*, 318.

6   Greenberg, *Nixon's Shadow*, 25; Stephen Ambrose, *Nixon*, vol. 1, *The Education of a Politician, 1913–1963* (New York: Simon & Schuster, 1988),126; William Lee Miller, "The Debating Career of Richard M. Nixon," *Reporter*, Aug 19, 1956, JVP, box 58, folder 21: Repercussions in Later Years, 11.

7   Irwin F. Gellman, *The Contender: Richard Nixon: The Congress Years, 1946–1952* (New York: Free Press, 1999), 58, 61–88.

8   "Endorsement of Voorhis by PAC Attacked," *Whittier News*, Apr 24, 1946, n.p., JVP, box 58, folder 13; "Report on Mass Meeting Held by Republican Nixon for Congress Committee at Huntington School," May 3, 1946, JVP, box 58, folder 13; "Nixon versus Voorhis," *South Pasadena Review*, May 24, 1946, JVP, box 89, folder 25: Campaign 1946; "Nixon versus Voorhis," *Pasadena Saturday Review*, May 24, 1946, 4, JVP, box 58, folder 10: Newspaper Articles Pro and Con; "Nixon versus Voorhis," *South Pasadena Review*, May 27, 1946, RNL, Campaign

1946, box 1, folder 4: Correspondence 1946, May–Jun; "Nixonites Offer Proof PAC Backing Voorhis; Congressman Denies," *Whittier News*, n.d., 8, JVP, box 58, folder 6: PAC-Communist Issue in Campaign; "Jerry Voorhis Returns," *South Pasadena Review*, Aug 23, 1946, 3, JVP, box 58, folder 10: Newspaper Articles Pro and Con; "Nixon Accepts Challenge of Pac Forces," *Monrovia News Post*, Sep 2, 1946, JVP, box 58, folder 13; Wilber Jerger, "The Real Nixon Story," *Los Angeles Free Press*, Oct 4, 1956; "Voorhis Denies Endorsement or Support of CIO-PAC," *Alhambra Post Advocate*, Sep 11, 1946, JVP, box 58, Folder 6: PAC-Communist Issue in Campaign; Jerry Voorhis campaign, position paper, n.d., JVP, box 58, folder 7: Communist Attacks; Farrell, *Richard Nixon*, 34.

9   Richard Nixon, *In the Arena: A Memoir of Victory, Defeat and Renewal* (New York: Pocket Books, 1991), 285.

10   "Nixon Makes Final Primary Statement to District Voters," *Monrovia Daily News-Post*, n.d., JVP, box 58, folder 13; Gellman, *Contender*, 64.

11   Deiter Groh, "The Temptation of Conspiracy Theory," in *Changing Conceptions of Conspiracy*, ed. Carl F. Graumann and Serge Moscovici (New York: Springer-Verlag, 1987), 1–7; David Brion Davis, *The Fear of Conspiracy: Images of Un-American Subversion from the Revolution to the Present* (Ithaca, NY: Cornell Univ Press, 1971); Graumman and Moscovici, introduction, *Changing Conspiracies*, vii–ix; Charles Paul Freund, "If History Is a Lie: America's Resort to Conspiracy Thinking," *Washington Post*, Jan 19, 1992, C1; Mark Fenster, *Conspiracy Theories: Secrecy and Power in American Culture* (Minneapolis: Univ of Minnesota Press, 1999).

12   Costello, "First Campaign"; Nixon-Gannon, Feb 9, 1983, part 5; Greenberg, *Nixon's Shadow*, 19.

13   Aitken, *A Life*, 113–14; Nixon-Gannon, Feb 9, 1983, part 4; Nixon, *Arena*, 211–12; Ambrose, *Education of a Politician*, 118; Will Swift, *Pat and Dick: The Nixons, an Intimate Portrait of a Marriage* (New York: Threshold, 2014), 59; Myra G. Gutin, *The President's Partner: The First Lady in the Twentieth Century* (Westport, CT: Greenwood Press, 1989), 63; Dorothy Schneider and Carl J. Schneider, *First Ladies: A Biographical Dictionary* (New York: Infobase Publishing, 2010), 292; Barber, *Presidential Character*, 133.

14   Nixon-Gannon, Feb 9, 1983, part 5; Rockwood C. Nelson to Roy Day, letter, Oct 26, 1945, RNL, Campaign 1946, box 1, folder 1: Correspondence 1945; Roy Day to Fellow Republican, letter, Oct 18, 1945, RNL, Campaign 1946, box 1, folder 1: Correspondence 1945; Costello, "First Campaign," 9–10; Aitken, *A*

Life, 113–14; Jeffrey Frank, *Ike and Dick: Portrait of a Strange Political Marriage* (New York: Simon & Schuster, 2013), 8; Tom Bewley to Richard Nixon, letter, Nov 7, 1945, RNL, Campaign 1946, box 1, folder 1: Correspondence 1945.

15 Swift, *Pat and Dick*, 64; Nixon-Gannon, Feb 9, 1983, part 5; Morris, *Richard Milhous Nixon*, 302; Paul Bullock, " 'Rabbits and Radicals': Richard Nixon's 1946 Campaign against Jerry Voorhis," *Southern California Quarterly* 55, no. 3 (Fall 1973): 319–59; Jonathan Michaels, *McCarthyism: The Realities, Delusions and Politics behind the 1950s Red Scare* (New York: Routledge, 2017), 106; Roy Day to Friends and Workers, letter, May 17, 1946, RNL, Campaign 1946, box 1, folder 4: Correspondence 1946, May–Jun; Richard Nixon to Roy Day, letter, Apr 29, 1946, RNL, Campaign 1946, box 1, folder 3: Correspondence 1946, Mar–Apr; Morris, *Richard Milhous Nixon*, 316; Brennan, *Pat Nixon*, 19.

16 Robert W. Griffith, *Politics of Fear* (Amherst: Univ of Massachusetts Press, 1987), 12; Chris Suellentrop, "Campaign Like It's 1946," *New York Times*, Mar 29, 2006; "What Have You Had Enough Of, Hunh?," *Harvard Crimson*, Oct 31, 1946; "Even Democrat Chiefs Have Had Enough," *Chicago Tribune*, Oct 31, 1946, 7; "Author of 'Had Enough,' " *New York Times*, Nov 7, 1946, 15; "GOP Women in Parley: Mrs. Suthers Says Housewives Have Had Enough of Truman," *New York Times*, Sep 26, 1946, 19; George Tagge, "GOP Slogan: 'Haven't You Had Enough?,' " *Chicago Tribune*, Sep 30, 1946, 8; William Strand, "Alaskans 'Had Enough,' " *Chicago Tribune*, Oct 13, 1946, 20; "Saunders, Young Win Election to State Assembly: Negro Voters Return to GOP in Tuesday's Election," *Cleveland Call and Post*, Nov 9, 1946, 1a; Richard Nixon to Contractors and Builders in the Twelfth District, pamphlet, n.d., RNL, Campaign 1946, box 1, folder 5: Correspondence Jul–Nov; "Are You Satisfied with Present Conditions," Nixon campaign advertisement, *Monrovia Daily News-Post*, Oct 18, 1946, JVP, box 58; "Nixon Tells Reform Aims," *Progress Bulletin*, May 16, 1946, JVP, box 58, folder 10: Newspaper Articles Pro and Con.

17 Morris, *Richard Milhous*, 302; "Report on Mass Meeting Held by Republican Nixon for Congress Committee at Huntington School," May 3, 1946, JVP, box 58, folder 13; "America Needs New Leadership Now," pamphlet, 1946, RNL, Campaign 1946, box 1, folder 7: Ephemera; "Nixon Tells Reform Aims," *Progress Bulletin*, May 16, 1946, JVP, box 58, folder 10: Newspaper Articles Pro and Con; "Nixon Says," pamphlet, n.d., RNL, Herman and Hubert Perry Collection, Campaign Materials: 1946–1968, box 16, folder 1; "Report on Mass

Meeting Held by Republican Nixon for Congress Committee at Huntington School"; "Nixon Tells Reform Aims"; "Had Enough?," Nixon campaign flyer, n.d., RNL, Pre-Presidential Papers: 1946 Campaign, box 1.

18 "Your Veteran Candidate," pamphlet, 1946, RNL, Campaign 1946, box 1, folder 7: Ephemera; Richard Nixon to Genevieve Blaisdell, letter, May 4, 1946, RNL, Campaign 1946, box 1, folder 4: Correspondence 1946, May–Jun; Costello, "First Campaign"; Kay Marten, "They're Proud of Nixon," *Chicago Tribune*, Oct 28, 1956, 35; Ambrose, *Education of a Politician*, 122; Aitken, *A Life*, 121: Greenberg, *Nixon's Shadow*, 15, 18; "Your Veteran Candidate."

19 "Who Is Richard M. Nixon?," advertisement, n.d., RNL, Campaign 1946, box 1, folder 7: Ephemera; "Praises Policy," *South Pasadena Review*, n.d., JVP, box 58, folder 10: Newspaper Articles Pro and Con; "Richard M. Nixon Is *One of Us*," Nixon campaign flyer, n.d., RNL, Campaign 1946, box 1, folder 7: Ephemera; "Your Veteran Candidate," pamphlet, 1946, RNL, Campaign 1946, box 1, folder 7: Ephemera.

20 Ambrose, *Education of a Politician*, 108; Conrad Black, *Richard M. Nixon: A Life in Full* (New York: PublicAffairs, 2007), 73; Vidal, *An Evening with Richard Nixon* (New York: Random House, 1972), 20; Spalding, *Nixon Nobody Knows*, 136; "Richard M. Nixon Is *One of Us*"; "Your Veteran Candidate."

21 "Elections: 1946," *New Republic*, Feb 11, 1946, 203–30, RNL, Campaign 1946, box 1, folder 17: Reflections 1947. For worries about an encroaching war, see Catherine Polk, "Nazi Plan for Another War Told by Solon," *Daily News*, May 22, 1946, JVP, box 58, folder 2: Campaign Material; "Questions about Germany," *St. Louis Dispatch*, Oct 5, 1945, JVP, box 58, folder 2: Campaign Material.

22 William Leuchtenberg, "New Faces of 1946," *Smithsonian Magazine*, Nov 2006; Morris, *Richard Milhous Nixon*, 265; Scott Pittman, "Lifting the Veil: Public-Private Surveillance Networks and the Red Scare in California Higher Education," *California History* 91, no. 4 (Winter 2014): 43–55; Costello, "First Campaign," 13; Michaels, *McCarthyism*, 5; Morris, *Richard Milhous*, 266.

23 Jon W. Anderson, "Conspiracy Theories, Premature Entextualization, and Popular Political Analysis," *Arab Studies Journal* 4, no. 1 (Spring 1996): 96–98; Victoria E. Pagán, "Toward a Model of Conspiracy Theory for Ancient Rome," *New German Critique*, no. 103 (Winter 2008): 27–49; "The Voorhis Program," Nixon campaign flyer, n.d., JVP, box 58, folder 13; Jack Marley, "'Smear' Told by Nixon Foe," *Chicago Daily News*, Oct 31, 1958; "A Man Can't Go Much Lower

Than This," JVP, box 58, folder 13; The Voorhis Program; Phil Kerby, "Richard Nixon Charts His Course," *Frontier: Voice of the New West*, Jun 1956, 7–12, JVP, box 58, folder 21: Repercussions in Later Years; Jerry Voorhis, *The Strange Case of Richard Milhous Nixon* (New York: Popular Library, 1972), 15.

24 "Richard M. Nixon," *Washington Post*, Dec 18, 1946, 12; Voorhis, *Strange Case*, 18; "Don't Be Fooled Again!," *Glendora Press-Gleaner*, Oct 25, 1946, 5, RNL, Pre-Presidential Papers: 1946 Campaign, box 1; Costello, "First Campaign"; "Are You Satisfied with Present Conditions"; "Veterans Don't Be Fooled!," Nixon campaign flyer, n.d., RNL, Pre-Presidential Papers: 1946 Campaign, box 1; "Don't Be Fooled Again!," B1; Jerry Voorhis, speech notes, JVP, box 58, folder 13; Jerry Voorhis position paper, n.d., JVP, box 58, folder 7: Communist Attacks; "Jerry Voorhis and His Voting Record in Congress," pamphlet, Oct 28, 1946, JVP, box 58, folder 1: Campaign and Election Material, Voorhis vs. Nixon.

25 Voorhis position paper; Jerry Voorhis, speech notes, JVP, box 58, folder 2: Campaign Material; "Voorhis Supports American Foreign Policy," Voorhis campaign pamphlet, JVP, box 58, folder 1: Campaign and Election Material, Voorhis vs. Nixon; "Voorhis Asks Withdrawal of Any Support by PAC," *Alhambra Post Advocate*, Sep 19, 1946, JVP, box 89, folder 25: Campaign 1946; "Congress Candidates Discuss Foreign Policy," *Whittier News*, Sep 19, 1946, JVP, box 89, folder 25, Campaign 1946; "Rep Voorhis Backs Byrnes in Address," *Post Advocate*, Sep 17, 1946, JVP, box 89, folder 25, Campaign 1946.

26 "Deception of the Voter Has No Place in American Politics," *San Gabriel Sun*, Nov 24, 1946; "Deception of the Voter Has No Place in American Politics," Voorhis campaign advertisement, *San Gabriel Sun*, Oct 24, 1946, JVP, box 89, folder 24: Campaign 1946 Ads; Jerry Voorhis, radio speech notes, n.d., JVP, box 58, folder 2: Campaign Material.

27 Earl Mazo, "GOP 'Amateurs' Started Nixon up the Ladder," *Akron Beacon Journal*, Oct 7, 1959, 1, JVP, box 58, folder 21: Repercussions in Later Years; Voorhis, *Strange Case*, 16.

28 Morris, *Richard Milhous Nixon*, 335; Farrell, *Richard Nixon*, 42; Mazo, "GOP 'Amateurs'"; "Nixon Makes Final Primary Statement to District Voters"; Costello, "First Campaign"; Gellman, *Contender*, 307.

29 Voorhis, *Strange Case*, 18, 20; "Why Mistrust Nixon?," *St. Louis-Dispatch*, n.d., JVP, box 58, folder 21: Repercussions in Later Years; Henry Steele Commager, "Issues 1972," *New York Times*, Sep 18, 1972.

30 Jerry Voorhis to William Lee Miller, letter, Mar 28, 1956, JVP, box 58, folder 21: Repercussions in Later Years; Jerry Voorhis to the editor of *Time*, notes of draft letter, n.d., JVP, box 58, folder 21: Repercussions in Later Years; Voorhis to Miller, Mar 28, 1956."

31 Voorhis, *Strange Case*, 8–9, 18; Pearson, "Ex-Rep. Jerry Voorhis Dies"; Fowler, "Jerry Voorhis, '46 Nixon Foe"; Joel Weisman, "Old Nixon Foe Voorhis Recalls Battle," *Chicago's American*, Jan 7, 1969, JVP, box 58, folder 21: Repercussions in Later Years"; "Nixon's First Political Victim Dies, *United Press International*, Sep 12, 1984.

32 "Nixon versus Voorhis," *South Pasadena Review*, May 27, 1946; Bullock, "Rabbits and Radicals,'" 252; Nixon campaign, memorandum, "Destination: Congress," n.d., RNL, Campaign 1946, box 1, folder 4: Correspondence 1946, May–Jun; "The Voorhis Program," n.d.; Voorhis to Miller, Mar 28, 1956; Pearson, "Ex-Rep. Jerry Voorhis Dies."

INTERLUDE TWO

1 Baron Byron, *Select Works of* Byron (Lucerne: H. L. Broenner, 1834), 6:435; Kay Redfield Jamison, *Touched with Fire* (New York: Free Press, 1993), 2.

2 Karl Jaspers, *General Psychopathology*, trans. J. Hoenig and Marian W. Hamilton (Baltimore: Johns Hopkins Univ Press, 1997), 2:577–81.

3 Debra Hershkowitz, *The Madness of Epic: Reading Insanity from Homer to Statius* (Oxford: Clarendon Press, 1988); Allen Thiher, *Revels in Madness* (Ann Arbor: Univ of Michigan Press, 2009); Andrew Solomon, *The Noonday Demon: An Atlas of Depression* (New York: Scribner Classics, 2014); Andrew Scull, *Madness in Civilization: A Cultural History of Insanity, from the Bible to Freud, from the Madhouse to Modern Science* (Princeton, NJ: Princeton Univ Press, 2016); James Whitehead, *Madness and the Romantic Poet* (Oxford: Oxford Univ Press, 2017).

4 H. R. Haldeman, with Joseph DiMona, *The Ends of Power* (New York: Dell Publishing, 1978), 81–83; Richard Nixon to Henry Kissinger, memorandum, Mar 22, 1969, in William Burr and Jeffrey P. Kimball, "Nixon, Kissinger and the Madman Strategy during the Vietnam War," National Security Archive Electronic Briefing Book no. 517, May 29, 2015, NSA.

5 Scull, *Madness*, 21; Homer, *The Iliad*, ed., Bernard Knox, trans. Robert Fagles (New York: Penguin, 1990), lines 407–409.

6   Scull, *Madness*, 115; Samuel Taylor Coleridge, *The Complete Works of Samuel Taylor Coleridge* (New York: Harper & Brothers, 1858), 140.

7   Niccolò Machiavelli, *Discourses in Livy*, vol. 3, part 2 (Chicago: Univ of Chicago Press, 1998), 213–14; Harvey Mansfield, *Machiavelli's New Modes and Orders: A Study of the Discourses of Livy* (Chicago: Univ of Chicago Press, 2001), esp. 305–12; Thomas Pangle and Timothy Burns, *The Key Texts of Political Philosophy* (Cambridge: Cambridge Univ Press, 2014), esp. 193–95.

8   John Milton, "Il Penseroso," in *Milton: Poems* (New York: Knopf Doubleday, 2012), 46; Solomon, *Noonday*, 300; Andrew Solomon, telephone interview with author, Oct 9, 2017.

9   J. M. Coetzee, *Youth* (New York: Penguin, 2003), 100; Byron, "Childe Harold's Pilgrimage," in *The Poetical Works of Lord Byron* (New York: Leavitt & Allen, 1858), 1:120; Whitehead, *Madness and the Romantic Poet*, 1–28; Peter Boerner, *Goethe* (London: Haus Publishing, 2015), Kindle; John Keats, "Ode on Melancholy," in *The Complete Poems*, ed. John Barnard (New York: Penguin Classics, 1977), 348.

10   Thiher, *Revels*, 214–21.

11   Elaine Showalter, *Representing Ophelia* (New York: Macmillan, 1994); William Shakespeare, *The Tragedy of Hamlet, Prince of Denmark*, 4.7, http://shakespeare.mit.edu/hamlet/full.html.

12   Shakespeare, *Hamlet*, 5.5.

13   Ellen Moers, *Literary Women: The Great Writers* (Oxford: Oxford Univ Press, 1977); Elaine Showalter, *A Literature of Their Own* (Princeton: Princeton Univ Press, 1998); Sandra M. Gilbert and Susan Gruber, *The Madwoman in the Attic* (New Haven: Yale Univ Press, 2020).

14   Jack Kerouac, *On the Road* (New York: Penguin Classics, 1999), 5; David Cooper, introduction to Michel Foucault, *Madness and Civilization* (New York: Routledge Classics, 2001), ix; Rick Perlstein, *Nixonland: The Rise of a President and the Fracturing of America* (New York: Scribner, 2009), 380.

15   Cooper, introduction, 1.

16   Thomas Szasz, *The Myth of Mental Illness: Foundations of a Theory of Personal Conduct* (New York: HarperCollins, 1974); R. D. Lang, *The Divided Self*, Divided Self: An Existential Study in Sanity and Madness* (New York: Penguin Books, 1965; Laing, *The Politics of Experience* (New York: Ballantine Books, 1972), esp. 102; Susie Scott and Charles Thorpe, "The Sociological Imagination of R. D. Laing,"

Sociological Theory 24, no. 4 (Dec 2006): 331–52; Howard Becker, *Outsiders: Studies in the Sociology of Deviance* (New York: Simon & Schuster, 2008), 9.

17   Benjamin Nelson, "A Medium with a Message: R. D. Laing," *Salmagundi*, no. 16 (Spring 1971): 199–201; Lionel Trilling, *Sincerity and Authenticity* (Cambridge: Harvard Univ Press, 1973), 171–72.

18   Pat Buchanan, *Nixon's White House Wars: The Battles That Made and Broke a President and Divided America Forever* (New York: Crown Forum, 2017), 81; David Remnick, "Nattering Nabobs," *New Yorker*, Jul 3, 2006; Juan de Onis, "Nixon Puts 'Bums' Label on Some College Radicals," *New York Times*, May 2, 1970, 1.

19   Adam Philips, "Acting Madness: The Diary of a Madman, Macbeth, King Lear," *Threepenny Review*, no. 126 (Summer 2011): 14.

20   Evan Thomas, "The Complexity of Being Richard Nixon," *Atlantic*, Jun 15, 2015.

21   Plato, *Plato in Twelve Volumes*, trans. Harold N. Fowler (Cambridge, MA: Harvard Univ Press, 1924), 9:244b.

5. MADNESS IN THE MIND

1   Joseph Lelyveld, "Kennedy Seeking to Bar Police from Prosecuting Him in Crash," *New York Times*, Jul 22, 1969, 18; Laurence Stern, "Drinking Possibility Probed," *Washington Post*, Jul 23, 1969, A1; *Boston Globe* cited in John Barron, "Chappaquiddick: The Still Unanswered Questions about Ted Kennedy's Fatal Car Crash of 1969," *Reader's Digest*, Apr 2, 2021; "Political Damage in Kennedy Accident," *Chicago Defender*, Jul 21, 1969, 3; "Teddy Escapes, Woman Drowns When Auto Plunges off Bridge," *Chicago Tribune*, Jul 20, 1969, 1; "Kennedy's Statement," *Washington Post*, Jul 20, 1969, A1; H. R. Haldeman, *Haldeman Diaries: Inside the Nixon White House* (New York: G. P. Putnam's Sons, 1994), Saturday, Jul 19, 1969, Monday, Jul 21, 1969, 72–75, Saturday, Jul 26, 1969, Monday, Aug 4, 1969, 79, Wednesday, Jun 9, 1971, 297.

2   "The Mysteries of Chappaquiddick," *Time*, Aug 1, 1969; Richard Tedrow and Thomas Tedrow, *Death at Chappaquiddick* (New Orleans: Pelican Publishing, 1976), 67.

3   "Kennedy Puts Political Future on Line," *Eugene Register-Guard*, Jul 26, 1969; Bill Gavin to Frank Shakespeare, memorandum, Jun 14, 1971, 4, RNL, box 11, folder 24: Ken Khachigian: Presidential Memos 1970.

4   Haldeman, *Diaries*, Monday, August 4, 1969, 79, emphasis in the original.

5   William Safire, *Before the Fall* (New York: Routledge, 2017), 154–55, 692; Haldeman, *Diaries*, Monday, August 4, 1969, 79.

6   Safire, *Before the Fall*, 154–55.

7   Carl Bernstein and Bob Woodward, "FBI Finds Nixon Aides Sabotaged Democrats," *Washington Post*, Oct 10, 1972, A1; Philip Roth, *Our Gang* (New York: Vintage, 1971).

8   Luke Nichter quoted in "Tapes Reveal Kept Eye on Senator," Associated Press, Aug 30, 2009; Richard Nixon, H. R. Haldeman and Ronald Ziegler, conversation, Apr 9 1971, http://nixontapes.org/emk/476-014_clipa.mp3; "How Nixon Gave Ted Kennedy Bodyguards–To Spy on His Personal Life," Associated Press, Aug 28, 2009; Richard Nixon and H. R. Haldeman, conversation, May 28, 1971, http://nixontapes.org/emk/505-018_clipa.mp3; Richard Nixon and John Ehrlichman, conversation, Sep 8, 1971, http://nixontapes.org/emk/276-044_clipa.mp3; Richard Nixon, H. R. Haldeman, John Mitchell, John Ehrlichman and Charles Colson, conversation, Aug 2, 1972, http://nixontapes.org/emk.html; Richard Nixon, H. R. Haldeman and Charles Colson, conversation, Oct 14, 1971, http://nixontapes.org/emk.html; Richard Nixon and H. R. Haldeman, conversation, May 28, 1971, http://nixontapes.org/emk/505-018_clipa.mp3; "Nixon to Haldeman: Dig up the Dirt on the Democrats," transcript of conversation, May 28, 1971, 9:00 am, SFGate, https://www.sfgate.com/news/article/NIXON-TO-HALDEMAN-DIG-UP-DIRT-ON-THE-DEMOCRATS-3138089.php.

9   Garry Wills, *Nixon Agonistes: The Crisis of the Self-Made Man* (New York: First Mariner Books, 2002), xiv–xv, 586; Will Swift, *Pat and Dick* (New York: Threshold Editions, 2014), 64; Henry Kissinger, *Years of Upheaval* (New York: Simon & Schuster, 2011), Kindle.

10 "Crippled epistemology" is what Cass Sunstein and Adrian Vermeule call such limited information as that which conspiracists draw upon for their theories. David Reynolds, *One World Divisible* (New York: W. W. Norton, 2000), 330; Cass Sunstein and Adrian Vermeule, "Conspiracy Theories: Causes and Cures," *Journal of Political Philosophy* 17, no. 2 (2009): 211.

11 Nixon, "Transcript of President's Speech to the Nation in Answer to Watergate Charge," *New York Times*, Aug 16, 1973.

12 Karl Popper, *The Open Society and Its Enemies* (London: Routledge, 1966), 2:94–99; Joan Didion, *White Album* (New York: FSG Adult, 2009), 11; Anita M.

Waters, "Conspiracy Theories as Ethnosociologies: Explanation and Intention in African American Political Culture," *Journal of Black Studies* 28, no. 1 (Sep 1997): 113; Brian L. Keeley, "Of Conspiracy Theories," *Journal of Philosophy* 96, no. 3 (Mar 1999): 123; Dieter Groh, "The Temptation of Conspiracy Theory, or: Why Do Good Things Happen to Bad People?," in *Changing Conceptions of Conspiracy*, ed. Carl F. Graumann and Serge Moscovici (New York: Springer-Verlag, 1987), 1. For recent scholarship on conspiracism, see also Lee Basham, "Malevolent Global Conspiracy," *Journal of Social Philosophy* 34, no. 1 (Feb 5, 2003): 91–103; David Coady, "Conspiracy Theories and Official Stories," *International Journal of Applied Philosophy* 17, no. 2 (Fall 2003): 197–209; Mark Fenster, *Conspiracy Theories: Secrecy and Power in American Culture* (Minneapolis: Univ Of Minnesota Press, 1999); Graumann and Moscovici, introduction, *Changing* Conceptions; Eric Oliver and Thomas J. Wood, "Conspiracy Theories and the Paranoid Style(s) of Mass Opinion," *American Journal of Political Science* 58, no. 4 (2014): esp. 953; Charles Pigden, "Popper Revisited; Or What Is Wrong with Conspiracy Theories?" *Philosophy of the Social Sciences* 25, no. 1 (1995): 3–34; E. Uscinski, *Conspiracy Theories: A Primer* (Mitchellville, MD: Rowman & Littlefield, 2020), 5.

13   David Brion Davis, *The Fear of Conspiracy: Images of Un-American Subversion from the Revolution to the Present* (Ithaca, NY: Cornell Univ Press, 1971); Uscinski, *Conspiracy Theories: A Primer*, 69; Daniel Pipes, *Conspiracy: How the Paranoid Style Flourishes and Where It Comes From* (New York: Touchstone, 1999), 18; Charles Paul Freund, "If History Is a Lie: America's Resort to Conspiracy Thinking," *Washington Post*, Jan 19, 1992, C1.

14   Richard Hofstadter, *The Paranoid Style in American Politics* (New York: Knopf, 2012), 3–40.

15   ABC News, "Tapes Reveal Nixon's Prejudices Again," Mar 22, 2018; John Farrell, *Richard Nixon: The Life* (New York: Doubleday, 2017), 378; Richard Nixon, H. R. Haldeman and Henry Kissinger, conversation, Apr 28, 1971, 9:28 a.m., in *The Nixon Tapes, 1971–1972*, ed. Douglas Brinkley and Luke A. Nichter (Boston: Houghton-Mifflin, 2014) 112–13.

16   Nixon, Haldeman and Kissinger, conversation, Apr 28, 1971, 9:28 a.m., in *Tapes, 1971–1972*, 113.

17   K. A. Cuordileone, "Politics in the Age of Anxiety," *Journal of American History* 87, no. 2 (Sept 2000): 531–34; David K. Johnson, *The Lavender Scare: The Cold*

War Persecution of Gays and Lesbians in the Federal Government (Chicago: Univ of Chicago Press, 2004), 76, 166; K. A. Cuordileone, *Manhood and American Political Culture in the Cold War* (Lawrence: Univ of Kansas Press, 2004), 64; Kathryn S. Olmsted, *Real Enemies: Conspiracy Theories and American Democracy, World War I to 9/11* (Oxford: Oxford Univ Press, 2009); Nixon, Haldeman and Kissinger, Apr 28, 1971, 9:28 a.m., in *Tapes, 1971–1972*, 112–13; ABC News, "Tapes Reveal Nixon's Prejudices Again."

18 ABC News, "Tapes Reveal Nixon's Prejudices Again"; Haldeman, *Diaries*, Wednesday, May 26, 1971, 292.

19 Tom Wicker, *One of Us* (New York: Random House, 1991), *One of Us*, 33; "Truman Had Names for Nixon," *Los Angeles Times*, Nov 23, 1973, 2; David Leeming, *James Baldwin: A Biography* (New York: Alfred A. Knopf, 1994), 382; Pat Buchanan, *Nixon's White House Wars: The Battles That Made and Broke a President and Divided America Forever* (New York: Crown Forum, 2017), 21; David Greenberg, *Nixon's Shadow* (New York: W. W. Norton, 2003), 61; Stewart Alsop, "The Mystery of Richard Nixon," *Saturday Evening Post*, Jul 12, 1958, 29.

20 W. H. Lawrence, "Democratic Keynote Talk Assails Nixon as 'Hatchet-Man,'" *New York Times*, Aug 14, 1956; Alsop, "Mystery."

21 Richard Nixon, *Six Crises* (New York: Doubleday, 1962), 70; H. R. Haldeman, with Joseph DiMona, *The Ends of Power* (New York: Dell Publishing, 1978), 83.

22 Hunter S. Thompson, *The Great Shark Hunt: Strange Tales from a Strange Time* (New York: Simon & Schuster, 2011), 185; Stephen Whitfield, "Richard Nixon as a Comic Figure," *American Quarterly* 1, no. 1 (Spring 1985): 122.

23 Safire, *Before the Fall*, 7; Tim Weiner, *One Man against the World: The Tragedy of Richard Nixon* (New York: Henry Holt and Co., 2015), 7; Gerald S. and Deborah H. Strober, *Nixon: An Oral History of His Presidency* (New York: HarperCollins, 1994), 72; H. R. Haldeman, OHP-RNL, Aug 13, 1987, 11, 84–85. For further examples of generalizing on Nixon's temper by his staff, see Jeb Stuart Magruder, *An American Life* (New York: Atheneum, 1974), 77; Dwight Chapin, interview by Timothy Naftali, OHP-RNL, Apr 2, 2007, 78; Charles Colson, interview by Fredrick J. Graboske and Paul A. Schmidt, OHP-RNL, Sep 21, 1988, 32.

24 Erikson is most often credited with the first use of the word *psychohistory*. Yet more than a decade before, in 1951, Isaac Asimov had used the term *psychohistory* in the opening chapter of *Foundation*, a science fiction novel. Asimov wrote of a

clique of psychohistorians looked to predict the future through mathematics, a very different definition of the word than Erikson's. Robert Jay Lifton and Eric Olson, eds., *Explorations in Psychohistory* (New York: Simon & Schuster, 1974), 17. Sigmund Freud, *The Interpretation of Dreams* (Stoughton, WI: Books on Demand, 2016), Kindle; Erik Erickson, *Young Man Luther* (New York: W. W. Norton, 1962), 14.

For analyses of the psychohistorical field contemporary of Nixon, see Albert Weeks, review of *In Search of Nixon: A Psychological Inquiry*, by Bruce Mazlish, *Annals of American Academy of Political and Social Science* 405 (Jan 1973): 211–12; Richard Noland, "Psychohistory, Theory and Practice," *Massachusetts Review* 18, no. 2 (Summer 1977): 295–322; Donna Arzt, "Psychohistory and Its Discontents," *Biography* 1, no. 3 (Summer 1978): 1–36; Mauricio Mazón, "Young Richard Nixon: A Study in Political Precocity," *Historian* 41, no. 1 (Nov 1978): 21–40; Newell Bringhurst, "Fawn Brodie's Richard Nixon: The Making of a Controversial Biography," *California History* 70, no. 4 (Winter 1991/92): 378–91.

25 Greenberg, *Nixon's Shadow*, 237–38; Thomas A. Kohut, "Psychohistory as History," *American Historical Review* 91, no. 2 (Apr 1986): 336–54.

26 Bruce Mazlish, "History, Psychology and Leadership," in *Leadership: Multidisciplinary Perspectives*, ed. Barbara Kellerman (Englewoods Cliffs, NJ: Prentice Hall, 1984), 16; Fawn Brodie, *Richard Nixon: The Shaping of His Character* (New York: W. W. Norton, 1981), 57; Winnicott quoted in Greenberg, *Nixon's Shadow*, 246; Bringhurst, "Fawn Brodie's Richard Nixon," 378–91; Harry Jeffrey, review of *Richard Nixon: The Shaping of His Character*, by Fawn M. Brodie, *Oral History Review* 10 (1982): 160–63; Ingrid Winther Scobie, review of *Richard Nixon: The Shaping of His Character*," by Fawn M. Brodie, *Pacific Historical Review* 52, no. 4 (Nov 1983): 474–76. For prominent psychohistories, see David Abrahamsen, *Nixon vs. Nixon: An Emotional Tragedy* (New York: Farrar, Straus and Giroux, 1977); James David Barber, "The Nixon Brush with Tyranny," *Political Science Quarterly* 92, no. 4 (Winter 1977–1978): 581–605; Brodie, *Shaping*; Bela Kornitzer and Richard Nixon, *The Real Nixon: An Intimate Biography* (Whitefish, MT: Literary Licensing, LLC, 2017); Earl Mazo and Stephen Hess, *Nixon: A Political Portrait* (New York: Harper and Row, 1968); and, more recently, Vamik Volkan et al., *Richard Nixon: A Psychobiography* (New York: Columbia Univ Press, 1997).

27 Kornitzer, *Real Nixon*, 45; Robert Dallek, *Nixon and Kissinger: Partners in Power* (New York: Harper Perennial, 2007), 6–7; Mark Feldstein, *Poisoning the Press:*

Richard Nixon, Jack Anderson and the Rise of Washington's Scandal Culture (New York: Farrar, Straus and Giroux, 2010), 17; Stephen Ambrose, *Nixon*, vol. 1, *The Education of a Politician, 1913–1963* (New York: Simon & Schuster, 1988), 63; Merle West, interview by Robert Davis, OHP-CSUF, 1977, "Richard Nixon as a Relative"; Roger Morris, *Richard Milhous Nixon: The Rise of an American Politician* (New York: Henry Holt & Co., 1989), 50, 76, 174–76.

28 Greenberg, *Nixon's Shadow*, 237–38, 252–53; Robert Lekachman, "Original Sin," *Nation*, Oct 17, 1981, 387. For critiques of psychohistory, see especially Gerald Izenberg, "Psychohistory and Intellectual History," *History and Theory* 14., no. 2 (May 1975): 139–55; Kohut, "Psychohistory as History"; Christopher Lasch, *The Culture of Narcissism* (New York: Norton, 1978); Lewis Perry, "Has Psychohistory Come of Age," *History Teacher* 20, no. 3 (May 1987): 401–23; Weeks, review of *In Search of Nixon*; Tom Wolfe, "The 'Me' Decade and the Third Great Awakening," *New York*, August 23, 1976.

29 Ambrose, *The Education*, 588. For notable longform biographies, see Jonathan Aitken, *Nixon: A Life* (New York: Regnery, 1994); Ambrose, *The Education*; Stephen Ambrose, *Nixon*, vol. 2, *The Triumph of a Politician, 1962–1972* (New York: Simon & Schuster, 1989); Stephen Ambrose, *Nixon* vol. 3, *Ruin and Recovery, 1973–1990* (New York: Simon & Schuster, 1991); Donald T. Critchlow, *Republican Character: From Nixon to Reagan* (Philadelphia: Univ of Pennsylvania Press, 2018); Irwin Gellman, *The President and the Apprentice* (New Haven, CT: Yale Univ Press, 2015); Irwin F. Gellman, *The Contender: Richard Nixon: The Congress Years, 1946–1952* (New York: Free Press, 1999); Morris, *Richard Milhous Nixon*; Herbert Parmet, *Richard M. Nixon and His America* (Boston: Little, Brown and Co., 1989); Wicker, *One of Us*.

30 Aitken, *A Life*, 32–34; Parmet, *Richard Nixon*, viii; Alsop, "Mystery," 58; Ambrose, *The Education*, 60–61; Morris, *Richard Milhous Nixon*, 117–121; Richard Nixon, *RN* (New York: Simon & Schuster, 1990), 17; Rick Perlstein, *Nixonland: The Rise of a President and the Fracturing of America* (New York: Scribner, 2009), 22–23, 67; Wicker, *One of Us*, 8–9.

31 Wicker, *One of Us*; Morris, *Richard Milhous Nixon*, 309; Ambrose, *Ruin and Recovery*, 588.

32 John Ehrlichman, *Witness to Power* (New York: Simon & Schuster, 1982), 12; Jules Witcover, *The Resurrection of Richard Nixon* (New York: G. P. Putnam's

Sons, 1970), 212; Monica Crowley, *Nixon off the Record* (New York: Random House, 1996), 5.

33   Nixon, *RN*, 625–28; Nixon-Gannon, Jun 13, 1983, part 3.

34   For examples of skullduggery, see, for the most charitable of readings, Aitken, *A Life*, 411–24, 467–528; or the first half of Ambrose, *Ruin and Recovery*. For more typically critical accounts of "thievery," see Stanley I. Kutler, *Abuse of Power: The New Nixon Tapes* (New York: Simon & Schuster, 1998); Farrell, *Richard Nixon*, 347–70, 397–434, 465–533. For Nixon wiretapping his staff and family, William Safire, interview by Timothy Naftali, OHP-RNL, May 27, 2008, 15; Walter Isaacson, *Kissinger: A Biography* (New York: Simon & Schuster, 1992), 227; Harrison Salisbury, *Without Fear or Favor* (New York: Times Books, 1980), 11; Olmsted, *Real Enemies*, 152; Carl Woodward and Bob Bernstein, "Nixon Wiretapped Brother," *Washington Post*, Sep 6, 1973.

35   For revisionism, see Jodie Allen, "Last of the Big Spenders," *Washington Post*, Feb 24, 1983; Gellman, *Contender*; Gellman, *Apprentice*; Greenberg, *Nixon's Shadow*, 304–37, Joan Hoff, *Reconsidered* (New York: Basic Books, 1995).

36   Hoff, *Reconsidered*, 3, 284, 454; Gellman, *Contender*, 343.

37   Gellman, *Contender*, 343, 360, 454; Hoff, *Reconsidered*, 1–16, 280–81; 740–41; Allen, "Big Spenders."

38   Iwan Morgan, *Nixon* (Oxfordshire, UK: Hodder Education Publishers, 2002), 194, emphasis in the original; Evan Thomas, *Being Nixon* (New York: Random House, 2016); Farrell, *Richard Nixon*.

39   Mark Feeney, *Nixon at the Movies* (Chicago: Univ of Chicago Press, 2004); Daniel Frick, *Reinventing Richard Nixon: A Cultural History of an American Obsession* (Lawrence: Univ Press of Kansas, 2008); Greenberg, *Nixon's Shadow*; Perlstein, *Nixonland*, 46.

40   Kathryn Olmsted, "Conspiracy Theories in US History," in *Conspiracy Theories and the People Who Believe Them*, ed. Joseph Uscinski (Oxford: Oxford Univ Press, 2019), 288–93; Olmsted, *Real Enemies*, 156–203.

41   Timothy Melley, "Brainwashed! Conspiracy Theory and Ideology in the Postwar United States," *New German Critique*, no. 103 (Winter 2008): 148–61; William H. Whyte, Jr., *The Organization Man* (New York: Touchstone Books, 1956), 6–7, 32, 46–47; Kevin Mattson, *Just Plain Dick: Richard Nixon's "Checkers" Speech and the "Rocking, Socking" Election of 1952* (London: Bloomsbury

Publishing, 2013), 47–48; C. Wright Mills, *White Collar* (New York: Oxford Univ Press, 1953), xii.

42 Mattson, *Plain Dick*; Perlstein, *Nixonland*. For a working definition of *anomie*, see Michael J. Wood and Karen M. Douglas, "Conspiracy Theory Psychology," in *Conspiracy Theories and the People Who Believe Them*, ed. Joseph E. Uscinski (Oxford: Oxford Univ Press, 2018), 249.

43 Rick Perlstein, *Before the Storm: Barry Goldwater and the Unmaking of the American Consensus* (New York: Bold Type Books, 2009), xi; Hofstadter, *Paranoid Style*; Daniel Bell, *The Radical Right* (New York: Anchor Books, 1964).

44 Alan Brinkley, "The Problem of America Conservatism," *American Historical Review* 99, no. 2 (Apr 1994): 409–29; Julian E. Zelizer, "Rethinking the History of American Conservatism," *Reviews in American History* 38, no. 2 (Jun 2010): 367–92; Russell Kirk, *The Conservative Mind*, 7th ed. (New York: Regnery Books, 1986); George H. Nash, *The Conservative Intellectual Tradition since 1945* (Wilmington, DE: Intercollegiate Studies Institute, 2005); Matthew Lassiter, "Inventing Family Values," in *Rightward Bound: Making America Conservative in the 1970s*, ed. Bruce Schulman and Zelizer (Cambridge, MA: Harvard Univ Press, 2008), 13–28; Jonathan Michaels, *McCarthyism: The Realities, Delusions and Politics behind the 1950s Red Scare* (Oxfordshire, UK: Routledge, 2017), 20. For particular critique of Hofstadter and his idea of the paranoid style, see Uscinski, "What Is a Conspiracy Theory," 47–52; M. R. X. Dentith, "Conspiracy Theories and Philosophy," in Uscinski, *People Who Believe*, 94–108. For revisionist analysis of conservatism as a traditional constituent of libertarianism, traditionalism and anticommunism, see Martin Durham, "On American Conservatism and Kim Philips-Fein's Survey of the Field," *Journal of American History* 98, no. 3 (Dec 2011): 756–59; Kim Phillips-Fein, "Conservatism: A State of the Field," *Journal of American History* 98, no. 3 (Dec 2011): 723–43; Matthew D. Lassiter and Joseph D. Crespino, eds., *The Myth of Southern Exceptionalism* (Oxford: Oxford Univ Press, 2010); Lisa McGirr, "Now That Historians Know So Much about the Right, How Should We Best Approach the Study of Conservatism," *Journal of American History* 98, no. 3 (Dec 2011): 765–70; Leo P. Ribuffo, "The Discovery and Rediscovery of American Conservatism Broadly Conceived," *OAH Magazine of History* 17, no. 2 (Jan 2003): 5–10.

45 Lisa McGirr, *Suburban Warriors: The Origins of the New American Right* (Princeton, NJ: Princeton Univ Press, 2002), esp. 147–86; Peter N. Carroll, *It Seemed*

Like Nothing Happened: The Tragedy and Promise of America in the 1970s (New York: Holt McDougal, 1982), 326–27; Donald T. Critchlow, *Phyllis Schlafly and Grassroots Conservatism* (Princeton, NJ: Princeton Univ Press, 2005), 1. For a review of the intellectual revolution in conservative thinking, see Donald T. Critchlow, "The Conservative Ascendancy," in Donald T. Critchlow and Nancy Maclean, *Debating the American Conservative Movement 1945 to the Present* (Lanham, MD: Rowman & Littlefield, 2009), 1–60; Daniel Stedman Jones, *Masters of the Universe: Hayek, Friedman, and the Birth of Neoliberal Politics* (Princeton, NJ: Princeton Univ Press, 2012).

46 Perlstein, *Before the Storm*, xiii, emphasis in the original; Alfred Moore, "On the Democratic Problems of Conspiracy Politics," in Uscinski, *People Who Believe*, 111–21; Barry Goldwater, *The Conscience of a Conservative* (Eastford, CT: Martino Fine Books, 2011), 20, 22, 70, 83–85.

47 Kevin Phillips, *The Emerging Republican Majority* (New Rochelle, NY: Arlington House, 1969); Wills, *Agonistes*, 265; Kevin M. Kruse, *White Flight: Atlanta and the Making of Modern Conservatism* (Princeton, NJ: Princeton Univ Press, 2005); Thomas J. Sugrue, *The Origins of the Urban Crisis: Race and Inequality in Postwar Detroit* (Princeton, NJ: Princeton Univ Press, 1996). For elite construction of ideological networks, see Nicole Hemmer, *Messengers of the Right: Conservative Media and the Transformation of American Politics* (Philadelphia: Univ of Pennsylvania Press, 2016); Kevin Kruse, *One Nation under God* (New York: Basic Books, 2015); Kim Phillips-Fein, *Invisible Hands: The Businessman's Crusade against the New Deal* (New York: W.W. Norton, 2009).

48 Robert Mason, "Political Realignment," in *A Companion to Richard M. Nixon*, ed. Melvin Small (Hoboken, NJ: Wiley and Blackwell, 2011), 252–69; Dean J. Kotlowski, *Nixon's Civil Rights* (Cambridge, MA: Harvard Univ Press, 2002), 215; "Transcript of Nixon's Acceptance Address," *New York Times*, Aug 24, 1972, and for video, "The Presidency: Richard Nixon 1972 Acceptance Speech," CSPAN, Aug 23, 1972, https://www.c-span.org/video/?3911-1/richard-nixon-1972-acceptance-speech; Reg Murphy and Hal Gulliver, *The Southern Strategy* (New York: Scribner, 1971), 3.

49 Stanley I. Kutler, *The Wars of Watergate* (New York: W. W. Norton, 1992), 70; Joe McGinnis, *The Selling of the Presidency* (New York: Penguin, 1968).

50 "Richard Nixon: Address Accepting the Presidential Nomination at the Republican National Convention in Miami Beach Florida," Aug 8, 1968,

American Presidency Project (hereinafter "Nixon 1968 Acceptance Speech") https://www.presidency.ucsb.edu/documents/address-accepting-the -presidential-nomination-the-republican-national-convention-miami.

51   David Greenberg, "Nixon as Statesman: The Failed Campaign," in *Nixon in the World: American Foreign Relations, 1969–1977*, ed. Fredrik Logevall and Andrew Preston (Oxford: Oxford Univ Press, 2008), 54; Dallek, *Nixon and Kissinger*, 368; Farrell, *Richard Nixon*, 337.

52   "Nixon 1968 Acceptance Speech"; Richard Nixon, "Address to the Nation on the War in Vietnam, November 3, 1969," *Public Papers of the Presidents of the United States: Richard M. Nixon (1969)* (Washington, DC: Government Printing Office, 1971), 909; "H. R. Haldeman: The Elections of '70 and '72 Buchanan," memorandum, n.d., WHSF-SMOF, box 6, folder 4; Safire, OHP-RNL, 8; Steve Bull, interview by Timothy Naftali, OHP-RNL, Jun 26, 20007, 5; Robert B. Semple Jr., "Speech Took Drafts and President Wrote All," *New York Times*, Nov 4, 1969, 17; Rowland Evans and Robert Novak, "Nixon's Appeal for Unity," *News-American*, Nov 3, 1969, 7b; Raymond Price Jr., interview by Timothy Naftali, OHP-RNL, Apr 4, 2007, 12; Nixon-Gannon, Apr 7, 1983, part 2.

53   "Polls Show the 'Silent Majority' Also Is Uneasy about War Policy," *Washington Post*, Nov 5, 1969, A19; "One Man Alone," *New York Times Book Review*, Nov 23, 1969, 10.

54   Richard Nixon, "Address to the Nation on Vietnam," Dec 15, 1969, Richard Nixon Foundation, https://www.nixonfoundation.org/2017/09/address -nation-vietnam-december-15-1969/. Richard Nixon, "Remarks on the CBS Radio Network: 'A New Alignment for America," May 16, 1968; Rob Kirkpat- rick, *1969: The Year That Changed the World* (New York: Skyhorse Publishing, 2011), Kindle; Mattson, *Plain Dick*, 59.

55   "Vets Day Observance in Milwaukee," *Milwaukee Star*, Oct 25, 1969; "Hail Us War Vets Today: 'Silent Majority' Urged to Join In," *Chicago Tribune*, Nov 11, 1969, 1; "Parades for Peace and Patriotism," *Time*, Nov 21, 1969.

56   "Veterans Day '69," *Los Angeles Sentinel*, Nov 13, 1969, A6; "Love It or Leave It," *National Affairs*, Nov 24, 1969, 35–36; Murray Schumach, "Support for the President Underlying Theme in City: Traditional Solemnity Marks Observance of Veterans Day Speeches Here Reflect Support of Nixon Policy," *New York Times*, Nov 12, 1969.

57 John Herbers, "Backers of Nixon Policy Rally in Capital," *New York Times*, Nov 12, 1969, 20; "Veterans Day Closes Most Banks; Courts," *Washington Post*, Nov 11, 1969, C2; Marie Smith, "Nixon Visits Veterans," *Washington Post*, Nov 12, 1969, B3; Philip D. Carter, "For Various Reasons," *Washington Post*, Nov 12, 1969; "Nixon's Unsilent Supporters," *Time*, Nov 21, 1969; Lee Edwards, "The Voice of the 'Silent Majority,'" *New York Times*, Nov 12, 1969, 20.

58 Andrew Katz, "Public Opinion and Foreign Policy," *Presidential Studies Quarterly* 27, no. 3 (Summer 1997): 510; Brittany Bounds, "The Right Response" (PhD diss., Texas A & M, 2015), 17, 135, 144.

59 In 1962 in the preface to *Six Crises*, a young Nixon had been quite frank about his desire for upward mobility. Writing, he explained, could afford him the "possibility of joining the 'literary' ranks" whose membership included the "distinguished" Jack Kennedy. Par for the course, Nixon was quick to distance himself. Although Nixon was attracted to Camelot, he remained steadfast in his own climb and rejected Kennedy's literary laurel just as he had shunned the Franklins of his college days. As he wrote, the type of fearlessness in crisis that he aimed for was a "learned" skill, "acquired and not inherited." The dream, however, might indeed be the same. Yet foremost, even as he reached for Kennedy-like success, Nixon stressed that he was different from them, that he believed hard work as central to success, that it was not the place one was born that mattered but dogged preparation. In this, Nixon was obedient in the pursuit of the prize but rebellious along the path. The observation characterizing Nixon as Schiff's "obedient rebel" is made by Bruce Mazlish, *In Search of Nixon: A Psychohistorical Inquiry* (New York: Basic Books, 1972), 71. Nixon, *Six Crises*, xxiii–xxv; Thomas, *Being Nixon*, xx.

60 Melvin Small, "The Election of 1968," in Small, *Companion*, 144; for Nixon's various membership cards to golf clubs, WHSF, box 2, folders 11–12, 22, 32, and box 4, folders 1–5.

61 Richard Nixon to John Ehrlichman, memorandum, Jan 9, 1969, 9, WHSF, box 1, folder 38; Richard Nixon to John Ehrlichman, memorandum, Jan 4, 1969, 2–3, WHSF, box 1, folder 38.

62 On thievery, see Kutler, *Abuse*, xvi, 8–10; Kutler, *Wars of Watergate*; John W. Dean, *The Nixon Defense: What He Knew and When He Knew It* (New York: Penguin Random House, 2015). On the Vietnam War, see Jeffrey P. Kimball, *The Vietnam War Files: Uncovering the Secret History of Nixon-Era Strategy*

(Lawrence: Univ Press of Kansas, 2004); Ken Hughes, *Chasing Shadows: The Nixon Tapes, the Chennault Affair and the Origins of Watergate* (Charlottesville: Univ of Virginia Press, 2014).

63 Ken Hughes, "A Rough Guide to Richard Nixon's Conspiracy Theories," Miller Center, https://millercenter.org/the-presidency/educational-resources/a-rough-guide-to-richard-nixon-s-conspiracy-theories; Bob Woodward, "White House Horrors," *New York Times*, Jul 13, 1973; "Bob Woodward Reviews *The Nixon Defense*, by John W. Dean," *Washington Post*, Jul 14, 2014.

64 Haldeman, *Diaries*, Thursday, August 3, 1972, 490, Wednesday, September 9, 1970, 192.

65 Rick Perlstein, "The Election of 1972," in Small *Companion*, 169–71; Thomas, *Being Nixon*, 210.

66 Richard Nixon, *In the Arena: A Memoir of Victory, Defeat and Renewal* (New York: Pocket Books, 1991), 292.

INTERLUDE THREE

1 Upon assuming the presidency in late January 1969, Nixon was similarly briefed on the U.S. nuclear war plan and informed that the United States and the Soviet Union would both suffer 90 million deaths in the event of such a conflict. Fred Kaplan, *The Bomb: Presidents, Generals, and the Secret History of Nuclear War* (New York: Simon & Schuster, 2020), 13; William Burr, "The Nixon Administration, the 'Horror Strategy,' and the Search for Limited Nuclear Options, 1969–1972: Prelude to the Schlesinger Doctrine," *Journal of Cold War Studies* 7, no. 3 (Summer 2005): 34.

2 Francis J. Gavin, "Nuclear Proliferation and Non-Proliferation during the Cold War," in *The Cambridge History of the Cold War*, ed. Melvin P. Leffler and Odd Arne Westad, vol. 2 (Cambridge: Cambridge Univ Press, 2010), 398.

3 Henry Kissinger, *Nuclear Weapons and Foreign Policy* (New York: Harper & Brothers, 1957), 3; John Lewis Gaddis, *Strategies of Containment* (Oxford: Oxford Univ Press, 1982), 128, emphasis in the original.

4 Arthur Schlesinger, Jr., *A Thousand Days: John F. Kennedy in the White House* (Boston: Houghton Mifflin, 2002), 311; Kissinger, *Nuclear Weapons and Foreign Policy*; Gaddis, *Strategies of Containment*; Mario Del Pero, *The Eccentric Realist: Henry Kissinger and the Shaping of American Foreign Policy* (Ithaca, NY: Cornell Univ Press, 2006), 52.

5   William Hitchcock, *The Age of Eisenhower: America and the World in the 1950s* (New York: Simon & Schuster, 2018), Kindle; Jeffrey P. Kimball and William Burr, *Nixon's Nuclear Specter: The Secret Alert of 1969, Madman Diplomacy, and the Vietnam War* (Lawrence: Univ Press of Kansas, 2015), 21–22, 82–83; Lester Brune, "Truman and Eisenhower: Strategic Options," in *The Korean War: Handbook of the Literature and Research*, ed. Lester H. Brune and Robin Higham (Westport, CT: Greenwood Publishing Group, 1996), 289; Jawaharlal Nehru and John Foster Dulles, memorandum of conversation, May 22, 1953, 1:00 p.m., *Foreign Relations of the United States, 1952–1954, The Near and Middle East*, vol. 9, part 1, ed. Paul Claussen et al. (Washington, DC: Government Printing Office, 1986), 1071.

6   William Hitchcock, "Ike Never Threatened to Use Nukes in North Korea," History News Network, Aug 11, 2017; William Hitchcock, "Trump Threatened to Nuke Korea. Did Ike Do The Same?," *Washington Post*, Aug 11, 2017; William Burr and Jeffrey P. Kimball, "Nixon, Kissinger and the Madman Strategy," NSA, May 29, 2015; Benjamin Read, memorandum, "Threat of the Use of Nuclear Weapons against China in Korean War," NSA, Mar 4, 1965.

7   Richard Nixon and Henry Kissinger, transcript of conversation, Apr 23, 1971, *Foreign Relations of the United States*, vol. 12, *Vietnam, 1969–1976*, eds. David Goldman and Erin R. Mahan (Washington, DC: Office of the Historian, Department of State, 2010), 581.

8   Evan Thomas, *Being Nixon* (New York: Random House, 2016), 208. For accounts of Nixon's excellent poker playing, see H. R. Haldeman, OHP-RNL, Apr 11, 1988, 129; Edward Nixon, interview by Timothy Naftali, OHP-RNL, Jan 9, 2007, 9; Nixon-Gannon, Feb 9, 1983, part 4; Roger Morris, *Richard Milhous Nixon: The Rise of an American Politician* (New York: Henry Holt & Co., 1989), 246; Burr and Kimball, *Nuclear Specter*, 85.

9   Fred Kaplan, *The Wizards of Armageddon* (Redwood City, CA: Stanford Univ Press, 1991).

10   Jonathan Schell, *The Fate of the Earth* (Stanford: Stanford Univ Press, 2000), 10; Kaplan, *Wizards*, 1; Aron quoted in Herman Kahn, *Thinking about the Unthinkable* (New York: Avon Library, 1962), 19; Herman Kahn, *On Thermonuclear War* (Piscataway, NJ: Transaction Publishers, 2011), 145–50; Kissinger, *Nuclear Weapons and Foreign Policy*, 3.

11   Arthur Schlesinger, Jr., *A Thousand Days* (New York: Random House, 1988), 313.

12 Niall Ferguson, *Kissinger, 1923–1968: The Idealist* (New York: Penguin, 2015), 463; Kaplan, *Wizards*.

13 Barry Scott Zellen, *State of Doom: Bernard Brodie, The Bomb, and the Birth of the Bipolar World* (London: A&C Black, 2011), ix, 49; Kaplan, *Wizards*, 31.

14 Kahn, *Thinking about the Unthinkable*, 24.

15 Norman Macrae, *John Von Neumann: The Scientific Genius Who Pioneered the Modern Computer, Game Theory, Nuclear Deterrence, and Much More* (Hinsdale, MA: Plunkett Lake Press, 1992); P. R. Halmos, "The Legend of John Von Neumann," *American Mathematical Monthly* 80, no. 4 (Apr 1973): 382–94; F. Forgó, "John Von Neumann's Contribution to Modern Game Theory," *Acta Oeconomica* 54, no. 1 (2004): 73–84; Kaplan, *Wizards*, 63.

16 Kahn, *Thinking about the Unthinkable*; James R. Schlesinger, "Defense Planning and Budgeting: The Issue of Centralized Control," Industrial College of the Armed Forces, May 1968, 28.

17 Andrew Cockburn, "The Defense Intellectual: Edward N. Luttwak," *Grand Street* 6, no. 3 (Spring 1987): 162; William Beecher, "Pentagon's 'Whiz Kids,'" *Wall Street Journal*, Sep 24, 1963, 18; Burr and Kimball, *Nuclear Specter*, 68; Richard H. Immerman, "Psychology," *Journal of American History* 77, no. 1 (June 1990): 171; Kahn, *Thinking about the Unthinkable*, 32–33.

18 John Farrell, *Richard Nixon: The Life* (New York: Doubleday, 2017); Thomas, *Being Nixon*, 294; Rick Perlstein, *Nixonland: The Rise of a President and the Fracturing of America* (New York: Scribner, 2009), 394; Greg Grandin, *Kissinger's Shadow: The Long Reach of America's Most Controversial Statesman* (New York: Macmillan, 2015), 56; Ferguson, *Kissinger*, 367.

19 Thomas C. Schelling, *The Strategy of Conflict* (Cambridge, MA: Harvard Univ Press, 1981), emphasis in the original; Thomas C. Schelling, *Arms and Influence* (New Haven, CT: Yale Univ Press, 1966); Robert Ayson, *Thomas Schelling and the Nuclear Age* (New York: Taylor & Francis, 2004); Todd Sechser and Matthew Fuhrmann, "The Madman and the Bomb: Nuclear Blackmail in the Trump Era," *Virginia Policy Review* 12, no. 1 (2017); Tyler Cowen, "Thomas Schelling, New Nobel Laureate," *Marginal Revolution*, Oct 10, 2005.

20 Kahn, *Thinking about the Unthinkable*, 92; Kaplan, *Wizards*, 47; Kissinger, *Nuclear Weapons and Foreign Policy*.

21 Kaplan, *Wizards*, 4; Albert Wohlstetter, "The Delicate Balance of Terror," RAND Corporation, 1958, https://www.rand.org/pubs/papers/P1472.html; Schelling, *Strategy of Conflict*, 6.

22 Schelling, *Arms and Influence*, 99; Michael Kinsley, "A Nobel Laureate Who's Got Game," *Washington Post*, Oct 12, 2005; Schelling, *Strategy of Conflict*, 187–204.

23 Kaplan, *The Bomb*, 104; Richard Nixon, *The Real War* (New York: Warner Books, 1980), 2, 254–56.

24 Kissinger, *Nuclear Weapons and Foreign Policy*; Daniel Ellsberg, "The Political Uses of Madness," Kahle/Austin Foundation, Internet Archive, Mar 25, 1959, https://archive.org/details/ThePoliticalUsesOfMadness/ELS005-001/page /n0/mode/2up, emphasis in the original.

25 Ellsberg, "Political Uses."

26 Jeffrey Kimball, "Did Thomas Schelling Invent the Madman Theory?," History News Network, n.d., https://historynewsnetwork.org/article/17183; Kissinger, *Nuclear Weapons and Foreign Policy*; Jann S. Wenner, "Daniel Ellsberg," *Rolling Stone*, Nov 8, 1973.

27 Kimball and Burr, *Nuclear Specter*, 52; Richard Nixon, *RN* (New York: Simon & Schuster, 1990), 52, 203, 406; Alsop, "Matter of Fact: Method in Khrushchev's Madness," *Washington Post*, Jul 20, 1959, A15.

28 Alsop, "Matter Of Fact," A15; "Russian's Words Cited: Harriman Sees Signs of Hope in Khrushchev Remarks," *New York Times*, Oct 5, 1959, 17; "Lodge Sees Shift in Kremlin Line," *New York Times*, Oct 5, 1959, 4; Thomas Whitney, "An End to the Iron Curtain?," *Problems of Communism* 8, no. 6 (1959): 57.

29 "West Is Warned by Khrushchev," *New York Times*, Jun 4, 1959; Salisbury, "Concern over Germany," *New York Times*, Jun 4, 1959; Khrushchev, "Khrushchev Remarks at the National Press Club," *Washington Post*, Sep 17, 1959, A16; Salisbury, "Khrushchev Remembers, *New York Times*, Jan 3, 1971; Burr and Kimball, *Nuclear Specter*, 52; Nixon-Gannon, May 12, 1983, part 2; Nina Khrushcheva, "The Return of the Madman Theory," *Jordan Times*, Sep 25, 2017; Khrushcheva, "The Return of the Madman Theory," *Japanese Times*, Oct 5, 2017.

30 Nixon, *RN*, 129; Hersh, *Price of Power*, 328; Wenner, "Daniel Ellsberg."

31 Jussi M. Hanhimäki, "An Elusive Grand Design" in *Nixon in the World: American Foreign Relations, 1969–1977*, ed. Fredrik Logevall and Andrew Preston (Oxford: Oxford Univ Press, 2008), 27; Thomas, *Being Nixon*, 190.

32 Schelling, *Strategy of Conflict*, 5–17, 187–204; Jonathan Schell, *The Unfinished Twentieth Century: The Crisis of Weapons of Mass Destruction* (New York: Verso, 2003), 112; Kimball, "Did Thomas C. Schelling Invent the Madman Theory?"; Stephen Quackenbush, "Deterrence Theory: Where Do We Stand?," *Review of International Studies* 37, no. 2 (April 2011): 741–62; Andrew Solomon, telephone interview by the author, Nov 8, 2017.

6. MADNESS IN PLAY

1   Leonard Garment, *Crazy Rhythm* (Boston: Perseus Press, 2001), 174–77.

2   Garment, *Crazy Rhythm*, 174–77.

3   Garment, *Crazy Rhythm*, 174–77.

4   Lewis Gaddis, "The Long Peace: Elements of Stability in the Postwar International System," *International Security* 10 (Spring 1986): 99–142; Raymond Garthoff, *Détente and Confrontation: American-Soviet Relations from Nixon to Reagan* (Washington, DC: Brookings Institution, 1985); John Lewis Gaddis, *Strategies of Containment* (Oxford: Oxford Univ Press, 1982); Jussi M. Hanhimäki, "An Elusive Grand Design," in *Nixon in the World: American Foreign Relations, 1969–1977*, ed. Fredrik Logevall and Andrew Preston (Oxford: Oxford Univ Press, 2008), 25–44.

5   I. F. Stone, "Nixon and the Arms Race: How Much Is 'Sufficiency,'" *New York Review of Books*, Mar 27, 1969; Robert D. Schulzinger, "Détente in the Nixon-Ford Years, 1969–1975," in *The Cambridge History of the Cold War*, ed. Melvin Leffler and Odd Arne Westad, vol. 2 (Cambridge, UK: 2012), 373–94; Burr and Kimball, *Nuclear Specter*, 328–29.

6   Jeffrey P. Kimball and William Burr, *Nixon's Nuclear Specter: The Secret Alert of 1969, Madman Diplomacy, and the Vietnam War* (Lawrence: Univ Press of Kansas, 2015); ; H. R. Haldeman, with Joseph DiMona, *The Ends of Power* (New York: Dell Publishing, 1978), 83; William Burr and Jeffrey P. Kimball, "Nixon, Kissinger and the Madman Strategy during Vietnam War," NSA, May 29, 2015.

7   Richard Nixon and Henry Kissinger, conversation, Dec 12, 1971, in William Burr, "Nixon/Kissinger Saw India as 'Soviet Stooge' in 1971 South Asia Crisis," NSA, Jun 29, 2005; Henry Kissinger, *The White House Years* (Boston: Little, Brown and Company, 1979), 614–15; Nixon and Kissinger, conversation, Apr 4, 1972, *Foreign Relations of the United States* (hereinafter *FRUS*), 1969–1976, vol. 8, *Vietnam* (Washington, DC: Office of the Historian, Department of State, 2010),

198–203; Richard Nixon to Henry Kissinger, message, Apr 23, 1971, *FRUS, 1969–1976*, vol. 8 *Vietnam*, 303–307.

8   Nixon-Gannon, Apr 7, 1983, part 2; Mike Gaetani, "50 Years Ago, Tragedy Helped Deliver Triumph," Center for Advanced Studies in Behavioral Sciences," Apr 24, 2020, https://casbs.stanford.edu/news/50-years-ago-tragedy -helped-deliver-triumph.

9   Richard Nixon to Daniel Patrick Moynihan, memorandum, Jan 3, 1968, 8, WHSF, box 1, folder 37; Juan de Onis, "Nixon Puts 'Bums' Label on Some College Radicals," *New York Times*, May 2, 1970, 1; Theodore White, "Making of the President," *Life*, Jul 18, 1969, 51; "Men of the Year," *Time*, Jan 3, 1969; Robert Dole, interview by Timothy Naftali, OHP-RNL, Mar 4, 2008, 5.

10 Anthony Lake to Henry Kissinger, letter, Electronic Briefing Book no. 517, NSA, Jul 16, 1969; Alexander Haig, interview by Timothy Naftali, OHP-RNL, Nov 30, 2007, 9; Burr and Kimball, "Nixon, Kissinger and the Madman Strategy"; Scott Sagan and Jeremi Suri, "The Madman Nuclear Alert: Secrecy, Signaling, and Safety in October 1969," *International Security* 27, no. 4 (Spring 2003); Evan Thomas, *Being Nixon* (New York: Random House, 2016), 234.

11 Haldeman, with DiMona, *Ends of Power*, 90; Sagan and Suri, "Madman Nuclear Alert."

12 "History of Strategic Air Command, Historical Study no. 117," NSA, 1970; Burr and Kimball, "Nixon White House"; Jeremi Suri, *Henry Kissinger and the American Century* (Cambridge, MA: Harvard Univ Press, 2009), 173, emphasis in the original.

13 Associated Press, Feb 17, 1978; David Rosenbaum, "Ex-President Is Accused of Initiating Break-In at the Watergate," *New York Times*, Feb 17, 1978; William Greider, "Carter's Unheralded Milestone," *Washington Post*, Feb 26, 1978; Seymour M. Hersh, *The Price of Power: Kissinger in the Nixon White House* (New York: Touchstone, 1984). For early examples of journalists and scholars analyzing Nixon's madman theory, see Richard Betts, "Misadventure Revisited," *Wilson Quarterly* 7, no. 3 (Summer 1983): esp. 102; Edward Said, "The Palestine Question and the American Context," *Arab Studies Quarterly* 2, no. 2 (Spring 1980): 130–31; Harrison Salisbury, "The 'Madman Theory' of Dealing with Communists," *Chicago Tribune*, Apr 22, 1979, E1; Jonathan Schell, *The Fate of the Earth* (New York: Knopf, 1982); William Shawcross, "The 'Madman Theory' of Politics," *New Statesman*, Jun 15, 1979, 860–63.

14   Hersh, *Price of Power*, esp. 52–53, 118–13; Richard Nixon, *No More Vietnams* (New York: Arbor House Publishing, 1987), 103–7.

15   For use of the term *madman theory*, see Hersh, *Price of Power*, 53, 60, 75, 119, 126, 133, 173, 185, 188, 192, 305, 328, 363, 368, 424, 568, 608, 636, 670; Walter Lafeber, "Henry Kissinger and the Web of Diplomacy," *Washington Post*, Jun 12, 1983, BW1.

16   Jeffrey P. Kimball, email interview by the author, Sep 28, 2017–Oct 2, 2017; Jeffrey P. Kimball, telephone interview by the author, Jun 11, 2020; Winston Lord, interview with the author, Cambridge, MA, Sep 30, 2019. For revisionists disavowal of the madman theory, see Joan Hoff, *Reconsidered* (New York: Basic Books, 1995), 177–80, 201; Fred Greenstein, "A Journalist's Vendetta," *New Republic*, Aug 1, 1983, 29. For examples of the Haldeman quote in newspapers, see "When the Sinister Writes of the Sinister," *Globe and Mail*, Feb 18, 1978, 6; Rosenbaum, "Ex-President Accused of Initiating Break-In."

17   Kimball delivered a series of talks and published scholarly articles on Nixon's use of the madman theory through the aughts. Sagan and Suri, "The Madman Nuclear Alert," also tie the SAC exercise with nuclear intimidation of Hanoi. Kimball, email interview, Sep 28, 2017–Oct 2, 2017; Jeffrey P. Kimball, "Nixon and Historians: Perspectives on Linebacker II and the Paris Treaty" (paper presented at the Society for Historians of American Foreign Relations 16th Annual Meeting, University of Maryland, College Park, MD, Aug 2, 1990); Jeffrey Kimball "'Peace with Honor': Richard Nixon and the Diplomacy of Threat and Symbolism," in *Shadow on the White House*, ed. David L. Anderson (Lawrence: Univ Press of Kansas, 1993), 155–61; William Burr, email interview by author, Jun 18, 2020; Kimball, email interview, Sep 28, 2017–Oct 2, 2017; Burr and Kimball, *Nuclear Specter*, 1–11; Jeffrey P. Kimball, *Nixon's Vietnam* (Lawrence: Univ Press of Kansas, 1998); Sagan and Suri, "Madman Nuclear Alert."

18   "George Bush Assails Bill Clinton's 'Judgment' for Protests Overseas," *Christian Science Monitor*, Oct 15, 1992; John Herbers, "Vietnam Moratorium Observed Nationwide," *New York Times*, Oct 16, 1969, 1; Charles Debenedetti, *An American Ordeal* (Syracuse, NY: Syracuse Univ Press, 1990), 254–55; "Millions March in US Vietnam Moratorium," BBC, Oct 15, 1969; "Are You Listening Nixon," https://www.youtube.com/watch?v=ZUn-EGsNt58; Charles Debenedetti, *American Ordeal: The Antiwar Movement of the Vietnam Era* (Syracuse, NY: Syracuse Univ Press, 1990), 254–55; John Wiener, "Nixon and the 1969 Vietnam

Moratorium," *Nation*, Jan 12, 2010; John Herbers, "Moratorium Backers Say Nixon Will Have to React," *New York Times*, Oct 17, 1969, 1; "Antiwar Protests Confront Nixon Administration," *Congressional Quarterly Almanac 1969*, 25th ed. (Washington, DC: Congressional Quarterly, 1970), 1017–20; Stanley Karnow, *Vietnam: A History* (New York: Penguin Books, 1984), 599, David Greenberg, *Nixon's Shadow* (New York: W. W. Norton, 2003), 87.

19   Katherine Scott, "Nixon and Dissent," in *A Companion to Richard M. Nixon*, ed. Melvin Small (Hoboken, NJ: Wiley and Blackwell, 2011), 313; Haldeman, with DiMona, *Ends of Power*, 121; Herbers, "Moratorium Backers, 1"; Debenedetti, *American Ordeal*, 256; Chalmers Roberts, "Nixon Weights Electoral Strategy for Victory in November: 'Law and Order' Issue," *Washington Post*, Aug 9, 1968, A12; "Millions March"; "George Bush Assails"; David Reynolds, *One World Divisible* (New York: W. W. Norton, 2000), 326; Penny Lewis, *Hardhats, Hippies And Hawks* (Ithaca, NY: Cornell Univ Press, 2013), 132.

20   Jeremi Suri, "Nukes of October," *Wired*, Feb 25, 2008; Sagan and Suri, "Madman Nuclear Alert"; Melvin Laird to assistant to the president for National Security Affairs, memorandum, Oct 16, 1969, NSA; CIA report quoted in *FRUS, 1969–1976*, vol. 34, *National Security Policy, 1969–1972*, ed. Edward Coltrin Keefer and M. Todd Bennett (Washington, DC: Office of the Historian, Department of State, 2011), 234; William Burr and Jeffrey P. Kimball, "Nixon's Nuclear Ploy," *Bulletin of the Atomic Scientists*, Jan 1, 2003, https://journals .sagepub.com/doi/full/10.2968/059001011.

21   Burr and Kimball, Nuclear *Specter*, 122; Burr and Kimball, "Nixon, Kissinger and the Madman Strategy"; Laird to Kissinger, memorandum, Apr 11, 1969, in Burr and Kimball, "Nixon, Kissinger and the Madman Strategy."

22   Max Frankel, "Moscow's Man Intrigues Washington," *New York Times*, Jul 29, 1962, 10, 14, 16; Anthony Austin, "Ambassador Dobrynin, Key Man in Arms Talks," *New York Times*, Jun 4, 1979, A6; Tom Dalyell, "Anatoly Dobrynin," *Independent*, Apr 12, 2010, 42; Robert McFadden, "Anatoly F. Dobrynin, 90, Is Dead," *New York Times*, Apr 9, 2010, A19; Matt Schudel, "Soviet Ambassador to US Was Known as a Master of Diplomacy," *Washington Post*, Apr 9, 2010, B6.

23   The memorandum of conversation as recorded by the Nixon administration relayed the same sprawling conversation as Dobrynin's account but without the alarm over Nixon's disorganized discussion. Anatoly Dobrynin, "Memorandum of Conversation (USSR)," Oct 20, 1969, in *Soviet-American Relations: The*

Detent Years, 1969–1972 (Washington, DC: Government Printing Office, 2007), 90–97; "Memorandum of Conversation (US)," Oct 20, 1969, in *FRUS, Détente Years*, 87–89.

24   Dobrynin, "Memorandum of Conversation," Oct 20, 1969, 97.

25   Richard Nixon, *RN* (New York: Simon & Schuster, 1990), 405–6; "Memorandum of Conversation (US)," Oct 20, 1969, 87.

26   Suri and Sagan, "Madman Nuclear Alert."

27   Burr and Kimball, Nuclear *Specter*, 307–9; Sagan and Suri, "Madman Nuclear Alert"; Suri, "Nukes of October"; Dobrynin, "Memorandum of Conversation," Oct 20, 1969, 97.

28   Haldeman, with DiMona, *Ends of Power*, 90.

29   Adam Garfinkle, "US Decision Making in the Jordan Crisis: Correcting the Record," *Political Science Quarterly* 100, no. 1 (Spring 1985): 117–38; Ziv Rubinovitz, "Blue and White 'Black September': Israel's Role in the Jordan Crisis of 1970," *International History Review* 32, no. 4 (Dec 2010): 687–706; Nixon, *RN*, 483–86.

30   Alan Dowty, *Middle East Crisis: US Decision-Making in 1958, 1970 and 1973* (Berkeley: Univ of California Press, 1984), 161; Nixon, *RN*, 486; Burr and Kimball, *Nuclear Specter*, 328–29; Jeffrey P. Kimball, *The Vietnam War Files: Uncovering the Secret History of Nixon-Era Strategy* (Lawrence: Univ Press of Kansas, 2004), 57–59; Walter Isaacson, *Kissinger: A Biography* (New York: Simon & Schuster, 1992), 295–315; Kissinger, *White House Years*, 600–631.

31   Burr and Kimball, *Nuclear Specter*, 328–29; Kissinger, *White House Years*, 614–15.

32   Sumit Ganguly, *Conflict Unending: India-Pakistan Tensions since 1947* (New Delhi: Oxford Univ Press, 2001), 51–78; Geoffrey Warner, "Nixon, Kissinger and the Breakup of Pakistan, 1971," *International Affairs* 81, no. 5 (Oct 2005): 1097–1118; Lorraine Boissoneault, "The Genocide the US Can't Remember, but Bangladesh Can't Forget," *Smithsonian Magazine*, Dec 16, 2016; Robert Dallek, *Nixon and Kissinger: Partners in Power* (New York: Harper Perennial, 2007), 335–59.

33   Ganguly, *Conflict Unending*, 51–78; *FRUS, 1969–1976*, vol. 11, *Southeast Asia Crisis, 1971*, ed. Louis J. Smith and Edward C. Keefer (Washington, DC: U.S. Government Printing Office, 2005), 34; Burr, "Soviet Stooge"; State Department to embassy in Pakistan, telegram, *FRUS, 1969–1976*, vol. 11, *Southeast Asia Crisis, 1971*, 605–6; editorial note, in *FRUS, 1969–1976*, vol. E–7, *Documents on South Asia, 1969–1972*, ed. Louis J. Smith (Washington: U.S. Government Printing

Office, 2005), 722; editorial note in *FRUS, 1969–1976*, vol. 11, *Southeast Asia Crisis, 1971*, 781; Richard Nixon and Henry Kissinger, transcript of conversation, Apr 4, 1972, in *FRUS, 1969–1976*, vol. 14, *Soviet Union, October 1971–May 1972*, ed. David C. Geyer et al. (Washington, DC: U.S. Government Printing Office, 2006), 258–60.

34 John Farrell, *Richard Nixon: The Life* (New York: Doubleday, 2017), 452–57; Warner "Breakup of Pakistan," 1100.

35 Ganguly, *Conflict Unending*, 51–78; Burr, "Soviet Stooge"; Nixon and Kissinger, conversation, Apr 4, 1972, in *FRUS, 1969–1976*, vol. 14, *Soviet Union, October 1971–May 1972*, 258–60.

36 Douglas Brinkley and Luke Nichter, eds., *The Nixon Tapes, 1971–1972* (Boston: Houghton-Mifflin, 2014), 385, 441, 458; H. R. Haldeman, *Haldeman Diaries: Inside the Nixon White House* (New York: G. P. Putnam's Sons, 1994), Thursday, May 11, 1972,, 459; Isaacson, *Kissinger*, 415–16; Sydney Schanberg, "Retreat Leaves Small Units of Marines Facing Enemy," *New York Times*, May 3, 1972.

37 Nixon, *RN*, 586, 590; Kissinger, *White House Years*, 1098, 1109; Richard Nixon and Henry Kissinger, conversation, Apr 13, 1972, 2:16 p.m., in Brinkley and Nichter, *Tapes, 1971–1972*, 463.

38 Nixon, *RN*, 588–89.

39 Richard Nixon et al., conversation, Apr 3, 1972, in *FRUS, 1969–1976*, vol. 8, *Vietnam, January–October 1972*, ed. John M. Carland (Washington, DC: Office of the Historian, Department of State, 2010), 250–53; Burr and Kimball, *Nuclear Specter*, 320.

40 Richard Nixon et al., conversation, May 4, 1972, 4:52 p.m., in *FRUS*, vol. 8, *Vietnam, January–October 1972*, 732–37; Rick Perlstein, *Nixonland: The Rise of a President and the Fracturing of America* (New York: Scribner, 2009), 656; Nixon, *RN*, 593.

41 Richard Nixon and Henry Kissinger, conversation, Apr 19, 1972, in *FRUS, 1969–1976*, vol. 8, *Vietnam, January–October 1972*, 427–48; Richard Nixon, John Connally, Thomas Moorer and Henry Kissinger, conversation, May 4, 1972, 3:04 p.m., in Brinkley and Nichter, *Tapes, 1971–1972*, 541; Nixon, Connally, Moorer and Kissinger, conversation, May 4, 1972, 3:04 p.m., in Brinkley and Nichter, *Tapes, 1971–1972*, 537.

42 Richard Nixon and Henry Kissinger, conversation, May 19, 1972, in *FRUS, 1969–1976*, vol. 8, *Vietnam, January–October 1972*; Nixon, *RN*, 602–7, emphasis in

the original; Michael Getler, "US Expands B-52 Force, Bombing List," *Washington Post*, May 25, 1972, A1; Lee Lescaze, "US Cites Heavy N. Viet Bomb Damage," *Washington Post*, May 17, 1972, A8; Charles Loeb, "World on View: A Calculated Risk," *Call and Post*, May 20, 1972, 2B.

43 Linda Charlton, "Antiwar Protests Rise Here and across the Country," *New York Times*, May 11, 1972, 1; John Darnton, "Hundreds Are Arrested in Antiwar Demonstrations," *New York Times*, May 11, 1972; Bart Barnes, "War Protest at Capitol Shuts Gallery," *Washington Post*, A1; "Protests Mount over Viet Harbor Mines," *Washington Post*, May 11, 1972, A16.

44 Nixon, *RN*, 600; Burr and Kimball, *Nuclear Specter*, 321; Nixon and Kissinger, conversation, Apr 19, 1972, *FRUS, 1969–1976*, vol. 8, *Vietnam, January–October 1972*, 427–48.

45 Nixon, *RN*, 607; emphasis in the original

46 James Chiles, "Go to Defcon 3," *Air & Space*, Mar 2014.

47 Dallek, *Nixon and Kissinger*, 515, 518; Craig Daigle, *The Limits of Détente* (New Haven, CT: Yale Univ Press, 2012), 319–22; David Morse, *Kissinger and the Yom Kippur War* (New York: McFarland, 2015), 149–51; Chiles, "Defcon 3"; Timothy Naftali, "CIA Reveals Its Secret Briefings to Presidents Nixon and Ford," CNN, Aug 26, 2016.

48 Abraham Rabinovich, "The Little-Known US-Soviet Confrontation during Yom Kippur War," *Global Post*, Oct 26, 2012; Dallek, *Nixon and Kissinger*, 525; Victor Israelian, "Nuclear Showdown as Nixon Slept," *Christian Science Monitor*, Nov 3, 1993.

49 Morse, *Kissinger and the Yom Kippur War*, 149, emphasis in the original; Daigle, *Limits of Détente*, 319–20.

50 Abraham Rabinovich, *The Yom Kippur War: The Epic Encounter That Transformed the Middle East* (New York: Schocken, 2005), 480; Dallek, *Nixon and Kissinger*, 530, 524; Alexander Haig, *Inner Circles: How America Changed the World: A Memoir* (New York: Grand Central, 1992), 415–16.

51 Memorandum for the record, Oct 24–25, 1973, 10:30 p.m.–3:30 a.m., in *FRUS, 1969–1976*, vol. 25, *Arab-Israeli Crisis and War, 1973*, ed. Nina Howland and Craig Daigle (Washington, DC: Government Printing Office, 2011), 737–41

52 Gerald S. Strober and Deborah H. Strober, *Nixon: An Oral History of His Presidency* (New York: HarperCollins, 1994), 156–57.

53 Memorandum for the record, Oct 24–25, 1973; Kissinger, *Years of Upheaval*, Kindle.

54   Israelian, "Nuclear Showdown"; Rabinovich, *Yom Kippur War*, 539–41; Morse, *Kissinger*, 156–160; Daigle, *Limits of Détente*, 324–26.

55   Israelian, "Nuclear Showdown"; Daigle, *Limits of Détente*, 325–28.

56   Israelian, "Nuclear Showdown."

57   Nixon-Gannon, May 27, 1983, part 4.

58   Burr and Kimball, Nuclear *Specter*, 333; Jeremi Suri, "Henry Kissinger and American Grand Strategy," in Logevall and Prescott, *Nixon in the World*, 75, emphasis in the original

59   Nixon and Kissinger, conversation, Dec 12, 1971, in Burr, "Soviet Stooge."

60   "The President's News Conference," Oct 26, 1973, transcript, American Presidency Project, https://www.presidency.ucsb.edu/documents/the -presidents-news-conference-84.

7. MADNESS CONTROLLED

1   "First Inaugural Address of Richard M. Nixon," Jan 20, 1969, Avalon Project, https://avalon.law.yale.edu/20th_century/nixon1.asp (hereinafter Nixon, "First Inaugural").

2   Nixon and Kissinger, conversation, Feb 14, 1972, 4:09–6:19 p.m., *FRUS, 1969–1976*, vol. 17, *China, 1969–1972*, ed. Stephen E. Philips (Washington, DC: Government Printing Office, 2006), 661–67; Richard Nixon, *RN* (New York: Simon & Schuster, 1990), 558–59; Nixon-Gannon, May 13, 1983, part 2.

3   Nixon and Kissinger, conversation, Feb 14, 1972, 4:09–6:19 p.m., 661–67.

4   Garry Wills, *Nixon Agonistes: The Crisis of the Self-Made Man* (New York: First Mariner Books, 2002), 432.

5   Schulzinger, "Détente, in the Nixon-Ford Years, 1969–1976," in *The Cambridge History of the Cold War*, ed. Melvin Leffler and Odd Arne Westad, vol. 2 (Cambridge: Cambridge Univ Press, 2012), 373–94; David Reynolds, *One World Divisible* (New York: W.W. Norton, 2000), 322–69; Daniel J. Sargent, *A Superpower Transformed: The Remaking of American Foreign Relations in the 1970s* (Oxford: Oxford Univ Press, 2015), 1–7; Mattias Fibiger, "The Nixon Doctrine and the Making of Authoritarianism in Island Southeast Asia," *Diplomatic History*, Aug 21, 2021; Stephen Daggett, "Costs of Major U.S. Wars," *Congressional Research Service Report*, June 29, 2010; Henry Kissinger, *The White House Years* (Boston: Little, Brown and Co., 1979), 222, emphasis in original; Kissinger to Nixon, memorandum, n.d., *Foreign Relations of the United States* (hereinafter

FRUS), *1969–1976*, vol. 1, *Foundations of Foreign Policy, 1969–1972*, ed. Louis J. Smith and David H. Herschler (Washington, DC: Government Printing Office, 2003), 111; Thomas C. Schelling, *Arms and Influence* (New Haven, CT: Yale Univ Press, 1966), 124–25; Henry Kissinger, *A World Restored: Metternich, Castlereagh and the Problems of Peace, 1812–22* (Washington, D.C.: Universal Library, 1964), 1; Zhou Enlai et al., memorandum of conversation, Jul 10, 1971, 12:10–6 p.m., *FRUS, 1969–1976*, vol. 17, *China, 1969–1972*, 403; Henry Kissinger, *Diplomacy* (New York: Simon & Schuster, 1994), 703; Fredrik Logevall and Andrew Preston, eds., introduction, *Nixon in the World: American Foreign Relations, 1969–1977* (Oxford: Oxford Univ Press, 2008), 5.

6   For a well-researched recent studies of Nixon's grand strategy as realpolitik, see Chris Tudda, *Cold War Turning Point*, and Fibiger, "Nixon Doctrine." For a similar but traditional assessment, see Robert S. Litwak, *Détente and the Nixon Doctrine* (Cambridge: Cambridge Univ Press, 1984), and Joan Hoff, *Reconsidered* (New York: Basic Books, 1995), 194–200. Tudda, *Turning Point*, 91; "Richard Nixon: Address Accepting the Presidential Nomination at the Republican National Convention in Miami Beach Florida," Aug 8, 1968, American Presidency Project, https://www.presidency.ucsb.edu/documents/address -accepting-the-presidential-nomination-the-republican-national-convention -miami (hereinafter, Nixon, "1968 Acceptance Speech"); Sargent, *Superpower Transformed*, 9–10; "Nixon's Report to Congress on Foreign Policy," *New York Times*, Feb 19, 1970; Kissinger, *World Restored*.

7   Fibiger, "Nixon Doctrine"; John Farrell, *Richard Nixon: The Life* (New York: Doubleday, 2017), 428.

8   By making peace with China, Nixon further calculated that he could coopt and fend off the challenge from his liberal flank, preempting his liberal adversaries like Senators Mike Mansfield and Ted Kennedy, who had been calling for just such a détente in Sino-U.S. relations. Indeed, an impetus for the trip was concern that Kennedy would go to China first. Jeremi Suri, *Power and Protest: Global Revolution and the Rise of Détente* (Cambridge, MA: Harvard Univ Press, 2005); James Mann, *About Face: A History of America's Curious Relationship with China, from Nixon to Clinton* (New York: Vintage, 2000), 28. For further analysis of détente between the United States, China and the Soviet Union as a sign of domestic weakness, see Keith L. Nelson, *The Making of Détente* (Baltimore: Johns Hopkins Univ Press, 1995); Sargent, *Superpower Transformed*.

9   Further, in Kissinger's judgment, better relations with China could shore up the socialist state as a stable power. A concurrent U.S.-Soviet détente would ease tensions, buying time for China to develop the capability to deter the Soviet Union on its own. If managed correctly, this two-track détente, the national security advisor estimated, could "gain time to paralyze" the Soviet Union with an assured China at its border. On triangulation, see Suri, *Power and Protest*, esp. 214, Logevall and Preston, introduction, *Nixon in the World*, 12; Nancy Bernkopf Tucker, "Taiwan Expendable? Nixon and Kissinger Go to China," *Journal of American History* 92, no. 1 (Jun 2005): 112. Mann, *About Face*, 56; Marc Trachtenberg, "The Structure of Great Power Politics, 1963–1975," in Leffler and Westad, *Cambridge History*, 498–99.

10 Walter Isaacson, *Kissinger: A Biography* (New York: Simon & Schuster, 1992), 334; H. R. Haldeman, interview by Raymond H. Geselbracht and Fred J. Graboske, OHP-RNL, Aug 13, 1987.

11 Nixon and Kissinger, conversation, Feb 14, 1972, 4:09–6:19 p.m., 661–67.

12 Richard Nixon et al., Beijing, memorandum of conversation, Feb 22, 1972, 2:10–6:00 p.m., *FRUS, 1969–1976*, vol. 17, *China, 1969–1972*, 694–718.

13 Stephen Ambrose, "Nixon and Vietnam: Vietnam and Electoral Politics," Kansas State University, Department of History, Eisenhower Lecture Series, n.d., https://www.k-state.edu/history/eisenlecture/3lecture.html; "Briefing Book Kissinger's Secret Trip," briefing book, July 1971, SCRIBD, https://www.scribd.com/document/58767074/Polo-I-Briefing-Book-Kissinger-s-Secret-Trip-to-China-July-1971, 62; Jeffrey P. Kimball, "Passport," *Society for Historians of American Foreign Relations*, Sep 2001, https://jewlscholar.mtsu.edu/items/65e9d72a-04fe-43e2-9586-aefea7e47920; Richard Nixon and Henry Kissinger, Aug 3, 1972, 8:28 a.m., conversation 760-006, excerpt A, *Presidential Recordings, Digital Edition*, Fatal Politics series, ed. Ken Hughes, Univ of Virginia Press, 2014–, http://prde.upress.virginia.edu/conversations/4006748.

14 Richard Nixon et al., memorandum of conversation, Feb 23, 1972, 2:00–6:00 p.m., *FRUS, 1969–1976*, vol. 17, *China, 1969–1972*, 719–52; H. R. Haldeman, *Haldeman Diaries: Inside the Nixon White House* (New York: G. P. Putnam's Sons, 1994), Wednesday, June 2, 1971, 295; Nixon-Gannon, Apr 8, 1983, part 1.

15 Haldeman, *Diaries*, Monday, January 20, 1969, 18; Jeffrey P. Kimball, "The Nixon Doctrine: A Saga of Misunderstanding," *Presidential Studies Quarterly* 36,

no. 1 (Mar 2006): 66; Rob Kilpatrick, *1969: The Year Everything Changed* (New York: Skyhorse, 2011), 1.

16   Richard Nixon, *In the Arena* (New York: Pocket, 1990), n.p.; Eleanor Harris, "The Darkest Hours of the Richard Nixons," *Washington Post*, Mar 4, 1956, AW1.

17   Nixon and Kissinger, conversation, Feb 14, 1972, 4:09–6:19 p.m., 661–67; Stanley Hoffman, *Gulliver's Troubles, or the Setting of American Foreign Policy* (New York: McGraw-Hill, 1968), xviii; "Malraux: Writer, War Hero, De Gaulle Aide," *New York Times*, Nov 24, 1976, 1; Joseph Kraft, "The Meaning of Malraux," *Washington Post*, Dec 5, 1976, 37; Douglas Brinkley and Luke Nichter, eds., *The Nixon Tapes, 1971–1972* (Boston: Houghton-Mifflin, 2014), 391, 402; Margaret MacMillan, *Nixon and Mao: The Week That Changed the World* (New York: Random House, 2007), 17.

18   Nixon-Gannon, May 27, 1983, part 1; Nixon, *RN*, 558–59; "Toasts of the President and Chairman Chang Ch'un-ch'iao at a Banquet in Shanghai," Feb 27, 1972, transcript, American Presidency Project, https://www.presidency.ucsb .edu/documents/toasts-the-president-and-chairman-chang-chun-chiao -banquet-shanghai, 374.

19   MacMillan, *Nixon and Mao*, 11; Farrell, *Richard Nixon*, 7, 66.

20   Tucker, "Taiwan Expendable," 116; "October 7, 1960, Debate Transcript," The Second Kennedy-Nixon Presidential Debate, Commission on Presidential Debates, https://www.debates.org/voter-education/debate-transcripts/october -7-1960-debate-transcript/; "Excerpts from Vice President's Radio and Television Speech," *U.S. News & World Report*, Jan 1, 1954, 68; Robert J. McMahon, *The Limits of Empire* (New York: Columbia Univ Press, 1999), 166.

21   Kissinger, *White House Years*, 1070; Mann, *About Face*, 16; Ross Terrill, "Facing the Dragon," *Australian Strategic Policy*, May 1, 2013, 11; Tudda, *Turning Point*, 22.

22   Richard Nixon, "Address to the Bohemian Club, San Francisco," Jul 29, 1967, *FRUS, 1969–1976*, vol. 1, *Foundations of Foreign Policy*, 2–4; Nixon, "First Inaugural"; Isaacson, *Kissinger*, 335.

23   "Initial Remarks in Guam with Newsman," Jul 25, 1969, transcript, American Presidency Project, https://www.presidency.ucsb.edu/documents/informal -remarks-guam-with-newsmen.

24   Nixon, "Initial Remarks in Guam"; Editorial Note 29, *FRUS*, vol. 1, *Foundations of Foreign Policy, 1969–1972*, 91–92; Nixon, *RN*, 395.

25   Jussi M. Hanhimäki, "An Elusive Grand Design," in Logevall and Preston, *Nixon in the World*, 38–40; Kimball, "Nixon Doctrine," 59–60.

26   Sargent, *Superpower Transformed*, 42; Fibiger, "Nixon Doctrine"; Kimball, "Nixon Doctrine," 59–60.

27   John Herbers, "Nixon Will Visit China before Next May to Seek a 'Normalization of Relations,'" *New York Times*, Jul 16, 1971, 1; "Text of Nixon Speech on China," *Chicago Tribune*, Jul 16, 1971, 2; Nicholas von Hoffman, "Shattering Jolt: China Visit," *Washington Post*, Jul 26, 1971, B1; Max Frankel, "Nixon Goes to China," *Media Studies Journal* 13 (1999): 40; Gerald S. Strober and Deborah Hart Strober, eds., *Nixon: An Oral History of His Presidency* (New York: Harper Collins, 1994), 132–33; John Lewis Gaddis, *Strategies of Containment* (Oxford: Oxford Univ Press, 1982), 275.

28   "Report from Hong Kong on Nixon Trip," transcript, *All Things Considered*, NPR, Jul 16, 1971, https://www.proquest.com/docview/2298263107 /48CAB4DE7E734F60PQ/1?accountid=14925; "Peking Reports on US 'Awakening,'" *Washington Post*, Jul 26, 1971, A20.

29   John W. Garver, *China's Quest: The History of the Foreign Relations of the People's Republic of China* (Oxford: Oxford Univ Press, 2016), 292; MacMillan, *Nixon and Mao*, 125; Nixon et al., memorandum of conversation, Feb 23, 1972, 2:00–6:00 p.m., 694–718; Sergey Radchenko, "The Sino-Soviet Split," in Leffler and Westad, *Cambridge History*, 349–72.

30   Barbara Barnouin and Yu Changgen, *Chinese Foreign Policy during the Cultural Revolution* (Totnes, UK: Kegan Paul International), 86–90; David Reynolds, *One World Divisible* (New York: W.W. Norton, 2000), 324.

31   Wen-Qing Ngoei, "'A Wide Anticommunist Arc': Britain, ASEAN and Nixon's Triangular Diplomacy, *Diplomatic History* 41, no. 5 (Nov 2017): 903–32; Guolin Yi, "The 'Propaganda State' and the Sino-American Rapprochement," *Journal of American-East Asian Relations* 20 (2013): 5–28; Marshall Green, self-interview, "Evolution of US-China Policy 1956–1973: Memoirs of an Insider," 1998, 27, FA-OHP; Henry Kissinger, interview by Susan Johnson, Jul 25, 2012, 3, FA-OHP; Nixon et al., Beijing, memorandum of conversation, Feb 22, 1972, 2:10–6 p.m., 694–718; Tudda, *Turning Point*, 93, 16–17; Jian Chin, *Mao's China and the Cold War* (Chapel Hill: Univ of North Carolina Press, 2010), 243–49; Evelyn Goh, "The China Card" in *A Companion to Richard M. Nixon*, ed. Melvin

Small (Hoboken, NJ: Wiley and Blackwell, 2011), 431; Henry Kissinger, *On China* (New York: Penguin, 2011), 23.

32   "China Speech, Fine Dinner Leave Nixon in Good Mood," *Chicago Tribune*, Jul 17, 1971, 3; Garry Wills, "Nixon's Approach to the Chinese," *Washington Post*, Jul 26, 1971; Isaacson, *Kissinger*, 347.

33   Tudda, *Turning Point*, 100; Selig S. Harrison, "Taiwan Protests Nixon Announcement," *Washington Post*, Jul 16, 1971, A18; Strober and Strober, *Oral History*, 132; MacMillan, *Nixon and Mao*, 295.

34   Richard Nixon, "Asia after Viet Nam," *Foreign Affairs*, Oct 1967; Kissinger, *White House Years*, 1049.

35   John Holdridge, *Crossing the Divide: An Insider's Account of the Normalization of U.S.-China Relations* (Lanham, MD, 1971), 87; Kissinger, *Diplomacy*, 723; Jung Chang and Jon Halliday, *Mao: The Unknown Story* (New York: Alfred A. Knopf, 2005), 580, 583; Yeh Chien-ying et al., Jul 11, 1971, 12:00–1:40 a.m., and 9:50 a.m.–10:35 a.m., NSA.

36   Kissinger claimed to have broached the idea of a détente with China in a discussion about a 1968 campaign speech he was writing for Nelson Rockefeller, then a candidate for the Republican nomination for president. Tudda, *Turning Point*, 8; Isaacson, *Kissinger*, 336; Chang and Halliday, *Mao*, 583; Margaret MacMillan, "Nixon, Kissinger, and the Opening to China," in Logevall and Prescott, *Nixon in the World*, 111; Strober and Strober, *Oral History*, 130; Nixon and Ehrlichman, conversation, Jan 24, 1972, 1:51 p.m., Brinkley and Nichter, *Nixon Tapes, 1971–1972*, 357; Kissinger, *Diplomacy*, 726; Mann, *About Face*, 25–26; Strober and Strober, *Oral History*, 129–33; Kissinger, *On China*, 296–97; Kissinger, *Diplomacy*, 721.

37   Strober and Strober, *Oral History*, 134; "Remarks to Midwestern News Media Executives Attending a Briefing on Domestic Policy in Kansas City," Jul 6, 1971, transcript, American Presidency Project; Chang and Halliday, *Mao*, 583; Yeh et al., memorandum, Jul 11, 1971, 12:00–1:40 a.m. and 9:50 a.m.–10:35 a.m., NSA.

38   Kissinger, *White House Years*, 187; Nixon et al., memorandum of conversation, Feb 23, 1972, 2:00–6:00 p.m., *FRUS, 1969–1976*, vol. 17, *China, 1969–1972*, 694–718; Nixon and Kissinger, conversation, Apr 23, 1971, 11:56 a.m., Brinkley and Nichter, *Nixon Tapes, 1971–1972*, 106.

39   Isaacson, *Kissinger*, 399–400; Tizoc Chavez, "'One Picture May Not Be Worth Ten Thousand Words, but the White House Is Betting It's Worth Ten Thousand

Votes': Richard Nixon and Diplomacy as Spectacle," in *The Cold War at Home and Abroad: Domestic Politics and U.S. Foreign Policy since 1945*, ed. Andrew Johns and Mitchell Lerner (Lexington: Univ Press of Kentucky, 2018), 146–72; MacMillan, *Nixon and Mao*, 273–74; Stanley Karnow, "Zhou Greets Nixon Amid Prospects of a Historic New Era," *Washington Post*, Feb 21, 1972; Dwight Chapin, interview by Timothy Naftali, OHP-RNL, Apr 2, 2007, 54; Kissinger, OHP-RNL, 49; Don Oberdorfer, "Life, from Peking . . . ," *Washington Post*, Jan 16, 1972, B7; Kissinger, *White House Years*, 1066.

40 Michelle Murray Yang, "President Nixon's Speeches and Toasts during His 1972 Trip to China," *Rhetoric and Public Affairs* 14, no. (Spring 2011): 9; Nixon and Kissinger, conversation, Feb 14, 1972, 4:09–6:19 p.m., 661–67.

41 Haldeman, *Diaries*, Thursday, February 17, 1972, 411; Stanley Karnow, "Nixon Sees Mao, Chou in Day of Cordiality," *Washington Post*, Feb 22, 1972, A1; Max Frankel, "Like a Trip to the Moon," *New York Times*, Feb 20, 1972, 1.

42 Nixon, *Arena*, 4; Richard Nixon et al., memorandum of conversation, Feb 21, 1972, 5:58–6:55 p.m., *FRUS, 1969–1976*, vol. 17, *China, 1969–1972*, 685–93; Jian, *Mao's China*, 274; Haldeman, *Diaries*, Sunday, February 20, and Monday, February 21, 1972, 412; MacMillan, *Nixon and Mao*, 150; Kissinger, *White House Years*, 1055; Nixon, *RN*, 559–560.

43 Nixon, *Arena*, 4–5, 10; Isaacson, *Kissinger*, 344; Kissinger, *White House Years*, 347; Kissinger, *On China*, 241; Haldeman, OHP-RNL, Aug 13, 1987, 75.

44 "Excerpts from Soviet Article about US-Chinese Relations," *New York Times*, Aug 11, 1971.

45 Richard Solomon, *Chinese Political Negotiating Behavior, 1967–1984* (Santa Monica, CA: RAND, 1995), 3–6; Kissinger, *On China*, 237–45; MacMillan, *Nixon and Mao*, 146, 208; Winston Lord, interview by Charles Stuart Kennedy and Nancy Bernkopf Tucker, Apr 28, 1998, FA-OHP.

46 Green, "China Policy," FA-OHP, 30.

47 Nixon, *RN*, 572–73; Haldeman, *Diaries*, Thursday, February 24, 1972, 419; Lord, FA-OHP; Jeremi Suri, *Henry Kissinger and the American Century* (Cambridge, MA: Harvard Univ Press, 2009), 181; Green, "China Policy," FA-OHP, 30.

48 Michelle Murray Yang, "President Nixon's Speeches and Toasts during His 1972 Trip to China," *Rhetoric and Public Affairs* 14, no. (Spring 2011): 3; Kissinger, *White House Years*; Richard Nixon and Henry Kissinger, conversation, Feb

14, 1972, 4:09 p.m., in Brinkley and Nichter, *Nixon Tapes, 1971–1972*, 402; Haldeman, *Diaries*, Friday, Oct 2, 1970, 200–201;; Nixon and Kissinger, conversation, Feb 14, 1972, 4:09–6:19 p.m., 661–67; Karnow, "Zhou Greets Nixon"; Terrill, "Facing the Dragon," 14; MacMillan, *Nixon and Mao*, 20.

49 MacMillan, *Nixon and Mao*, 22–24; Kissinger, *White House Years*, 1055–62.

50 Haldeman, *Diaries*, Sunday, February 20, 1972, 412, Monday, February 21, 1972, 413; MacMillan, *Nixon and Mao*, 22.

51 Karnow, "Nixon Sees Mao," A1; Kissinger, *On China*, 255; Kissinger, *White House Years*, 1057; Chang and Halliday, *Mao*, 584; Strober and Strober, *Oral History*, 135.

52 Kissinger, *On China*, 256; Nixon, *RN*, 572–73; Haldeman, *Diaries*, Sunday, February 20, 412, Monday, February 21, 1972, 413; Kissinger, *White House Years*, 1084; Roderick MacFarquhar, "Nixon's China Pilgrimage," *World Today* 28, no. 4 (Apr 1972): 155.

53 Kissinger, *White House Years*, 1159; Kissinger, *Diplomacy*, 727, 730; Suri, *Kissinger*, 234.

54 Karnow, "Nixon Sees Mao" A1; Kissinger, *White House Years*, 1057, 1059; Kissinger, *On China*, 257; Isaacson, *Kissinger*, 401; Yang, "President Nixon's Speeches," 10–11; Mao Zedong et al., memorandum of conversation, Feb 21, 1972, 2:50–3:55 p.m., *FRUS*, vol. 17, *China, 1969–1972*, 681–83; Chang and Halliday, *Mao*, 583; MacMillan, *Nixon and Mao*, 65.

55 Mao et al., memorandum of conversation, Feb 21, 1972, 2:50–3:55 p.m., 679–84.

56 Mao et al., memorandum of conversation, Feb 21, 1972, 2:50–3:55 p.m., 697–84.

57 Nixon, *RN*, 561, 572–72; Mao et al., memorandum of conversation, Feb 21, 1972, 2:50 p.m.–3:55 p.m., 679–84.

58 Mao et al., memorandum of conversation, Feb 21, 1972, 2:50–3:55 p.m., 679–84; Nixon-Gannon, May 27, 1983, part 1.

59 Kissinger, *White House Years*, 1057; Nixon-Gannon, May 13, 1983, part 3; Nixon et al., Beijing, Feb 22, 1972, memorandum of conversation, 2:10–6:00 p.m., , 694–718; Mao et al., memorandum of conversation, Feb 21, 1972, 2:50 p.m.–3:55 p.m., 697–84; Strober and Strober, *Oral History*, 135–36.

60 Karnow, "Nixon Sees Mao," A1; "China Band Draws Nixon Raves," *Chicago Tribune*, Feb 22, 1972, 3; Haldeman, *Diaries*, Tuesday, Feb 22, 1972, 416, Chapin, OHP-RNL, 53.

61 Yang, "Nixon's Speeches," 24.

62 MacMillan, *Nixon and Mao*, 148; Lord, FA-OHP; MacFarquhar, "China Pilgrimage," 154; Isaacson, *Kissinger*, 402; Nixon-Gannon, May 13, 1983, part 4; Anne Collins Walker, *China Calls: Paving the Way for Nixon's Historic Journey to China* (Seattle: Madison Books, 2012), 229; Haldeman, *Diaries*, Sunday, February 20, and Monday, February 21, 1972, 415–16; Nixon et al., memorandum of conversation, Feb 22, 1972, 2:10–6:00 p.m., 694–718.

63 Haldeman, *Diaries*, Wednesday, Feb 23, 1972, 418; Lord, FA-OHP.

64 Nixon, *RN*, 572–73; Nixon et al, conversation, Mar 13, 1972, 10:15 a.m., Brinkley and Nichter, *Nixon Tapes, 1971–1972*, 417–18; "2 Mush [sic] Oxen Are Going to China as Nixon Gifts," *New York Times*, Feb 18, 1972.

65 Nixon-Gannon, May 13, 1983, part 3; Kissinger, *On China*; Nixon et al., memorandum of conversation, Feb 21, 1972, 5:58–6:55 p.m., 685–93; Nixon et al., memorandum of conversation, Feb 22, 1972, 2:10–6:00 p.m., 694–718; Nixon et al., memorandum of conversation, Feb 23, 1972, 2:00–6:00 p.m., 694–718; Richard Nixon et al., memorandum of conversation, Feb 24, 1972, 5:15–8:05 p.m., *FRUS, 1969–1976*, vol. 17, *China, 1969–1972*, 761–85; Nixon et al., memorandum of conversation, Feb 25, 1972, 5:45–6:45 p.m., *FRUS, 1969–1976*, vol. 17, *China, 1969–1972*, 785–94; Richard Nixon et al., memorandum of conversation, Feb 26, 1972, 9:20–10:05 a.m., *FRUS, 1969–1976*, vol. 17, *China, 1969–1972*, 795–801; Richard Nixon et al., memorandum of conversation, Feb 28, 1972, 8:30–9:30 a.m., *FRUS, 1969–1976*, vol. 17, *China, 1969–1972*, 817–24.

66 Nixon, *On China*, Kindle; Nixon et al., memorandum of conversation, Feb 21, 1972, 5:58–6:55 p.m., 685–93; Nixon et al., memorandum of conversation, Feb 22, 1972, 2:10–6 p.m.; Nixon et al., memorandum of conversation, Feb 23, 1972, 2:00–6:00 p.m.; MacMillan, *Nixon and Mao*, 246–60.

67 Kissinger, *Diplomacy*, 728; "Joint Statement Following Discussions with Leaders of the People's Republic of China," *FRUS, 1969–1976*, vol. 17, *China, 1969–1972*, 812–16.

68 "Joint Statement Following Discussions with Leaders of the People's Republic of China," 812–16.

69 Goh, "China Card," 434.

70 Stanley Karnow, "Chou Greets Nixon Amid Prospects of a Historic New Era," *Washington Post*, Feb 21, 1972; John W. Finney, "Congress Chiefs Pleased," *New York Times*, Jul 16, 1971, 1; Frankel, "Nixon Goes to China," 40; Kissinger, *White House Years*, 769; Kissinger, *On China*, 270.

71 Kissinger, *Diplomacy*, 728–30.

72 Strober and Strober, *Oral History*, 132; Mann, *About Face*, 53–54; Reynolds, *One World*, 329; Nixon et al., memorandum of conversation, Feb 22, 1972, 2:10–6:00 p.m.," 694–718; Nixon et al., memorandum of conversation, Feb 24, 1972, 5:15–8:05 p.m.," 761–85; Winston Lord to Kissinger, "Memcon of Your Conversation with Chou En-Lai," Jul 29, 1971, NSA; Tucker, "Taiwan Expendable," 109–35.

73 Chang and Halliday, *Mao*, 586–87; Chen Jian, "China and the Cold War after Mao," in Leffler and Westad, *Cambridge Companion*, 186.

74 Jussi Hanhimäki, "Foreign Policy Overview," in Small, *Companion*, 353–55; Sargent, *Superpower Transformed*, 155; Gaddis, *Strategies*, 310–29.

75 Nixon, "1968 Acceptance Speech"; "Report by President Nixon to the Congress," Feb 18, 1970, *FRUS, 1969–1976*, vol. 1, *Foundations of Foreign Policy, 1969–1972*, 195; Sargent, *Superpower Transformed*, 68–69, 155.

76 Fibinger, "Nixon Doctrine"; Sargent, *Superpower Transformed*, 68; Kissinger, *A World Restored* (Washington, D.C.: Universal Library, 1964), 2, 316; Kissinger, "Peace, Legitimacy, and the Equilibrium: A Study of the Statesmanship of Castlereagh and Metternich" (PhD diss., Harvard Univ, 1954); Kissinger, *White House Years*, 1074–75.

77 Robert Sam Anson, *Exile: The Unquiet Oblivion of Richard Nixon* (New York: Simon & Schuster, 1984); "Text of Nixon Toast at Shanghai Dinner," *New York Times*, Feb 27, 1972, 16.

78 Haldeman, *Diaries*, Wednesday, Jun 2, 1971, 295; Nixon-Gannon, May 13, 1983, part 3; Richard Reeves, *Richard Nixon: Alone in the White House* (New York: Simon & Schuster, 2001), 343.

79 Haldeman, *Diaries*, Wednesday, Jun 2, 1971, 295.

80 Nixon-Gannon, May 13, 1983, part 3; Kenneth Thompson, *The Nixon Presidency: Twenty-Two Intimate Perspectives on Richard M. Nixon* (Ann Arbor: Univ of Michigan Press, 1987), 128.

81 Kissinger, *Diplomacy*, 51–53, 707–42.

82 Kissinger, *Diplomacy*, 707–42; William Safire, *Before the Fall* (New York: Routledge, 2017), 4.

83 Hanhimäki, "Elusive Grand Strategy," 25–44.

84 Nixon and Kissinger, conversation, Apr 19, 1972, 3:27 p.m., Brinkley and Nichter, *Nixon Tapes, 1971–1972*, 495; Richard Nixon et al., conversation, May 4,

1972, 3:04 p.m., Brinkley and Nichter, *Nixon Tapes, 1971–1972*, 537; Kimball, "Nixon Doctrine."

85 "15,000 Welcome President," *Washington Post*, Feb 29, 1972; "With Varying Motives 15,000 Gather at Andrews for President's Arrival," *Washington Post*, Feb 29, 1972; MacMillan, *Nixon and Mao*, 149, 321; "President Home after China Trip," *New York Times*, Feb 29, 1972, 1.

86 Haldeman, *Diaries*, Tuesday, October 12, 1971, 363; Isaacson, *Kissinger*, 406.

87 Reeves, *Alone in the White House*, 22.

CONCLUSION

1 Marshall McLuhan, "The Debates," *New York Times*, Sep 23, 1976.

2 Stanley I. Kutler, *The Wars of Watergate* (New York: W. W. Norton, 1992), 617; Gerald S. Strober and Deborah H. Strober, eds., *Nixon: An Oral History of His Presidency* (New York: HarperCollins, 1994), 345.

3 Frank Leonard, memorandum, "There's Something about the Guy I Just Don't Like," Mar 29, 1971, WHSF-CMC, box 1, folder 2; Jonathan Aitken, *Nixon: A Life* (New York: Regnery, 1994), 2.

4 Marvin Kalb, *The Nixon Memo* (Chicago: Univ of Chicago Press, 1994), 1216; John Herbers, "He Wanted a More Open White House, Didn't Get It," *New York Times*, Mar 3, 1974; Strober and Strober, *Oral History*, 449; Nicholas von Hoffman, "When Push Comes to Shove," *Washington Post*, Aug 24, 1973; Melvin Small, *The Presidency of Richard Nixon* (Lawrence, KS: Univ of Kansas Press); David Greenberg, *Nixon's Shadow* (New York: W. W. Norton, 2003), 256–60; Stewart Alsop, "Mr. Nixon under Stress," *Newsweek*, Aug 27, 1973; Mark Feeney, *Nixon at the Movies* (Chicago: Univ of Chicago Press, 2004), 250.

5 Strober and Strober, *Oral History*, 459; Small, *Presidency*, Kindle; Keith Olson, "Watergate," in *A Companion to Richard M. Nixon*, ed. Melvin Small (Hoboken, NJ: Wiley and Blackwell, 2011), 482–86; "5 Lowest Job Approval Ratings for US President," *U.S. News & World Report*, Oct 3, 2008.

6 Aitken, *A Life*, 533, 536–37; Ambrose, *Ruin and Recovery*, 465; Martz et al., "Long Road Back"; John Farrell, *Richard Nixon: The Life* (New York: Doubleday, 2017), 535–37, 547–48.

7 Ambrose, *Ruin and Recovery*, 465; Baumgold, "Nixon's New Life"; David M. Alpern and John J. Lindsay, "Watching Nixon," *Newsweek*, May 16, 1977, 29;

Michael Reese and John J. Lindsay, "Nixon: 'Never Look Back,'" *Newsweek*, Jun 14, 1982, 38.

8   Aitken, *A Life*, 531, Julie Baumgold, "Nixon's New Life in New York," *New York Magazine*, Jun 9, 1980; Stephen Ambrose, *Nixon*, vol. 3, *Ruin and Recovery, 1973–1990* (New York: Simon & Schuster, 1991); 584, 590; Richard Nixon, *Leaders* (New York: Warner Books, 1982), 70–71.

9   "White House: A Stout If Rambling Defense," *Time*, May 27, 1974, 16"; "An Old China Hand," *Newsweek*, March 8, 1976, 38; Baumgold, "Nixon's New Life"; "Nixon Comes Back into the Limelight—and Controversy," *U.S. News & World Report*, March 1, 1976; Larry Martz et al., "Nixon's Long Road Back," *Newsweek*, May 19, 1986; "The Sage of Saddle River," *Newsweek*, May 19, 1986, 32.

10   Richard Nixon, *RN* (New York: Simon & Schuster, 1990); Ambrose, *Ruin and Recovery*, 482, 508–11; Carl Bernstein and Bob Woodward, *The Final Days* (New York: Simon & Schuster, 1976); Frost-Nixon Interview Collection, RNL, subseries D, Program Transcripts, program no. 1-5, May 4, May 12, May 19, May 26, Sep 10, 1977, https://www.nixonlibrary.gov/finding-aids/frost-nixon -interview-collection-donated-materials. Carl Bernstein and Bob Woodward, *All the President's Men* (New York: Simon & Schuster, 1974); Aitken, *A Life*, 541, 560–61; Farrell, *Richard Nixon*, 547; Alpern and Lindsay, "Watching Nixon"; Kalb, *Memo*, 20.

11   "Old China Hand"; Ambrose, *Ruin and Recovery*, 490, 516; Farrell, *Richard Nixon*, 549; "Limelight—and Controversy."

12   Baumgold, "Nixon's New Life"; Kalb, *Memo*, 12; Ambrose, *Ruin and Recovery*, 539; Martz et al., "Road Back"; Aitken, *A Life*, 562–64; Farrell, *Richard Nixon*, 541–42, 549.

13   Baumgold, "Nixon's New Life"; Farrell, *Richard* Nixon, 541–42; Ambrose, *Ruin and Recovery*, 556–60; "Sage of Saddle River."

14   "He's Back: The Rehabilitation of Richard Nixon," *Washington Post*, May 19, 1986; Aitken, *A Life*; Joan Hoff, *Reconsidered* (New York: Basic Books, 1995), esp. ix–x, 345–46.

15   "Sage of Saddle River; Kalb, *Memo*, 23; Baumgold, "Nixon's New Life"; Ambrose, *Ruin and Recovery*, 560.

16   Monica Crowley, *Nixon in Winter* (New York: Random House, 1998), 8; "Sage of Saddle River"; Martz et al., "Long Road Back"; Ambrose, *Ruin and Recovery*,

466, 476; Aitken, *A Life*, 534–35; Farrell, *Richard Nixon*, 535, emphasis in the original

17 Baumgold, "Nixon's New Life"; Kalb, *Memo*, 20, 26, 29–30; Ambrose, *Ruin and Recovery*, 545, 554; "The Private Travels of Nixon," *Time*, Nov 2, 1981.

18 Aitken, *A Life*, 542, 552, 558, 560–61; Ambrose, *Ruin and Recovery*, 529; Jonathan Friendly, "Nixon Wins Applause," *New York Times*, May 10, 1984; "Private Travels"; Martz et al., "Long Road Back." For examples of Nixon's mainstream opinion pieces, see Richard Nixon, "Don't Let Salvador Become Another Vietnam," *Wall Street Journal*, May 2, 1983, 30; "Test Candidates on Moral Lessons of Vietnam War," *Wall Street Journal*, Aug 31, 1988, 1; "Cut the Chain of Greed, Poverty, Self-Indulgence," *Los Angeles Times*, Apr 12, 1990, B7; "Drugs our Second Civil War," *Los Angeles Times*, Apr 12, 1990, 7; "Clinton's Greatest Challenges," *New York Times*, Mar 5, 1993; "Moscow, March '94: Chaos and Hope," *New York Times*, Mar 25, 1994.

19 "Notes and Comments," *New Yorker*, May 26, 1986; Feeney, *Nixon at the Movies*; Daniel Frick, *Reinventing Richard Nixon: A Cultural History of an American Obsession* (Lawrence: Univ Press of Kansas, 2008); Greenberg, *Shadow*, xxvi; Stewart Alsop, "The Mystery of Richard Nixon," *Saturday Evening Post*, Jul 12, 1958; Reese and Lindsay, "Nixon: 'Never Look Back,'" 38.

20 Monica Crowley, *Nixon off the Record* (New York: Random House, 1996), 5.

21 Crowley, Record, 6; Nixon-Gannon, Apr 8, 1983, part 1; Crowley, *Winter*, 286–87, 290; Kutler, *Wars of Watergate*, 10; Nixon-Gannon, Sep 7, 1983, part 2.

22 Richard Nixon, *The Real War* (New York: Touchstone, 1980), 4, 9; Richard Nixon, *Real Peace* (Boston: Little, Brown and Co., 1984); Richard Nixon, *No More Vietnams* (New York: Arbor House Publishing, 1987); Richard Nixon, *1999: Victory without War* (New York: Simon & Schuster, 1988); Richard Nixon, *Beyond Peace* (Boston, MA: Little, Brown and Co., 1994); Ambrose, *Ruin and Recovery*, 565.

23 Nixon, *Real Peace*, 4, 19; Nixon, *Beyond Peace*, 15, 33; Ambrose, *Ruin and Recovery*, 550–52.

24 Kalb, *Memo*, 68–90; Thomas Friedman, "Nixon 'Save Russia Memo': Bush Feels the Sting," *New York Times*, Mar 11, 1992.

25 Arthur Schlesinger, Jr., *The Imperial Presidency* (New York: Houghton Mifflin, 1973); William Bundy, *A Tangled Web* (New York: Hill & Wang, 1998); Martz et al., "Nixon's Long Road"; Arthur Schlesinger, Jr., "Dealing with an Out-of-Control

President, in 1973," *Atlantic*, Nov 1, 1973; Richard Pipes, *US-Soviet Relations in the Era of Détente* (New York: Routledge, 1981).

26 Crowley, *Winter*, 407; William Boot, "Nixon Resurrectus," *Columbia Journalism Review* 26, no. 3 (1987); "Notes and Comments," *New Yorker*, May 26, 1986.

27 Greenberg, *Shadow*, xxvi; Frick, *Reinventing*; Feeney, *At the Movies*; Alsop, "Mystery"; Hoff, *Reconsidered*, 345–46.

28 Hunter S. Thompson, *The Great Shark Hunt: Strange Tales from a Strange Time* (New York: Simon & Schuster, 2011), 177.

29 Tom Wicker, *One of Us* (New York: Random House, 1991), xi–xii.

30 Rogers Worthington, "The Paradox That Is Tom Wicker: Tom Wicker's Wide-Ranging Column Is a Pillar of the Times," *Chicago Tribune*, May 23, 1978, A1; Rupert Cornwell, "Tom Wicker," *Independent*, Dec 1, 2011, 53; Garry Boulard, "Tom Wicker Reminisces," *Editor & Publisher*, Mar 7, 1992, 20; Anthony Lane, "Tom Wicker, 1926–2011," *New York Times*, Nov 27, 2011, Sr9; Arthur Unger, "Tom Wicker Speaks Out," *Christian Science Monitor*, Mar 5, 1982; "Tom Wicker, Times Columnist, Dies at Vermont Home, *Bennington Banner*, Nov 25, 2011; Wicker, *One of Us*, xi–xii.

31 Wicker, *One of Us*, xi–xii.

Index

Page numbers in *italics* refer to photos.

charisma: of JFK, 22; of Mao, 300; of Nixon, 22, 329; postmodern focus on, 51, 52; of Zhou, 292

Checkers speech, 40–43, 52, 97

childhood: and loneliness, 66–67, 68; of Pat Nixon, 90–92; and real Nixon, 11–12; and sentimentalism, 61, 62, 64–77, 79, 81; similarities with JFK, 22; work during, 111–12

China: and Dulles ploy, 216–17; and Indo-Pakistani War (1971), 251–52; madman strategy by, 292–93; nuclear development by, 284; Shanghai Communiqué, 306–7, 313; and Vietnam War, 243, 246, 279, 307–8, 311. See also détente with China

China trip (1972): banquet, 302–3, 309, 313; and handshakes, 291–92; and hospitality, 293, 302–3, 304; lack of pomp in, 294–96; and legacy, 267–68, 275–76, 336; and Malraux, 267–68, 277–78; and Mao meeting, 296–302; and media, 282–83, 289–91, 302, 303, 305, 308, 309, 317–18; and performance, 289–91, 319; planning for, 287–89; return from, 317–18; Shanghai Communiqué, 306–7, 313; and work ethic, 110–11. See also détente with China

China trip (1976), 327–28

Chisholm, Shirley, 135

CIA, 194, 321

CIO-PAC, 142–47, 154, 157

civil rights, 94, 132–36, 194, 198, 201, 202

Civil Rights Act of 1957, 132

Civil Rights Act of 1964, 94, 136

Civil Rights Act of 1965, 133

class: in biographies, 190–91, 192; and campaigns, 38, 150–53, 156, 157, 159, 175, 176–77, 178; and Chappaquiddick incident, 174–75; and conspiracies, 4, 176–80, 208–10; and counterculture, 198; and cultural conservatism, 197–200; and DC social scene, 116–17; and education, 190–91; and "forgotten man," 108–10, 150, 197–98, 203; and Hiss, 176, 178; and pain, 81; and Pat Nixon, 90–92, 103–4; and performance, 3; and post-Watergate career, 209–10, 328; and sentimentalism, 81; and work focus, 108; and writing, 391n59. See also poverty; welfare

Clement, Frank G., 184

Clinton, William Jefferson, 118, 242

clumsiness, 115–16

Cohn, Roy, 53

COININTELPRO, 134

Cold War: and Eisenhower, 214–18; Nixon as cooling, 232–33; and sentimentalism, 55–60, 78–80; and Truman, 42; and work, 111. See also détente with China; madman strategy; nuclear deterrence

college, 29–30, 31, 108, 190

Colson, Charles, 124

Committee for the Re-election of the President (CREEP), 193

communism. See anticommunism and red-baiting; Cold War; détente with China

336; overview, 269–72; and post-Watergate career, 334–35; and Soviet Union, 269–72, 283–84, 286, 299, 306, 308, 310; and Vietnam War, 271–72, 274–76, 296, 306–8. *See also* China trip (1972)

Dewey, Thomas, 39

Diplomacy (Kissinger), 308, 315–17

Dobrynin, Anatoly, 243–46, 253, 257–58, 259–60, 262, 286, 318

Dole, Robert, 235

domestic policy: affirmative action, 110, 135–36; and détente, 271–72; disinterest in, 128; as progressive, 126–28, 194–95, 198; welfare, 110, 126, 128–32, 134–35, 137–38, 194, 201; and work, 128–36

Domestic Policy Council, 120

Douglas, Helen Gahagan, 50, 126, 157–58, 176–77, 178, 183

Drowns, Helene, 97

drugs, 168, 169, 183

Duck Hook, Operation, 235–36, 238, 282

Dulles, John Foster, 291

Dulles ploy, 216–17

Eagleburger, Lawrence, 122

East Pakistan, 250–52

economic aid, 281–82, 311–13, 335

education of Nixon: and acting, 29–30; and class, 190–91; and debate, 31; and parents, 74–75, 108, 112, 137; remembrances by classmates, 30, 68, 188; and work, 108, 111–12

Egypt and Arab-Israeli War (1973), 258–63

Ehrlichman, John, *118*; background and career of, 119–20; and campaigns, 56, 120; and China trip, 285; on demonstrations, 242; and executive branch reorganization, 120; on family interactions, 98; on Nixon's management style, 49; on Pat Nixon, 101; on psychohistories, 191–92; and Watergate scandal, 322, 323

Eisenhower, Dwight D., 25, 37–38, 41–44, 214–18, 282, 315

Eisenhower, Julie Nixon: on 1960 loss, 97; and China trip, 303, 318; and class, 209; and desegregation, 134; on Nixon's relations with women, 94–95; on parents, 88, 90, 93, 97; on post-Watergate period, 324; and Watergate, 100

Eisenhower, Mamie, 103

Ellsberg, Daniel, 84, 193, 225–26, 228

emasculation, 109, 129–30

emotions: and authenticity, 10–11; as binary, 9; discomfort with, 10–11, 17–18, 24; history of, 9–10; Mao and Zhou's control of, 292–93; and Pat Nixon, 89–90; and sentimentalism, 61–64; theory on, 9–10, 17. *See also* affect and affective control; anger; performance

enemies: and biographies, 193–95, 213; and class, 208–10; Congress as, 127; conspiracy as tool to delegitimize, 146–47; counterculture as, 181–83; and Hiss case, 36–37; imitation of, enemies (*cont.*)

    180, 207; and inability to enjoy success, 203–4; Jewish people as, 208–9; and Kissinger, 122; and Latin America tour (1953), 43–44; Mao and China as, 279–80; media and journalists as, 125, 177, 209; need for, 3–4, 209; and performance, 53–54; and presidential campaign (1972), 175–76, 193; and presidential plans, 106; protestors as, 170, 193, 204–8, 235, 236, 247; reactions of, 183–85; and real Nixon, 12; and representative campaign (1946), 145–47, 153, 159–60; and sentimentalism, 63–64, 81–83; shifting of, 3–4, 178–79, 211; surveillance of, 83, 175–76, 193; "useful enemies," 145–47, 159–60; and vice-presidential campaign scandal (1952), 38, 42; and Watergate scandal, 210–13, 332–33

Enthoven, Alain, 221

environmental policy, 127–28

Environmental Protection Agency, 127

Equal Rights Amendment (ERA), 94

Erikson, Erik, 130, 186, 189

executive branch, reorganization of, 106, 120–21

face, 269, 274, 275, 313–14

family: deaths in, 22, 61, 66, 70, 73, 74; interactions, 97–98; as key to real Nixon, 11–12; psychohistories on, 187–88; and sentimentalism, 61, 62, 64, 65, 66, 70–77, 79, 90; surveillance of, 193

Family Assistance Plan (FAP), 110, 129–32, 134–35

Farrell, John, 195

fathers and welfare reform, 129–30

Febvre, Lucien, 4, 17

feminism, 87–89, 90, 94, 95–96, 102–5, 109

Finch, Bob, 324

Florence, Ola, 30, 68, 112

food stamps, 126, 128

football, 112

Ford, Gerald, 101

foreign policy: and aid, 281–82, 311–13, 335; anti-communist focus of, 279–80; and authoritarianism, 271, 311–13, 317, 331; in first presidential term, 106, 270, 280–82; as focus, 128; inconsistency in, 5, 282, 315–17; Kissinger's approach to, 121–23; and legacy, 267–68, 273, 275–76, 314–15, 336; Nixon Doctrine, 280–82, 283, 311; and post-Watergate career, 331–35; pragmatism in, 268–69; and rejection of pacifism, 278–79, 316; and work ethic, 110–11. *See also* détente with China; madman strategy

"forgotten man," 108–10, 150, 197–98, 203

Freud, Sigmund, 130, 186, 189

Frost, David, 326–27

Fulbright, J. William, 243

Gaddis, John Lewis, 232, 283, 310

game theory: and détente, 269, 272, 273; development of, 220–25; and madman

249–50; overview, 233–34; reliance on, 218, 264; and Vietnam War, 234, 238, 245–46, 247, 252–58

Klein, Herbert, 46, 51–52, 53, 208

Knowland, William, 42, 113

Kopechne, Mary Jo, 172–73

Korean War, 216–17

Kotlowski, Dean J., 133–34

Kutler, Stanley I., 11, 45, 211, 322

Laing, R. D., 169

Laird, Melvin, 236, 241

Laird, William, 281

Laos and Vietnam War, 313

Latin America goodwill tour (1953), 43–44

law school, 112, 188, 190–91

Leaders (Nixon), 54, 334

legacy of Nixon: disagreement on, 335–39; and foreign policy, 267–68, 273, 275–76, 314–15, 336; and loneliness, 269, 273, 276, 315, 339; and peace, 115, 318–19; post-Watergate career, 325–35; rehabilitation of, 328–32; and Vietnam War, 314–15; and Watergate scandal, 324, 327

LGBTQ people. *See* homosexuality

liberalism: fear of, 312–13; and progressiveness as president, 126–28, 194–95, 198

libertarianism, 150, 199–201

Lincoln, Abraham, 40, 267–68, 312–13

Linebacker, Operation, 252–58, 265

Lipset, Seymour Martin, 198, 199

Lodge, Henry Cabot, 227

loneliness: and childhood, 66–67, 68; and DC social scene, 116–17; and legacy, 269, 273, 276, 315, 339; and sentimentalism, 62; and use of seclusion, 13–14

Long, Russell, 135

longform biographies, 12, 190–96

Longworth, Alice Roosevelt, 101

Lord, Winston, 240, 282, 293, 297, 303, 304

MacMillan, Margaret, 278, 295

MAD (mutual assured destruction), 215, 219–20, 232

madman strategy: and anger, 162–64, 184, 247; and Arab-Israeli War (1973), 258–66; in biographies, 237–41; by China, 292–93; denial as reaction to, 6; effectiveness of, 8–9; and game theory, 217, 225–26, 264–66; and Garment, 230–32, 237; and Haldeman, 1–2, 5–6, 18, 237, 239–40, 255; and Indo-Pakistani War (1971), 250–52, 264, 265; and Jordan, 216–17, 234, 248–50; and Khrushchev, 226–29; origins and development of, 1–2, 5–6, 18, 228–29, 237, 239–40; overview of, 14–18, 230–34; and performance, 239, 244–45, 247–48, 265–66; poles of, 4–5; reliance on, 264–66; scholarly interest in, 218–26; and unpredictability, 171; and utility of madness, 7–9, 225–26, 229. *See also* Kissinger, Henry Alfred, and madman strategy; madness

Philadelphia Plan, 135. *See also* affirmative action

philanthropy, 60, 96

Philippines, aid to, 311

Philips, Adam, 171

Phillips, Kevin, 201

Plato, 161, 171

poker, 5, 217, 220, 225, 237, 264, 273, 335

political action committees. *See* CIO-PAC; National Citizens Political Action Committee (NCPAC)

Popper, Karl, 179

postmodernism, 2, 27–29, 46, 50–51, 187

post-revisionist biographies, 210–11

poverty: and focus on work, 131; of Nixon, 190–91; and Pat Nixon, 90–92; and sentimentalism, 66, 70, 74. *See also* welfare

premature entextualization, 153, 178

presidency: and Chappaquiddick incident, 172–75; and management style, 49, 106, 117–18, 124; and performance in first term, 107–18; and progessivism, 126–28; and reorganization of executive branch, 106, 120–21. *See also* domestic policy; foreign policy; madman strategy

presidential campaign (1960): and civil rights, 133; and class, 177; debates, 45–47, 279; and Haldeman, 120; and Pat Nixon, 45, 97; and performance, 22, 45–47; and sentimentalism, 62–63

presidential campaign (1968): acceptance speech, 203–4, 270; ads, 202, 206; and civil rights, 133; and Ehrlichman, 120;

and ERA, 94; red-baiting in, 158; and Robert F. Kennedy, 192

presidential campaign (1972): and Chappaquiddick incident, 173–75; and civil rights, 133; and conspiracy, 175–76, 210–13; and martyrdom theory, 212; and performance, 56–60; and sentimentalism, 56–60, 78–80, 83–85; and surveillance, 175–76, 193; and Thompson, 338

Price, Raymond, Jr., 28, 124

Price of Power, The (Hersh), 238–39

psychohistories, 11–13, 186–90, 191–92, 195, 213, 336

Pumpkin Papers, 36

race: and affirmative action, 110, 135–36; black unemployment, 134; and civil rights, 132–36, 138, 193, 194, 198, 201, 202; and cultural conservatism, 197–200; and domestic policy, 126; Nixon's attitudes on, 132–34; and representative campaign (1946), 132, 150; Southern strategy, 133, 184, 194; and welfare reform, 129–32, 134–35. *See also* whites

radical right, 199, 200

RAND Corporation, 219, 221, 222

Rather, Dan, 303

Reagan, Ronald, 24, 194–95, 199, 201, 333–34

real Nixon: and cultural biographies, 197; and foreign policy, 317; interest in, 11–13, 27, 210, 326, 337–38; Kennedy on, 3; and performance, 23–24, 26–27;

313–14; Nixon on military performance in, 185; nuclear alert in 1969, 6–7, 237, 238, 240–41, 243–46; Operation Duck Hook, 235–36, 238, 282; Operation Linebacker, 252–58, 265; protests, 83–85, 234–35, 236, 241–42, 247, 256–57, 271–72; in revisionist biographies, 194; and Shanghai Communiqué, 306–8; silent majority speech, 204–8. *See also* madman strategy and Vietnam War

volunteerism, 96–97

von Neumann, John, 220–21

Voorhis, Horace Jeremiah "Jerry," 141–48, 154–57, *155*, 158–60, 176, 178

Voorhis Act, 154–55, 159

Walters, Barbara, 51–53, 87, 290

Watergate scandal: in biographies, 193, 195; and enemies, 210–13, 332–33; events of, 321–24; and legacy, 324, 327; Nixon on, 332–33; and pranks, 212; Saturday Night Massacre, 258, 323

welfare, 110, 126, 128–32, 134–35, 137–38, 194, 201

Wheeler, Earle, 170

White Collar (Mills), 196

White House, 100

whites: and cultural conservatism, 197–200; and representative campaign (1946), 150; and Southern strategy, 133, 184, 194; and Veterans Day march, 207; and welfare reform, 131–32

Whyte, William H., Jr., 196–97

Wicker, Tom, 138, 191, 197, 338–39

Wilde, Oscar, 77

Wilkins, Roy, 133

Williams College. *See* college

Wills, Garry, 11, 61, 62, 107, 177, 269, 285

Wilson, Woodrow, 268–69, 313, 315–17, 335

Winnicott, D. W., 188

wiretaps, 176, 193. *See also* surveillance

Witness to Power (Ehrlichman), 191–92

women: and affirmative action, 135; appointed by Nixon, 94; backlash against women's rights, 201, 202; and emasculation of men, 109, 129–30; and madness, 167–68; Nixon's interactions with, 93–95; and nuclear deterrence theory, 222. *See also* feminism

Woods, Rose Mary, 186

Woodward, Bob, 211, 322, 327

work ethic: and campaigning, 113–16, 149; and civil rights, 133; and domestic policy, 128–36; and early work, 111–13; focus on, 108, 136–38, 177; and foreign policy, 110–11; and modern conservatism, 199; and parents, 70, 72, 136–37; post-Watergate career, 325–26, 330; and sentimentalism, 70, 72, 82; shifting goals of, 113–15; work habits, 123–25 writings: and class, 391n59; on détente with China, 286–87; on nuclear deterrence, 224–25; and performance, 49–50, 54; post-Presidency, 209, 326, 333–34; with Safire, 286–87; and sentimentalism, 82. See also *specific titles*

Zhou Enlai: and China trip (1972), 274–75, 287–88, 291–93, 294, 297, 300, 304, 305–6, 309; and handshakes, 291–92; and Mao, 300; warning from, 269

Ziegler, Ronald, 50–52, 53, 124, 323, 324, 325